BRIGGS LAND ™

"Given the current political state of the country, this series feels very relevant indeed." —*IGN*

"[*Briggs Land*] promises to be the backdrop for some deeply compelling drama." —*PASTE MAGAZINE*

"*Briggs Land* got me thinking how such a crazy idea is really close to happening nowadays. I'm almost scared to see what happens next. Almost scared, but I'm very curious." —*FÁBIO MOON*

"Thoughtful world-building and complex characters." —*COMICS BULLETIN*

"AMC knew what they were doing in picking up the rights to this one. If any story deserves to be told in live action, it's this well-oiled crime family saga." —*BLACK NERD PROBLEMS*

"[*Briggs Land* is the] *Sopranos* of secession." —*GEEKS WORLDWIDE*

"I feel like I am reading a leaked script and storyboard for the next big thing. AMC is developing the show for television, and when you read it you can see why." —*GRAPHIC POLICY*

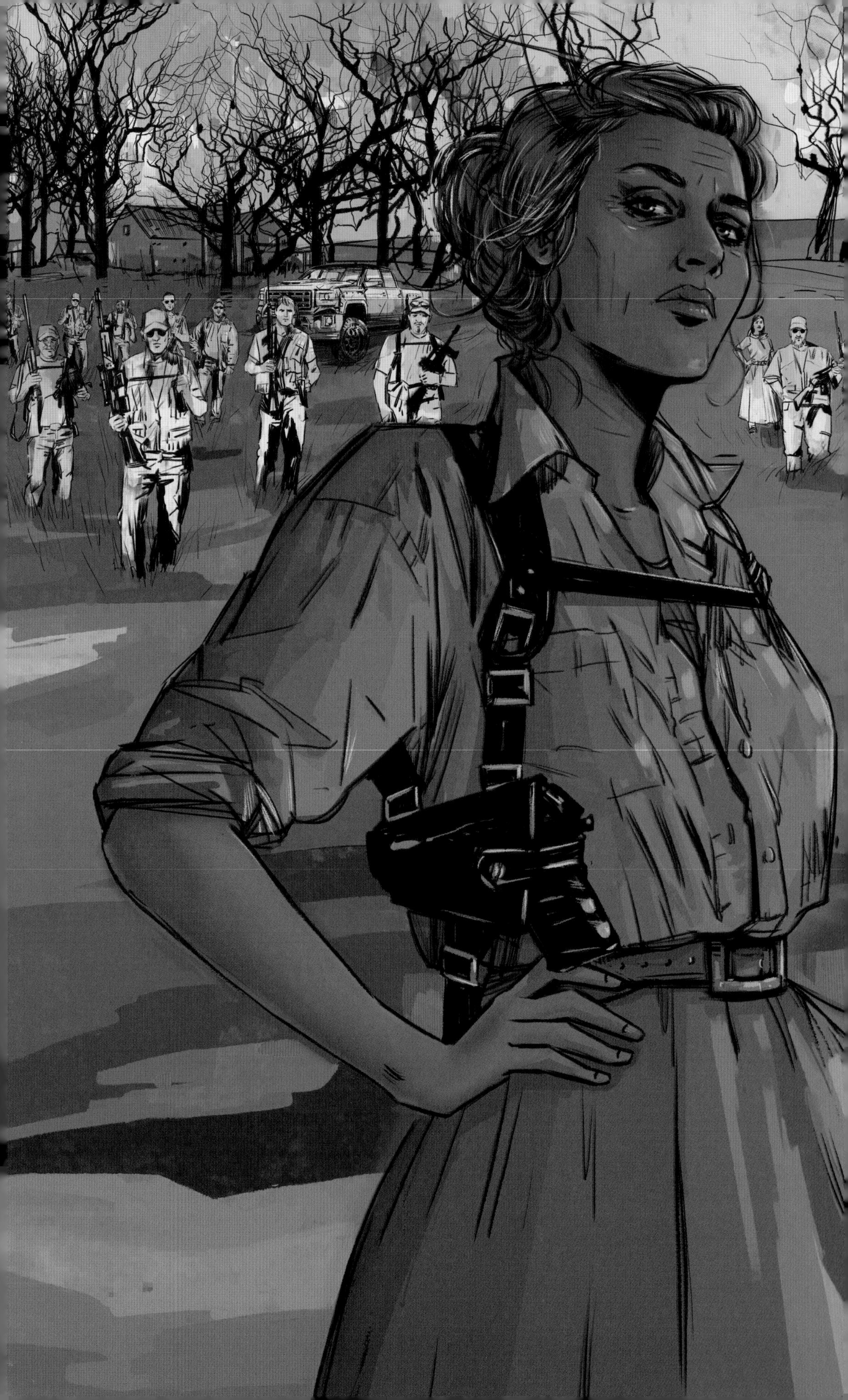

VOLUME 1
STATE OF GRACE

SCRIPT / BRIAN WOOD
ART / MACK CHATER
COLORS / LEE LOUGHRIDGE AND JEREMY COLWELL
LETTERING / NATE PIEKOS OF BLAMBOT®
CHAPTER BREAK ART / TULA LOTAY
COVER / MACK CHATER AND BRIAN WOOD

BRIGGS LAND CREATED BY BRIAN WOOD

BRIGGS█▌▌LAND™

DARK HORSE BOOKS

PRESIDENT AND PUBLISHER / MIKE RICHARDSON
EDITOR / SPENCER CUSHING
ASSISTANT EDITOR / KEVIN BURKHALTER
COLLECTION DESIGNER / BRENNAN THOME
DIGITAL ART TECHNICIAN / ALLYSON HALLER

SPECIAL THANKS TO BRIAN BOCKRATH AND BEN DAVIS OF AMC, JOHN HODGES AND RAVI NANDAN OF A24, ANGELA CHENG CAPLAN, HARRIS M. MILLER II, AND MEREDITH, AUDREY, AND IAN.

NEIL HANKERSON Executive Vice President / TOM WEDDLE Chief Financial Officer / RANDY STRADLEY Vice President of Publishing / MATT PARKINSON Vice President of Marketing / DAVID SCROGGY Vice President of Product Development / DALE LaFOUNTAIN Vice President of Information Technology / CARA NIECE Vice President of Production and Scheduling / NICK McWHORTER Vice President of Media Licensing / MARK BERNARDI Vice President of Digital and Book Trade Sales / KEN LIZZI General Counsel / DAVE MARSHALL Editor in Chief / DAVEY ESTRADA Editorial Director / SCOTT ALLIE Executive Senior Editor / CHRIS WARNER Senior Books Editor / CARY GRAZZINI Director of Specialty Projects / LIA RIBACCHI Art Director / VANESSA TODD Director of Print Purchasing / MATT DRYER Director of Digital Art and Prepress / SARAH ROBERTSON Director of Product Sales / MICHAEL GOMBOS Director of International Publishing and Licensing

Briggs Land Volume 1: State of Grace

This volume collects the Dark Horse comic book series *Briggs Land* #1–#6, originally published August 2016–January 2017.

Published by Dark Horse Books
A division of Dark Horse Comics, Inc.
10956 SE Main Street
Milwaukie, OR 97222

DarkHorse.com

International Licensing: 503-905-2377
To find a comics shop in your area, call the Comic Shop Locator Service toll-free at 1-888-266-4226.

Library of Congress Cataloging-in-Publication Data
Names: Wood, Brian, 1972- author. | Chater, Mack, artist. | Loughridge, Lee,
  colourist. | Piekos, Nate, letterer. | Lotay, Tula, artist.
Title: Briggs Land. Volume 1, State of grace / script, Brian Wood ; art, Mack
  Chater ; colors, Lee Loughridge ; lettering, Nate Piekos of Blambot ;
  cover art, Tula Lotay.
Other titles: State of grace
Description: First edition. | Milwaukie, OR : Dark Horse Books, 2017. | "This
  volume collects the Dark Horse comic book series Briggs Land #1–#6,
  originally published August 2016-January 2017"--Title page verso.
Identifiers: LCCN 2016044135 | ISBN 9781506700595 (paperback)
Subjects: LCSH: Comic books, strips, etc. | BISAC: COMICS & GRAPHIC NOVELS /
  Crime & Mystery.
Classification: LCC PN6728.B69 W66 2017 | DDC 741.5/973--dc23
LC record available at https://lccn.loc.gov/2016044135

First edition: April 2017
ISBN 978-1-50670-059-5

10 9 8 7 6 5 4 3 2 1

Printed in China

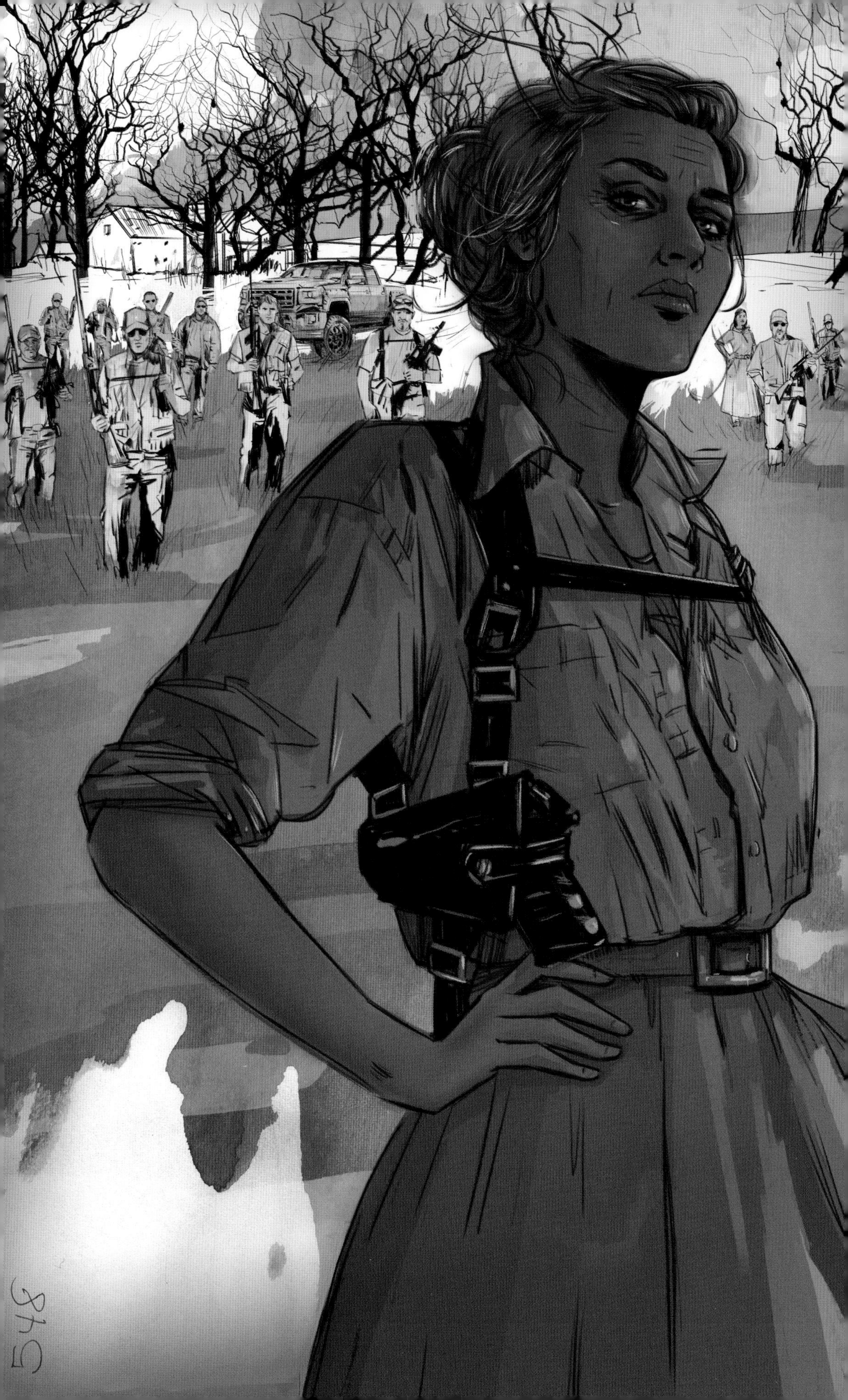

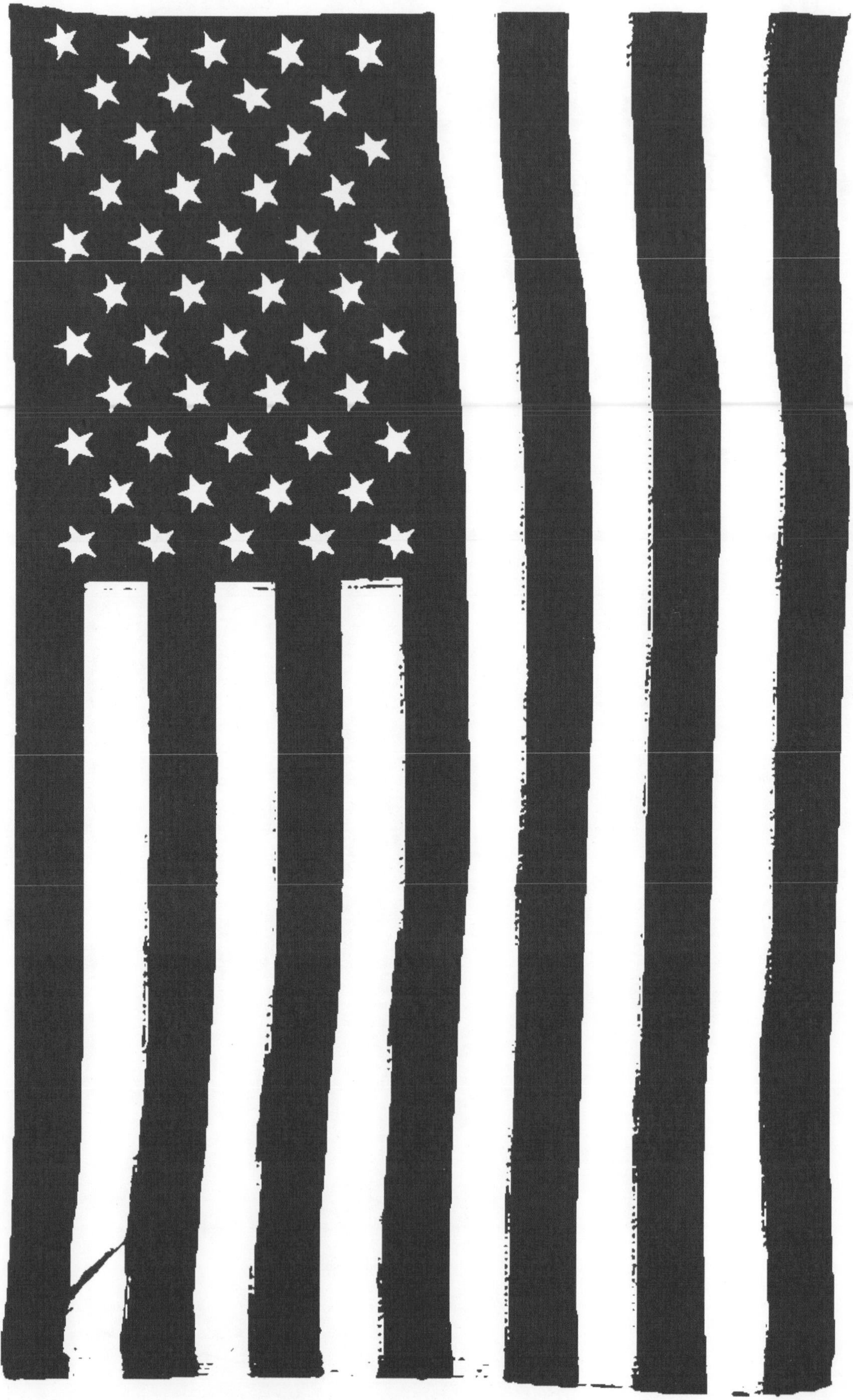

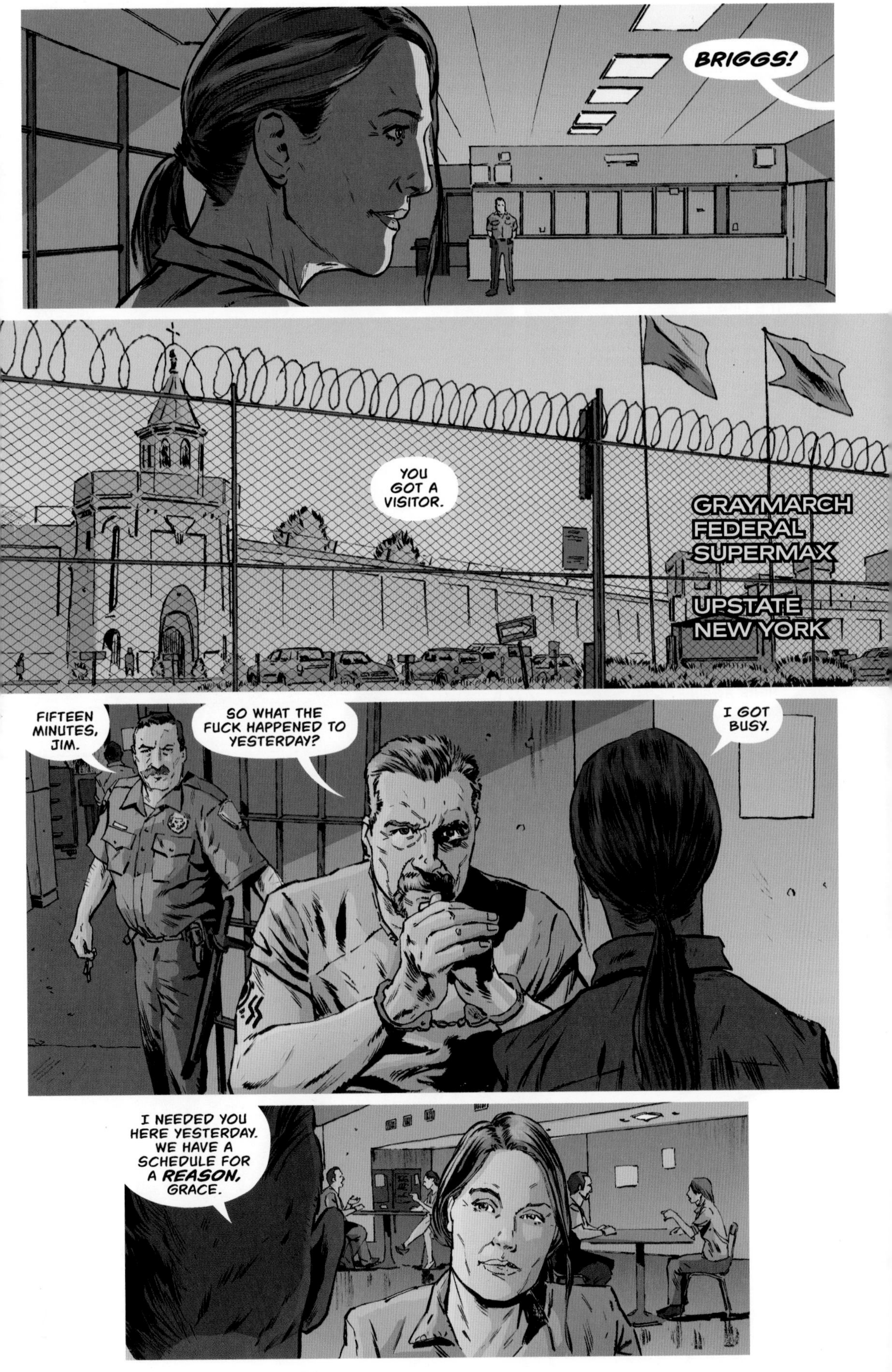
BRIGGS!
YOU GOT A VISITOR.
GRAYMARCH FEDERAL SUPERMAX
UPSTATE NEW YORK
FIFTEEN MINUTES, JIM.
SO WHAT THE FUCK HAPPENED TO YESTERDAY?
I GOT BUSY.
I NEEDED YOU HERE YESTERDAY. WE HAVE A SCHEDULE FOR A *REASON,* GRACE.

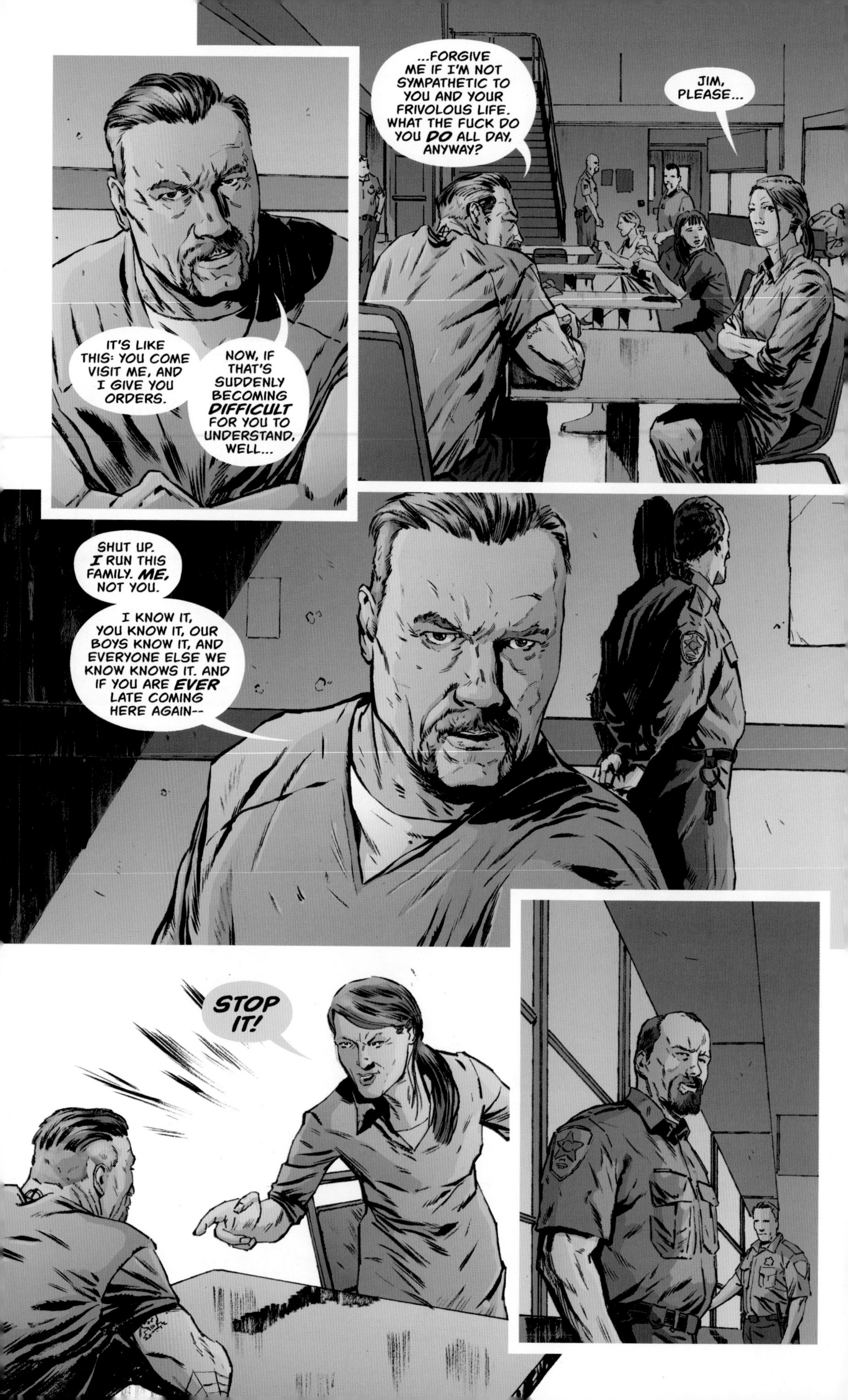
IT'S LIKE THIS: YOU COME VISIT ME, AND I GIVE YOU ORDERS.
NOW, IF THAT'S SUDDENLY BECOMING *DIFFICULT* FOR YOU TO UNDERSTAND, WELL...
...FORGIVE ME IF I'M NOT SYMPATHETIC TO YOU AND YOUR FRIVOLOUS LIFE. WHAT THE FUCK DO YOU *DO* ALL DAY, ANYWAY?
JIM, PLEASE...
SHUT UP. *I* RUN THIS FAMILY. *ME,* NOT YOU.
I KNOW IT, YOU KNOW IT, OUR BOYS KNOW IT, AND EVERYONE ELSE WE KNOW KNOWS IT. AND IF YOU ARE *EVER* LATE COMING HERE AGAIN--
STOP IT!

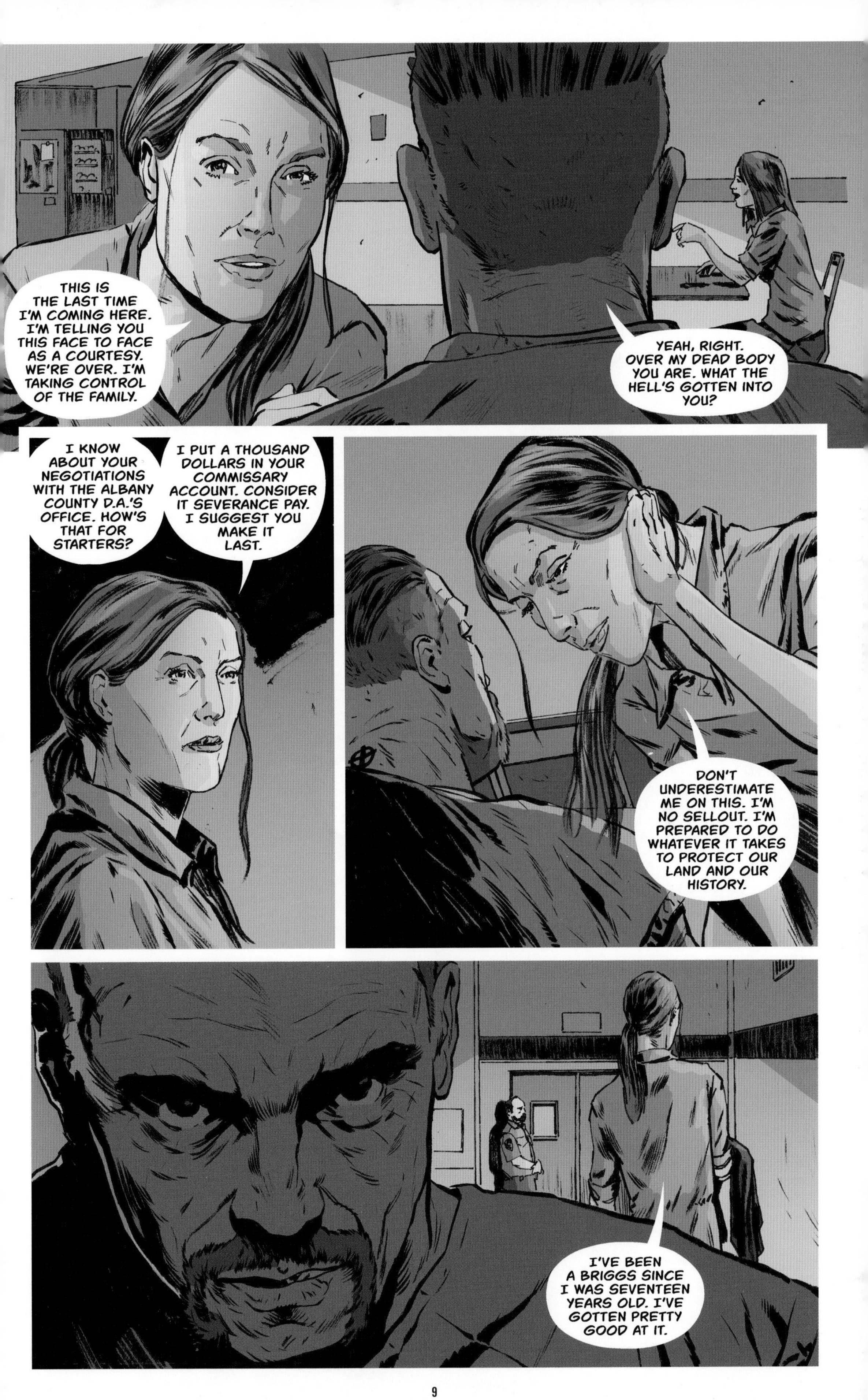
THIS IS THE LAST TIME I'M COMING HERE. I'M TELLING YOU THIS FACE TO FACE AS A COURTESY. WE'RE OVER. I'M TAKING CONTROL OF THE FAMILY.
YEAH, RIGHT. OVER MY DEAD BODY YOU ARE. WHAT THE HELL'S GOTTEN INTO YOU?
I KNOW ABOUT YOUR NEGOTIATIONS WITH THE ALBANY COUNTY D.A.'S OFFICE. HOW'S THAT FOR STARTERS?
I PUT A THOUSAND DOLLARS IN YOUR COMMISSARY ACCOUNT. CONSIDER IT SEVERANCE PAY. I SUGGEST YOU MAKE IT LAST.
DON'T UNDERESTIMATE ME ON THIS. I'M NO SELLOUT. I'M PREPARED TO DO WHATEVER IT TAKES TO PROTECT OUR LAND AND OUR HISTORY.
I'VE BEEN A BRIGGS SINCE I WAS SEVENTEEN YEARS OLD. I'VE GOTTEN PRETTY GOOD AT IT.

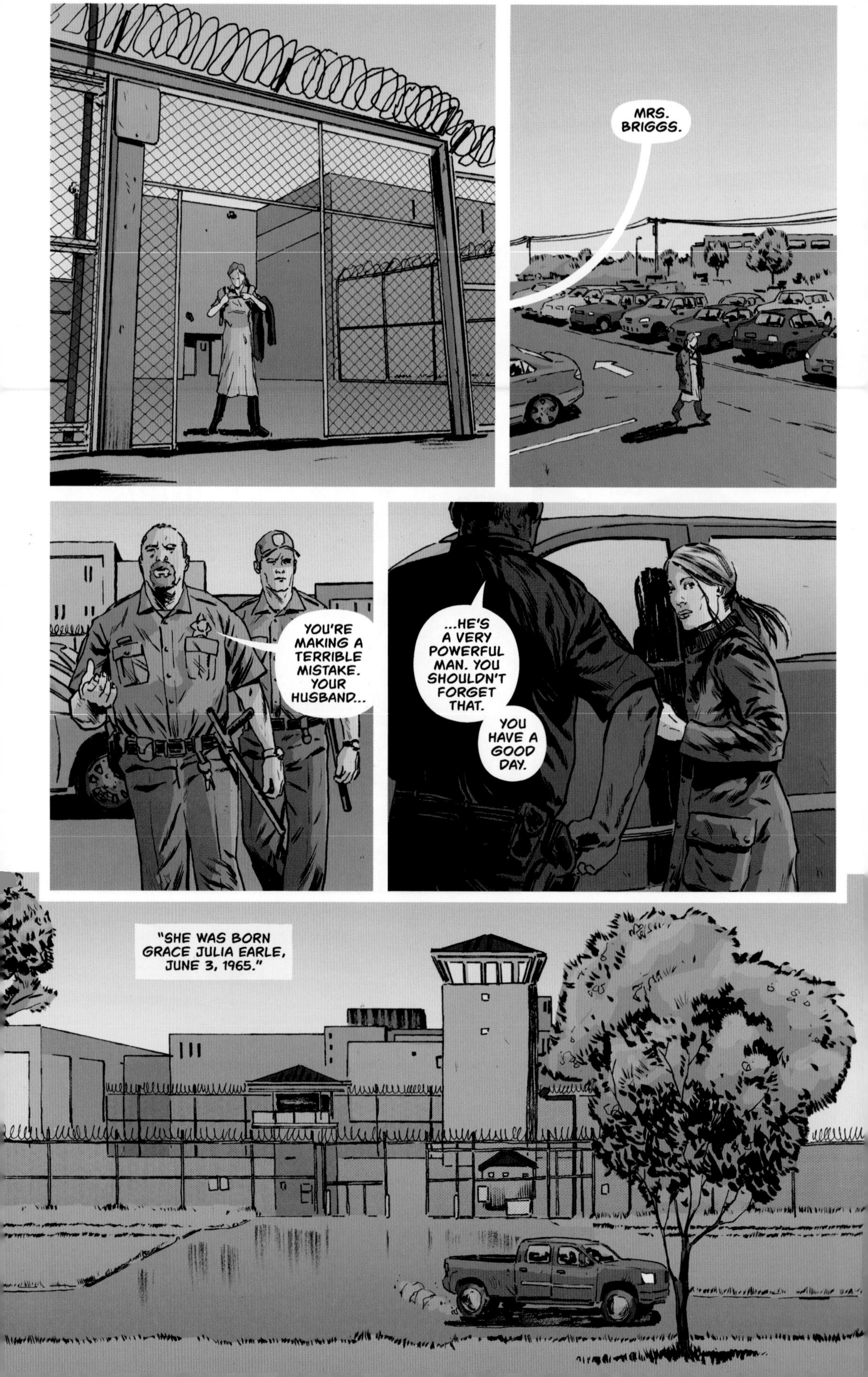
MRS. BRIGGS.
YOU'RE MAKING A TERRIBLE MISTAKE. YOUR HUSBAND...
...HE'S A VERY POWERFUL MAN. YOU SHOULDN'T FORGET THAT.
YOU HAVE A GOOD DAY.
"SHE WAS BORN GRACE JULIA EARLE, JUNE 3, 1965."

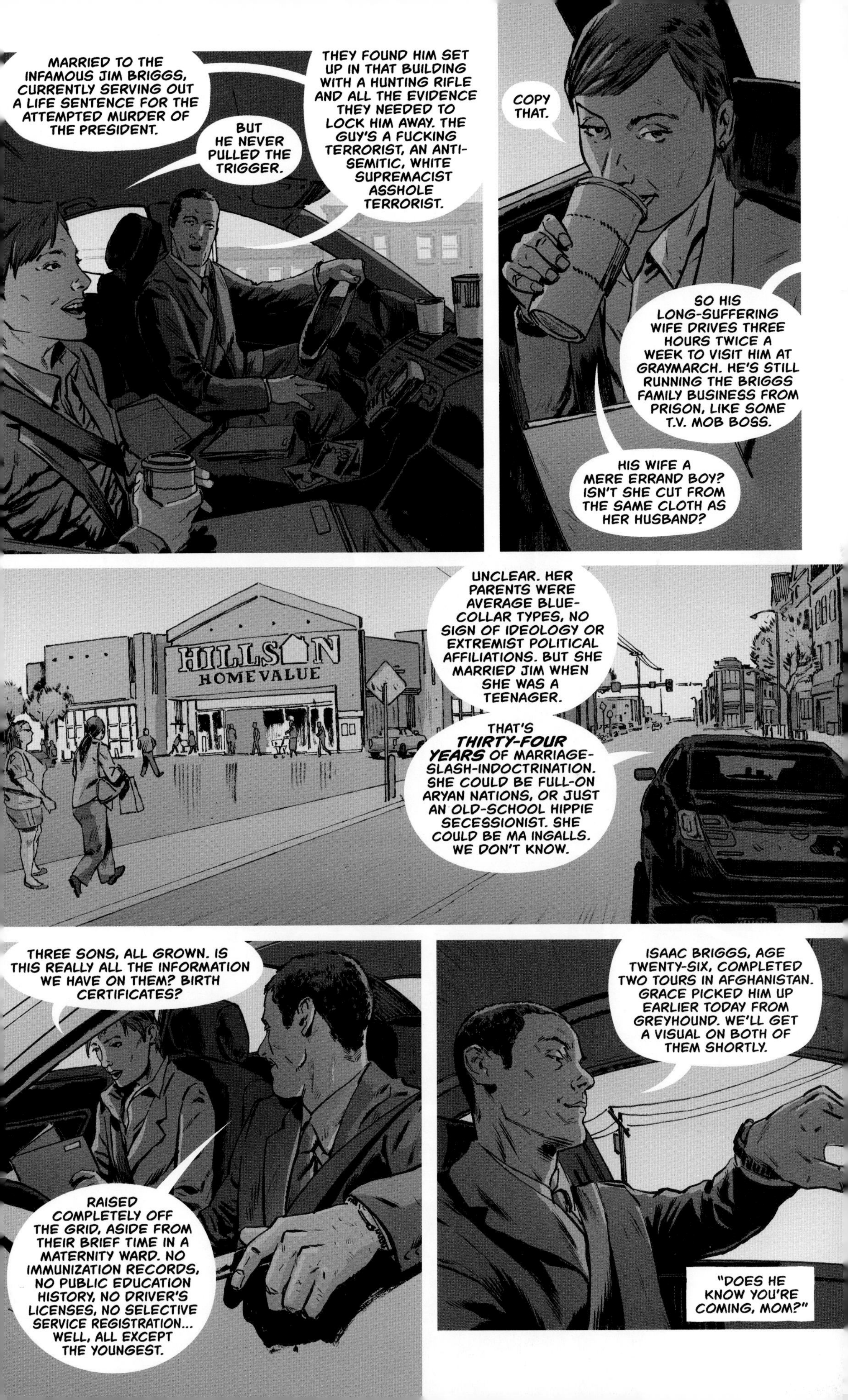
MARRIED TO THE INFAMOUS JIM BRIGGS, CURRENTLY SERVING OUT A LIFE SENTENCE FOR THE ATTEMPTED MURDER OF THE PRESIDENT.
BUT HE NEVER PULLED THE TRIGGER.
THEY FOUND HIM SET UP IN THAT BUILDING WITH A HUNTING RIFLE AND ALL THE EVIDENCE THEY NEEDED TO LOCK HIM AWAY. THE GUY'S A FUCKING TERRORIST, AN ANTI-SEMITIC, WHITE SUPREMACIST ASSHOLE TERRORIST.
COPY THAT.
SO HIS LONG-SUFFERING WIFE DRIVES THREE HOURS TWICE A WEEK TO VISIT HIM AT GRAYMARCH. HE'S STILL RUNNING THE BRIGGS FAMILY BUSINESS FROM PRISON, LIKE SOME T.V. MOB BOSS.
HIS WIFE A MERE ERRAND BOY? ISN'T SHE CUT FROM THE SAME CLOTH AS HER HUSBAND?
HILLSON
HOMEVALUE
UNCLEAR. HER PARENTS WERE AVERAGE BLUE-COLLAR TYPES, NO SIGN OF IDEOLOGY OR EXTREMIST POLITICAL AFFILIATIONS. BUT SHE MARRIED JIM WHEN SHE WAS A TEENAGER.
THAT'S ***THIRTY-FOUR YEARS*** OF MARRIAGE-SLASH-INDOCTRINATION. SHE COULD BE FULL-ON ARYAN NATIONS, OR JUST AN OLD-SCHOOL HIPPIE SECESSIONIST. SHE COULD BE MA INGALLS. WE DON'T KNOW.
THREE SONS, ALL GROWN. IS THIS REALLY ALL THE INFORMATION WE HAVE ON THEM? BIRTH CERTIFICATES?
RAISED COMPLETELY OFF THE GRID, ASIDE FROM THEIR BRIEF TIME IN A MATERNITY WARD. NO IMMUNIZATION RECORDS, NO PUBLIC EDUCATION HISTORY, NO DRIVER'S LICENSES, NO SELECTIVE SERVICE REGISTRATION... WELL, ALL EXCEPT THE YOUNGEST.
ISAAC BRIGGS, AGE TWENTY-SIX, COMPLETED TWO TOURS IN AFGHANISTAN. GRACE PICKED HIM UP EARLIER TODAY FROM GREYHOUND. WE'LL GET A VISUAL ON BOTH OF THEM SHORTLY.
"DOES HE KNOW YOU'RE COMING, MOM?"

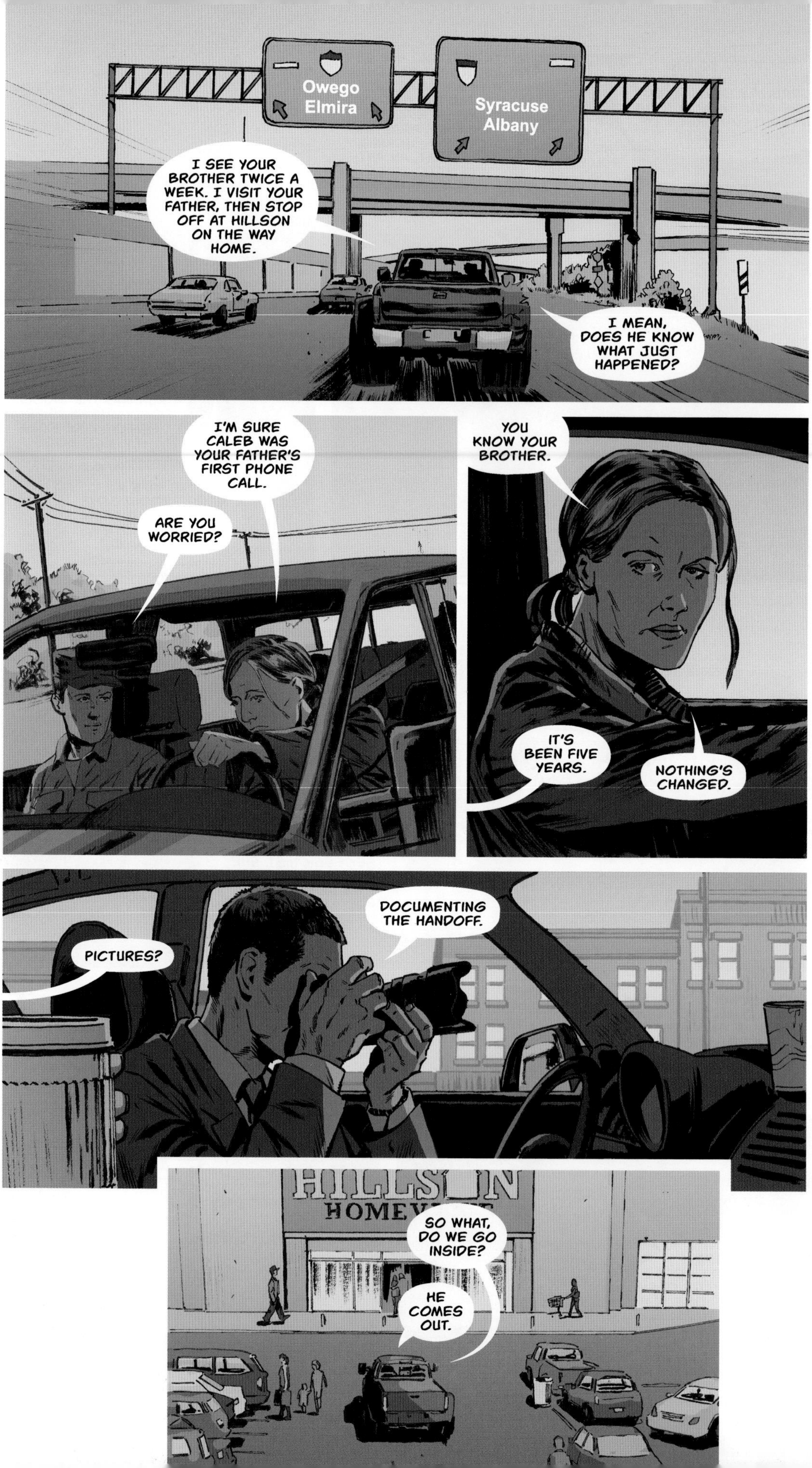
Owego
Elmira
Syracuse
Albany
I SEE YOUR BROTHER TWICE A WEEK. I VISIT YOUR FATHER, THEN STOP OFF AT HILLSON ON THE WAY HOME.
I MEAN, DOES HE KNOW WHAT JUST HAPPENED?
I'M SURE CALEB WAS YOUR FATHER'S FIRST PHONE CALL.
ARE YOU WORRIED?
YOU KNOW YOUR BROTHER.
IT'S BEEN FIVE YEARS.
NOTHING'S CHANGED.
PICTURES?
DOCUMENTING THE HANDOFF.
HOME
SO WHAT, DO WE GO INSIDE?
HE COMES OUT.

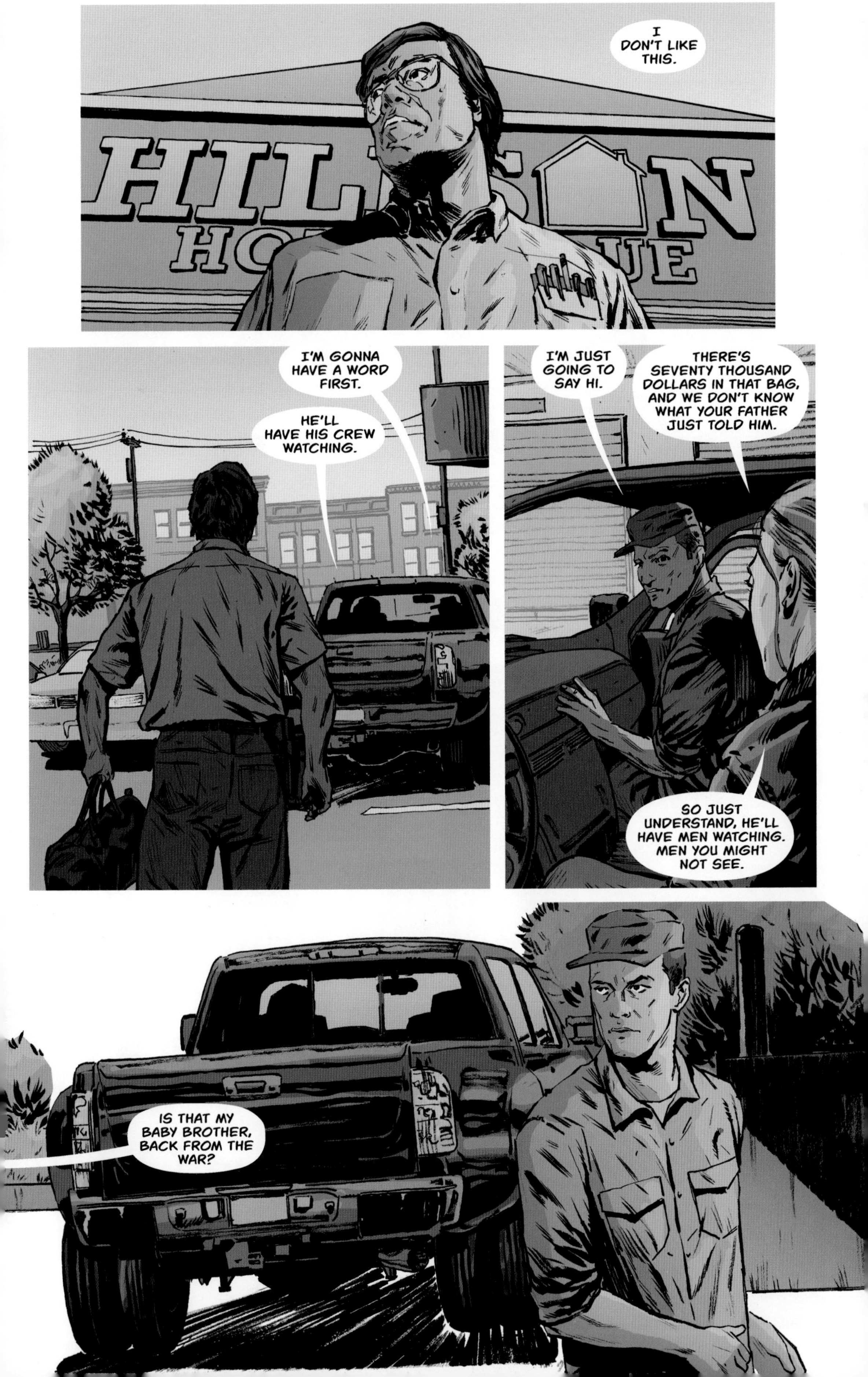
I DON'T LIKE THIS.
I'M GONNA HAVE A WORD FIRST.
HE'LL HAVE HIS CREW WATCHING.
I'M JUST GOING TO SAY HI.
THERE'S SEVENTY THOUSAND DOLLARS IN THAT BAG, AND WE DON'T KNOW WHAT YOUR FATHER JUST TOLD HIM.
SO JUST UNDERSTAND, HE'LL HAVE MEN WATCHING. MEN YOU MIGHT NOT SEE.
IS THAT MY BABY BROTHER, BACK FROM THE WAR?

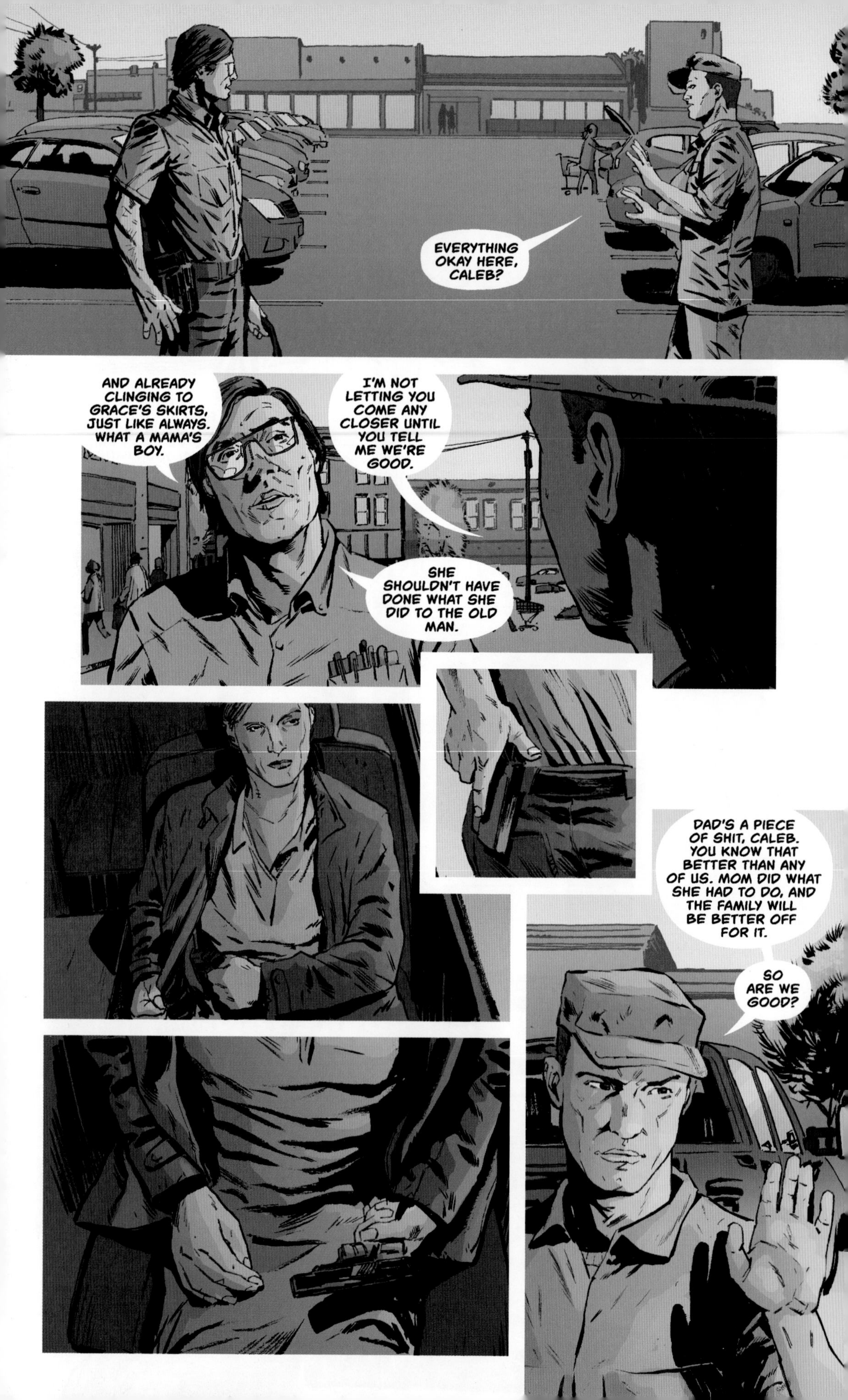
EVERYTHING OKAY HERE, CALEB?
AND ALREADY CLINGING TO GRACE'S SKIRTS, JUST LIKE ALWAYS. WHAT A MAMA'S BOY.
I'M NOT LETTING YOU COME ANY CLOSER UNTIL YOU TELL ME WE'RE GOOD.
SHE SHOULDN'T HAVE DONE WHAT SHE DID TO THE OLD MAN.
DAD'S A PIECE OF SHIT, CALEB. YOU KNOW THAT BETTER THAN ANY OF US. MOM DID WHAT SHE HAD TO DO, AND THE FAMILY WILL BE BETTER OFF FOR IT.
SO ARE WE GOOD?

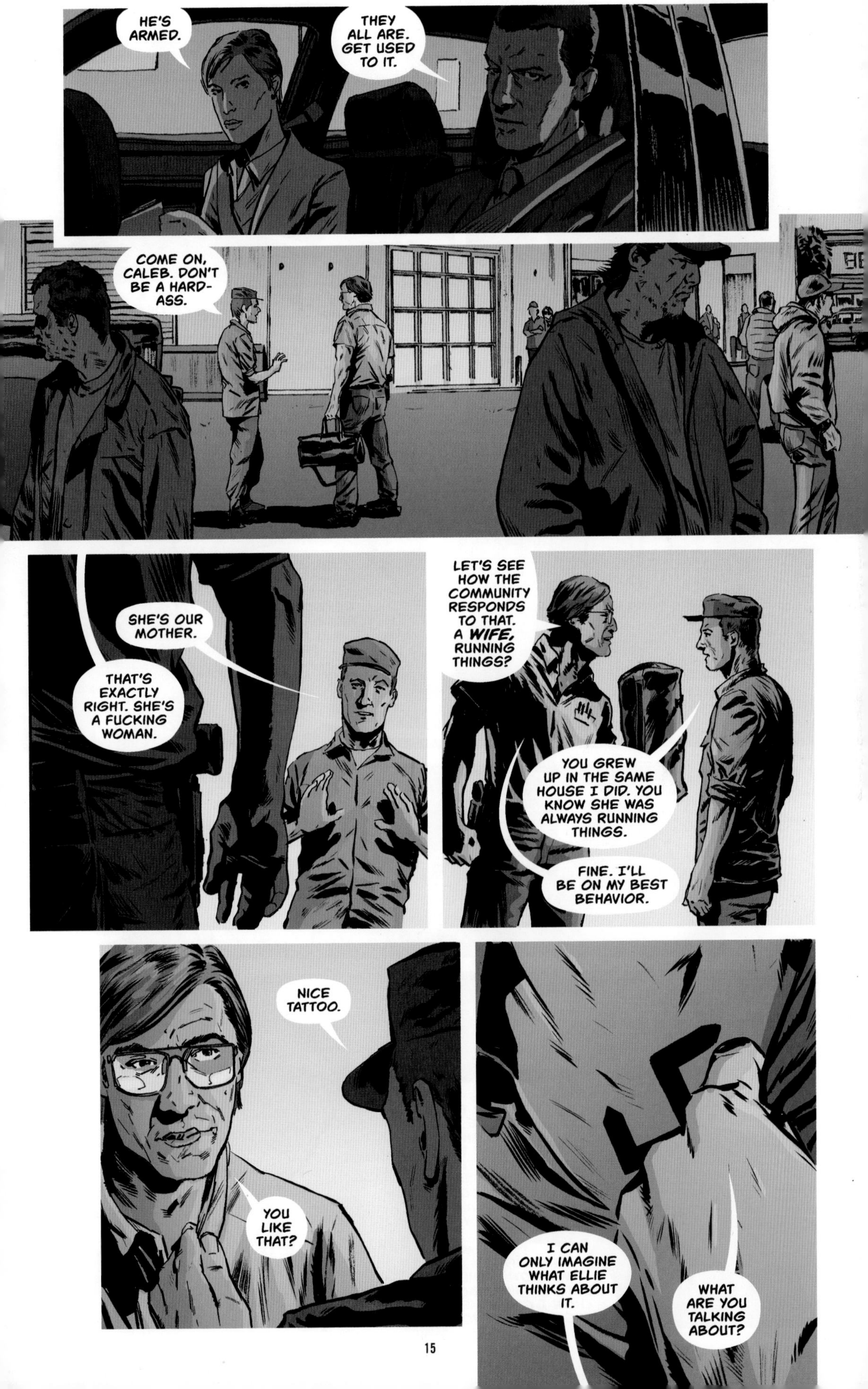
HE'S ARMED.
THEY ALL ARE. GET USED TO IT.
COME ON, CALEB. DON'T BE A HARD-ASS.
SHE'S OUR MOTHER.
THAT'S EXACTLY RIGHT. SHE'S A FUCKING WOMAN.
LET'S SEE HOW THE COMMUNITY RESPONDS TO THAT. A *WIFE,* RUNNING THINGS?
YOU GREW UP IN THE SAME HOUSE I DID. YOU KNOW SHE WAS ALWAYS RUNNING THINGS.
FINE. I'LL BE ON MY BEST BEHAVIOR.
NICE TATTOO.
YOU LIKE THAT?
I CAN ONLY IMAGINE WHAT ELLIE THINKS ABOUT IT.
WHAT ARE YOU TALKING ABOUT?

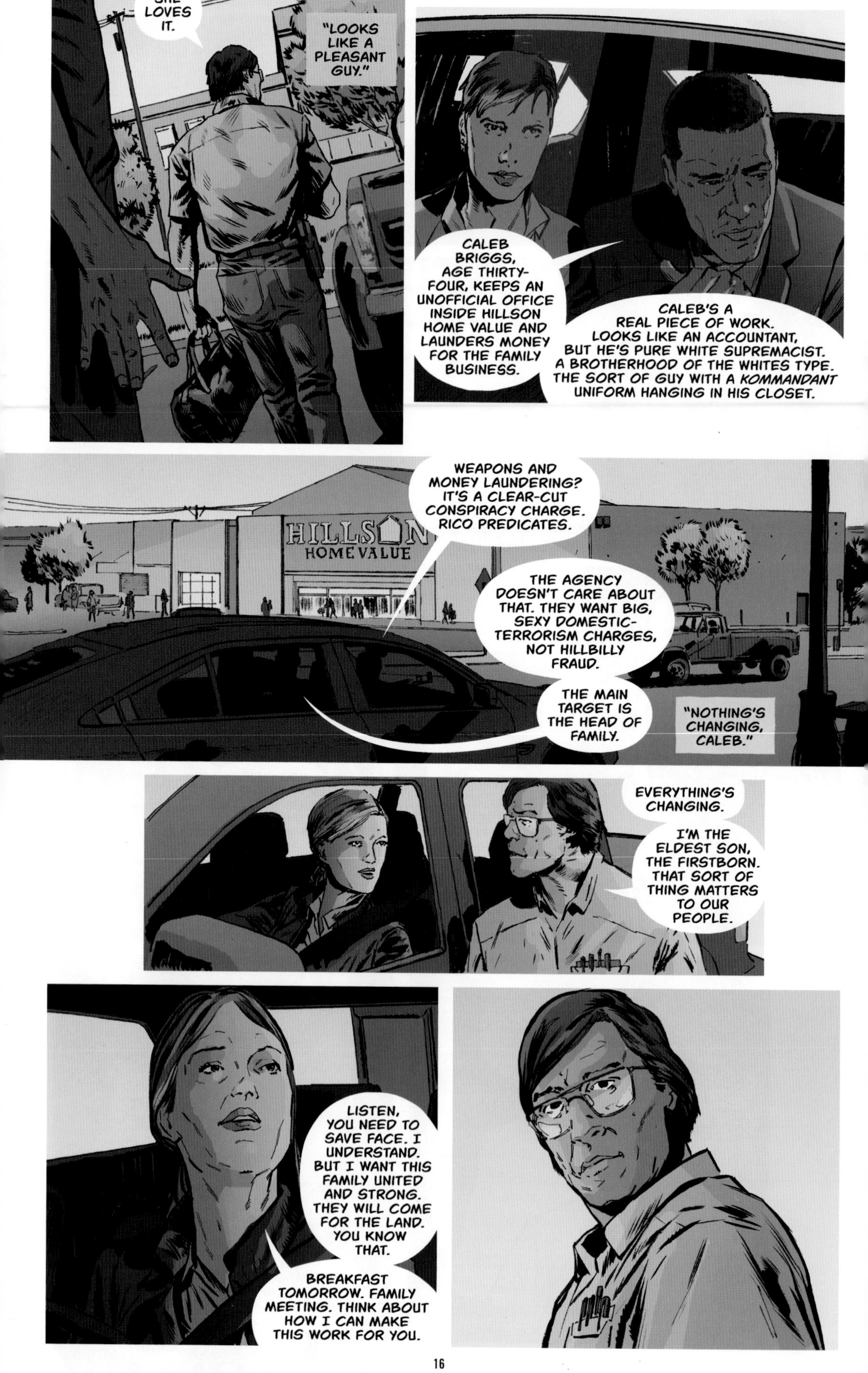
SHE LOVES IT.
"LOOKS LIKE A PLEASANT GUY."
CALEB BRIGGS, AGE THIRTY-FOUR, KEEPS AN UNOFFICIAL OFFICE INSIDE HILLSON HOME VALUE AND LAUNDERS MONEY FOR THE FAMILY BUSINESS.
CALEB'S A REAL PIECE OF WORK. LOOKS LIKE AN ACCOUNTANT, BUT HE'S PURE WHITE SUPREMACIST. A BROTHERHOOD OF THE WHITES TYPE. THE SORT OF GUY WITH A *KOMMANDANT* UNIFORM HANGING IN HIS CLOSET.
HILLSON HOME VALUE
WEAPONS AND MONEY LAUNDERING? IT'S A CLEAR-CUT CONSPIRACY CHARGE. RICO PREDICATES.
THE AGENCY DOESN'T CARE ABOUT THAT. THEY WANT BIG, SEXY DOMESTIC-TERRORISM CHARGES, NOT HILLBILLY FRAUD.
THE MAIN TARGET IS THE HEAD OF FAMILY.
"NOTHING'S CHANGING, CALEB."
EVERYTHING'S CHANGING.
I'M THE ELDEST SON, THE FIRSTBORN. THAT SORT OF THING MATTERS TO OUR PEOPLE.
LISTEN, YOU NEED TO SAVE FACE. I UNDERSTAND. BUT I WANT THIS FAMILY UNITED AND STRONG. THEY WILL COME FOR THE LAND. YOU KNOW THAT.
BREAKFAST TOMORROW. FAMILY MEETING. THINK ABOUT HOW I CAN MAKE THIS WORK FOR YOU.

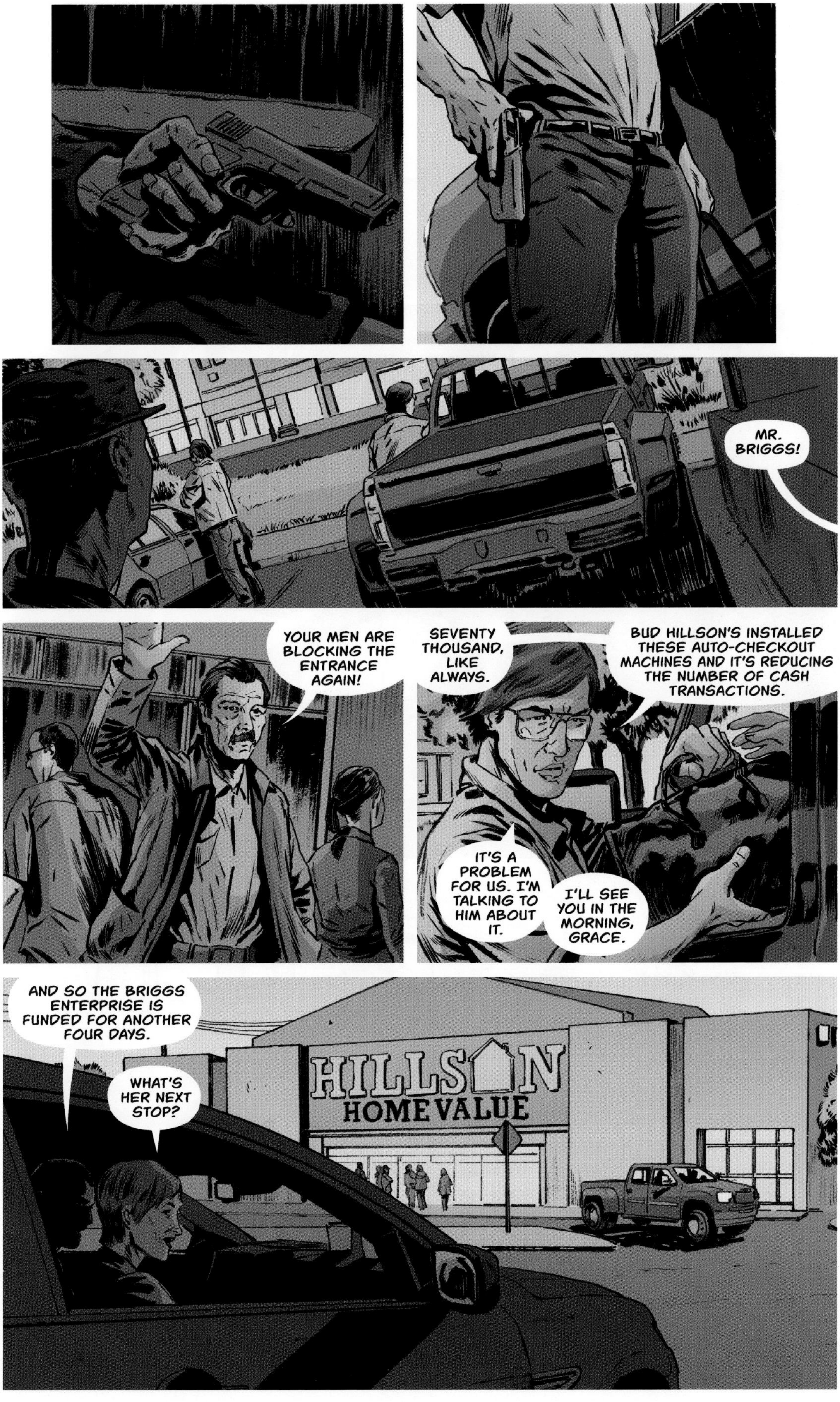
MR. BRIGGS!
YOUR MEN ARE BLOCKING THE ENTRANCE AGAIN!
SEVENTY THOUSAND, LIKE ALWAYS.
BUD HILLSON'S INSTALLED THESE AUTO-CHECKOUT MACHINES AND IT'S REDUCING THE NUMBER OF CASH TRANSACTIONS.
IT'S A PROBLEM FOR US. I'M TALKING TO HIM ABOUT IT.
I'LL SEE YOU IN THE MORNING, GRACE.
AND SO THE BRIGGS ENTERPRISE IS FUNDED FOR ANOTHER FOUR DAYS.
WHAT'S HER NEXT STOP?
HILLSON
HOME VALUE

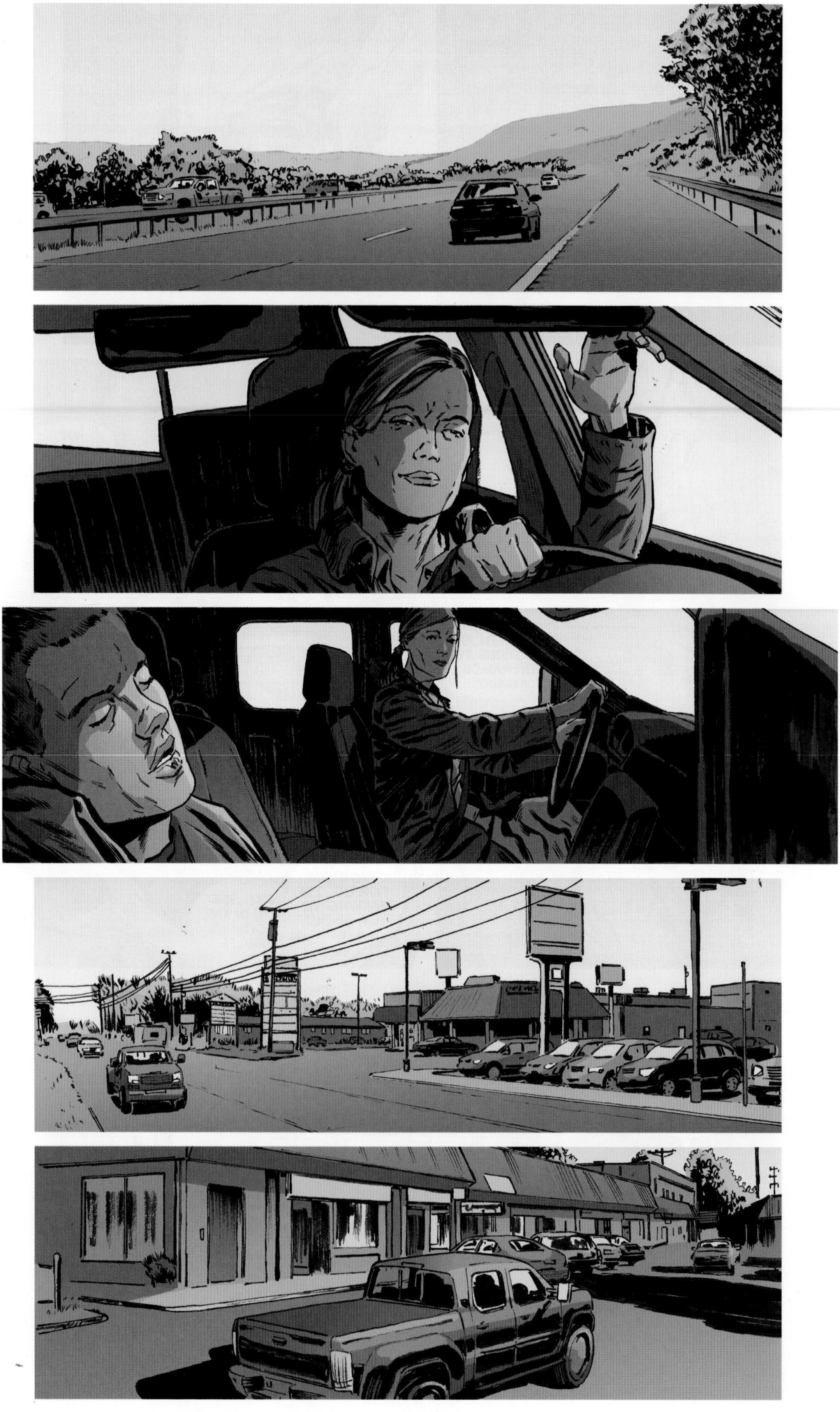

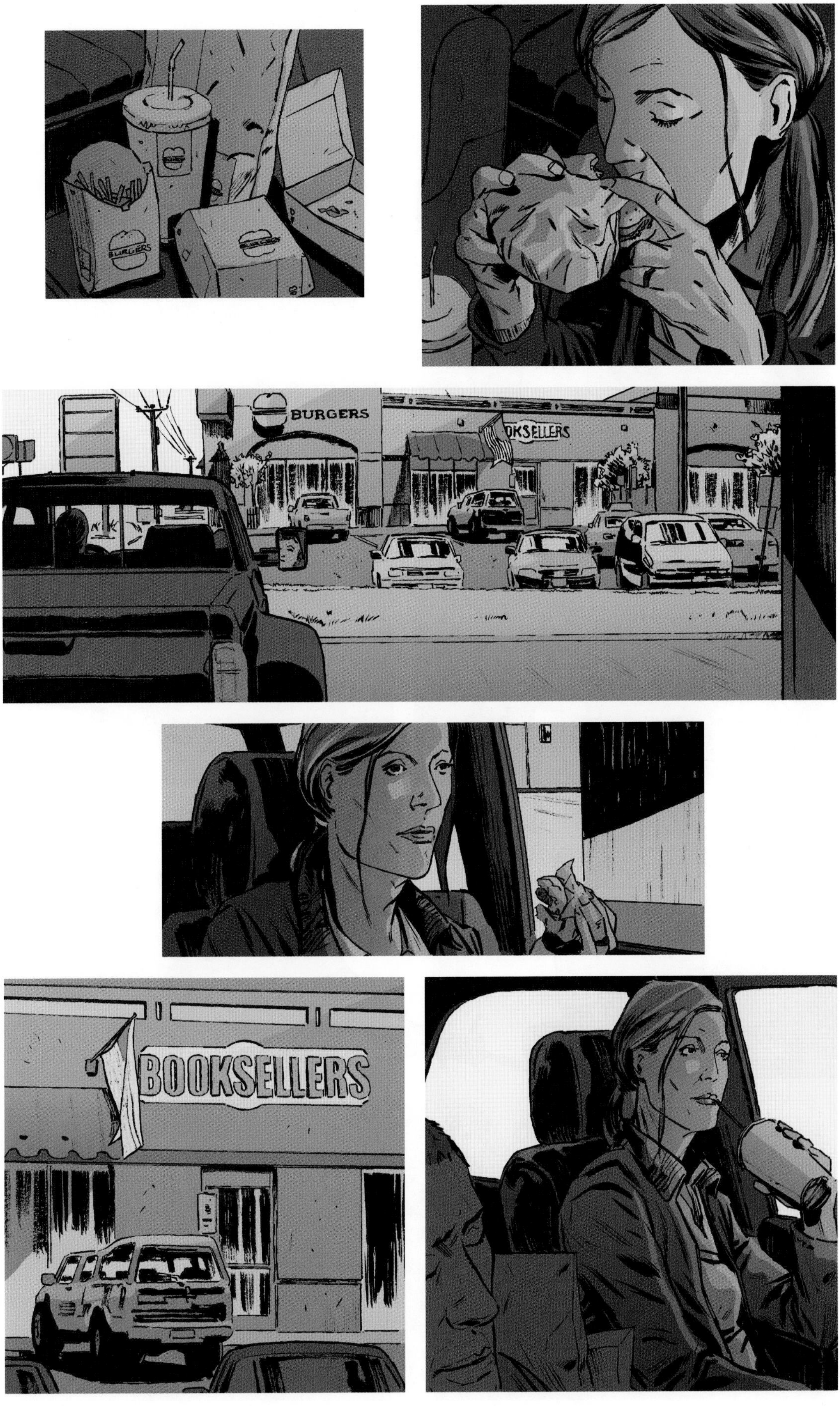
BURGERS
BURGERS
BOOKSELLERS

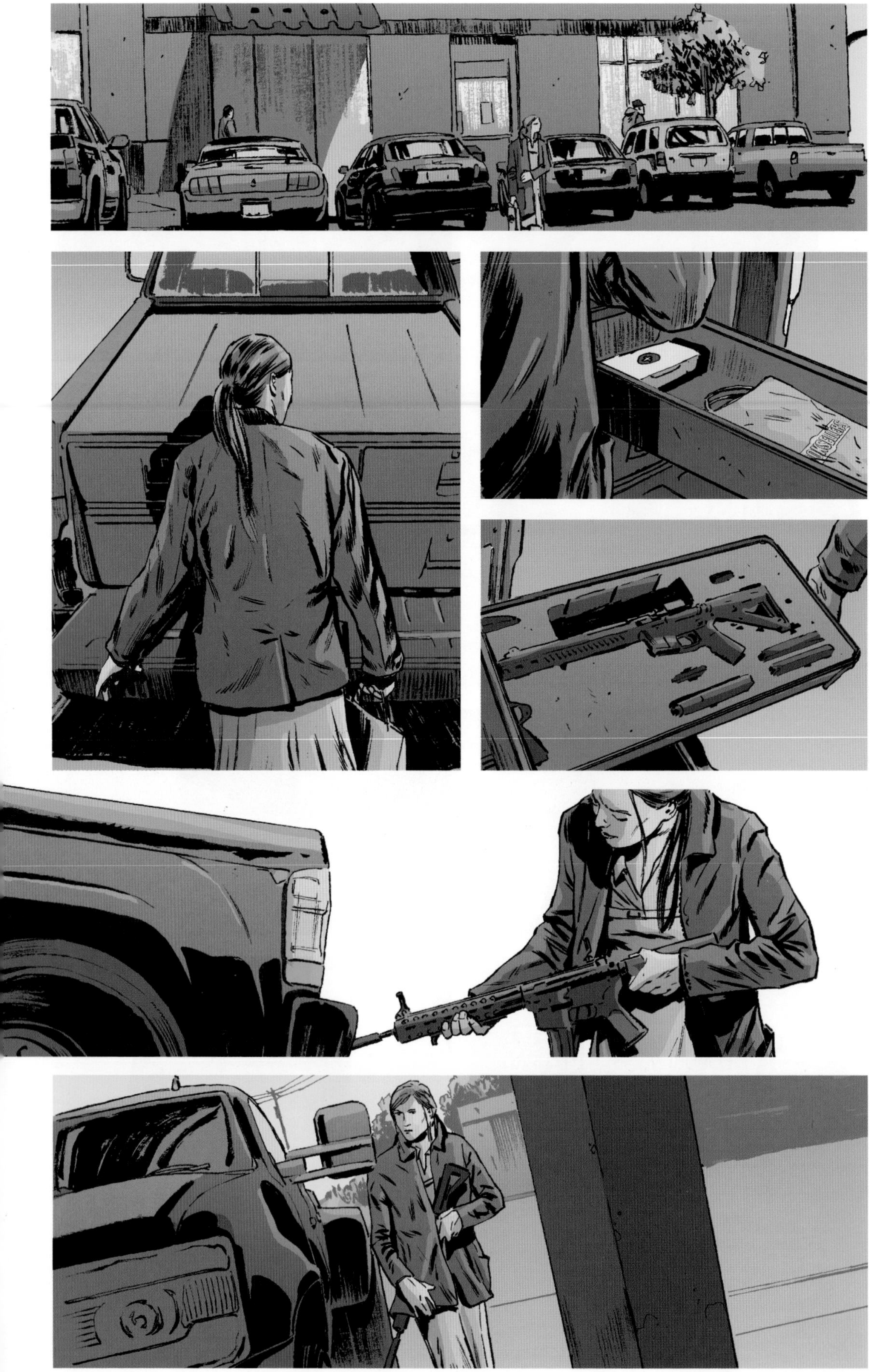

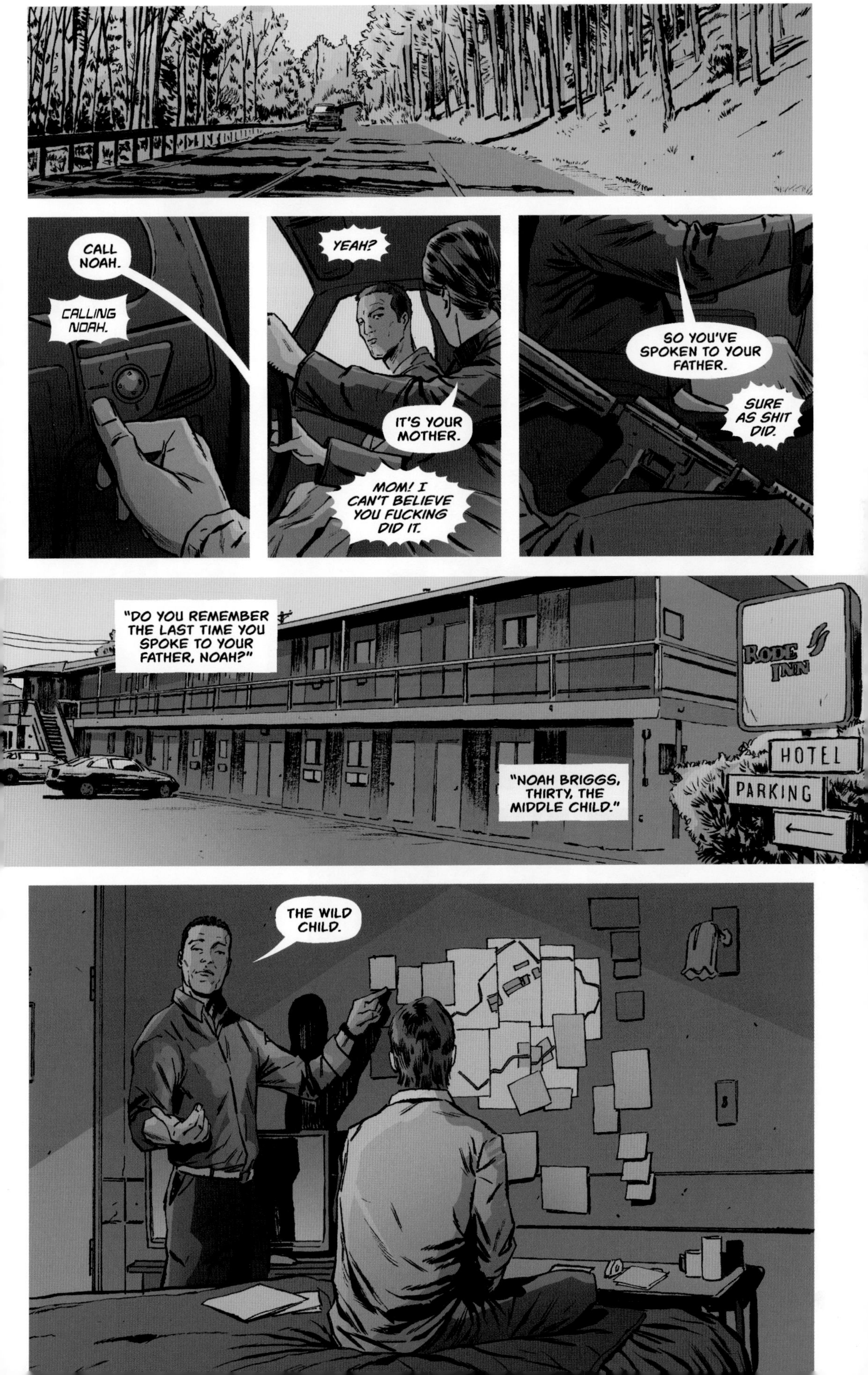
CALL NOAH.
CALLING NOAH.
YEAH?
IT'S YOUR MOTHER.
MOM! I CAN'T BELIEVE YOU FUCKING DID IT.
SO YOU'VE SPOKEN TO YOUR FATHER.
SURE AS SHIT DID.
"DO YOU REMEMBER THE LAST TIME YOU SPOKE TO YOUR FATHER, NOAH?"
RODE INN
HOTEL
PARKING
"NOAH BRIGGS, THIRTY, THE MIDDLE CHILD."
THE WILD CHILD.

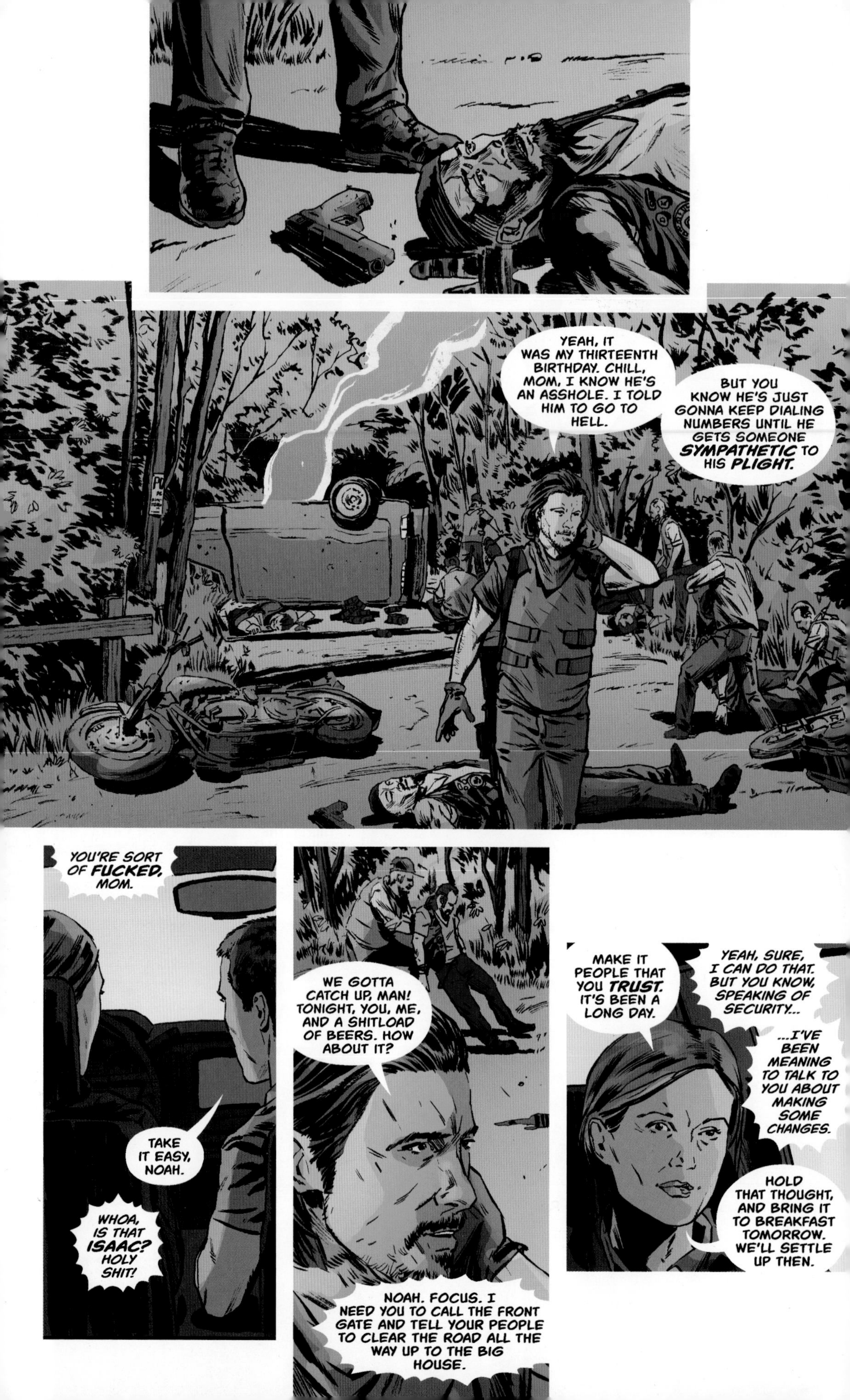
YEAH, IT WAS MY THIRTEENTH BIRTHDAY. CHILL, MOM, I KNOW HE'S AN ASSHOLE. I TOLD HIM TO GO TO HELL.
BUT YOU KNOW HE'S JUST GONNA KEEP DIALING NUMBERS UNTIL HE GETS SOMEONE SYMPATHETIC TO HIS PLIGHT.
YOU'RE SORT OF FUCKED, MOM.
TAKE IT EASY, NOAH.
WHOA, IS THAT ISAAC? HOLY SHIT!
WE GOTTA CATCH UP, MAN! TONIGHT, YOU, ME, AND A SHITLOAD OF BEERS. HOW ABOUT IT?
NOAH. FOCUS. I NEED YOU TO CALL THE FRONT GATE AND TELL YOUR PEOPLE TO CLEAR THE ROAD ALL THE WAY UP TO THE BIG HOUSE.
MAKE IT PEOPLE THAT YOU TRUST. IT'S BEEN A LONG DAY.
YEAH, SURE, I CAN DO THAT. BUT YOU KNOW, SPEAKING OF SECURITY...
...I'VE BEEN MEANING TO TALK TO YOU ABOUT MAKING SOME CHANGES.
HOLD THAT THOUGHT, AND BRING IT TO BREAKFAST TOMORROW. WE'LL SETTLE UP THEN.

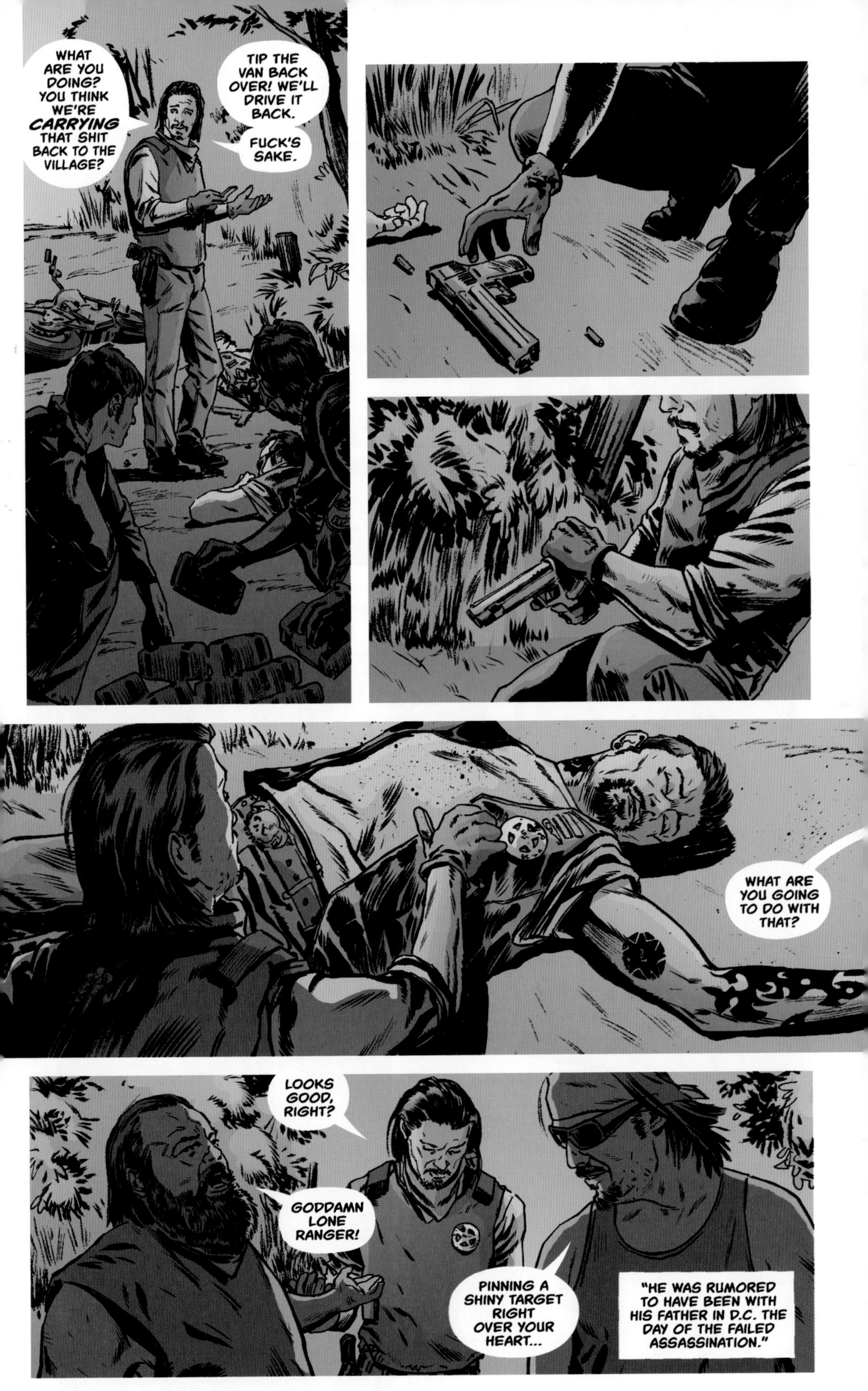

WHAT ARE YOU DOING? YOU THINK WE'RE CARRYING THAT SHIT BACK TO THE VILLAGE?
TIP THE VAN BACK OVER! WE'LL DRIVE IT BACK.
FUCK'S SAKE.
WHAT ARE YOU GOING TO DO WITH THAT?
LOOKS GOOD, RIGHT?
GODDAMN LONE RANGER!
PINNING A SHINY TARGET RIGHT OVER YOUR HEART...
"HE WAS RUMORED TO HAVE BEEN WITH HIS FATHER IN D.C. THE DAY OF THE FAILED ASSASSINATION."

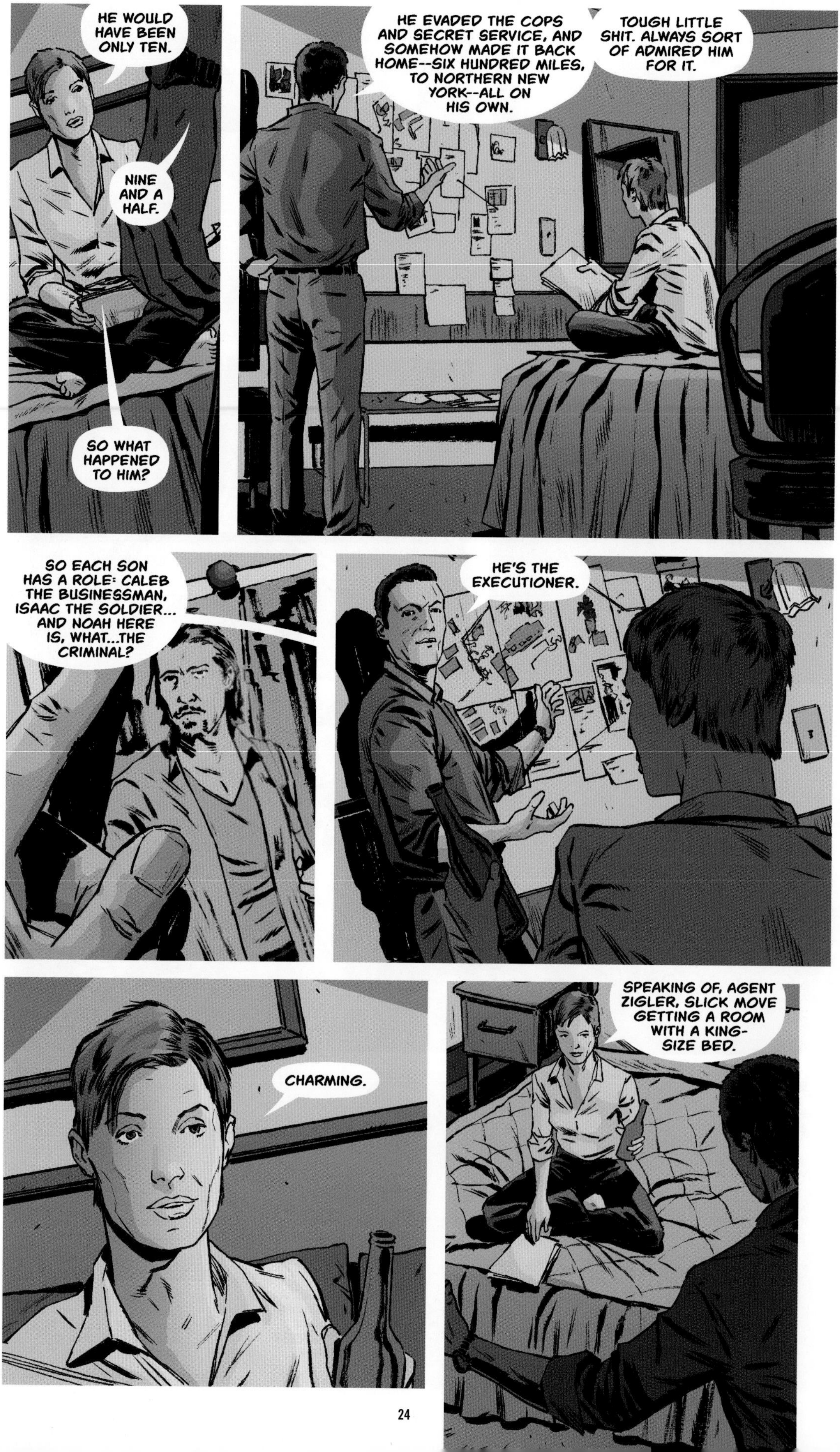
HE WOULD HAVE BEEN ONLY TEN.
NINE AND A HALF.
SO WHAT HAPPENED TO HIM?
HE EVADED THE COPS AND SECRET SERVICE, AND SOMEHOW MADE IT BACK HOME--SIX HUNDRED MILES, TO NORTHERN NEW YORK--ALL ON HIS OWN.
TOUGH LITTLE SHIT. ALWAYS SORT OF ADMIRED HIM FOR IT.
SO EACH SON HAS A ROLE: CALEB THE BUSINESSMAN, ISAAC THE SOLDIER... AND NOAH HERE IS, WHAT...THE CRIMINAL?
HE'S THE EXECUTIONER.
CHARMING.
SPEAKING OF, AGENT ZIGLER, SLICK MOVE GETTING A ROOM WITH A KING-SIZE BED.

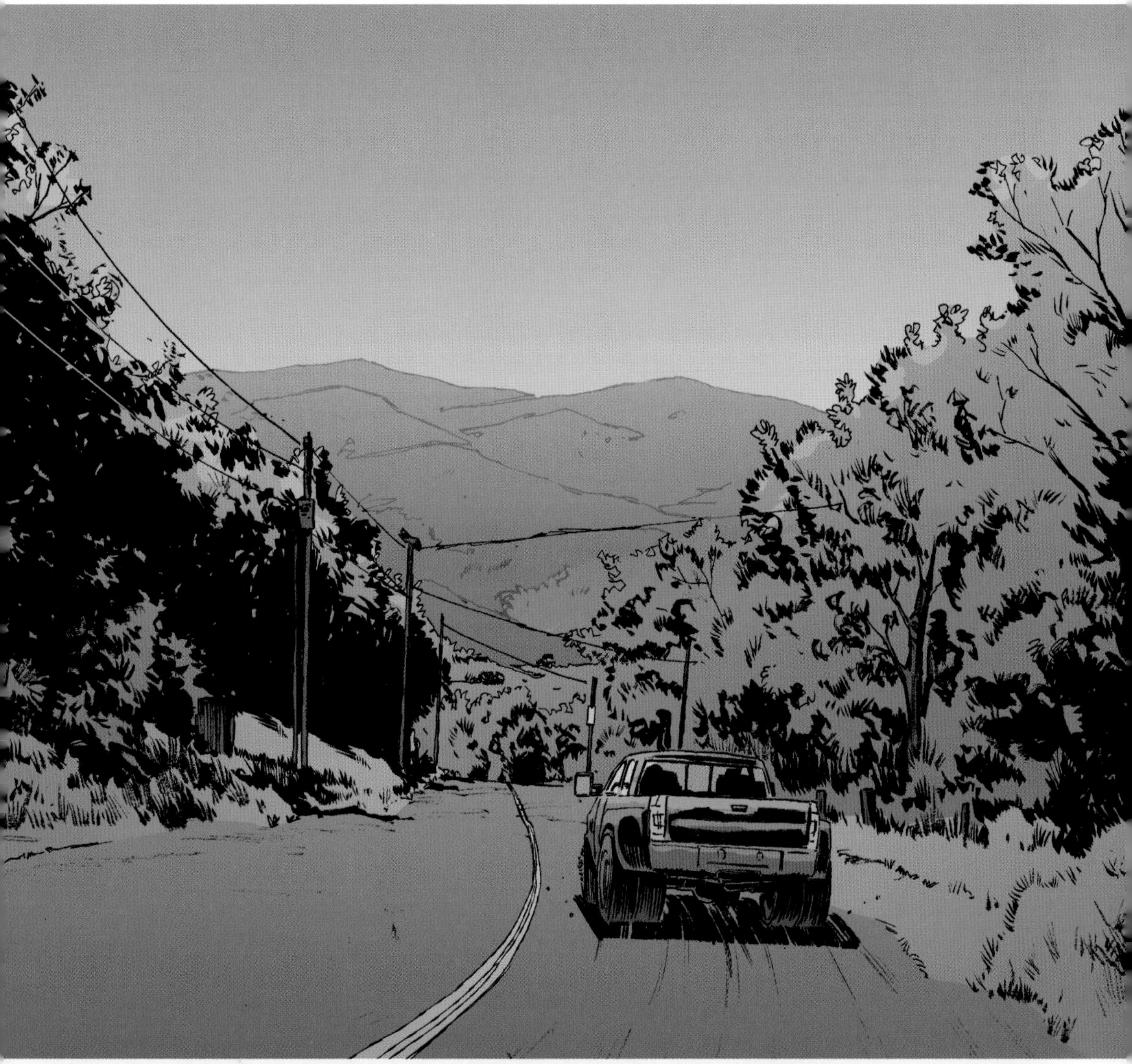

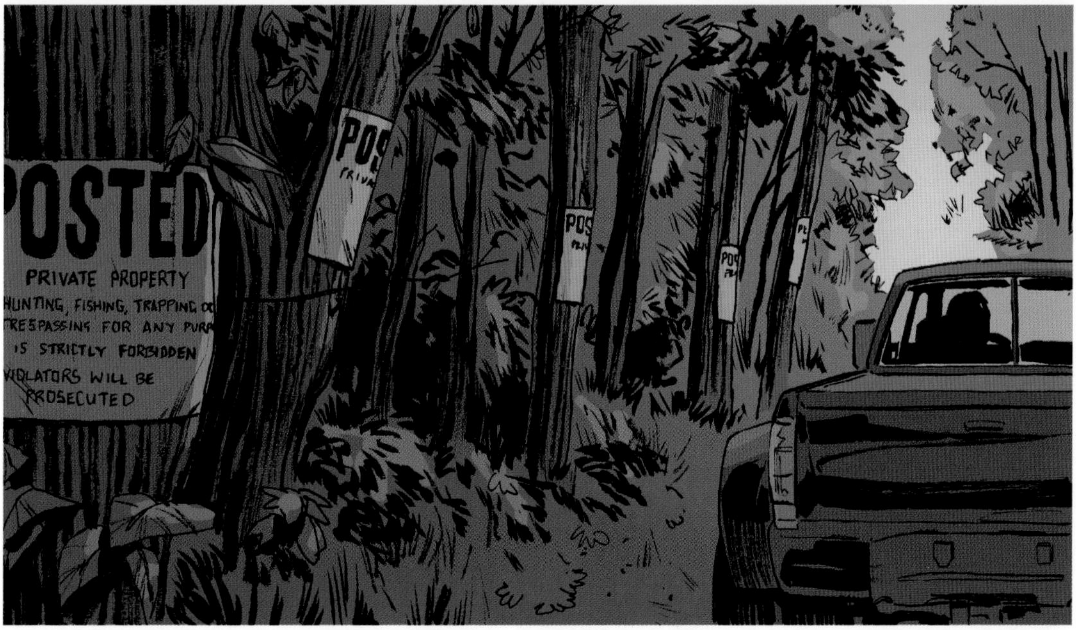
POSTED
PRIVATE PROPERTY
HUNTING, FISHING, TRAPPING
TRESPASSING FOR ANY
IS STRICTLY FORBIDDEN
VIOLATORS WILL BE
PROSECUTED

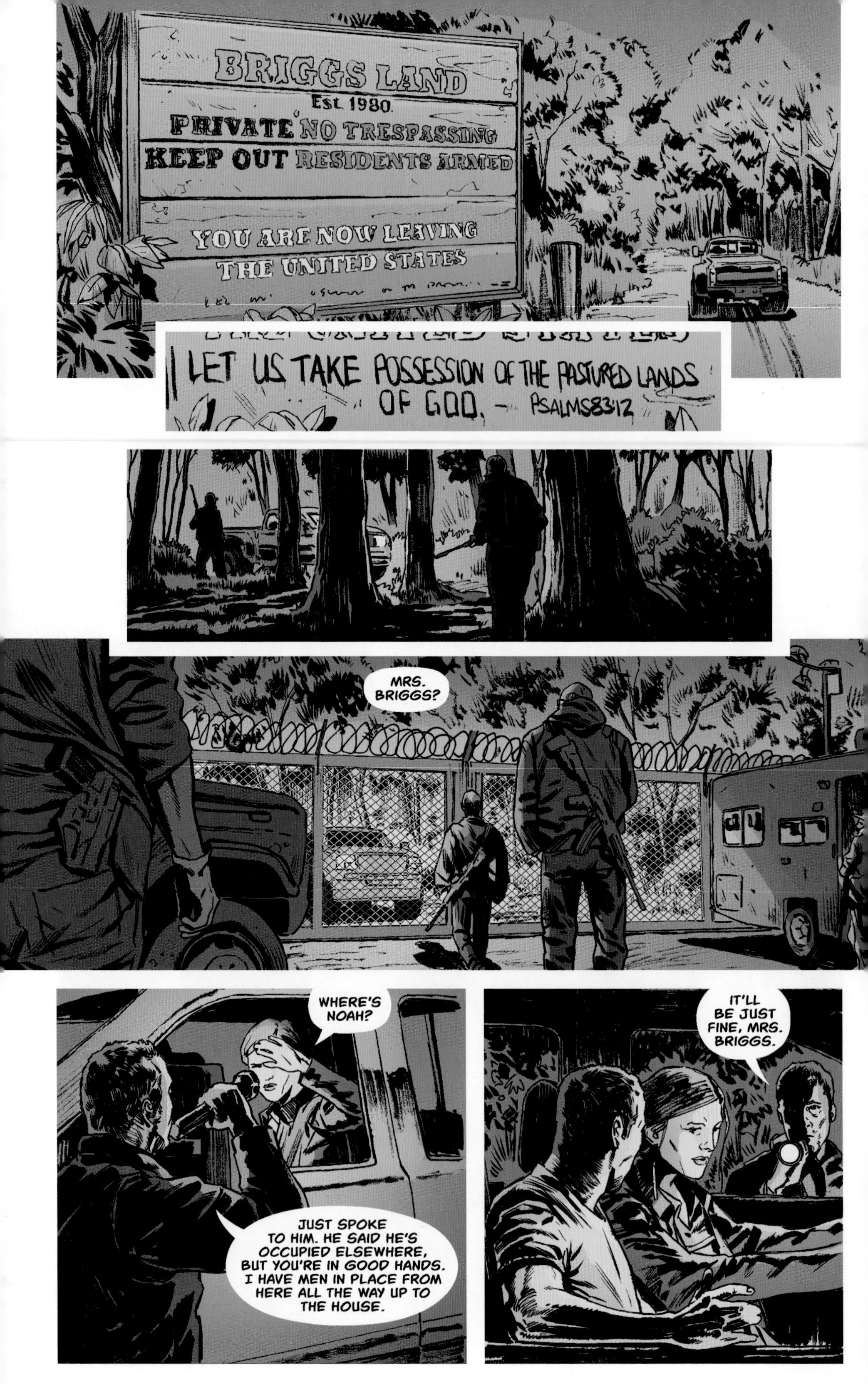
BRIGGS LAND
Est. 1980.
PRIVATE NO TRESPASSING
KEEP OUT RESIDENTS ARMED
YOU ARE NOW LEAVING
THE UNITED STATES
LET US TAKE POSSESSION OF THE PASTURED LANDS OF GOD. - PSALMS 83:12
MRS. BRIGGS?
WHERE'S NOAH?
JUST SPOKE TO HIM. HE SAID HE'S OCCUPIED ELSEWHERE, BUT YOU'RE IN GOOD HANDS. I HAVE MEN IN PLACE FROM HERE ALL THE WAY UP TO THE HOUSE.
IT'LL BE JUST FINE, MRS. BRIGGS.

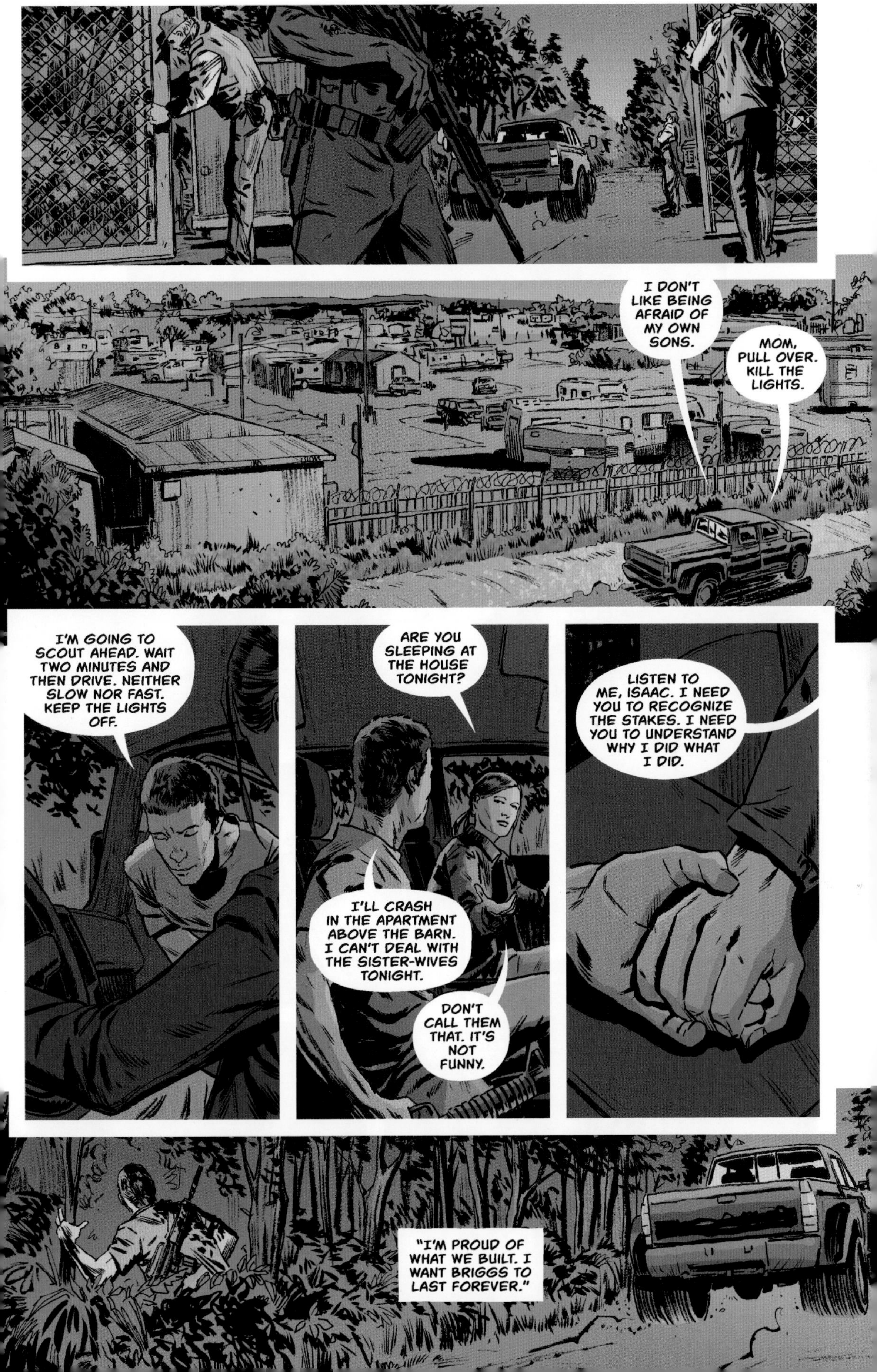
I DON'T LIKE BEING AFRAID OF MY OWN SONS.
MOM, PULL OVER. KILL THE LIGHTS.
I'M GOING TO SCOUT AHEAD. WAIT TWO MINUTES AND THEN DRIVE. NEITHER SLOW NOR FAST. KEEP THE LIGHTS OFF.
ARE YOU SLEEPING AT THE HOUSE TONIGHT?
I'LL CRASH IN THE APARTMENT ABOVE THE BARN. I CAN'T DEAL WITH THE SISTER-WIVES TONIGHT.
DON'T CALL THEM THAT. IT'S NOT FUNNY.
LISTEN TO ME, ISAAC. I NEED YOU TO RECOGNIZE THE STAKES. I NEED YOU TO UNDERSTAND WHY I DID WHAT I DID.
"I'M PROUD OF WHAT WE BUILT. I WANT BRIGGS TO LAST FOREVER."

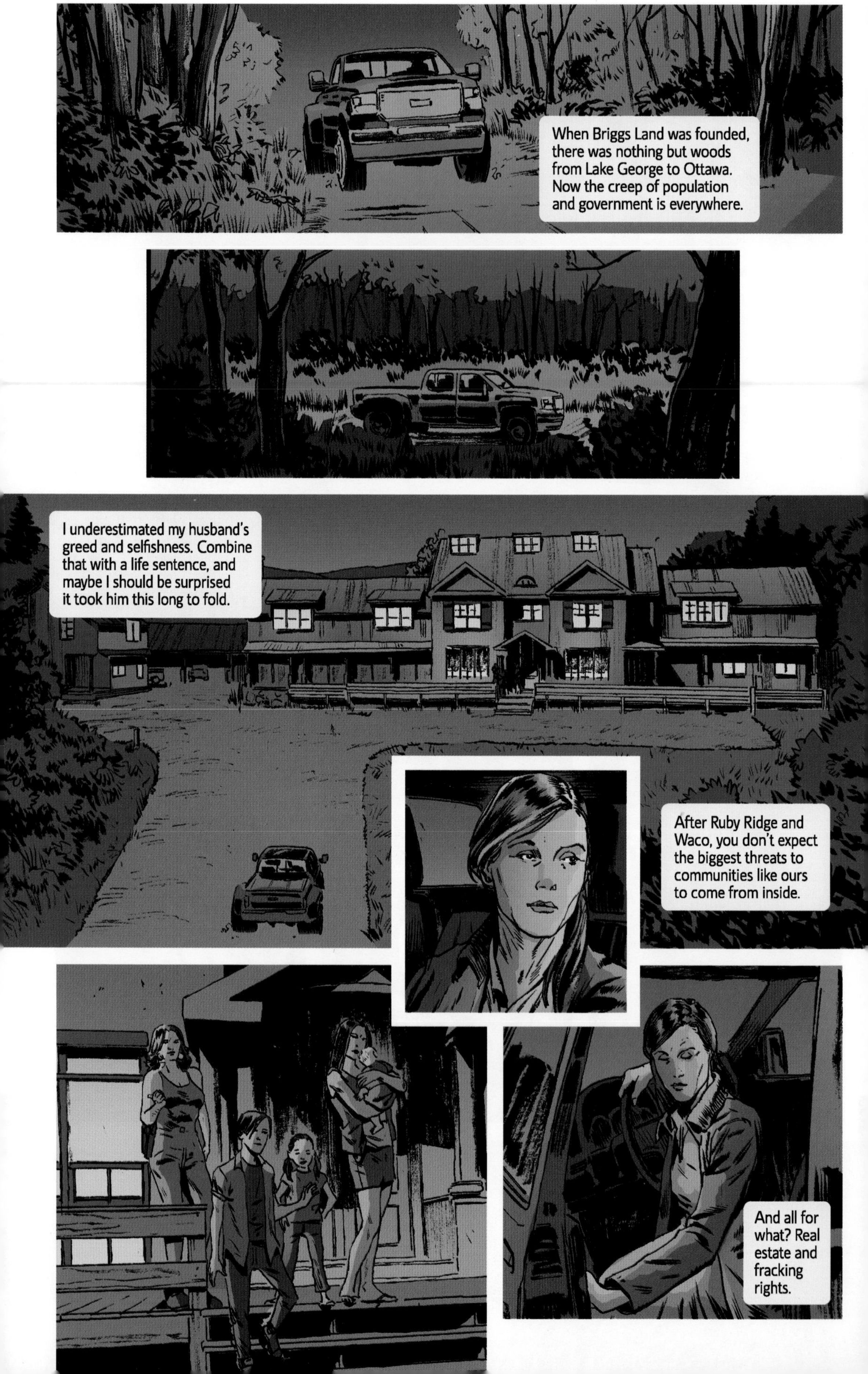
When Briggs Land was founded, there was nothing but woods from Lake George to Ottawa. Now the creep of population and government is everywhere.
I underestimated my husband's greed and selfishness. Combine that with a life sentence, and maybe I should be surprised it took him this long to fold.
After Ruby Ridge and Waco, you don't expect the biggest threats to communities like ours to come from inside.
And all for what? Real estate and fracking rights.

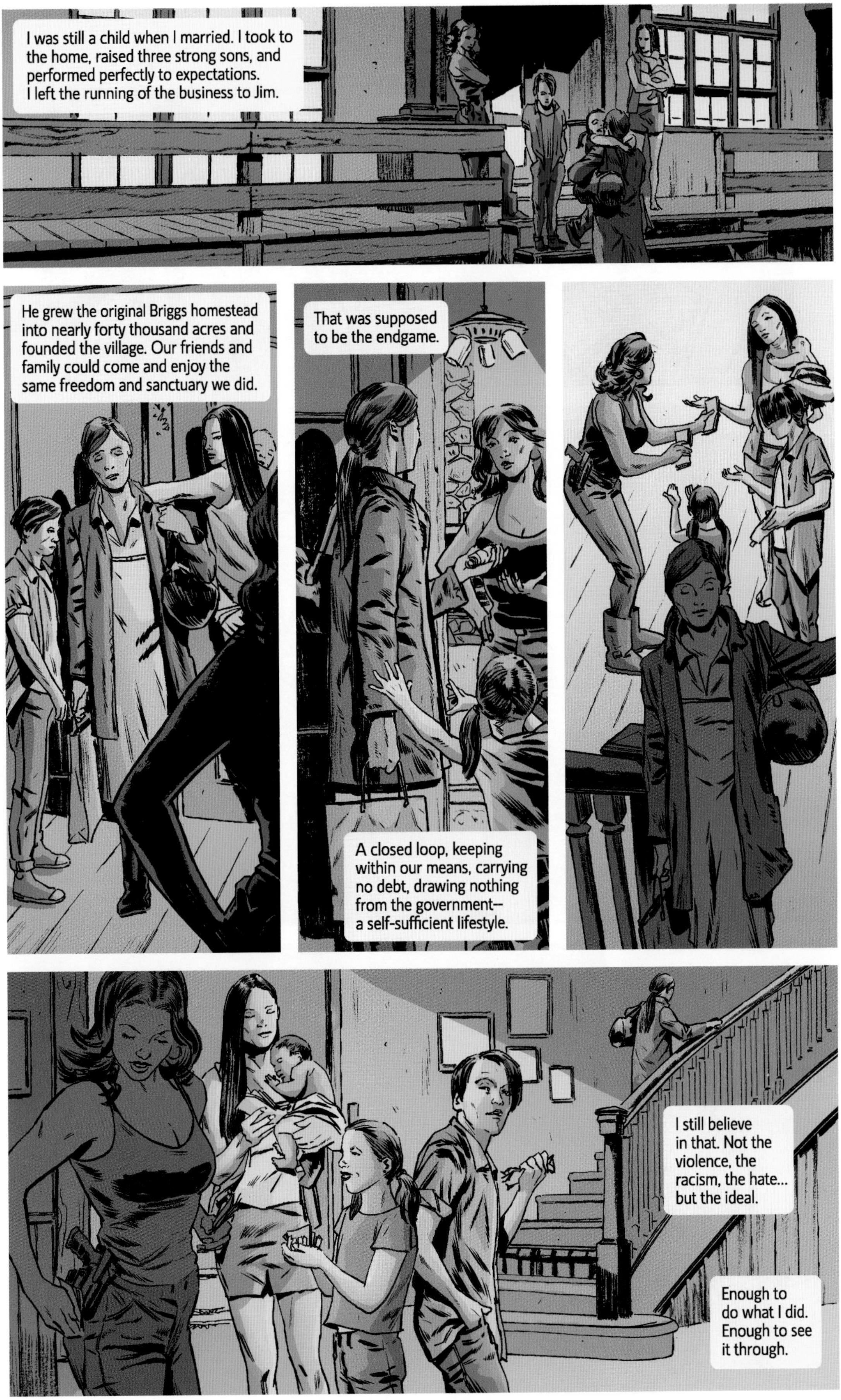
I was still a child when I married. I took to the home, raised three strong sons, and performed perfectly to expectations. I left the running of the business to Jim.
He grew the original Briggs homestead into nearly forty thousand acres and founded the village. Our friends and family could come and enjoy the same freedom and sanctuary we did.
That was supposed to be the endgame.
A closed loop, keeping within our means, carrying no debt, drawing nothing from the government--a self-sufficient lifestyle.
I still believe in that. Not the violence, the racism, the hate... but the ideal.
Enough to do what I did. Enough to see it through.

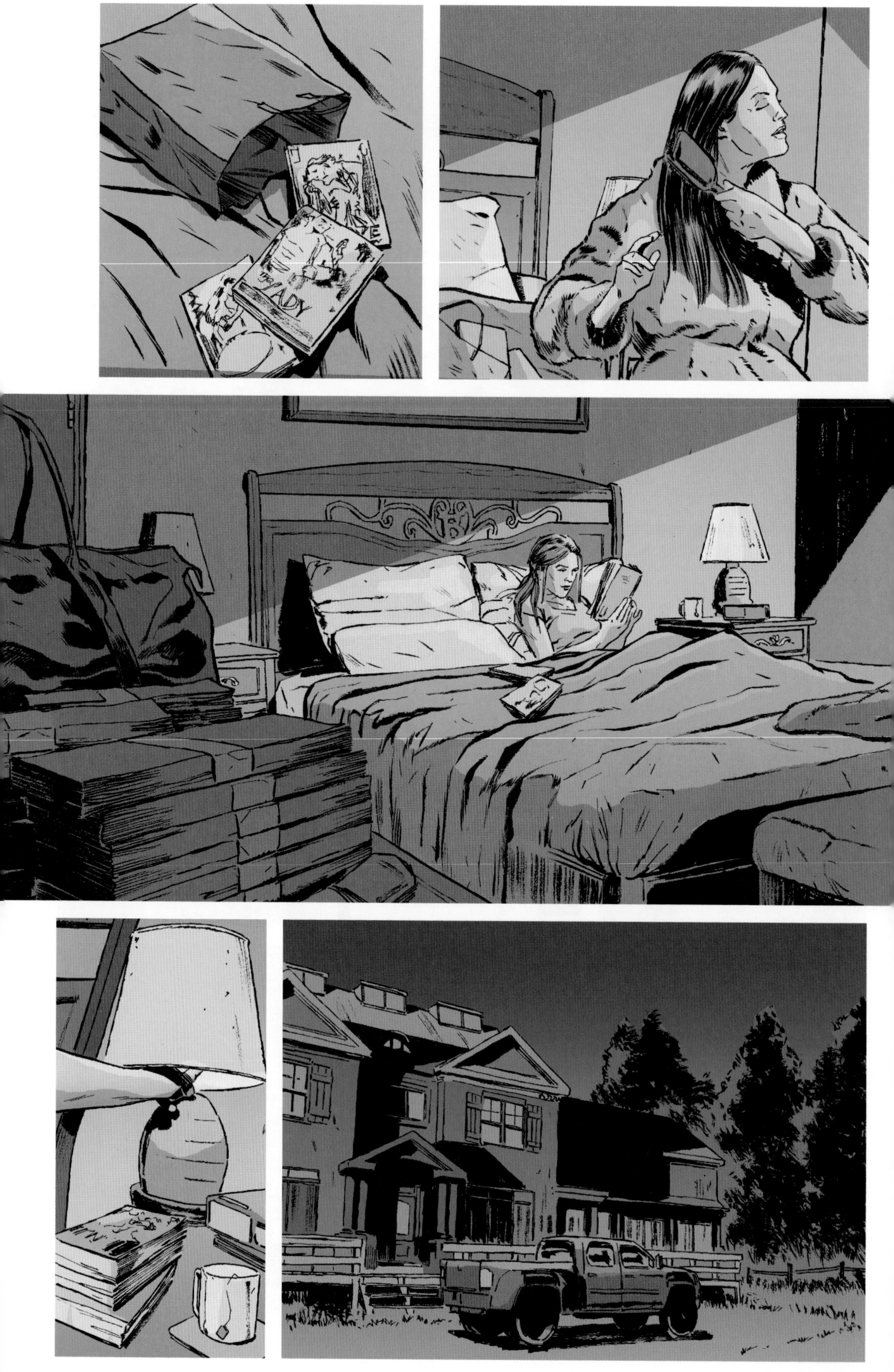

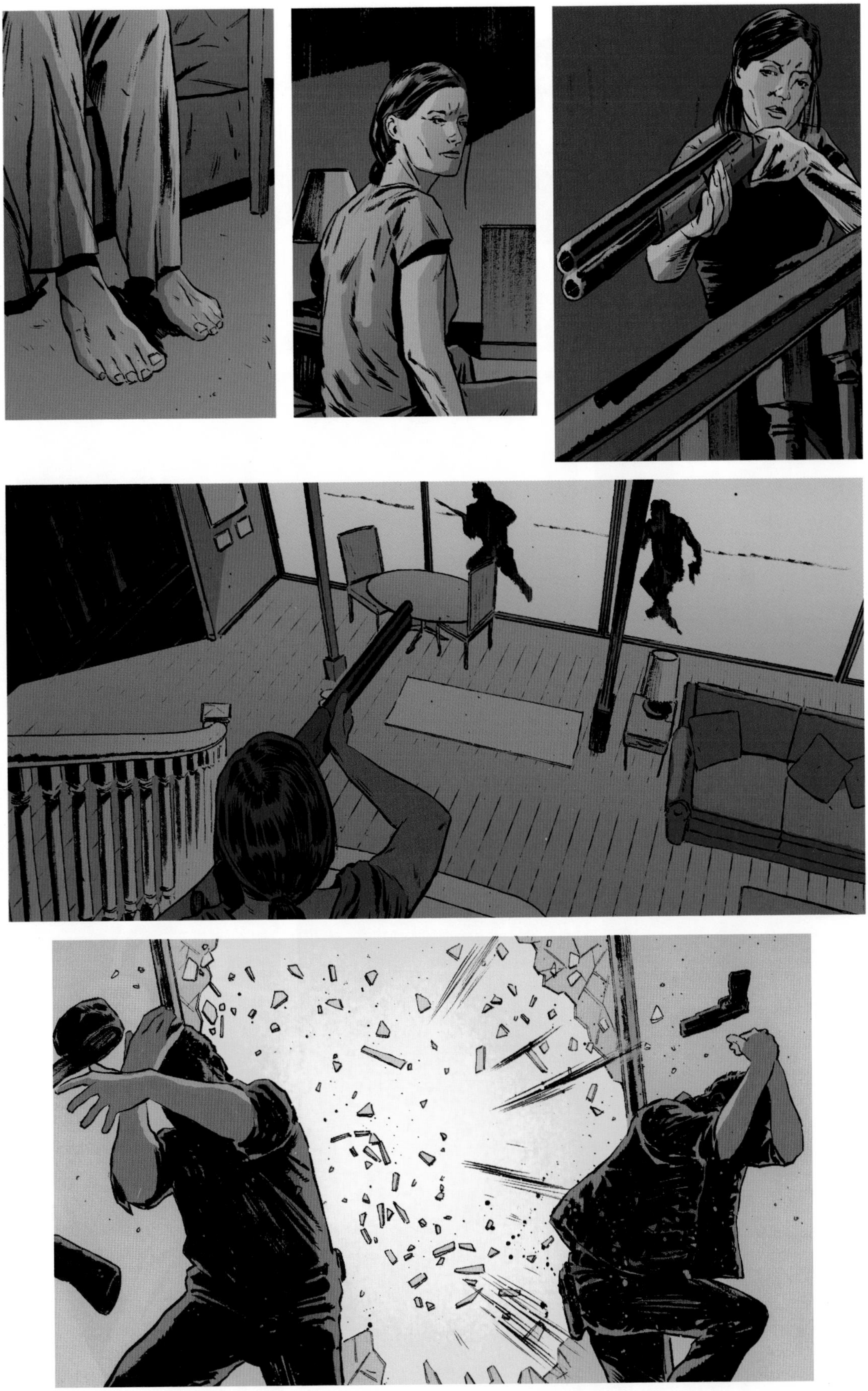

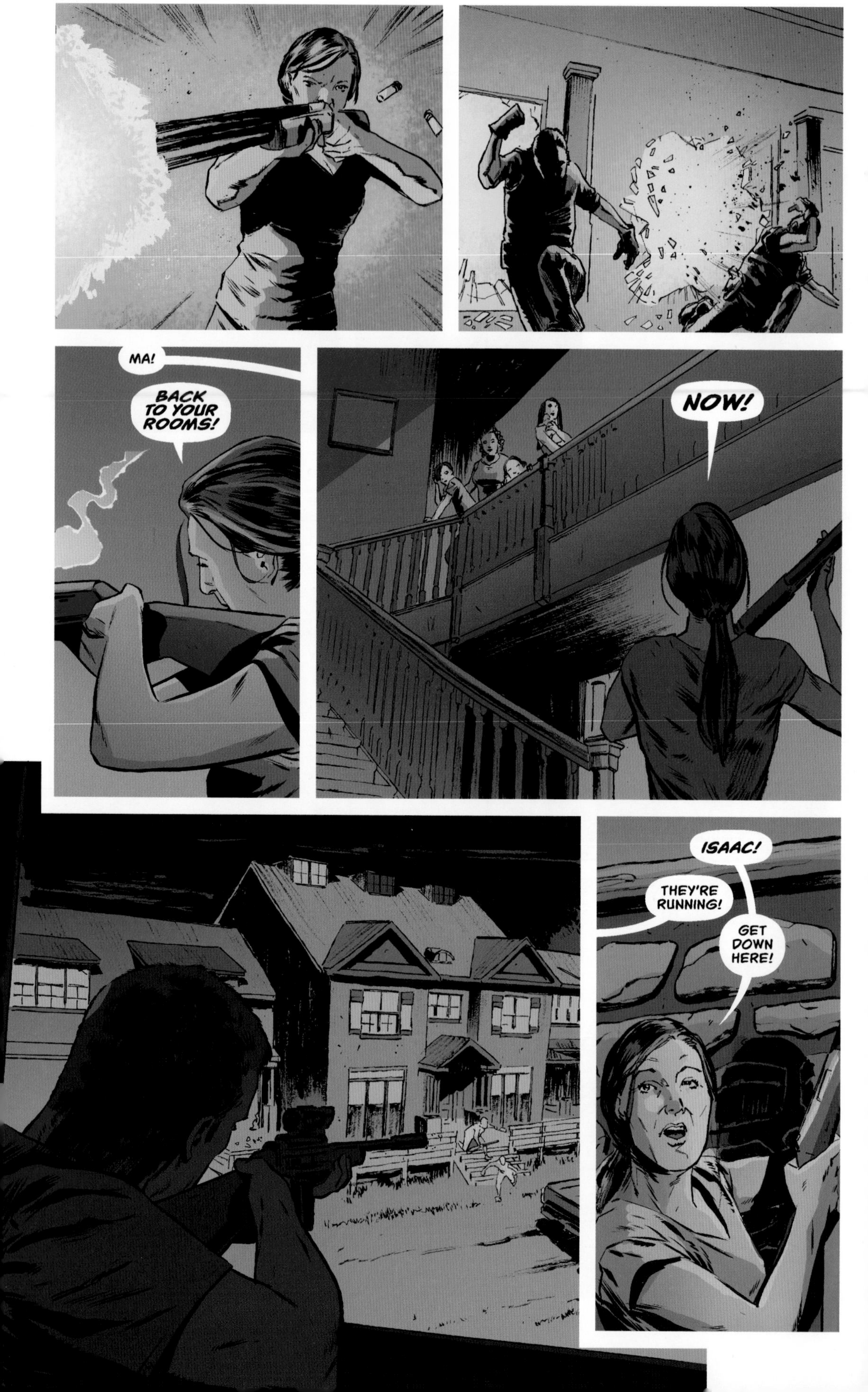
MA!
BACK TO YOUR ROOMS!
NOW!
ISAAC!
THEY'RE RUNNING!
GET DOWN HERE!

DID YOU SEE WHO IT WAS?

TWO MEN. TOO DARK TO IDENTIFY. DON'T YOU HAVE FLOOD-LIGHTS? MOTION SENSORS?

THIS IS OUR **HOME**. I CAN'T BELIEVE HE'D DO THIS.

YOU DON'T KNOW FOR SURE WHO DID THIS.

OF COURSE I KNOW WHO DID THIS! AND SO DO YOU!

WE **RAISED** YOU HERE! HIS **GRANDKIDS** LIVE IN THIS HOUSE!

OH MY GOD.

MOM...

OH MY GOD, IS THIS MY FAULT? I PROVOKED HIM...

MOM.

YOU DID THE RIGHT THING.

LISTEN...

I'LL NEVER STOP HIM! HE'S A FUCKING MONSTER!

LOOK AT THE HOUSE.

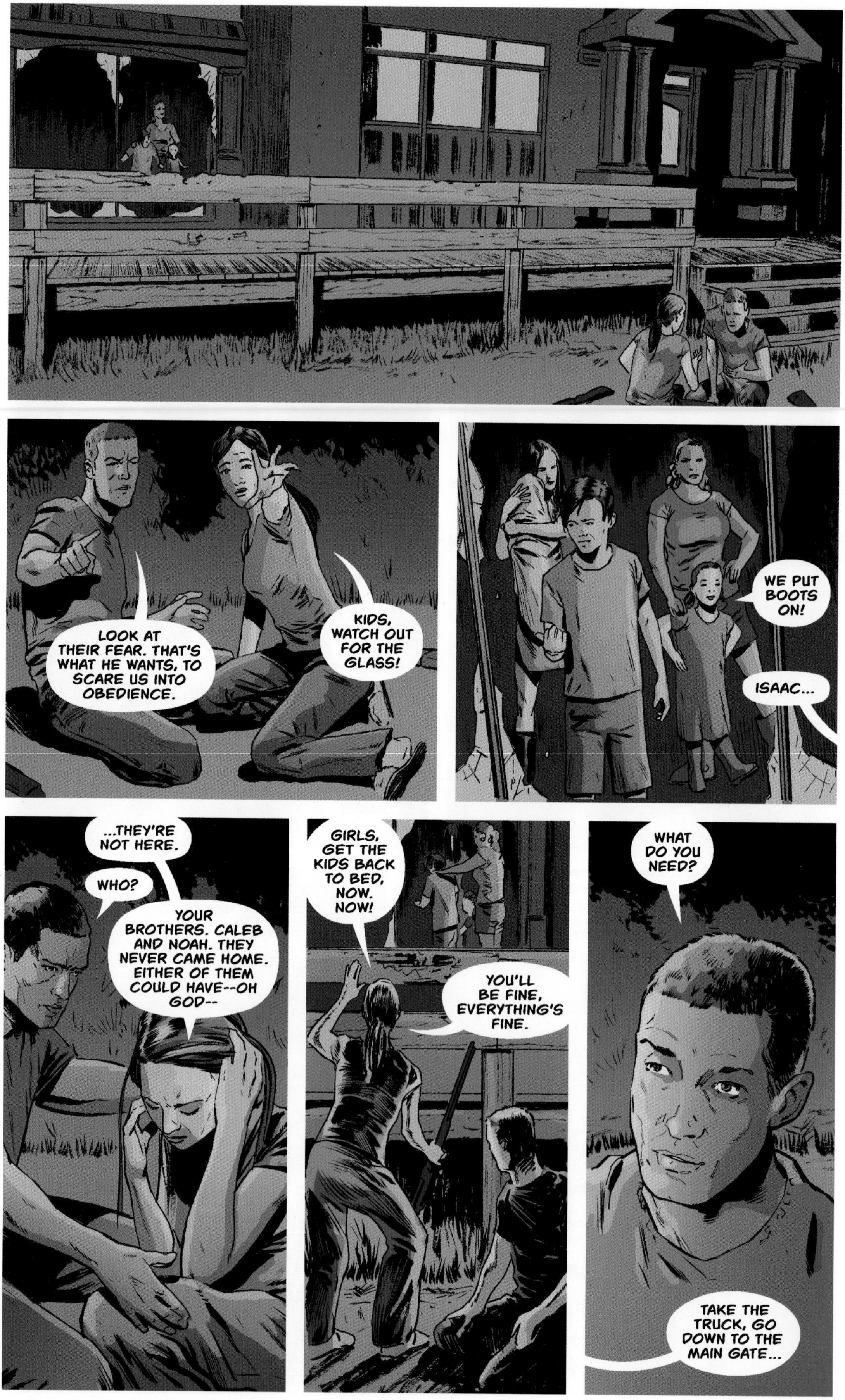
LOOK AT THEIR FEAR. THAT'S WHAT HE WANTS, TO SCARE US INTO OBEDIENCE.
KIDS, WATCH OUT FOR THE GLASS!
WE PUT BOOTS ON!
ISAAC...
...THEY'RE NOT HERE.
WHO?
YOUR BROTHERS. CALEB AND NOAH. THEY NEVER CAME HOME. EITHER OF THEM COULD HAVE--OH GOD--
GIRLS, GET THE KIDS BACK TO BED, NOW. NOW!
YOU'LL BE FINE, EVERYTHING'S FINE.
WHAT DO YOU NEED?
TAKE THE TRUCK, GO DOWN TO THE MAIN GATE...

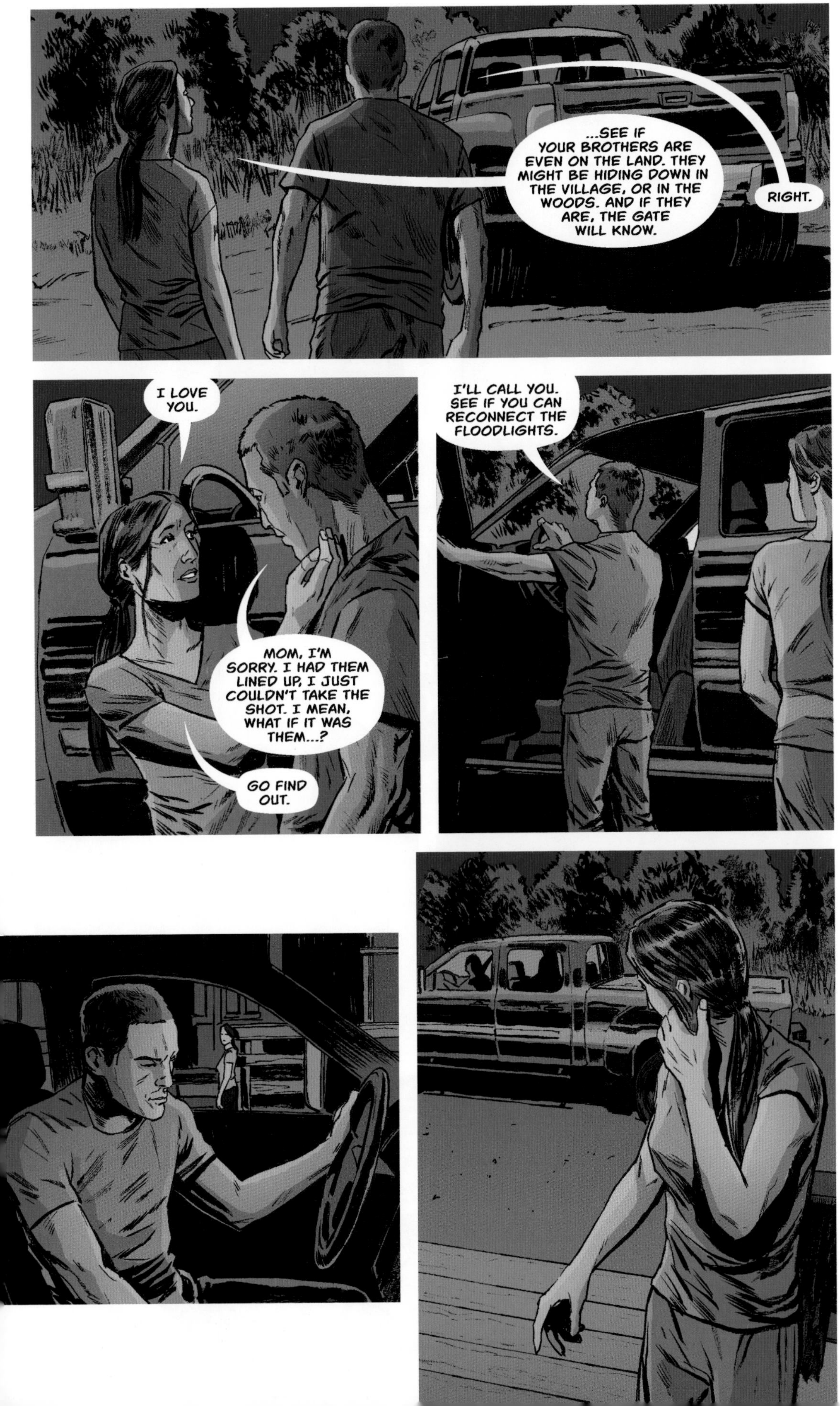
...SEE IF YOUR BROTHERS ARE EVEN ON THE LAND. THEY MIGHT BE HIDING DOWN IN THE VILLAGE, OR IN THE WOODS. AND IF THEY ARE, THE GATE WILL KNOW.
RIGHT.
I LOVE YOU.
MOM, I'M SORRY. I HAD THEM LINED UP, I JUST COULDN'T TAKE THE SHOT. I MEAN, WHAT IF IT WAS THEM...?
GO FIND OUT.
I'LL CALL YOU. SEE IF YOU CAN RECONNECT THE FLOODLIGHTS.

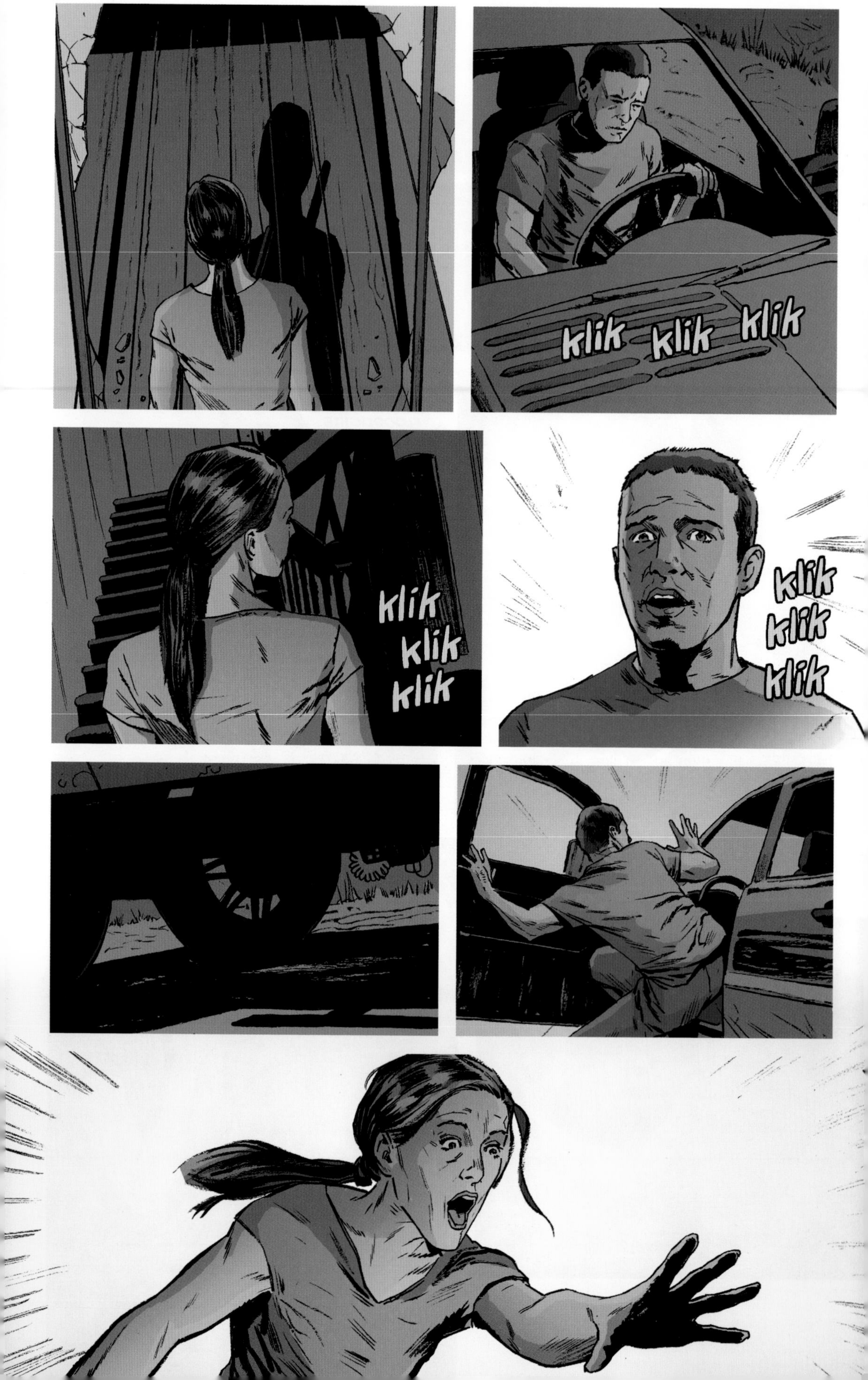
klik klik klik
klik
klik
klik
klik
klik
klik

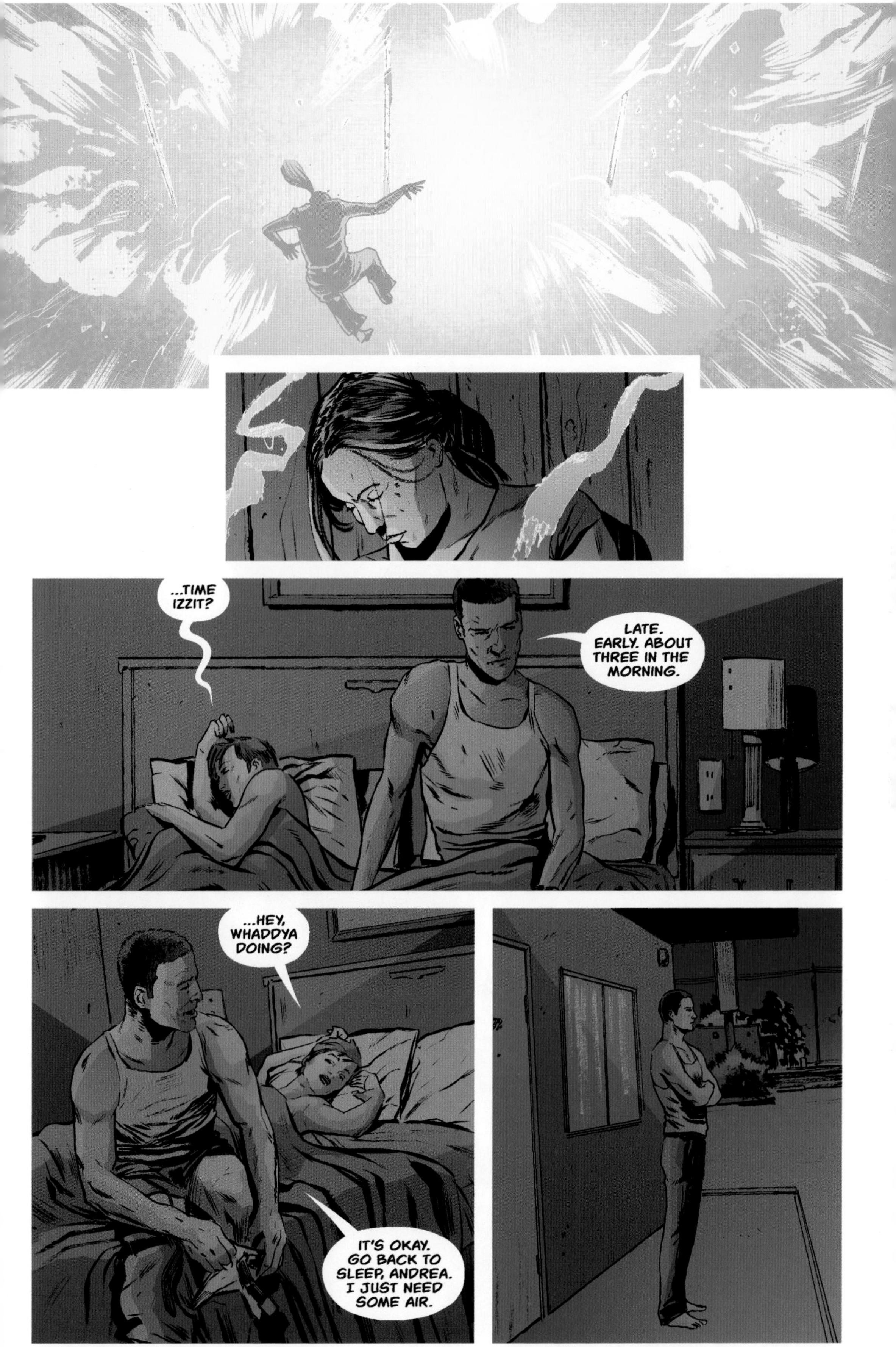
...TIME IZZIT?
LATE. EARLY. ABOUT THREE IN THE MORNING.
...HEY, WHADDYA DOING?
IT'S OKAY. GO BACK TO SLEEP, ANDREA. I JUST NEED SOME AIR.

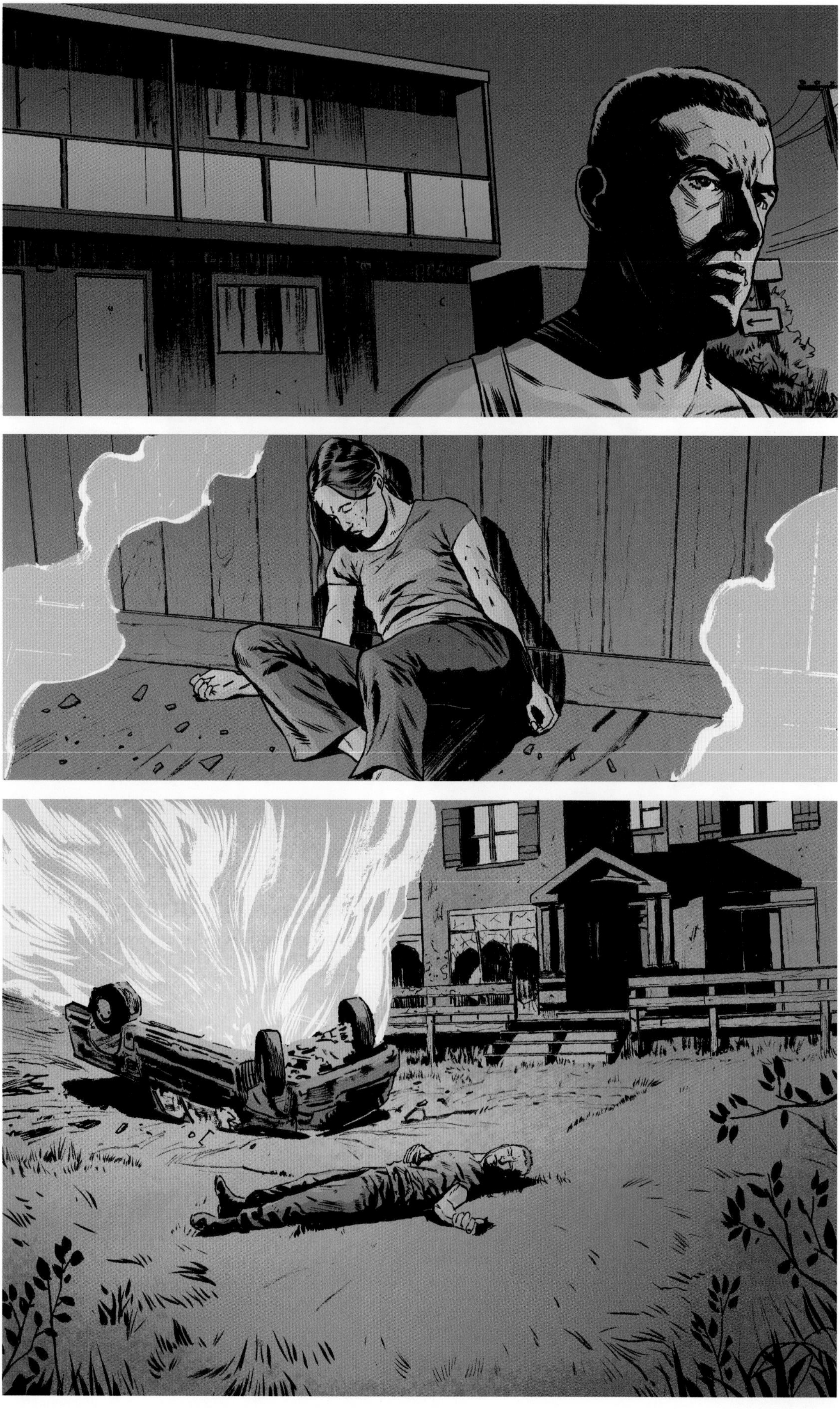

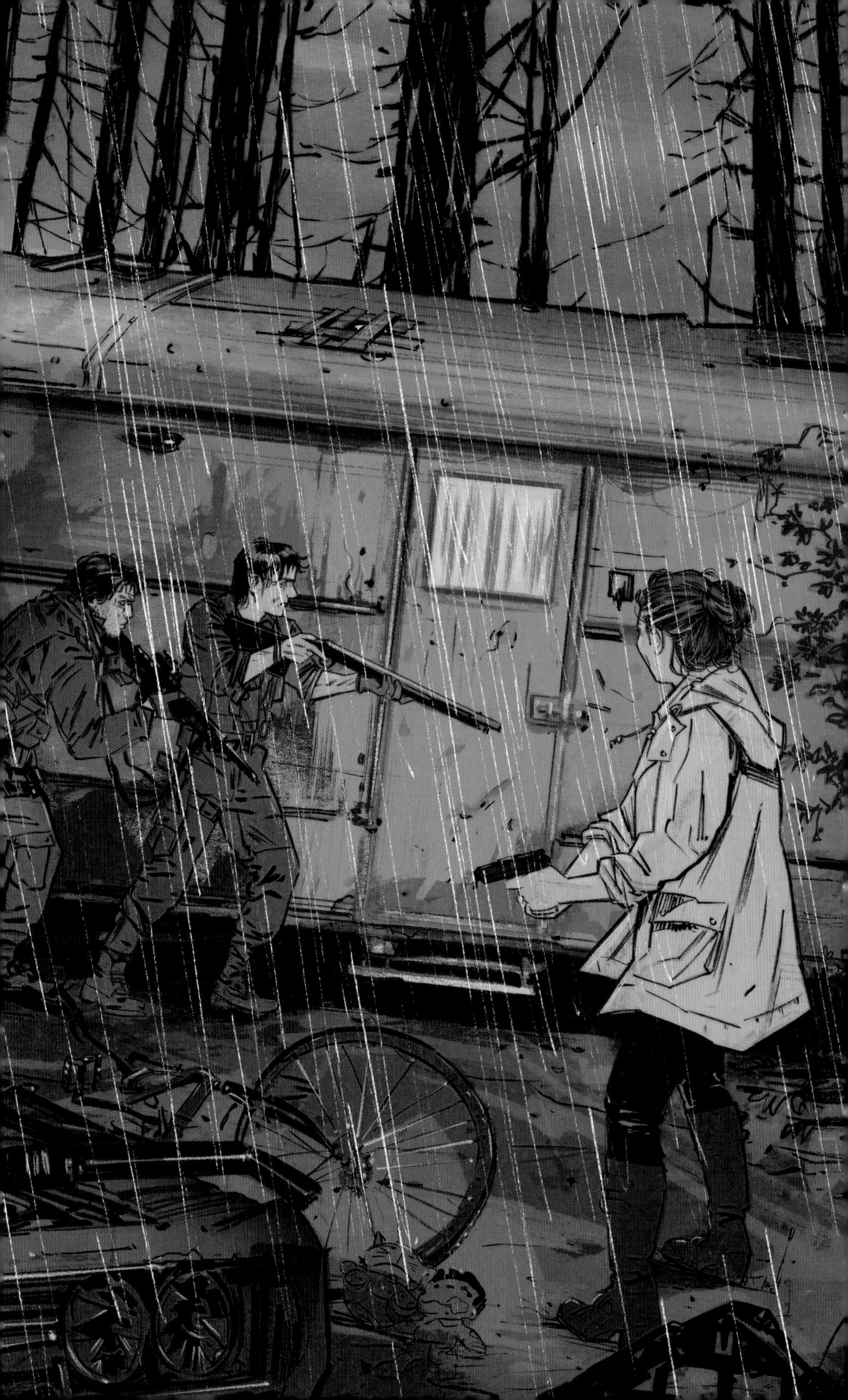

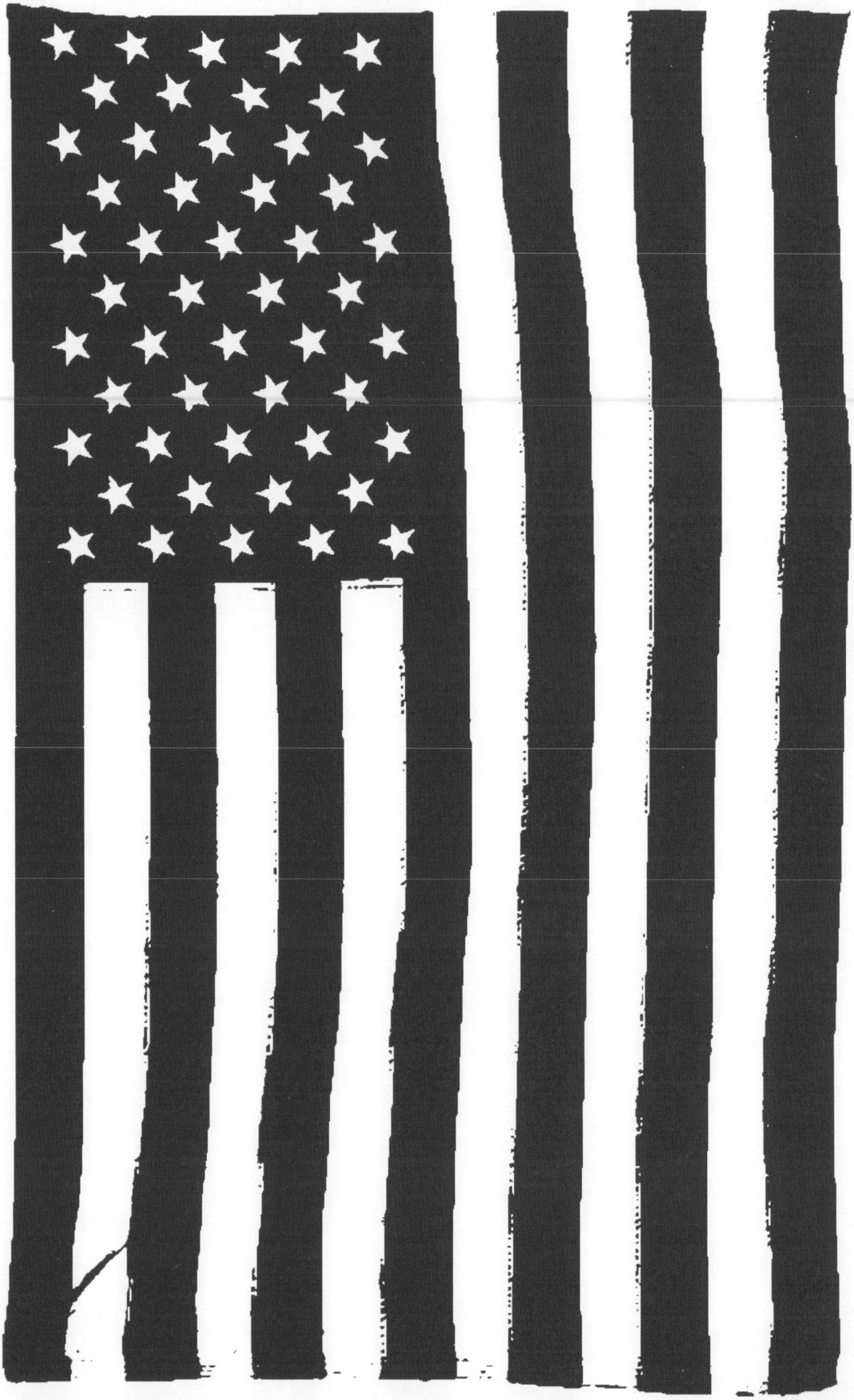

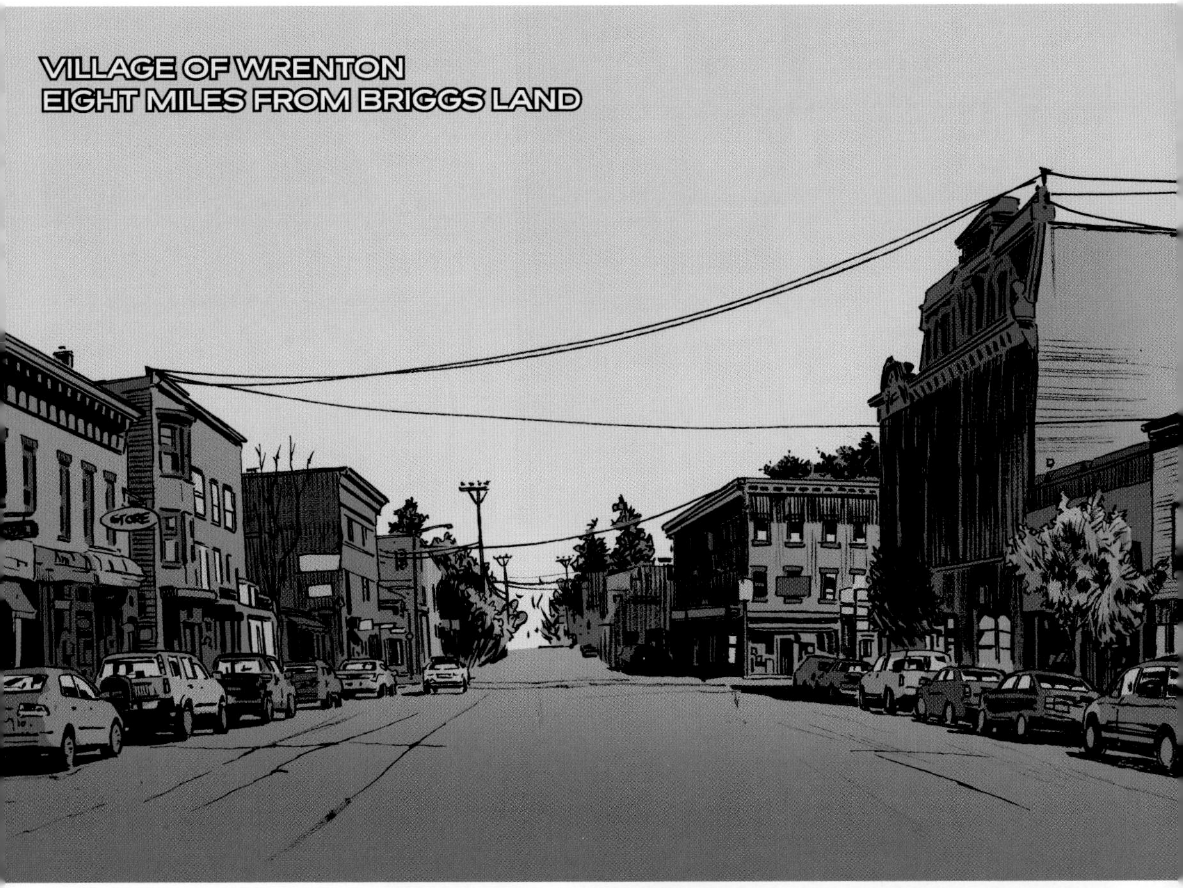
VILLAGE OF WRENTON
EIGHT MILES FROM BRIGGS LAND
STORE

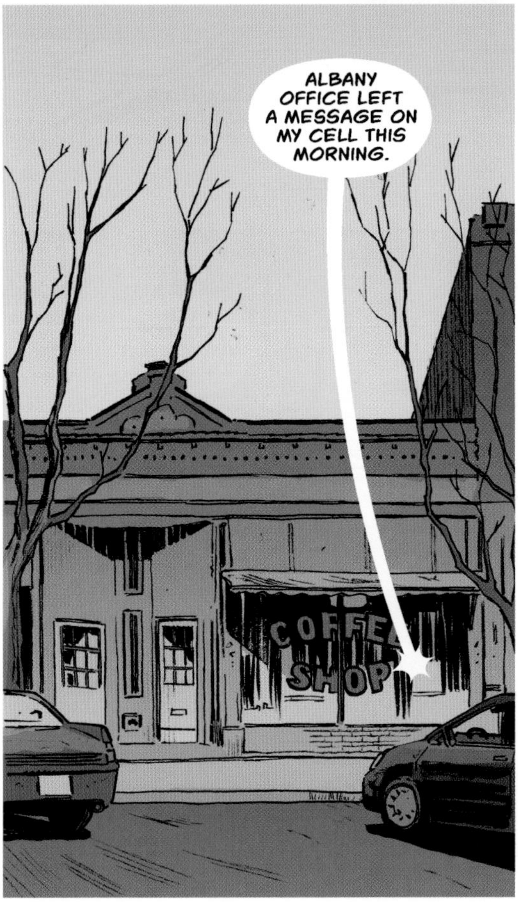
ALBANY OFFICE LEFT A MESSAGE ON MY CELL THIS MORNING.
COFFEE SHOP

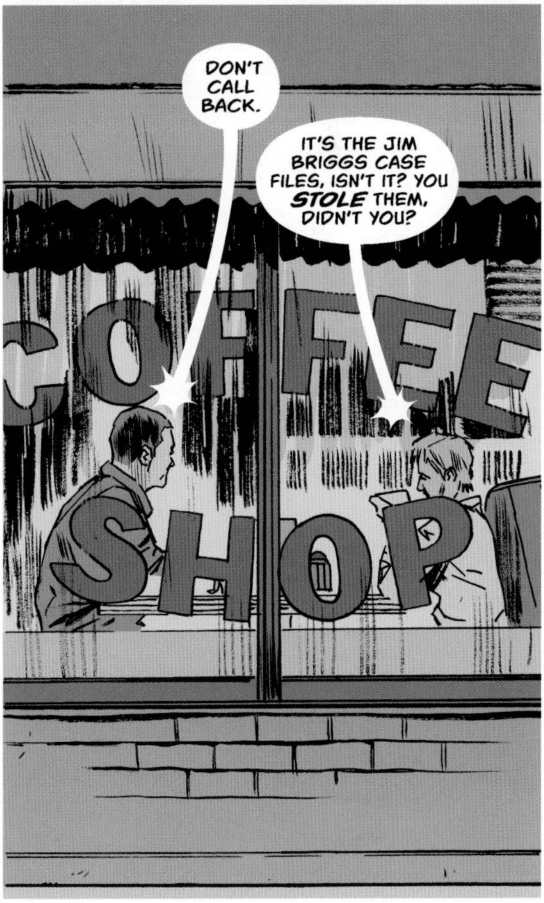
DON'T CALL BACK.
IT'S THE JIM BRIGGS CASE FILES, ISN'T IT? YOU **STOLE** THEM, DIDN'T YOU?
COFFEE SHOP

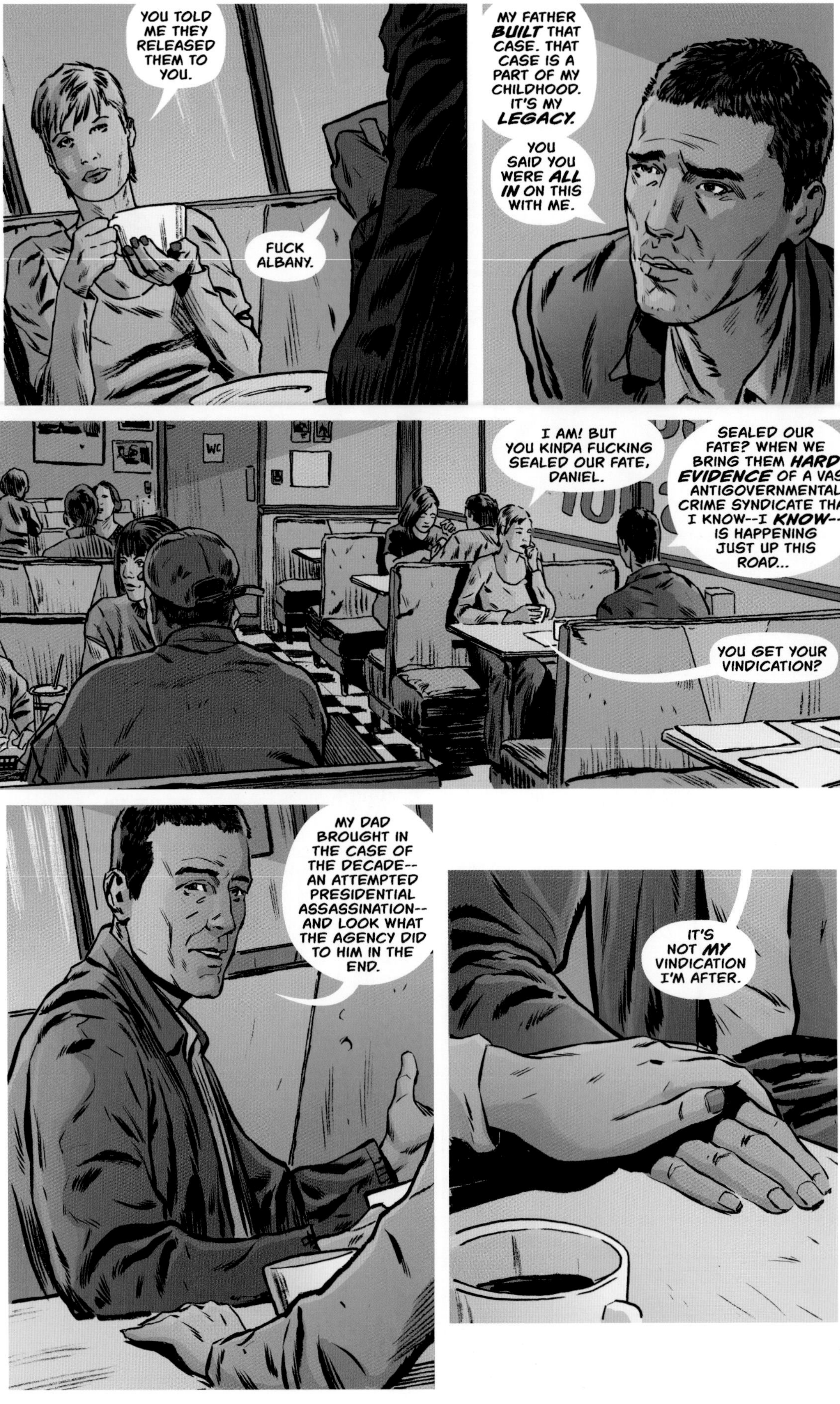
YOU TOLD ME THEY RELEASED THEM TO YOU.
FUCK ALBANY.
MY FATHER BUILT THAT CASE. THAT CASE IS A PART OF MY CHILDHOOD. IT'S MY LEGACY.
YOU SAID YOU WERE ALL IN ON THIS WITH ME.
I AM! BUT YOU KINDA FUCKING SEALED OUR FATE, DANIEL.
SEALED OUR FATE? WHEN WE BRING THEM HARD EVIDENCE OF A VAST ANTIGOVERNMENTAL CRIME SYNDICATE THAT I KNOW--I KNOW--IS HAPPENING JUST UP THIS ROAD...
YOU GET YOUR VINDICATION?
MY DAD BROUGHT IN THE CASE OF THE DECADE--AN ATTEMPTED PRESIDENTIAL ASSASSINATION--AND LOOK WHAT THE AGENCY DID TO HIM IN THE END.
IT'S NOT MY VINDICATION I'M AFTER.
WC

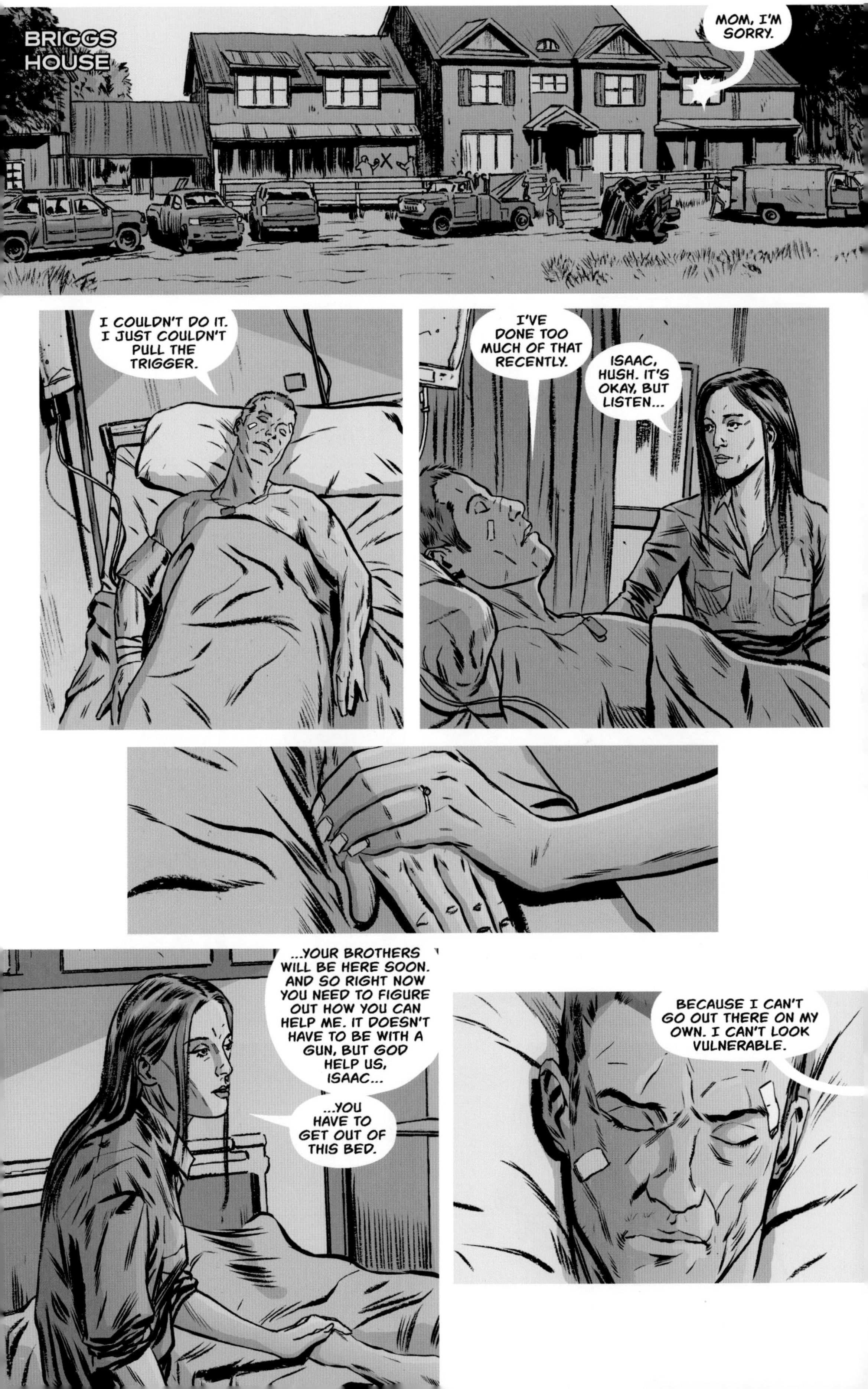
BRIGGS HOUSE
MOM, I'M SORRY.
I COULDN'T DO IT. I JUST COULDN'T PULL THE TRIGGER.
I'VE DONE TOO MUCH OF THAT RECENTLY.
ISAAC, HUSH. IT'S OKAY, BUT LISTEN...
...YOUR BROTHERS WILL BE HERE SOON. AND SO RIGHT NOW YOU NEED TO FIGURE OUT HOW YOU CAN HELP ME. IT DOESN'T HAVE TO BE WITH A GUN, BUT GOD HELP US, ISAAC...
...YOU HAVE TO GET OUT OF THIS BED.
BECAUSE I CAN'T GO OUT THERE ON MY OWN. I CAN'T LOOK VULNERABLE.

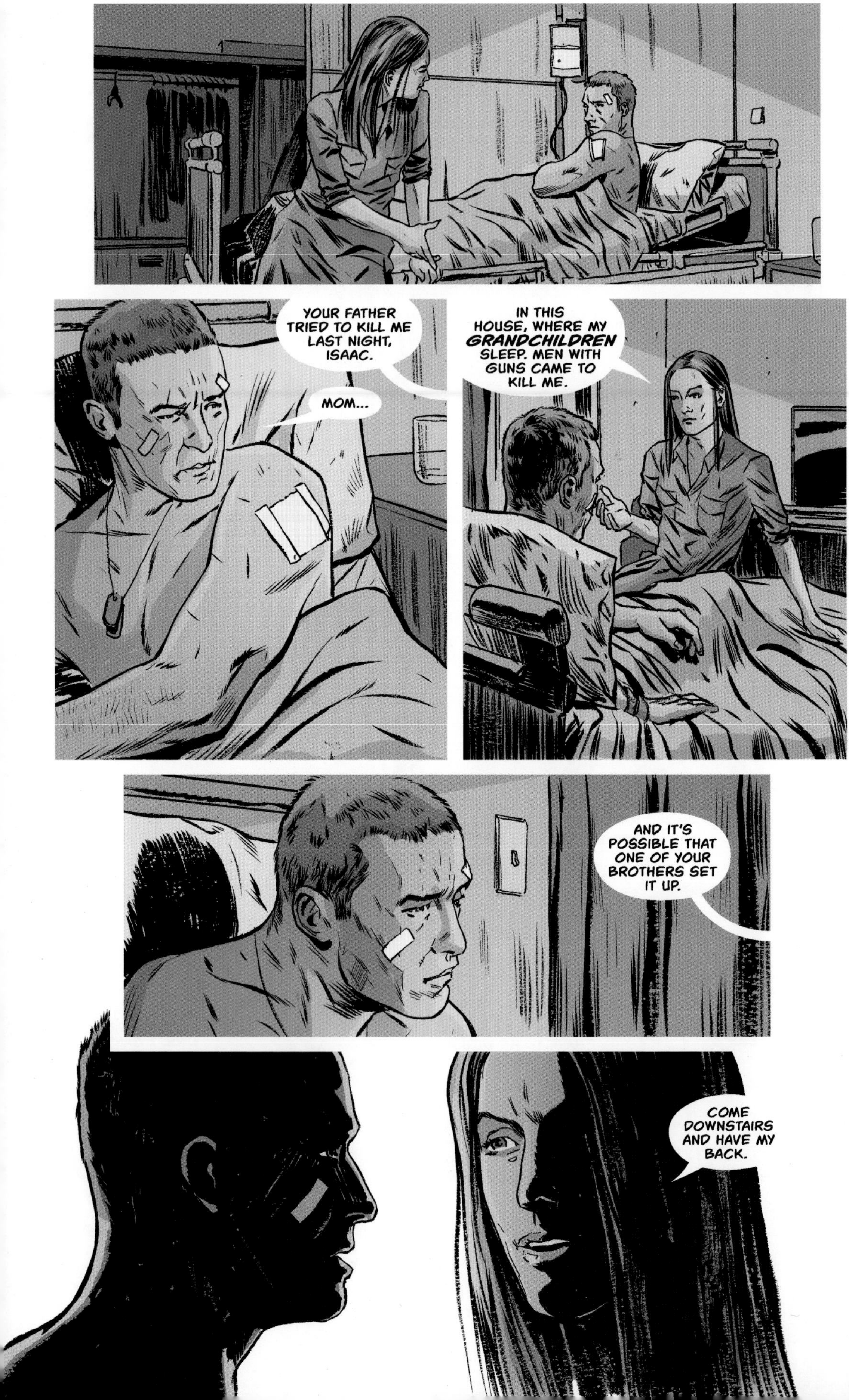
YOUR FATHER TRIED TO KILL ME LAST NIGHT, ISAAC.
MOM...
IN THIS HOUSE, WHERE MY GRANDCHILDREN SLEEP. MEN WITH GUNS CAME TO KILL ME.
AND IT'S POSSIBLE THAT ONE OF YOUR BROTHERS SET IT UP.
COME DOWNSTAIRS AND HAVE MY BACK.

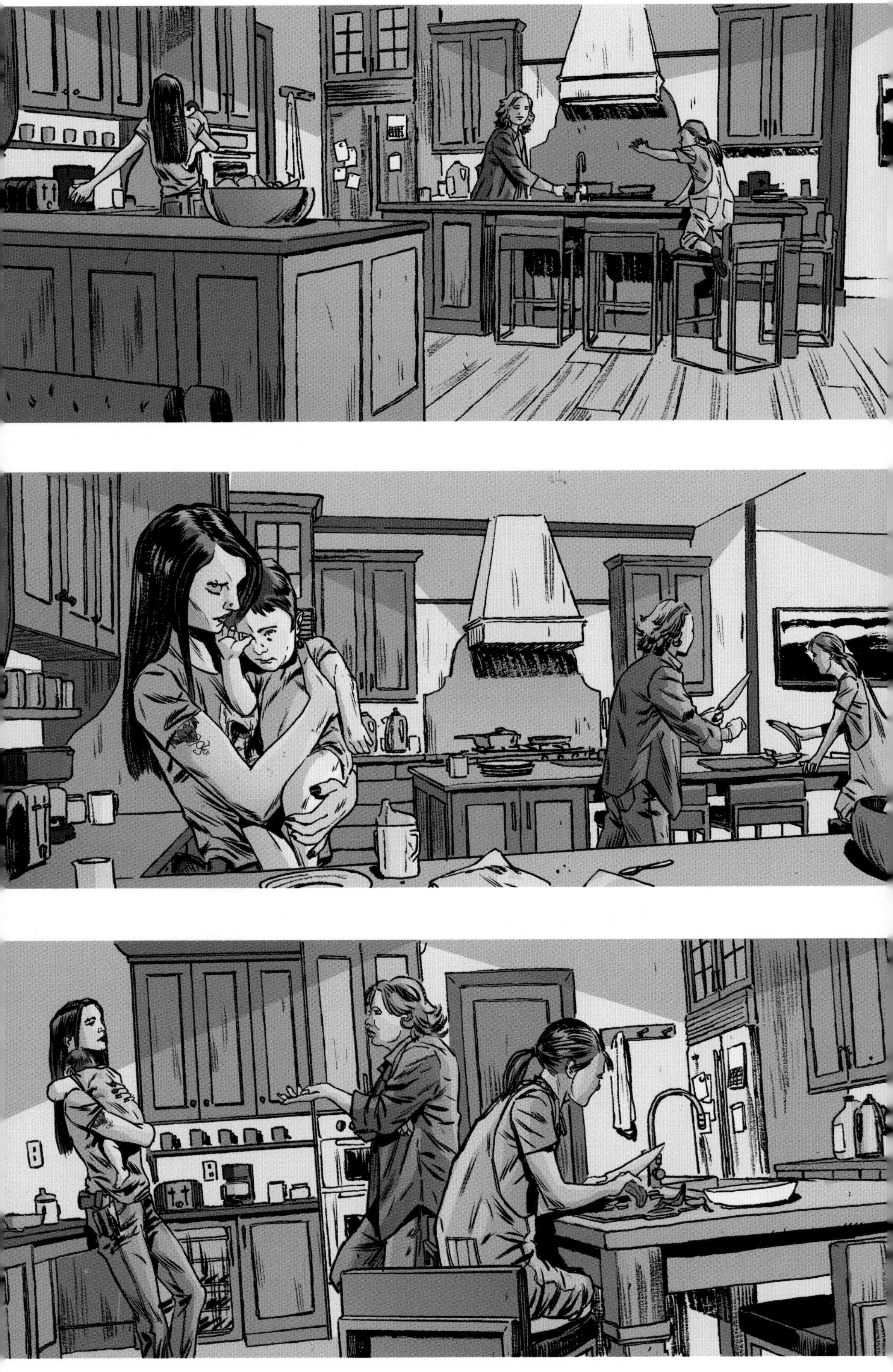

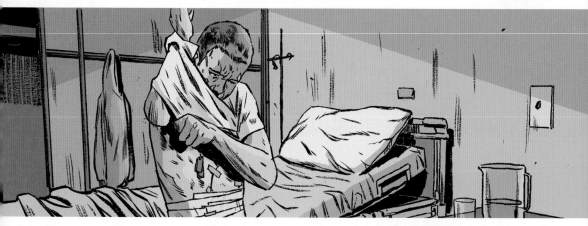

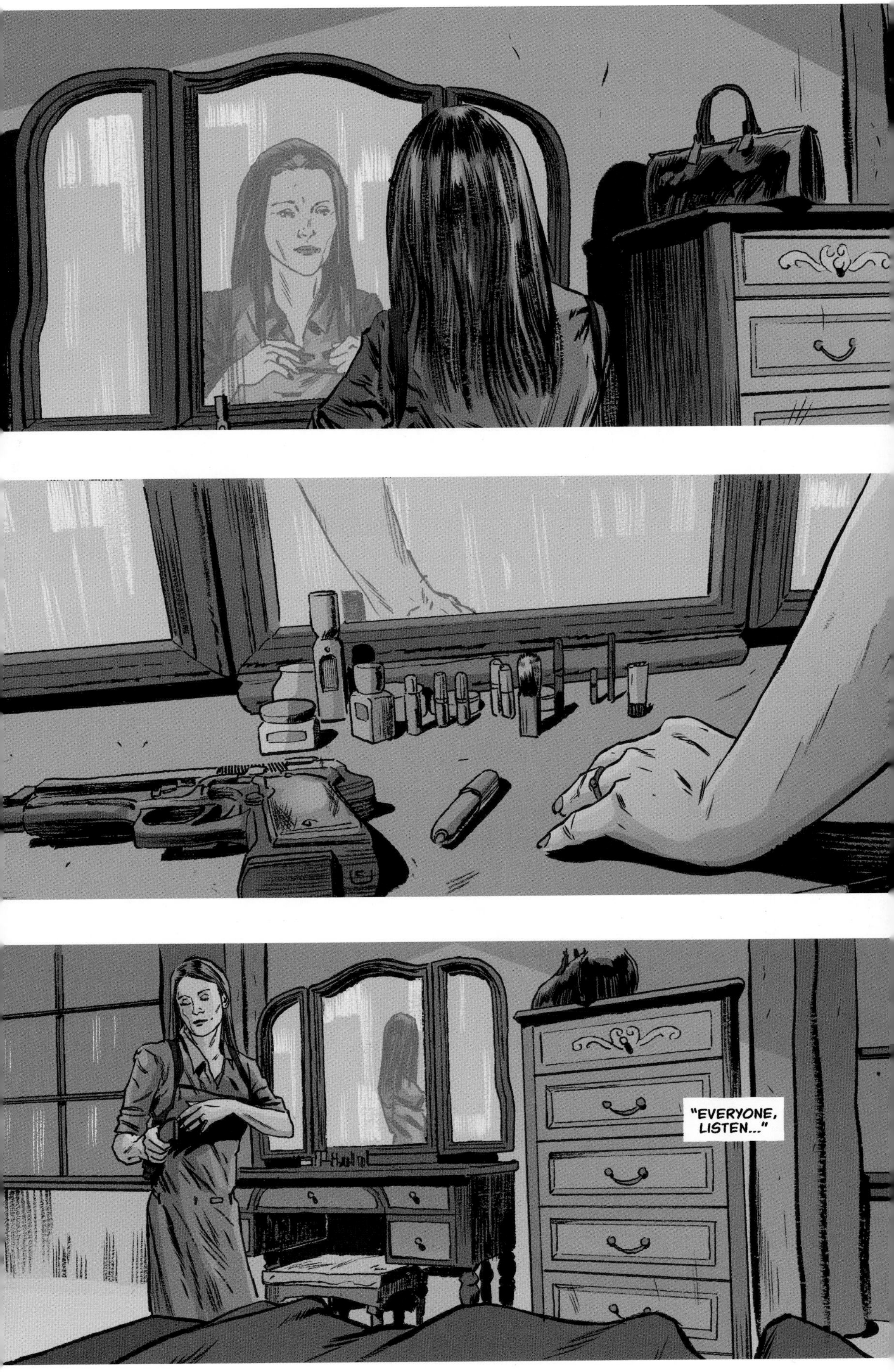
"EVERYONE, LISTEN..."

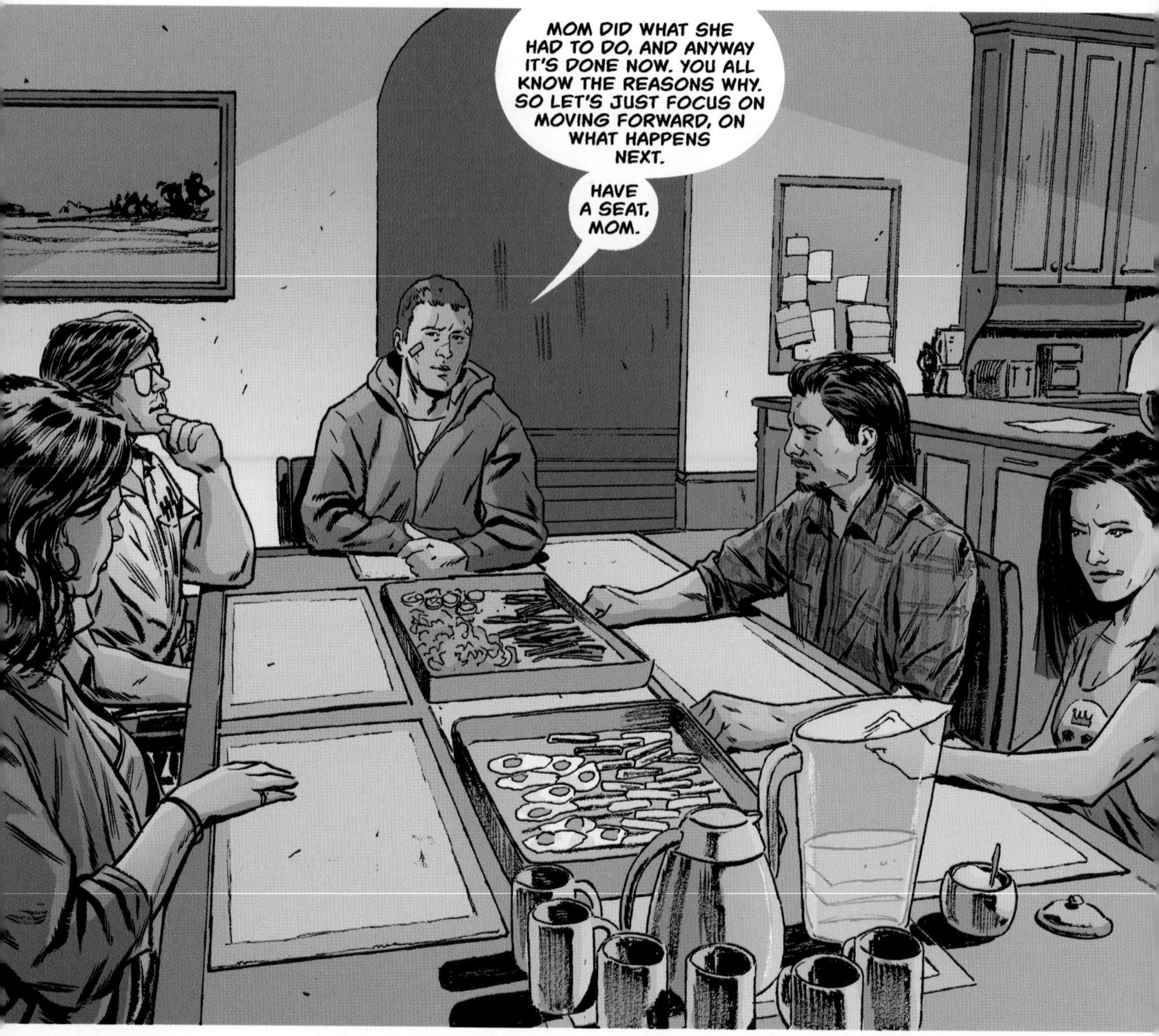
MOM DID WHAT SHE HAD TO DO, AND ANYWAY IT'S DONE NOW. YOU ALL KNOW THE REASONS WHY. SO LET'S JUST FOCUS ON MOVING FORWARD, ON WHAT HAPPENS NEXT.
HAVE A SEAT, MOM.

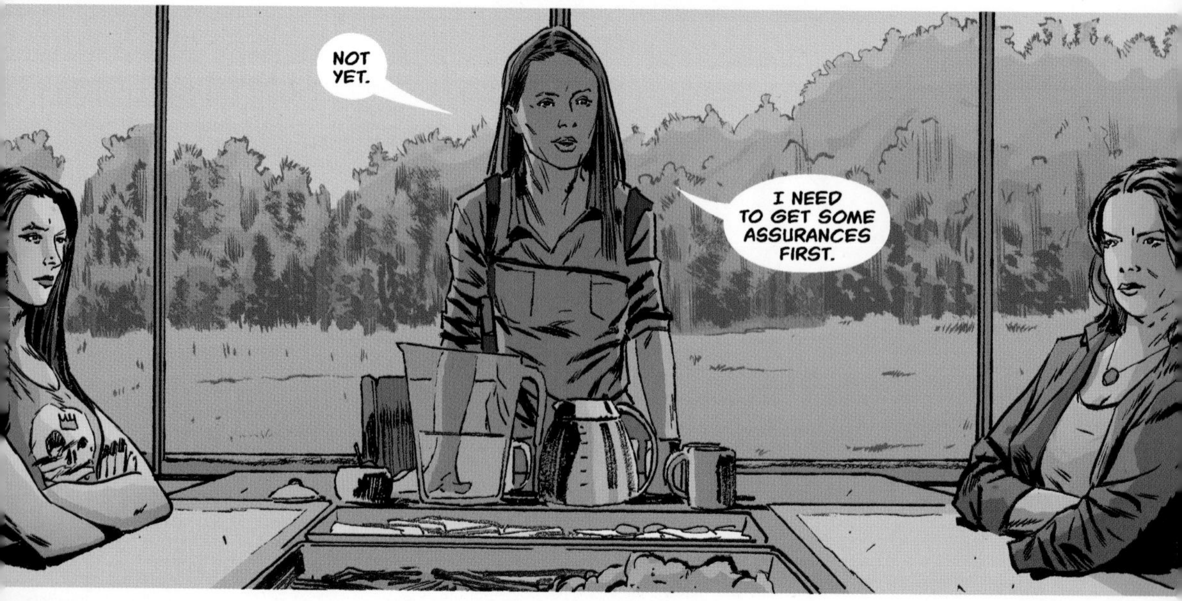
NOT YET.
I NEED TO GET SOME ASSURANCES FIRST.

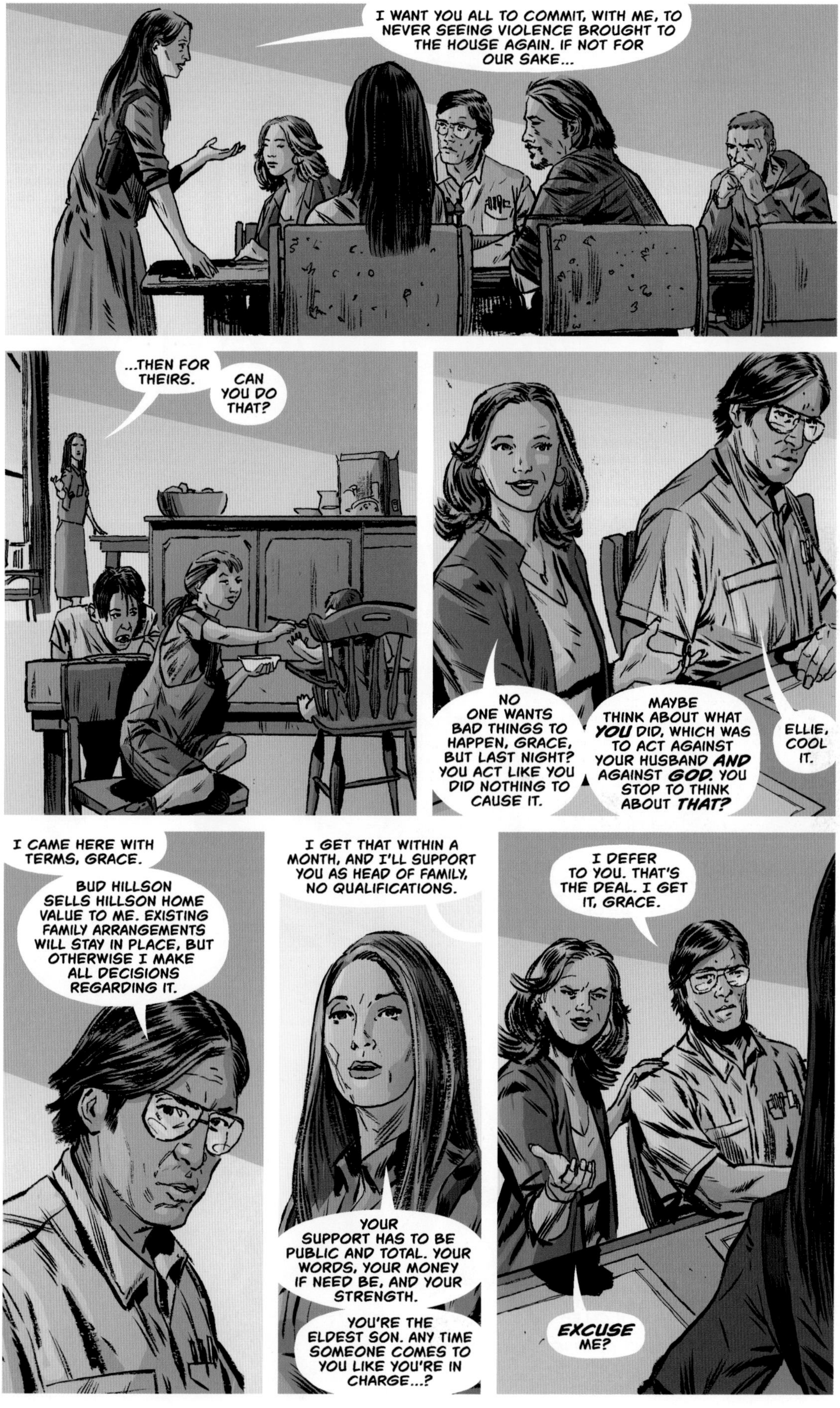

I WANT YOU ALL TO COMMIT, WITH ME, TO NEVER SEEING VIOLENCE BROUGHT TO THE HOUSE AGAIN. IF NOT FOR OUR SAKE...
...THEN FOR THEIRS.
CAN YOU DO THAT?
NO ONE WANTS BAD THINGS TO HAPPEN, GRACE, BUT LAST NIGHT? YOU ACT LIKE YOU DID NOTHING TO CAUSE IT.
MAYBE THINK ABOUT WHAT YOU DID, WHICH WAS TO ACT AGAINST YOUR HUSBAND AND AGAINST GOD. YOU STOP TO THINK ABOUT THAT?
ELLIE, COOL IT.
I CAME HERE WITH TERMS, GRACE.
BUD HILLSON SELLS HILLSON HOME VALUE TO ME. EXISTING FAMILY ARRANGEMENTS WILL STAY IN PLACE, BUT OTHERWISE I MAKE ALL DECISIONS REGARDING IT.
I GET THAT WITHIN A MONTH, AND I'LL SUPPORT YOU AS HEAD OF FAMILY, NO QUALIFICATIONS.
YOUR SUPPORT HAS TO BE PUBLIC AND TOTAL. YOUR WORDS, YOUR MONEY IF NEED BE, AND YOUR STRENGTH.
YOU'RE THE ELDEST SON. ANY TIME SOMEONE COMES TO YOU LIKE YOU'RE IN CHARGE...?
I DEFER TO YOU. THAT'S THE DEAL. I GET IT, GRACE.
EXCUSE ME?

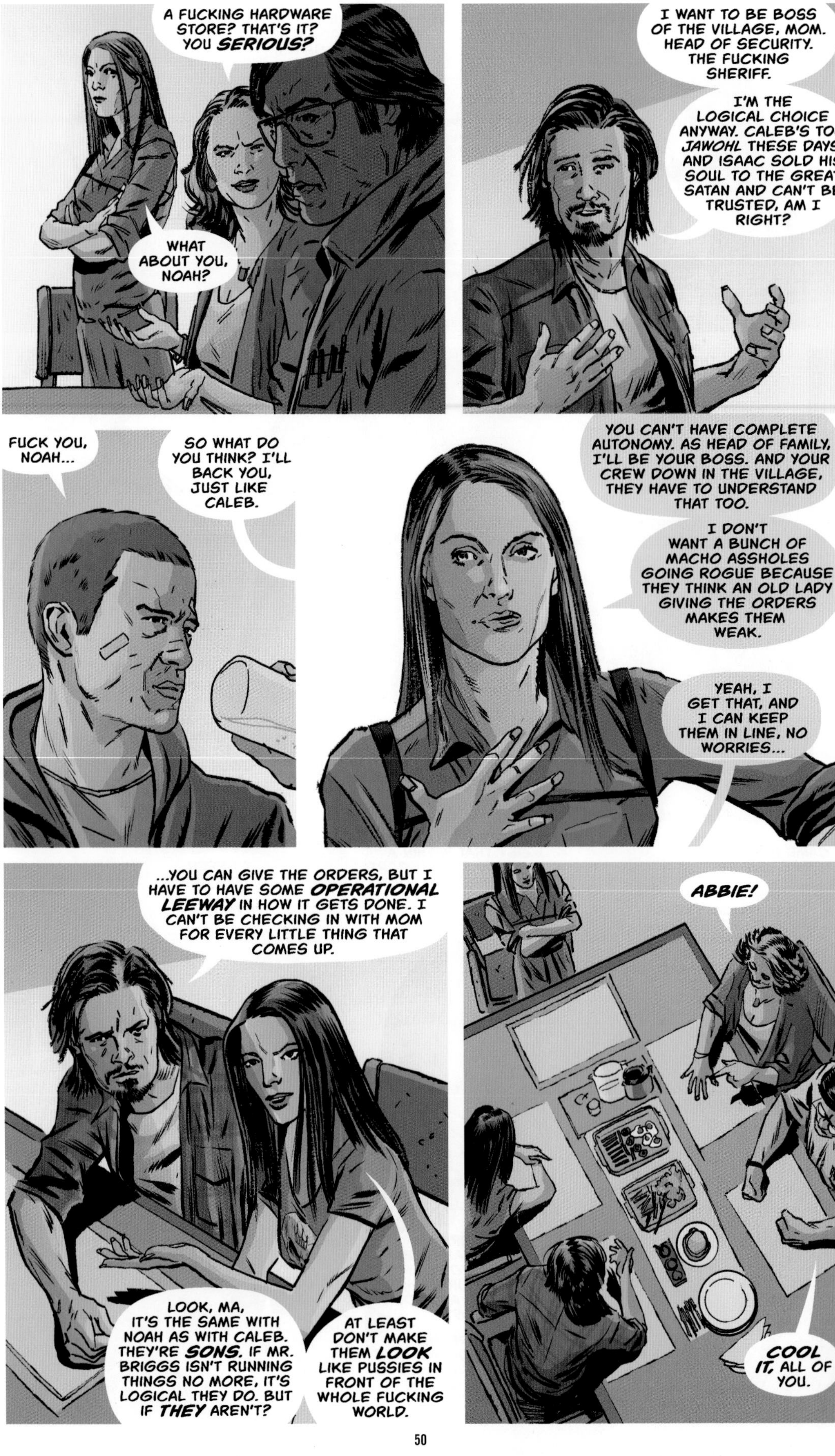
A FUCKING HARDWARE STORE? THAT'S IT? YOU SERIOUS?
WHAT ABOUT YOU, NOAH?
I WANT TO BE BOSS OF THE VILLAGE, MOM. HEAD OF SECURITY. THE FUCKING SHERIFF.
I'M THE LOGICAL CHOICE ANYWAY. CALEB'S TOO JAWOHL THESE DAYS, AND ISAAC SOLD HIS SOUL TO THE GREAT SATAN AND CAN'T BE TRUSTED, AM I RIGHT?
FUCK YOU, NOAH...
SO WHAT DO YOU THINK? I'LL BACK YOU, JUST LIKE CALEB.
YOU CAN'T HAVE COMPLETE AUTONOMY. AS HEAD OF FAMILY, I'LL BE YOUR BOSS. AND YOUR CREW DOWN IN THE VILLAGE, THEY HAVE TO UNDERSTAND THAT TOO.
I DON'T WANT A BUNCH OF MACHO ASSHOLES GOING ROGUE BECAUSE THEY THINK AN OLD LADY GIVING THE ORDERS MAKES THEM WEAK.
YEAH, I GET THAT, AND I CAN KEEP THEM IN LINE, NO WORRIES...
...YOU CAN GIVE THE ORDERS, BUT I HAVE TO HAVE SOME OPERATIONAL LEEWAY IN HOW IT GETS DONE. I CAN'T BE CHECKING IN WITH MOM FOR EVERY LITTLE THING THAT COMES UP.
LOOK, MA, IT'S THE SAME WITH NOAH AS WITH CALEB. THEY'RE SONS. IF MR. BRIGGS ISN'T RUNNING THINGS NO MORE, IT'S LOGICAL THEY DO. BUT IF THEY AREN'T?
AT LEAST DON'T MAKE THEM LOOK LIKE PUSSIES IN FRONT OF THE WHOLE FUCKING WORLD.
ABBIE!
COOL IT, ALL OF YOU.

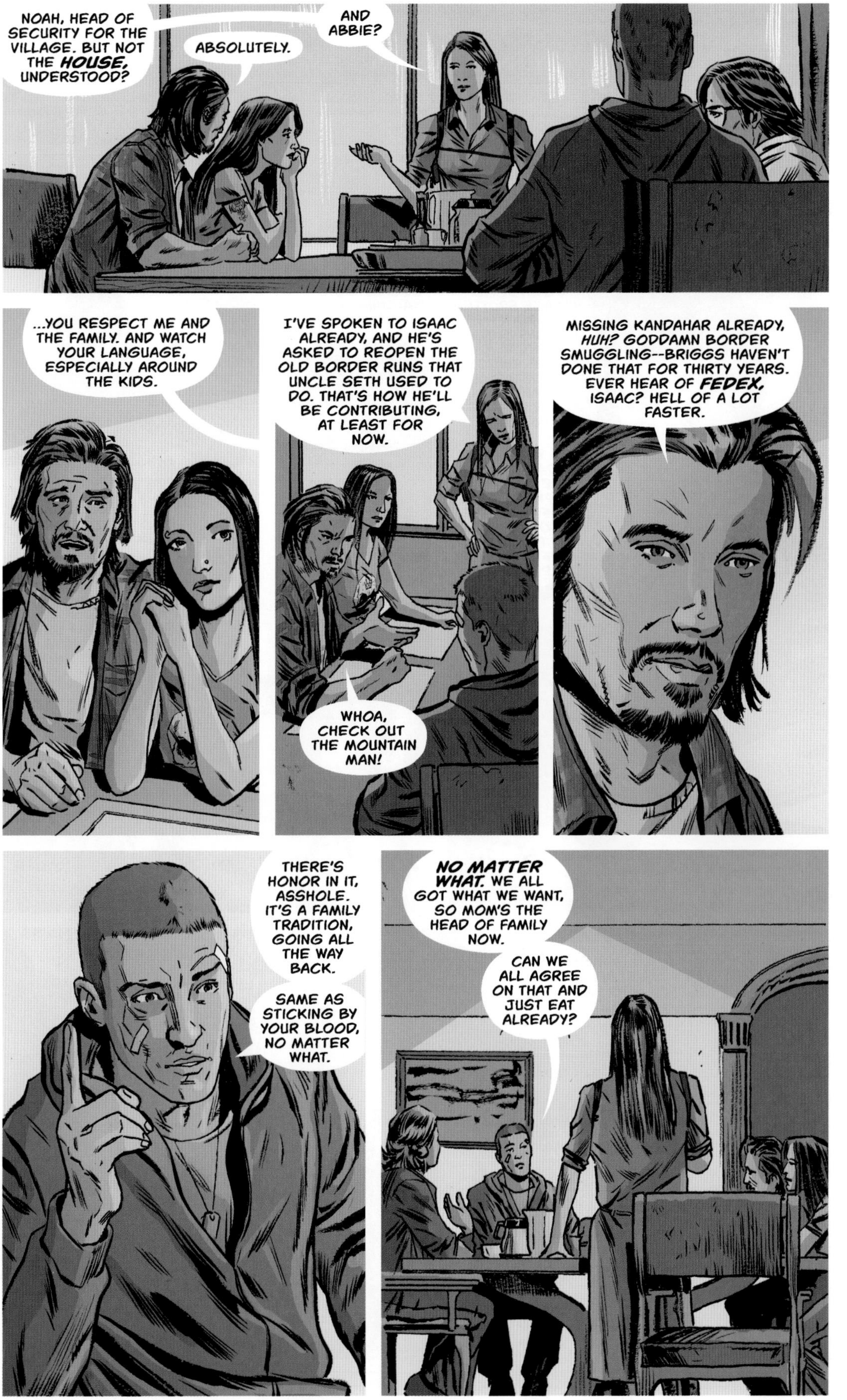

NOAH, HEAD OF SECURITY FOR THE VILLAGE. BUT NOT THE **HOUSE,** UNDERSTOOD?
ABSOLUTELY.
AND ABBIE?
...YOU RESPECT ME AND THE FAMILY. AND WATCH YOUR LANGUAGE, ESPECIALLY AROUND THE KIDS.
I'VE SPOKEN TO ISAAC ALREADY, AND HE'S ASKED TO REOPEN THE OLD BORDER RUNS THAT UNCLE SETH USED TO DO. THAT'S HOW HE'LL BE CONTRIBUTING, AT LEAST FOR NOW.
WHOA, CHECK OUT THE MOUNTAIN MAN!
MISSING KANDAHAR ALREADY, *HUH?* GODDAMN BORDER SMUGGLING--BRIGGS HAVEN'T DONE THAT FOR THIRTY YEARS. EVER HEAR OF ***FEDEX,*** ISAAC? HELL OF A LOT FASTER.
THERE'S HONOR IN IT, ASSHOLE. IT'S A FAMILY TRADITION, GOING ALL THE WAY BACK.
SAME AS STICKING BY YOUR BLOOD, NO MATTER WHAT.
NO MATTER WHAT. WE ALL GOT WHAT WE WANT, SO MOM'S THE HEAD OF FAMILY NOW.
CAN WE ALL AGREE ON THAT AND JUST EAT ALREADY?

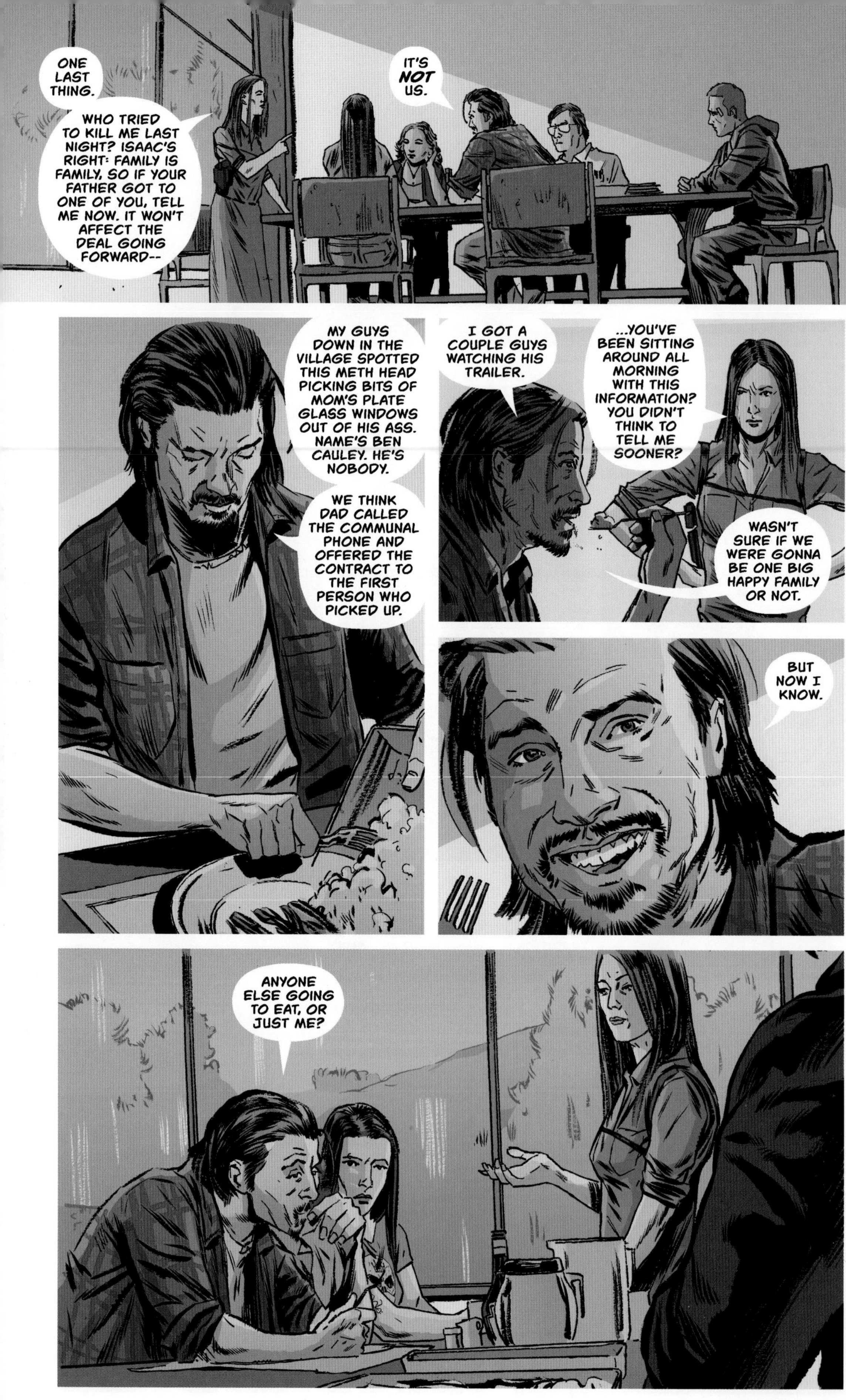
ONE LAST THING.
WHO TRIED TO KILL ME LAST NIGHT? ISAAC'S RIGHT: FAMILY IS FAMILY, SO IF YOUR FATHER GOT TO ONE OF YOU, TELL ME NOW. IT WON'T AFFECT THE DEAL GOING FORWARD--
IT'S NOT US.
MY GUYS DOWN IN THE VILLAGE SPOTTED THIS METH HEAD PICKING BITS OF MOM'S PLATE GLASS WINDOWS OUT OF HIS ASS. NAME'S BEN CAULEY. HE'S NOBODY.
WE THINK DAD CALLED THE COMMUNAL PHONE AND OFFERED THE CONTRACT TO THE FIRST PERSON WHO PICKED UP.
I GOT A COUPLE GUYS WATCHING HIS TRAILER.
...YOU'VE BEEN SITTING AROUND ALL MORNING WITH THIS INFORMATION? YOU DIDN'T THINK TO TELL ME SOONER?
WASN'T SURE IF WE WERE GONNA BE ONE BIG HAPPY FAMILY OR NOT.
BUT NOW I KNOW.
ANYONE ELSE GOING TO EAT, OR JUST ME?

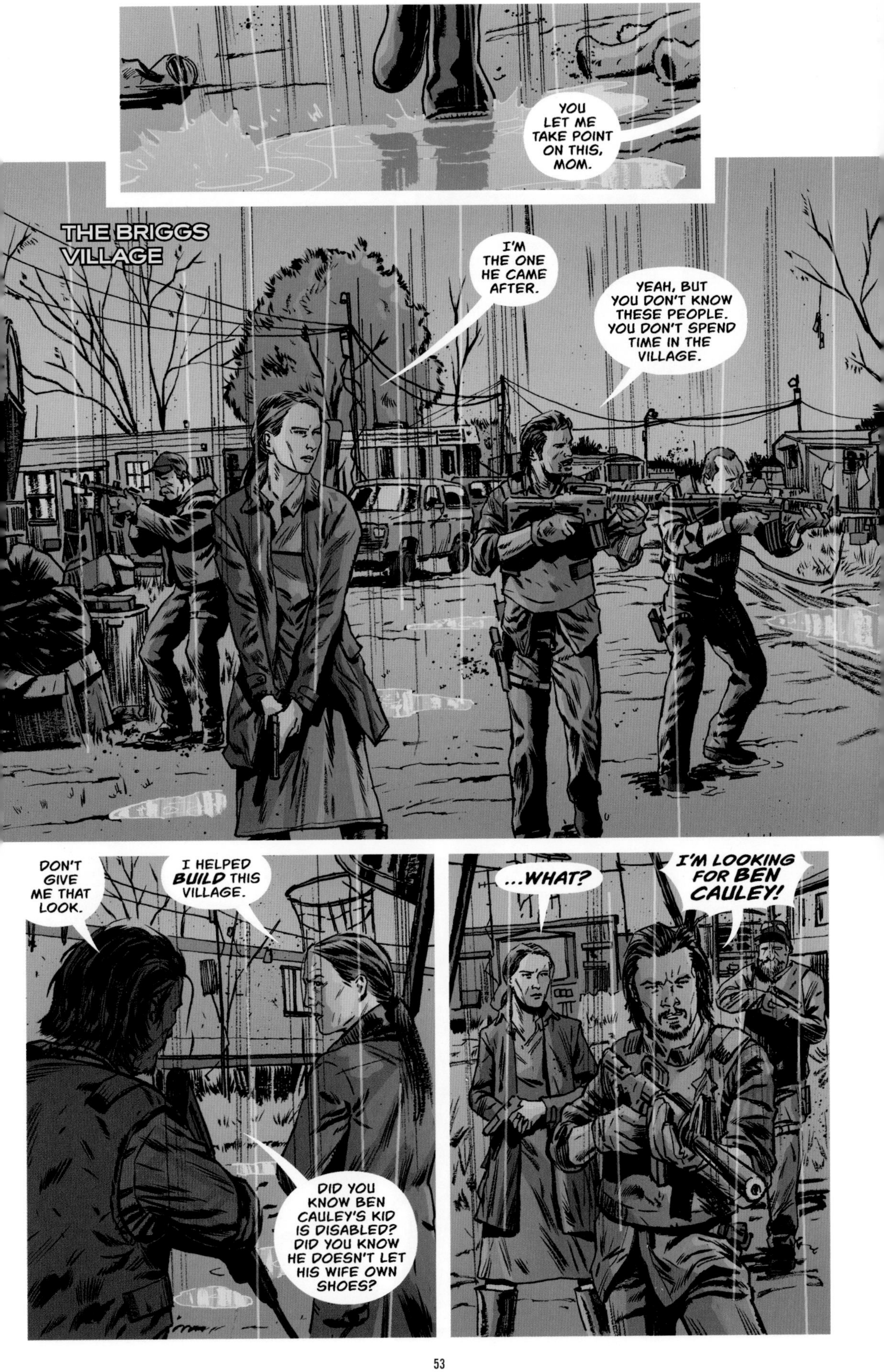
YOU LET ME TAKE POINT ON THIS, MOM.
THE BRIGGS VILLAGE
I'M THE ONE HE CAME AFTER.
YEAH, BUT YOU DON'T KNOW THESE PEOPLE. YOU DON'T SPEND TIME IN THE VILLAGE.
DON'T GIVE ME THAT LOOK.
I HELPED **BUILD** THIS VILLAGE.
DID YOU KNOW BEN CAULEY'S KID IS DISABLED? DID YOU KNOW HE DOESN'T LET HIS WIFE OWN SHOES?
...WHAT?
I'M LOOKING FOR **BEN CAULEY!**

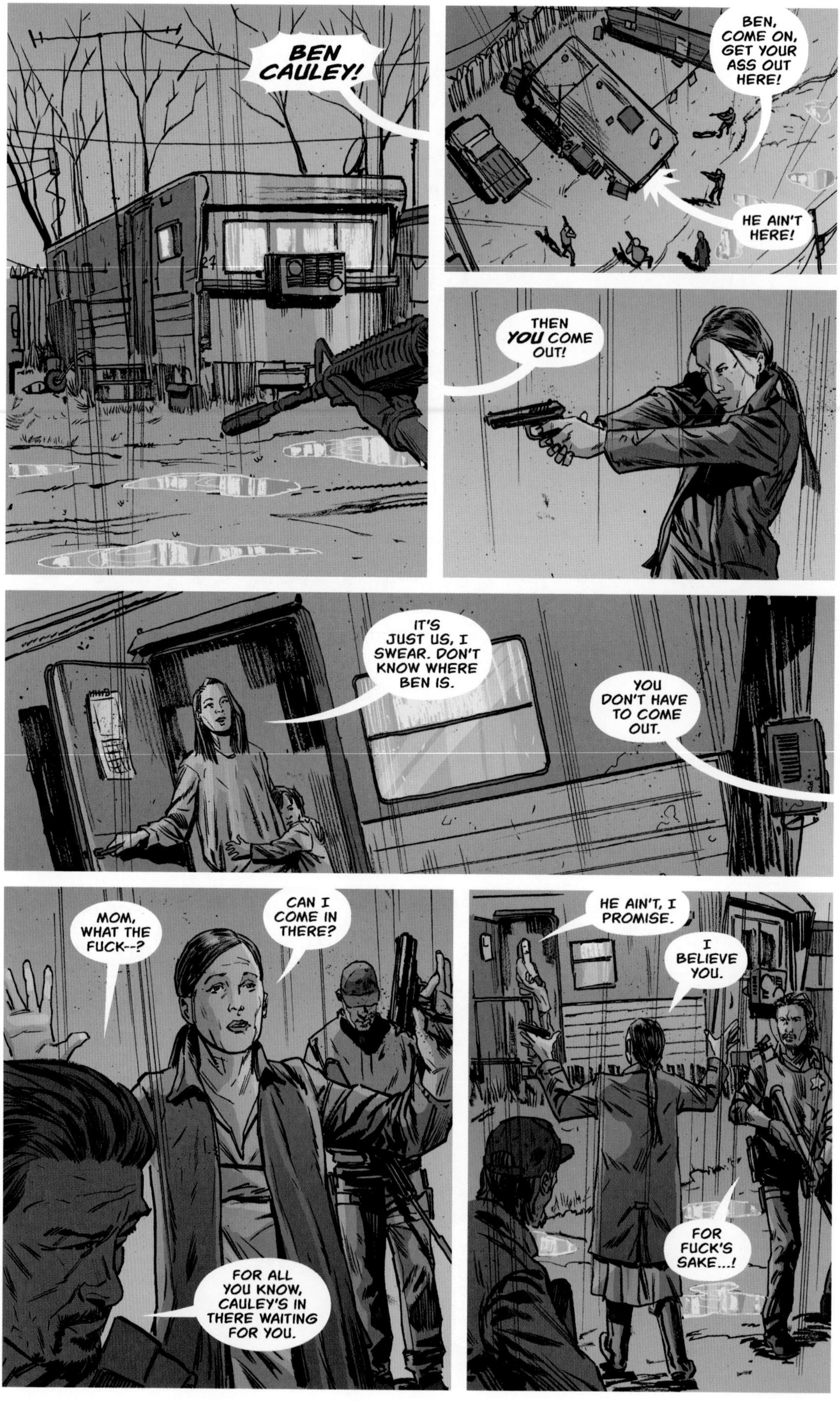
BEN CAULEY!
BEN, COME ON, GET YOUR ASS OUT HERE!
HE AIN'T HERE!
THEN YOU COME OUT!
IT'S JUST US, I SWEAR. DON'T KNOW WHERE BEN IS.
YOU DON'T HAVE TO COME OUT.
MOM, WHAT THE FUCK--?
CAN I COME IN THERE?
FOR ALL YOU KNOW, CAULEY'S IN THERE WAITING FOR YOU.
HE AIN'T, I PROMISE.
I BELIEVE YOU.
FOR FUCK'S SAKE...!

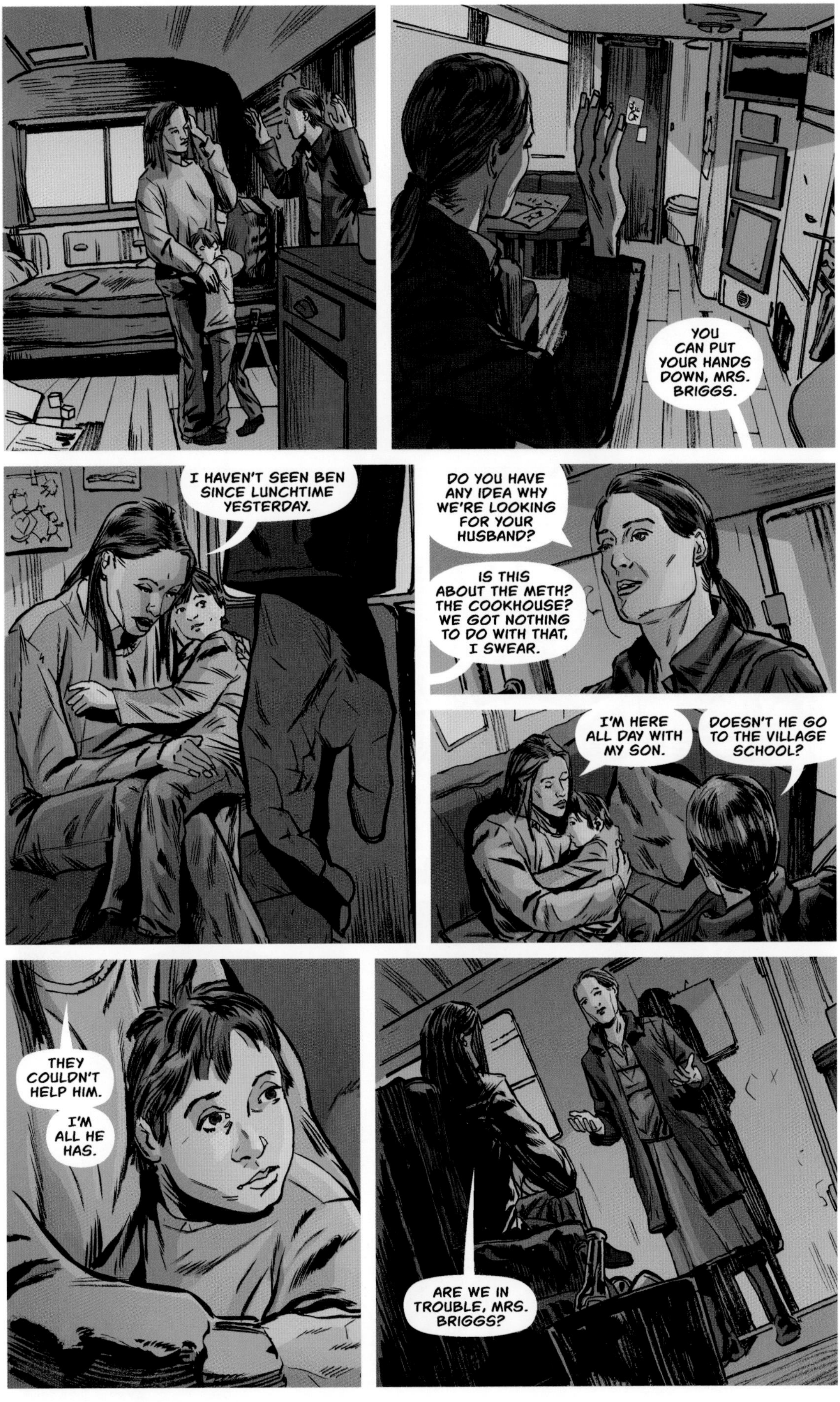
YOU CAN PUT YOUR HANDS DOWN, MRS. BRIGGS.
I HAVEN'T SEEN BEN SINCE LUNCHTIME YESTERDAY.
DO YOU HAVE ANY IDEA WHY WE'RE LOOKING FOR YOUR HUSBAND?
IS THIS ABOUT THE METH? THE COOKHOUSE? WE GOT NOTHING TO DO WITH THAT, I SWEAR.
I'M HERE ALL DAY WITH MY SON.
DOESN'T HE GO TO THE VILLAGE SCHOOL?
THEY COULDN'T HELP HIM.
I'M ALL HE HAS.
ARE WE IN TROUBLE, MRS. BRIGGS?

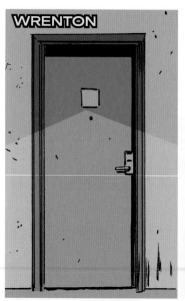

HEY, HAVE YOU EVER CONSIDERED GRACE AS A POTENTIAL BOSS OF THE FAMILY?

SHE'S NOT THE BOSS. JIM BRIGGS IS.

YEAH, BUT HOW ABOUT IT? WANNA GAME IT OUT?

WHAT'S THE POINT? THESE EXTREMIST COMMUNITIES ARE ALL PATRIARCHIES. CALEB BRIGGS IS NEXT IN LINE WHENEVER THE OLD MAN KICKS THE BUCKET.

GRACE IS A HOUSEWIFE.

MAYBE THERE'S MORE TO HER THAN WE THINK.

DID YOU KNOW ABOUT THIS?

... HOW THE FUCK DID YOU FIND THIS?

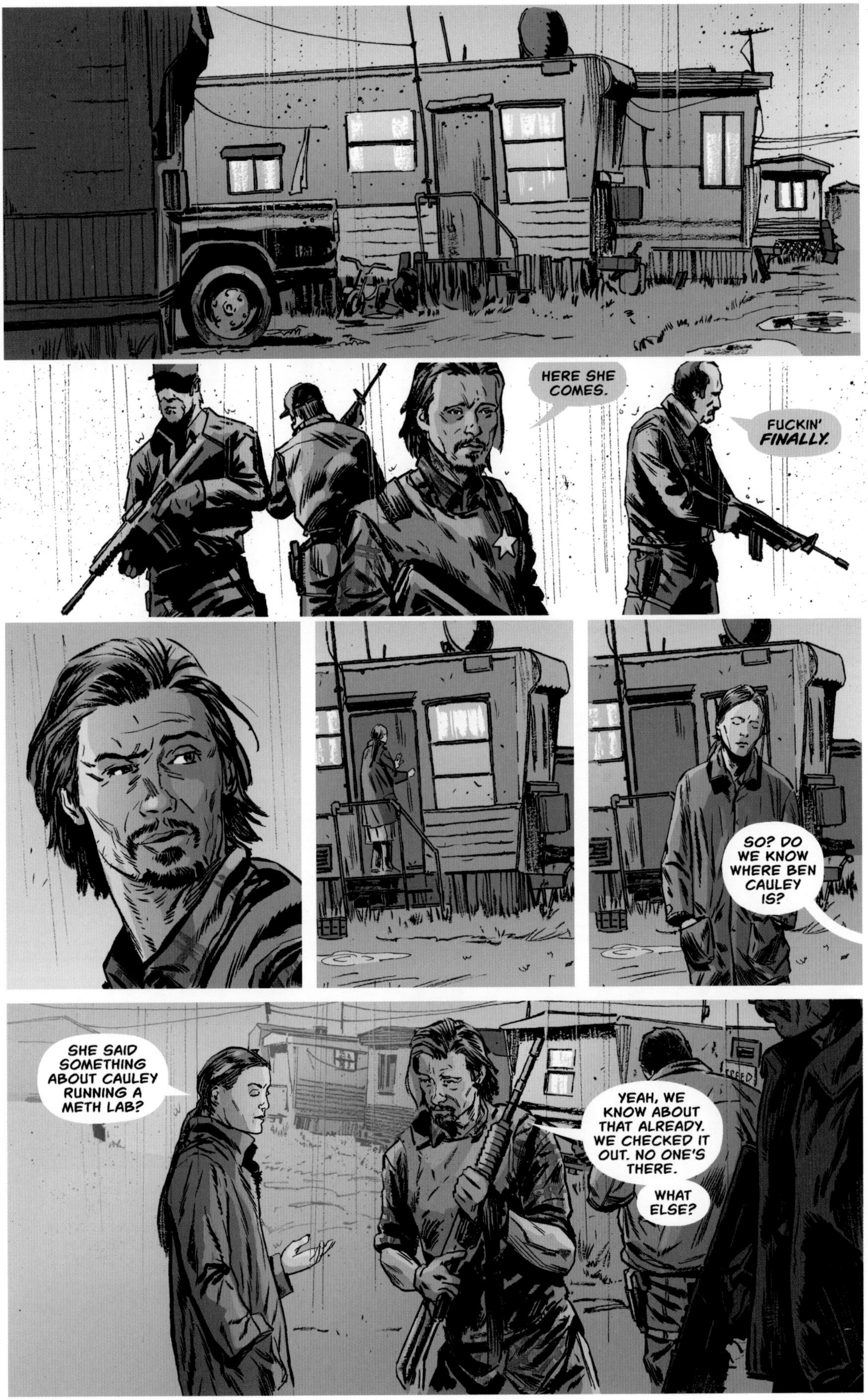
HERE SHE COMES.
FUCKIN' *FINALLY.*
SO? DO WE KNOW WHERE BEN CAULEY IS?
SHE SAID SOMETHING ABOUT CAULEY RUNNING A METH LAB?
YEAH, WE KNOW ABOUT THAT ALREADY. WE CHECKED IT OUT. NO ONE'S THERE.
WHAT ELSE?

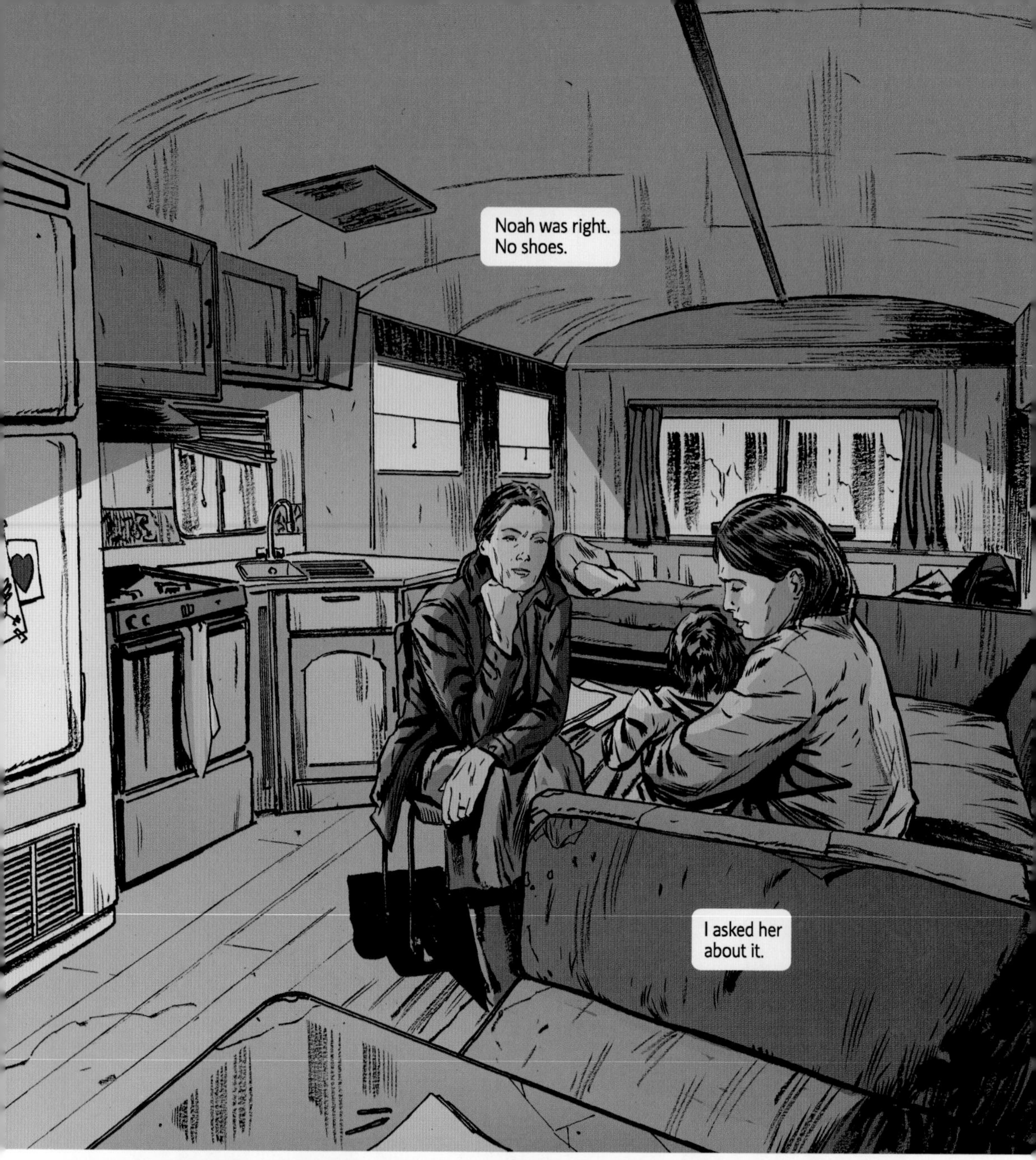
Noah was right.
No shoes.
I asked her
about it.

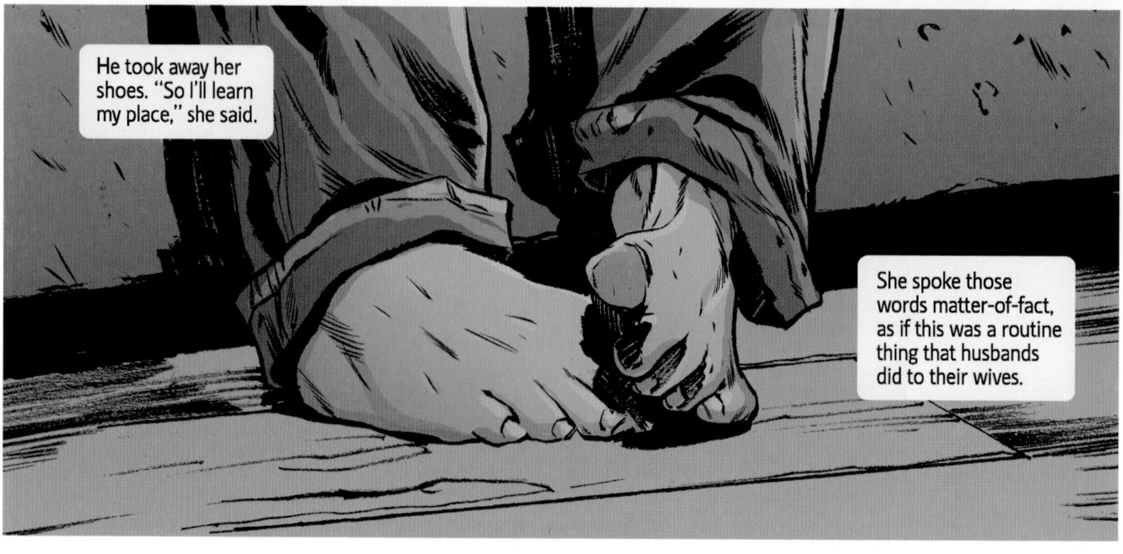
He took away her
shoes. "So I'll learn
my place," she said.
She spoke those
words matter-of-fact,
as if this was a routine
thing that husbands
did to their wives.

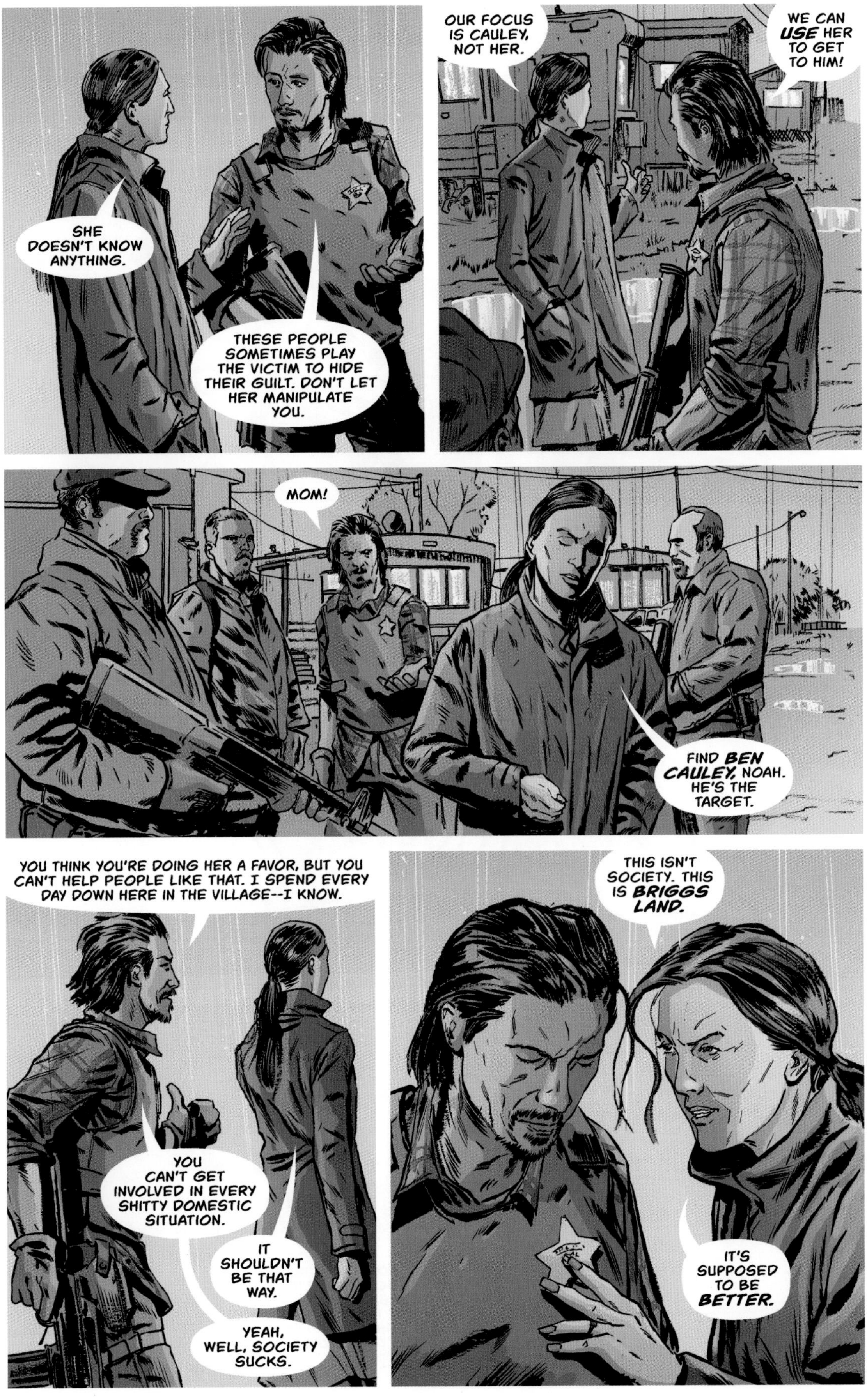
SHE DOESN'T KNOW ANYTHING.
THESE PEOPLE SOMETIMES PLAY THE VICTIM TO HIDE THEIR GUILT. DON'T LET HER MANIPULATE YOU.
OUR FOCUS IS CAULEY, NOT HER.
WE CAN USE HER TO GET TO HIM!
MOM!
FIND BEN CAULEY, NOAH. HE'S THE TARGET.
YOU THINK YOU'RE DOING HER A FAVOR, BUT YOU CAN'T HELP PEOPLE LIKE THAT. I SPEND EVERY DAY DOWN HERE IN THE VILLAGE--I KNOW.
YOU CAN'T GET INVOLVED IN EVERY SHITTY DOMESTIC SITUATION.
IT SHOULDN'T BE THAT WAY.
YEAH, WELL, SOCIETY SUCKS.
THIS ISN'T SOCIETY. THIS IS BRIGGS LAND.
IT'S SUPPOSED TO BE BETTER.

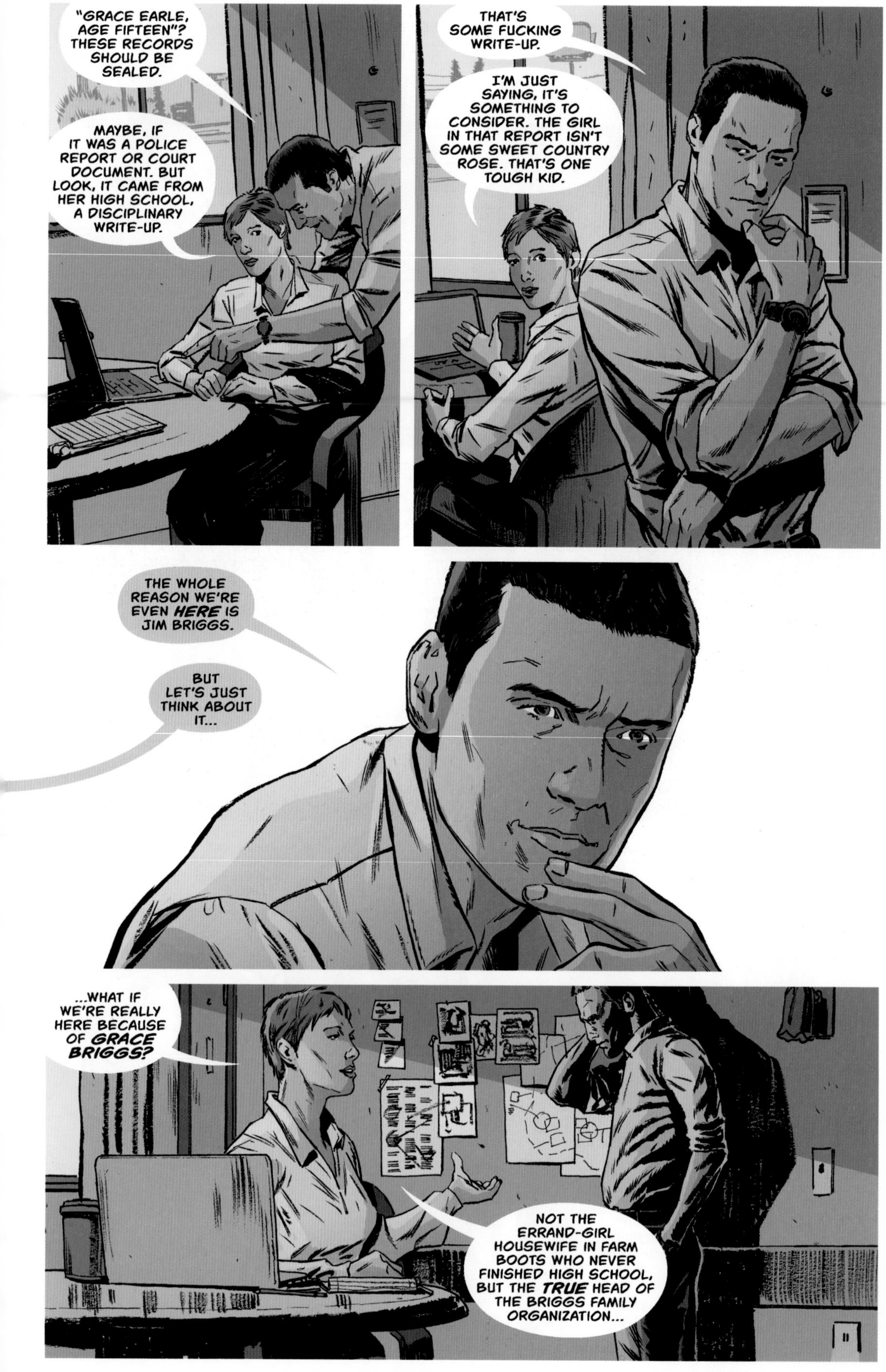
"GRACE EARLE, AGE FIFTEEN"? THESE RECORDS SHOULD BE SEALED.
MAYBE, IF IT WAS A POLICE REPORT OR COURT DOCUMENT. BUT LOOK, IT CAME FROM HER HIGH SCHOOL, A DISCIPLINARY WRITE-UP.
THAT'S SOME FUCKING WRITE-UP.
I'M JUST SAYING, IT'S SOMETHING TO CONSIDER. THE GIRL IN THAT REPORT ISN'T SOME SWEET COUNTRY ROSE. THAT'S ONE TOUGH KID.
THE WHOLE REASON WE'RE EVEN *HERE* IS JIM BRIGGS.
BUT LET'S JUST THINK ABOUT IT...
...WHAT IF WE'RE REALLY HERE BECAUSE OF *GRACE BRIGGS?*
NOT THE ERRAND-GIRL HOUSEWIFE IN FARM BOOTS WHO NEVER FINISHED HIGH SCHOOL, BUT THE *TRUE* HEAD OF THE BRIGGS FAMILY ORGANIZATION...

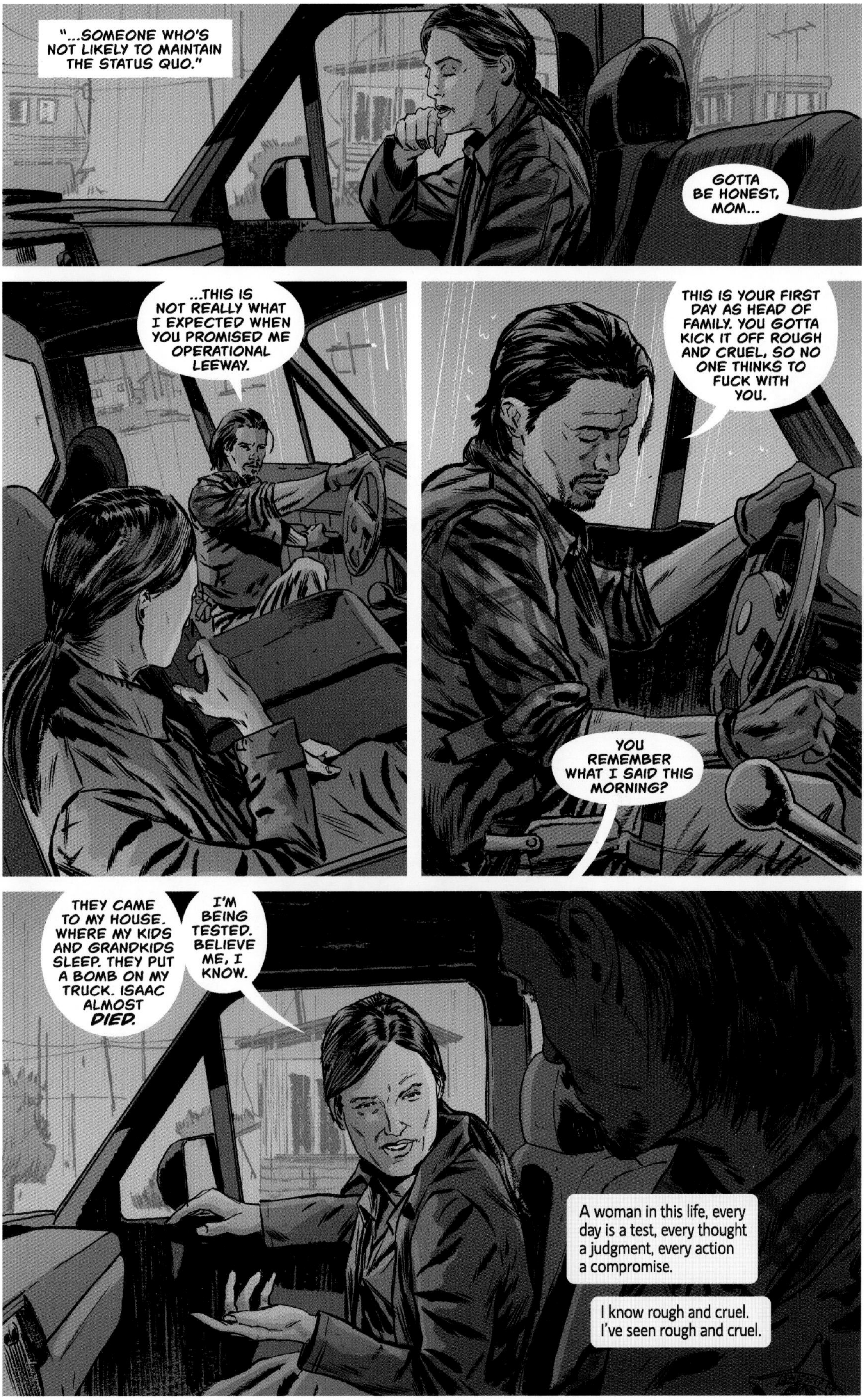
"...SOMEONE WHO'S NOT LIKELY TO MAINTAIN THE STATUS QUO."
GOTTA BE HONEST, MOM...
...THIS IS NOT REALLY WHAT I EXPECTED WHEN YOU PROMISED ME OPERATIONAL LEEWAY.
THIS IS YOUR FIRST DAY AS HEAD OF FAMILY. YOU GOTTA KICK IT OFF ROUGH AND CRUEL, SO NO ONE THINKS TO FUCK WITH YOU.
YOU REMEMBER WHAT I SAID THIS MORNING?
THEY CAME TO MY HOUSE. WHERE MY KIDS AND GRANDKIDS SLEEP. THEY PUT A BOMB ON MY TRUCK. ISAAC ALMOST DIED.
I'M BEING TESTED. BELIEVE ME, I KNOW.
A woman in this life, every day is a test, every thought a judgment, every action a compromise.
I know rough and cruel. I've seen rough and cruel.

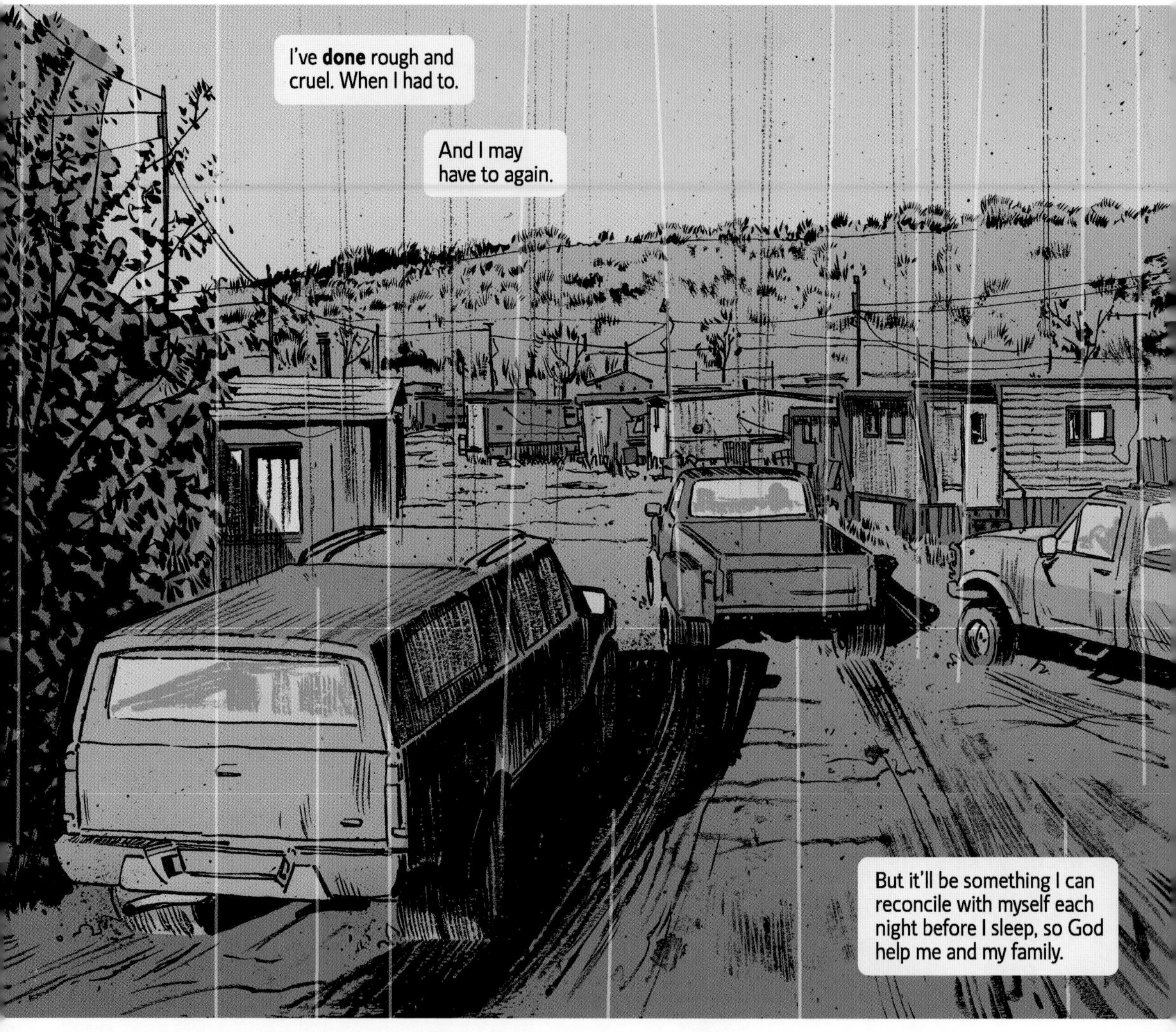
I've **done** rough and cruel. When I had to.
And I may have to again.
But it'll be something I can reconcile with myself each night before I sleep, so God help me and my family.

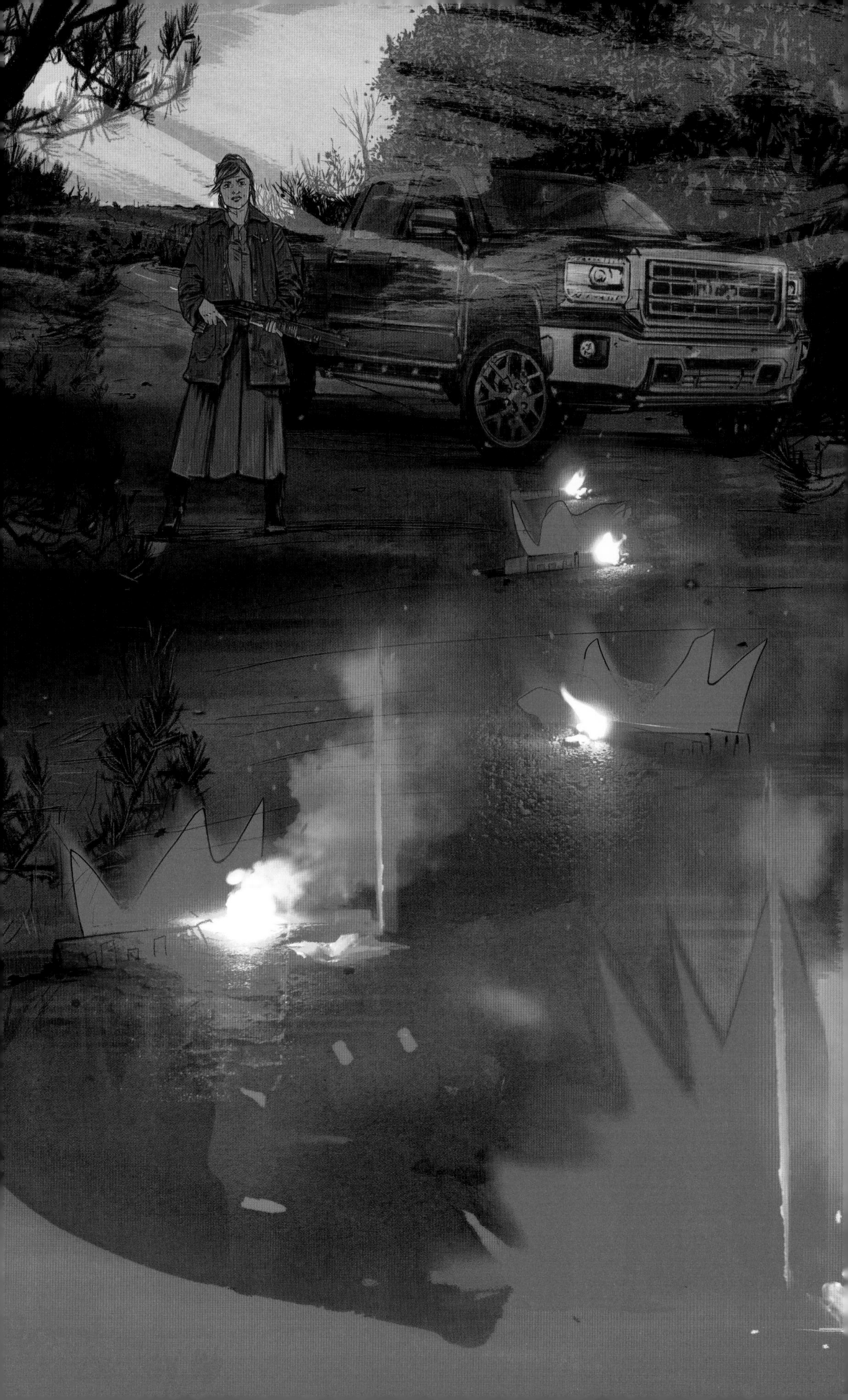

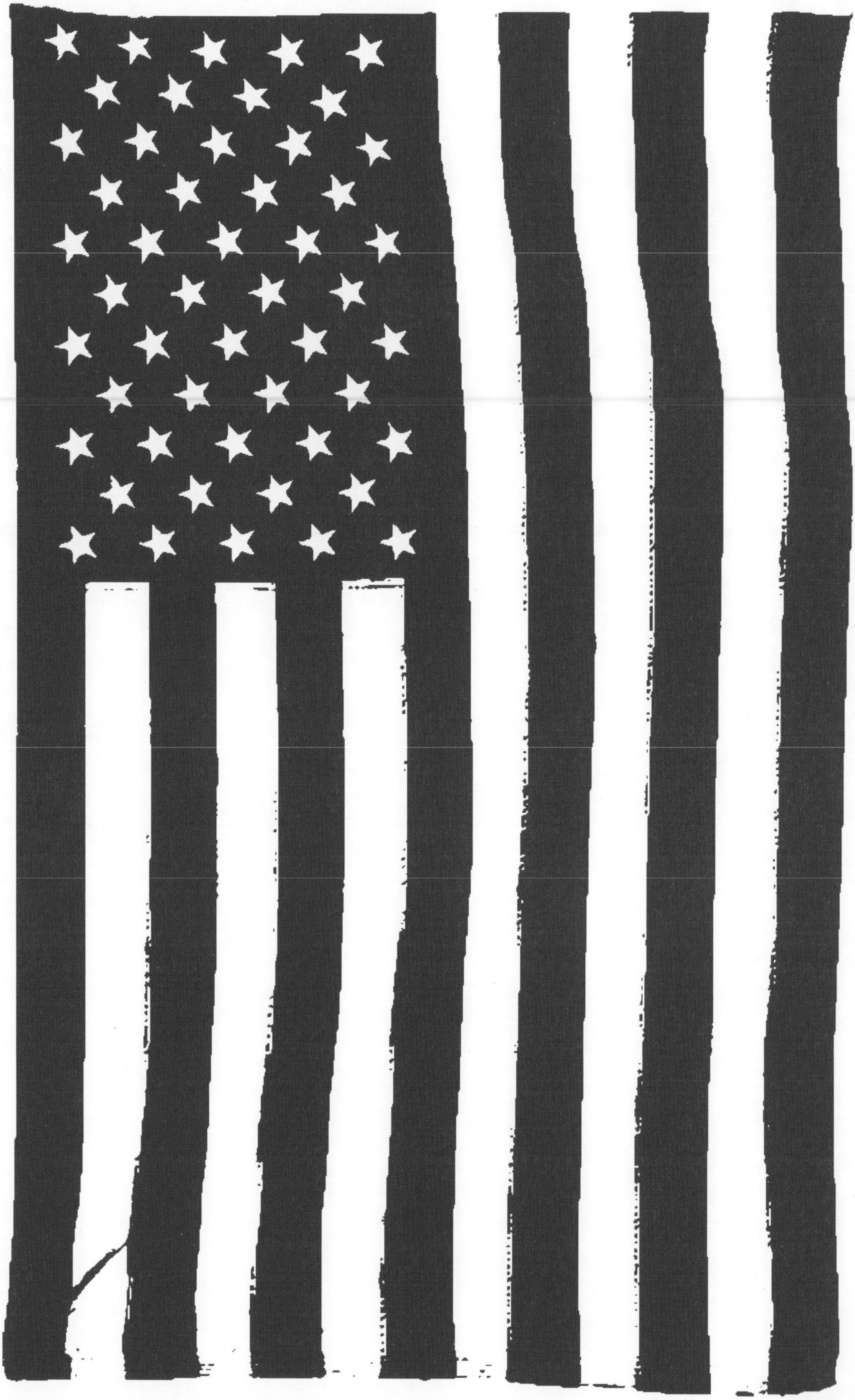

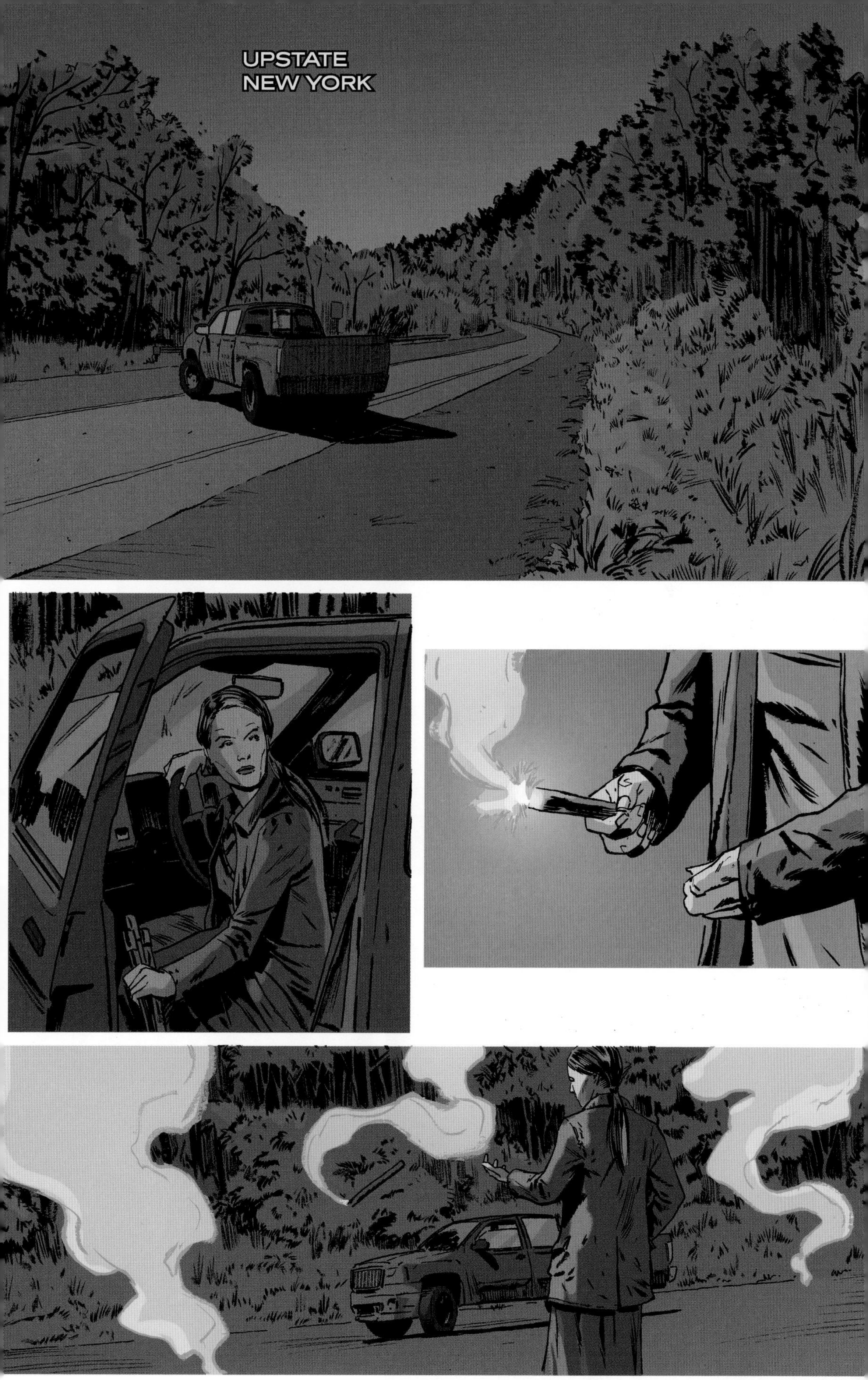
UPSTATE NEW YORK

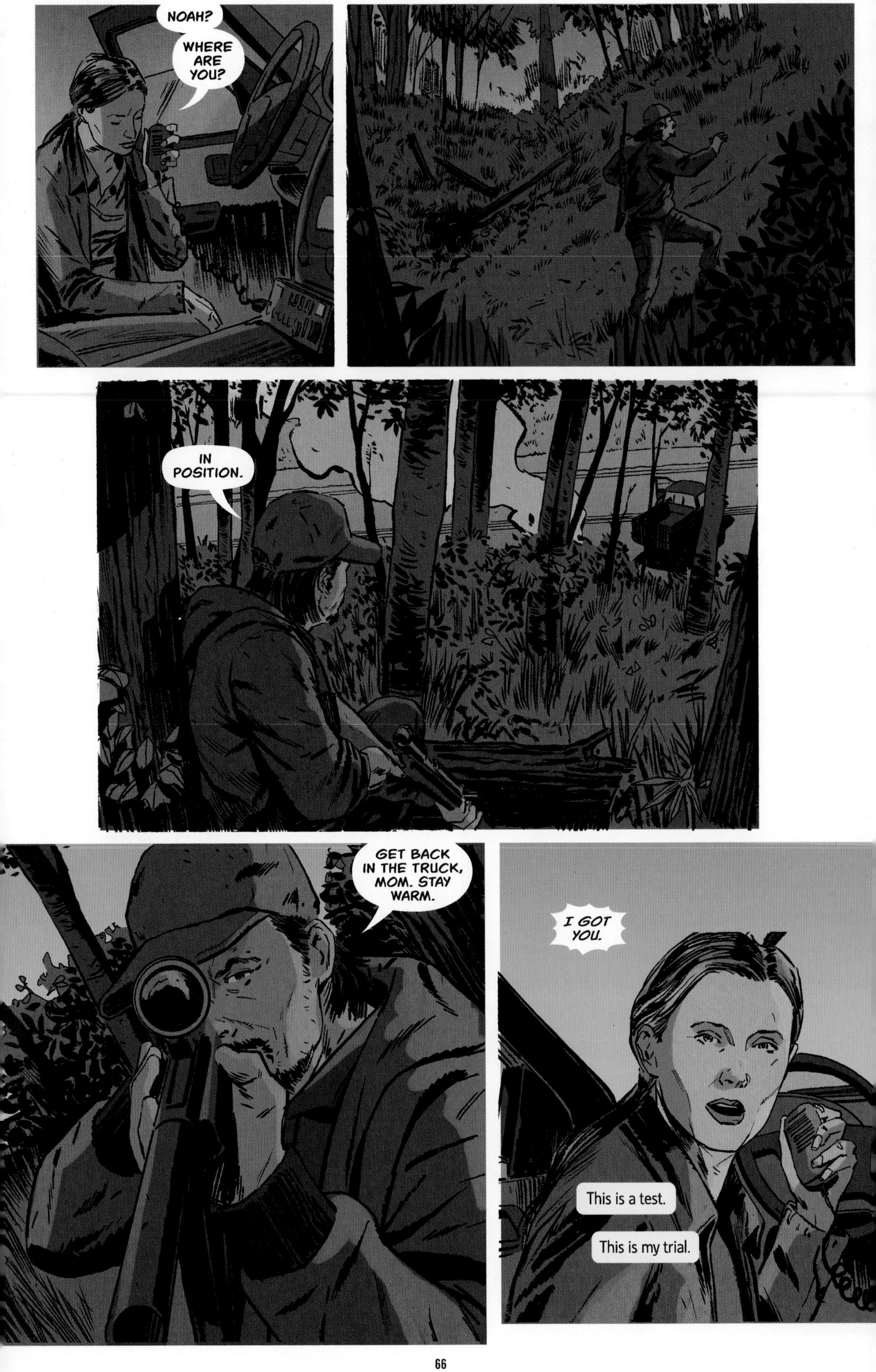
NOAH?
WHERE ARE YOU?
IN POSITION.
GET BACK IN THE TRUCK, MOM. STAY WARM.
I GOT YOU.
This is a test.
This is my trial.

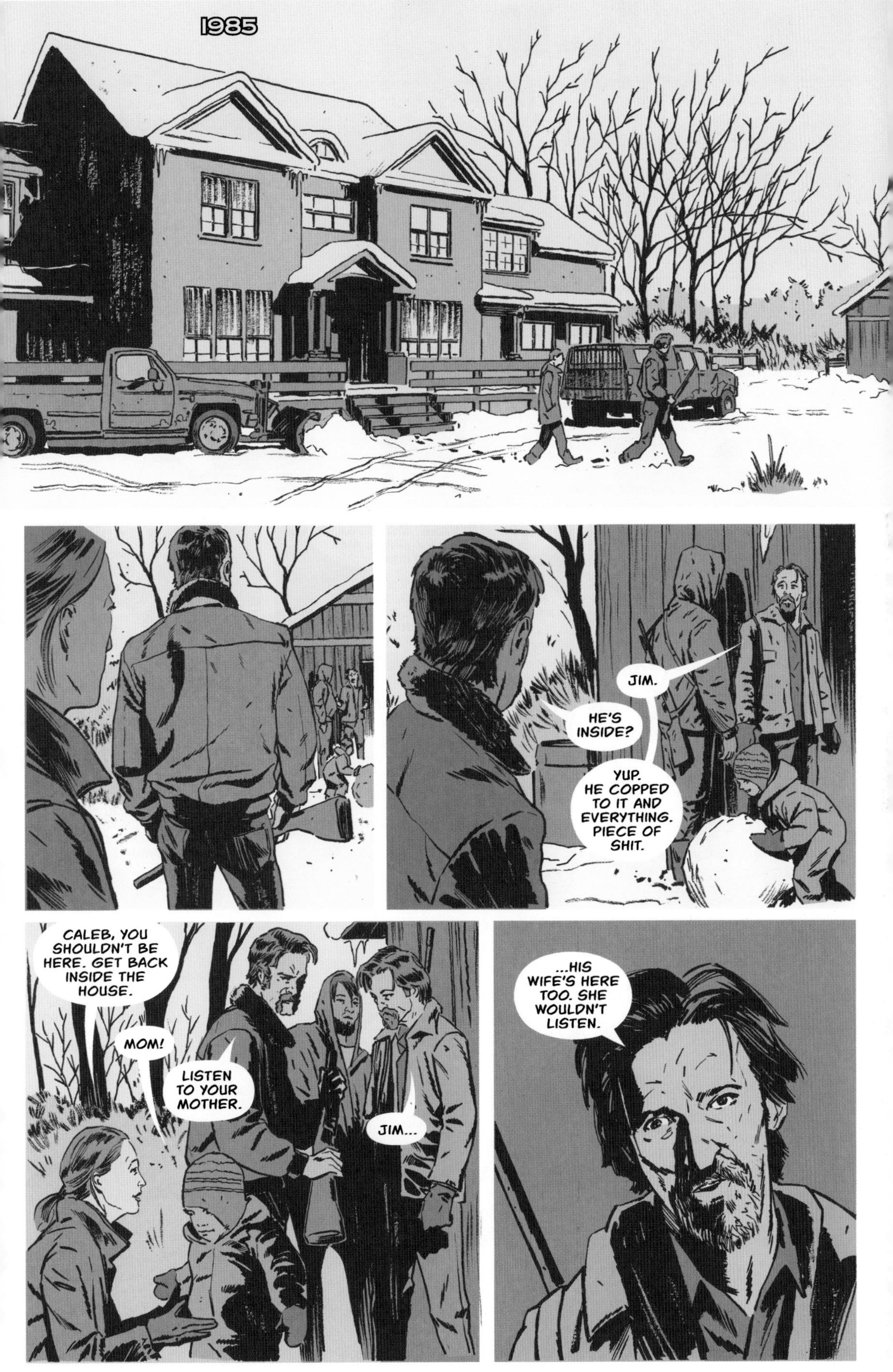
1985
JIM.
HE'S INSIDE?
YUP. HE COPPED TO IT AND EVERYTHING. PIECE OF SHIT.
CALEB, YOU SHOULDN'T BE HERE. GET BACK INSIDE THE HOUSE.
MOM!
LISTEN TO YOUR MOTHER.
JIM...
...HIS WIFE'S HERE TOO. SHE WOULDN'T LISTEN.

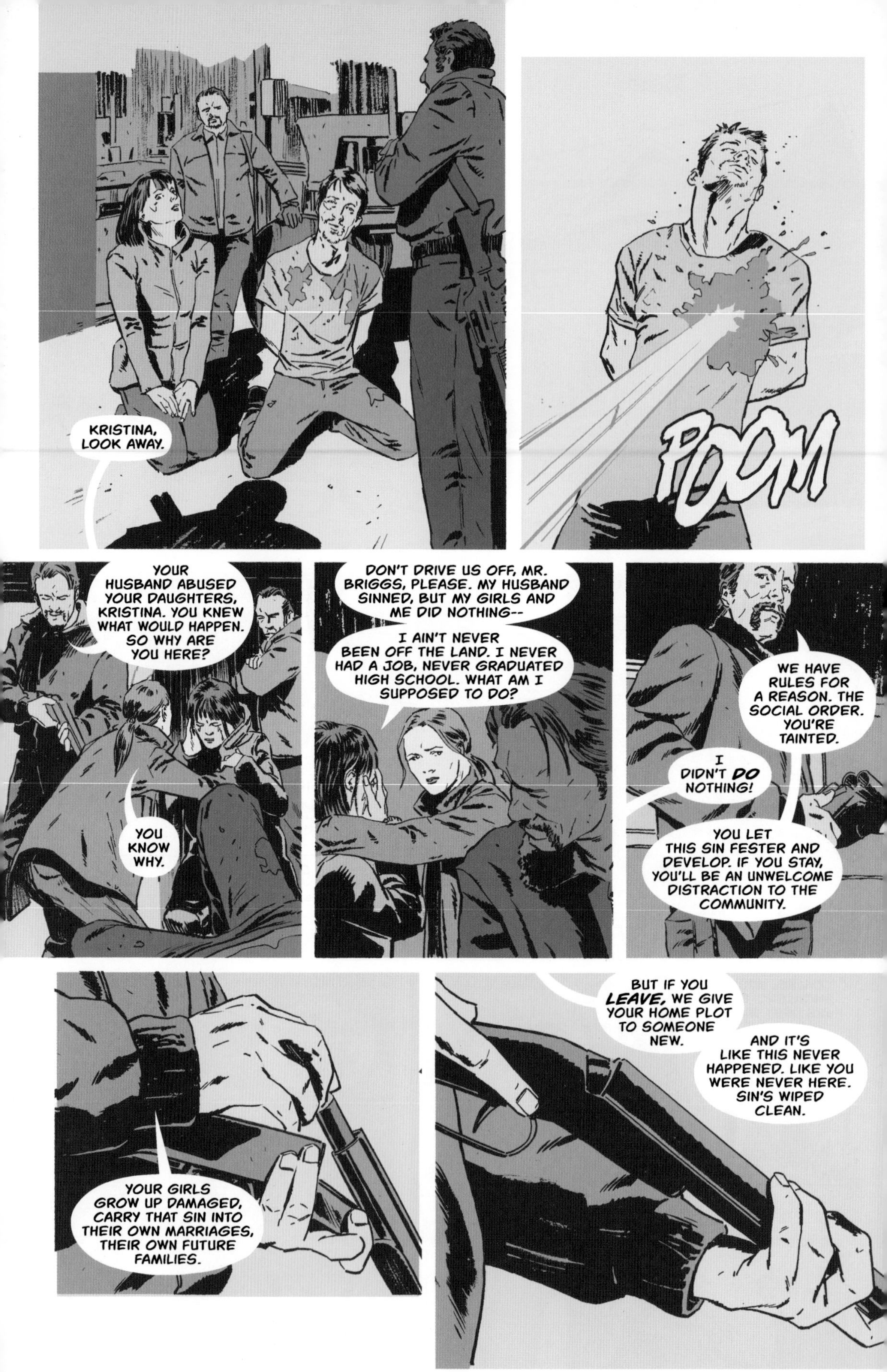
KRISTINA, LOOK AWAY.
POOM
YOUR HUSBAND ABUSED YOUR DAUGHTERS, KRISTINA. YOU KNEW WHAT WOULD HAPPEN. SO WHY ARE YOU HERE?
YOU KNOW WHY.
DON'T DRIVE US OFF, MR. BRIGGS, PLEASE. MY HUSBAND SINNED, BUT MY GIRLS AND ME DID NOTHING--
I AIN'T NEVER BEEN OFF THE LAND. I NEVER HAD A JOB, NEVER GRADUATED HIGH SCHOOL. WHAT AM I SUPPOSED TO DO?
WE HAVE RULES FOR A REASON. THE SOCIAL ORDER. YOU'RE TAINTED.
I DIDN'T *DO* NOTHING!
YOU LET THIS SIN FESTER AND DEVELOP. IF YOU STAY, YOU'LL BE AN UNWELCOME DISTRACTION TO THE COMMUNITY.
YOUR GIRLS GROW UP DAMAGED, CARRY THAT SIN INTO THEIR OWN MARRIAGES, THEIR OWN FUTURE FAMILIES.
BUT IF YOU ***LEAVE,*** WE GIVE YOUR HOME PLOT TO SOMEONE NEW.
AND IT'S LIKE THIS NEVER HAPPENED. LIKE YOU WERE NEVER HERE. SIN'S WIPED CLEAN.

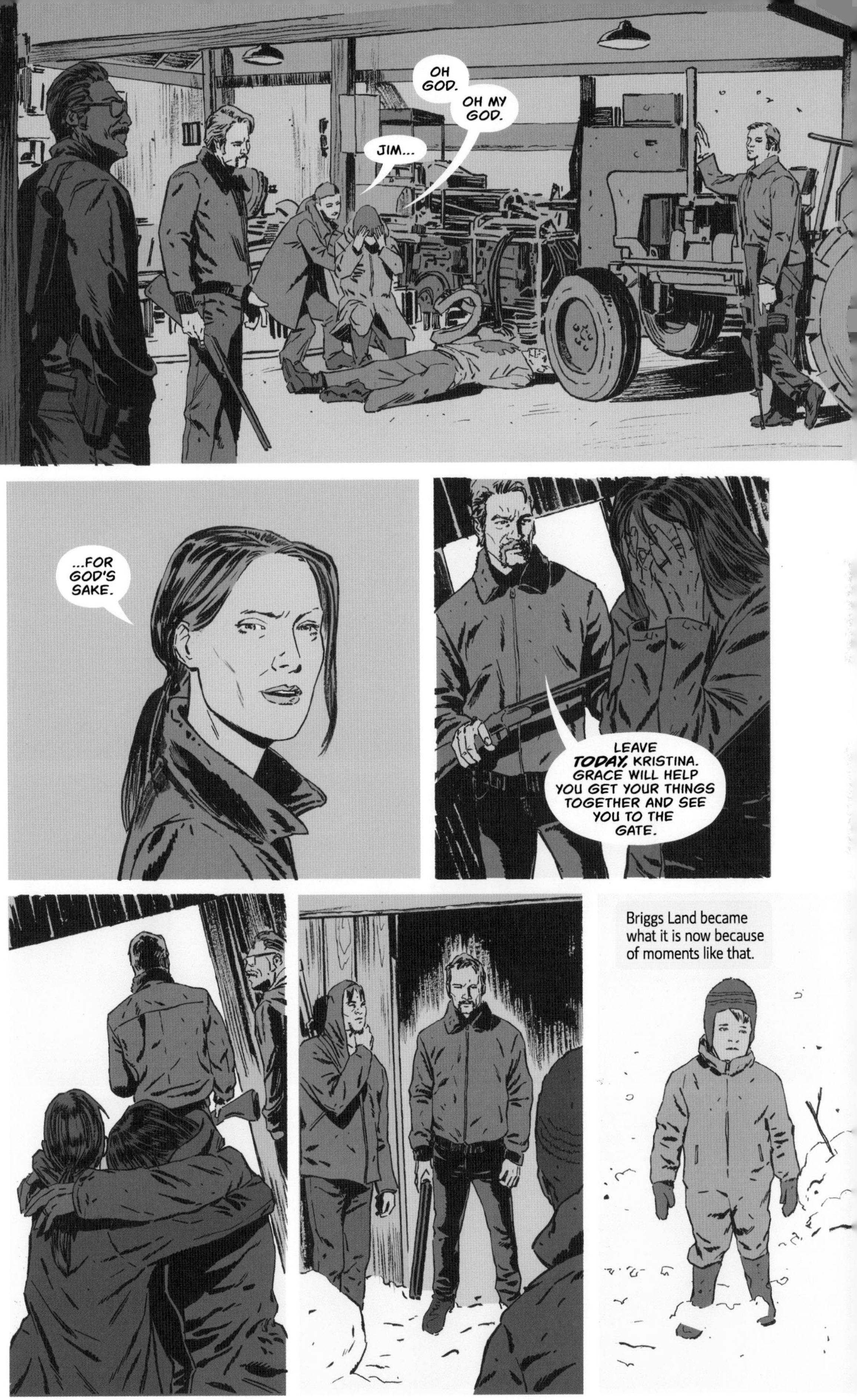
OH GOD.
OH MY GOD.
JIM...
...FOR GOD'S SAKE.
LEAVE *TODAY,* KRISTINA. GRACE WILL HELP YOU GET YOUR THINGS TOGETHER AND SEE YOU TO THE GATE.
Briggs Land became what it is now because of moments like that.

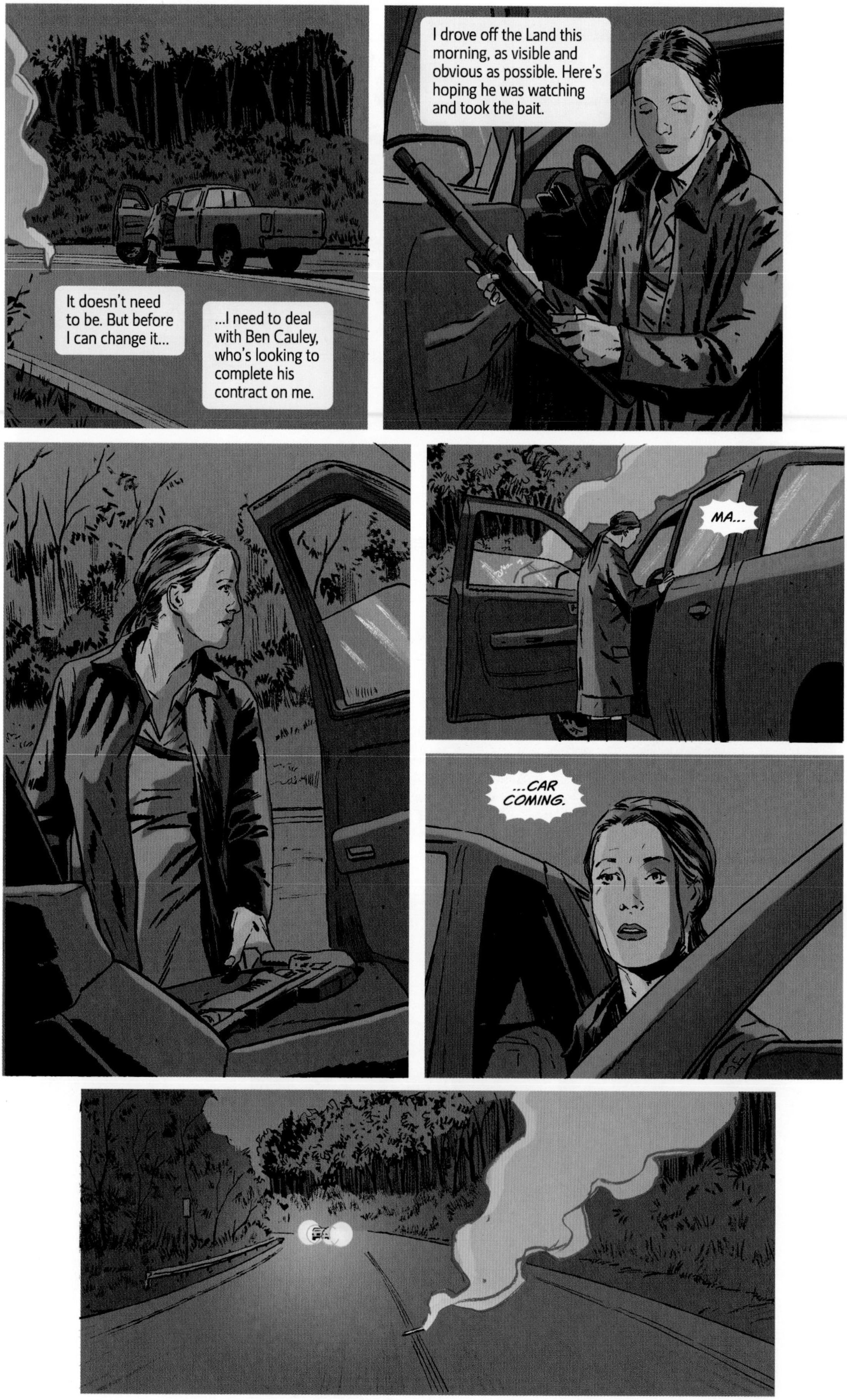
It doesn't need to be. But before I can change it...
...I need to deal with Ben Cauley, who's looking to complete his contract on me.
I drove off the Land this morning, as visible and obvious as possible. Here's hoping he was watching and took the bait.
MA...
...CAR COMING.

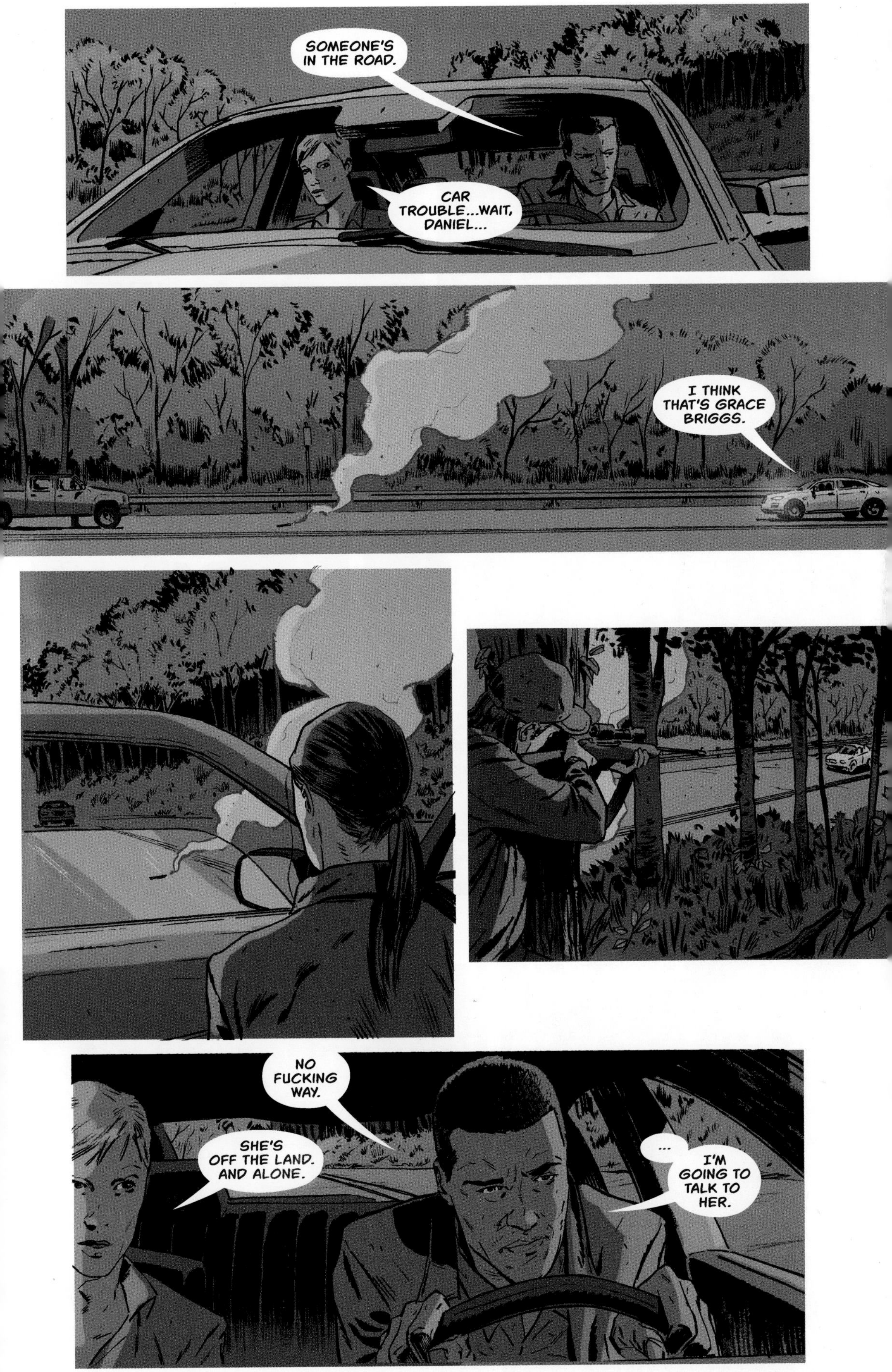

SOMEONE'S IN THE ROAD.
CAR TROUBLE...WAIT, DANIEL...
I THINK THAT'S GRACE BRIGGS.
NO FUCKING WAY.
SHE'S OFF THE LAND. AND ALONE.
...
I'M GOING TO TALK TO HER.

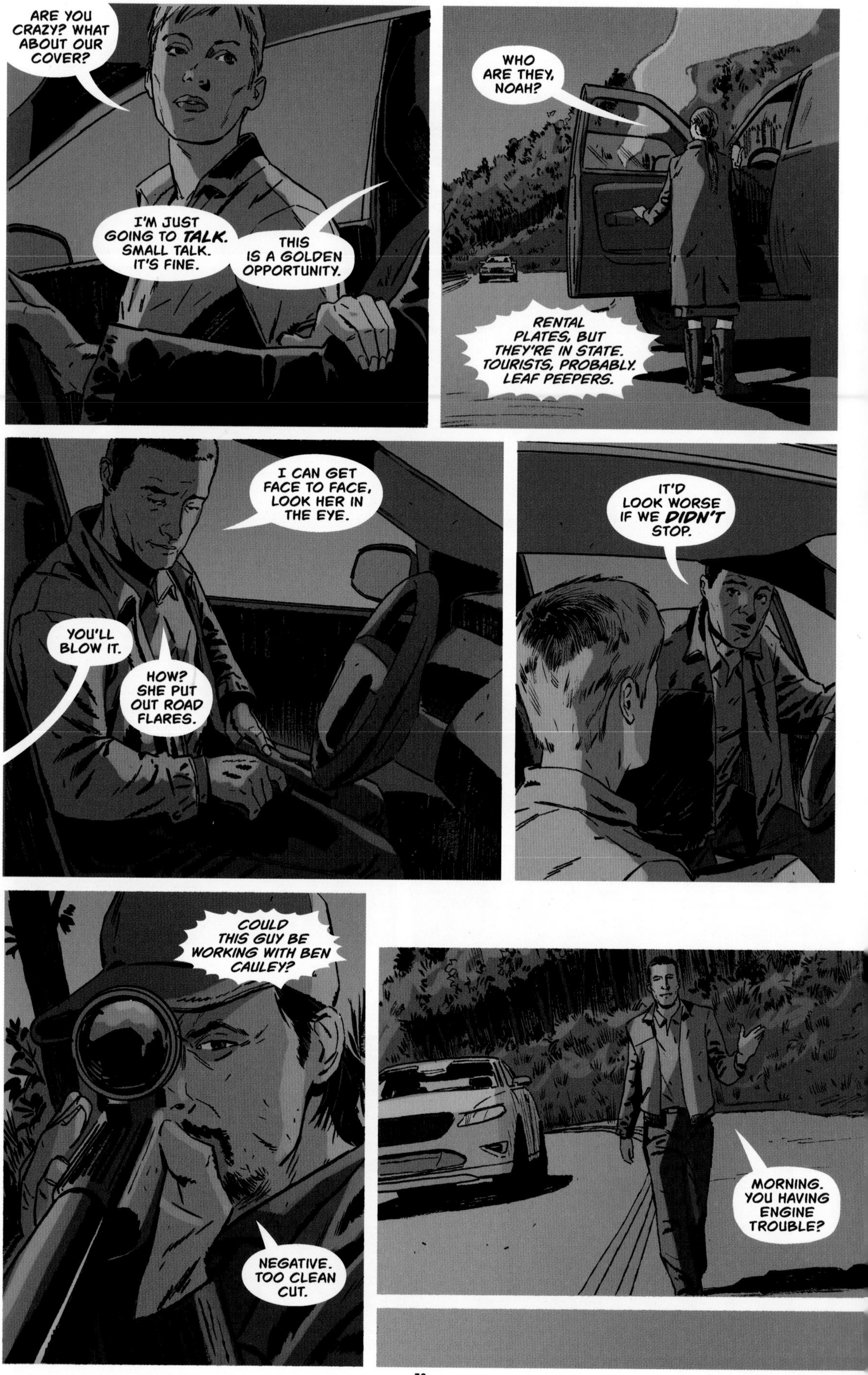
ARE YOU CRAZY? WHAT ABOUT OUR COVER?
I'M JUST GOING TO TALK. SMALL TALK. IT'S FINE.
THIS IS A GOLDEN OPPORTUNITY.
WHO ARE THEY, NOAH?
RENTAL PLATES, BUT THEY'RE IN STATE. TOURISTS, PROBABLY. LEAF PEEPERS.
I CAN GET FACE TO FACE, LOOK HER IN THE EYE.
YOU'LL BLOW IT.
HOW? SHE PUT OUT ROAD FLARES.
IT'D LOOK WORSE IF WE DIDN'T STOP.
COULD THIS GUY BE WORKING WITH BEN CAULEY?
NEGATIVE. TOO CLEAN CUT.
MORNING. YOU HAVING ENGINE TROUBLE?

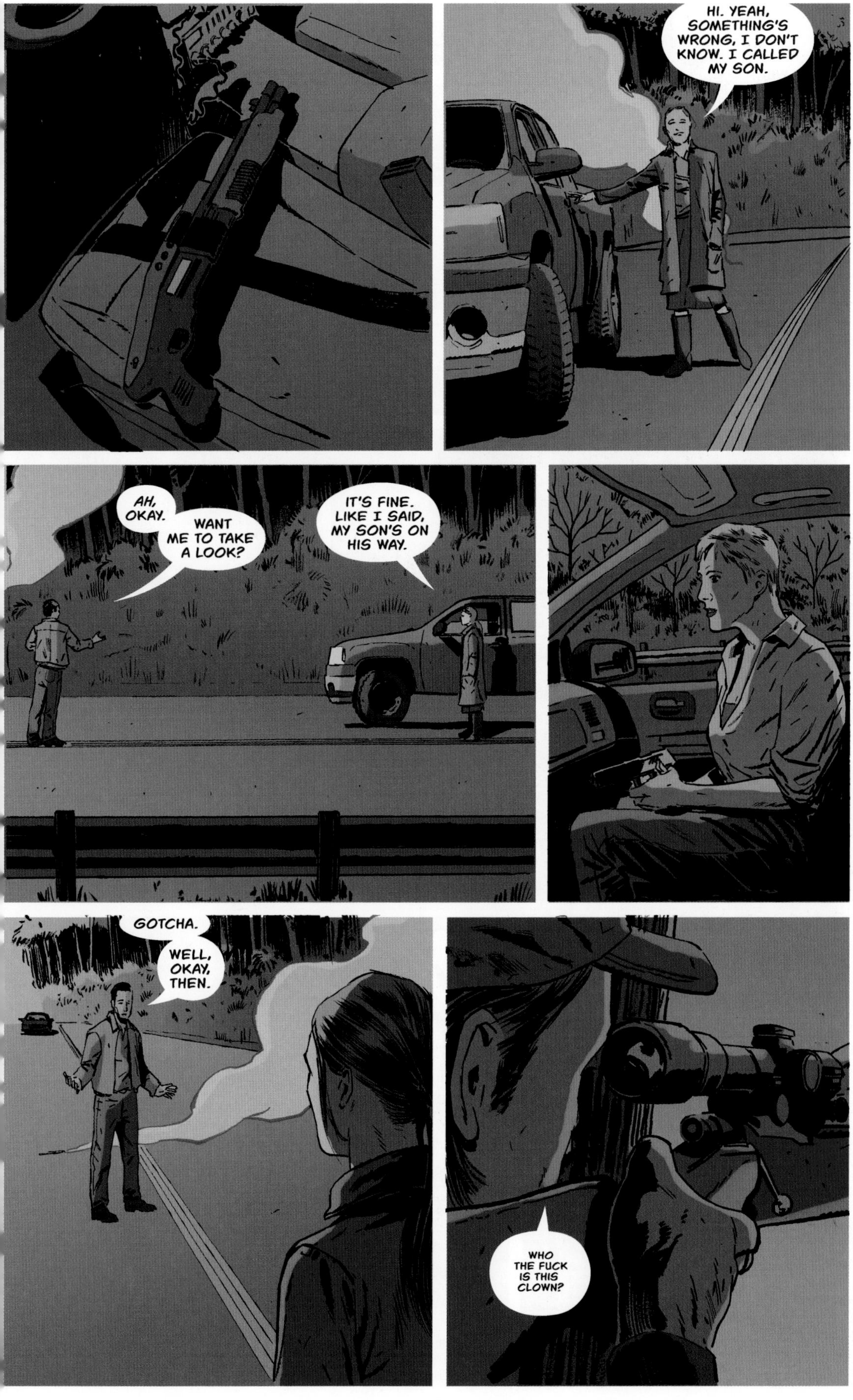
HI. YEAH, SOMETHING'S WRONG, I DON'T KNOW. I CALLED MY SON.
AH, OKAY.
WANT ME TO TAKE A LOOK?
IT'S FINE. LIKE I SAID, MY SON'S ON HIS WAY.
GOTCHA.
WELL, OKAY, THEN.
WHO THE FUCK IS THIS CLOWN?

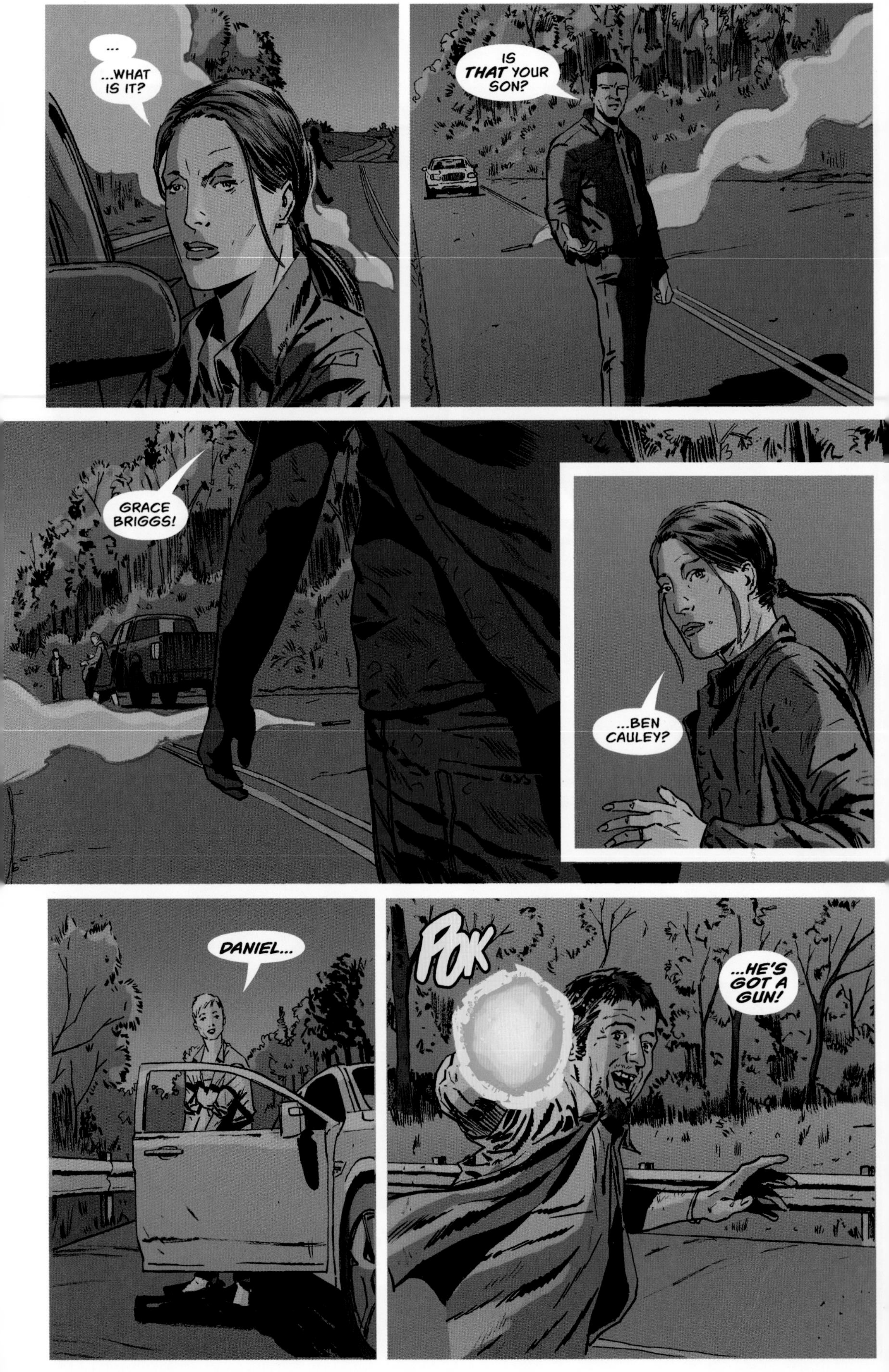
...
...WHAT IS IT?
IS THAT YOUR SON?
GRACE BRIGGS!
...BEN CAULEY?
DANIEL...
POK
...HE'S GOT A GUN!

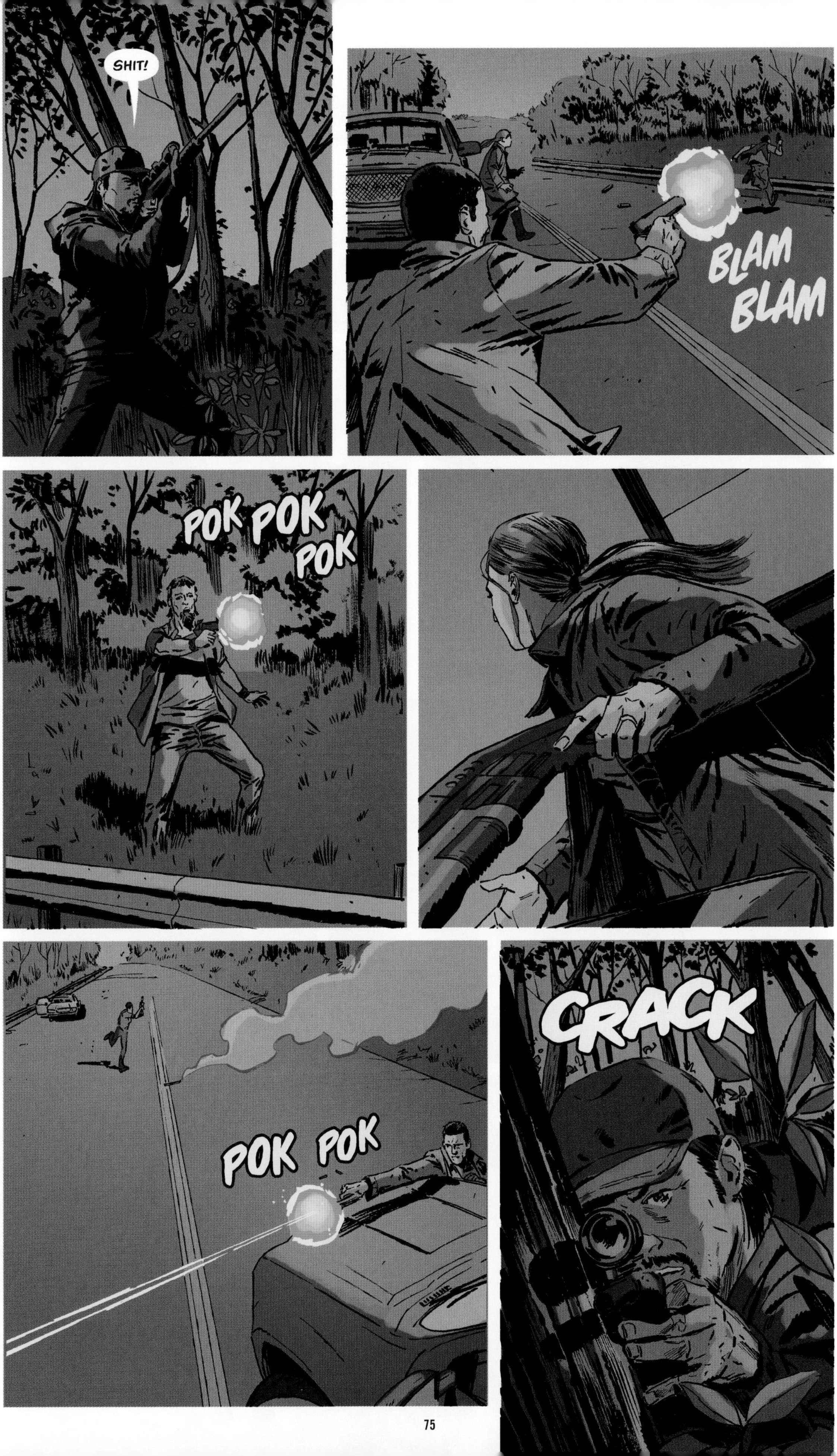
SHIT!
BLAM
BLAM
POK POK
POK
POK POK
CRACK

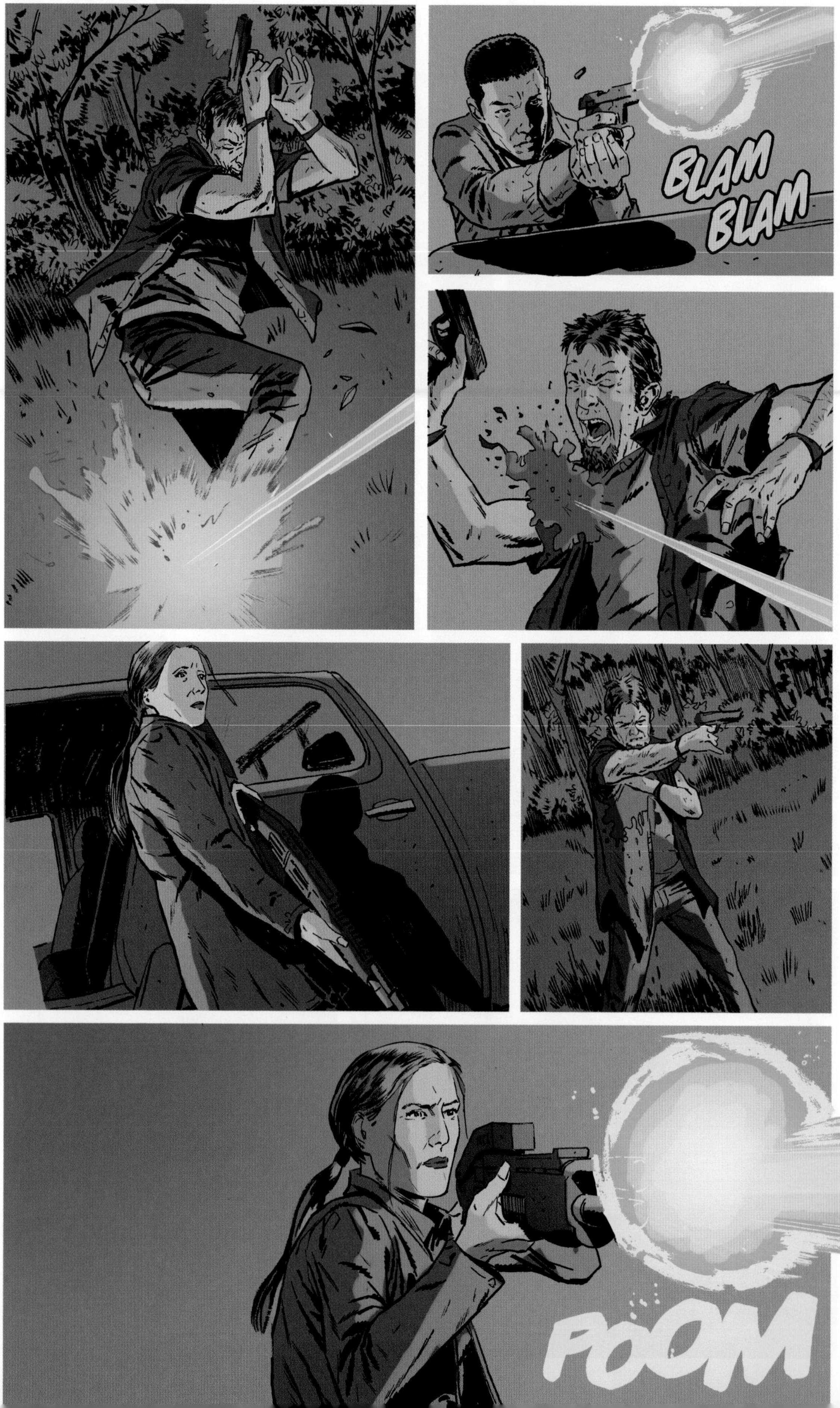
BLAM
BLAM
POOM

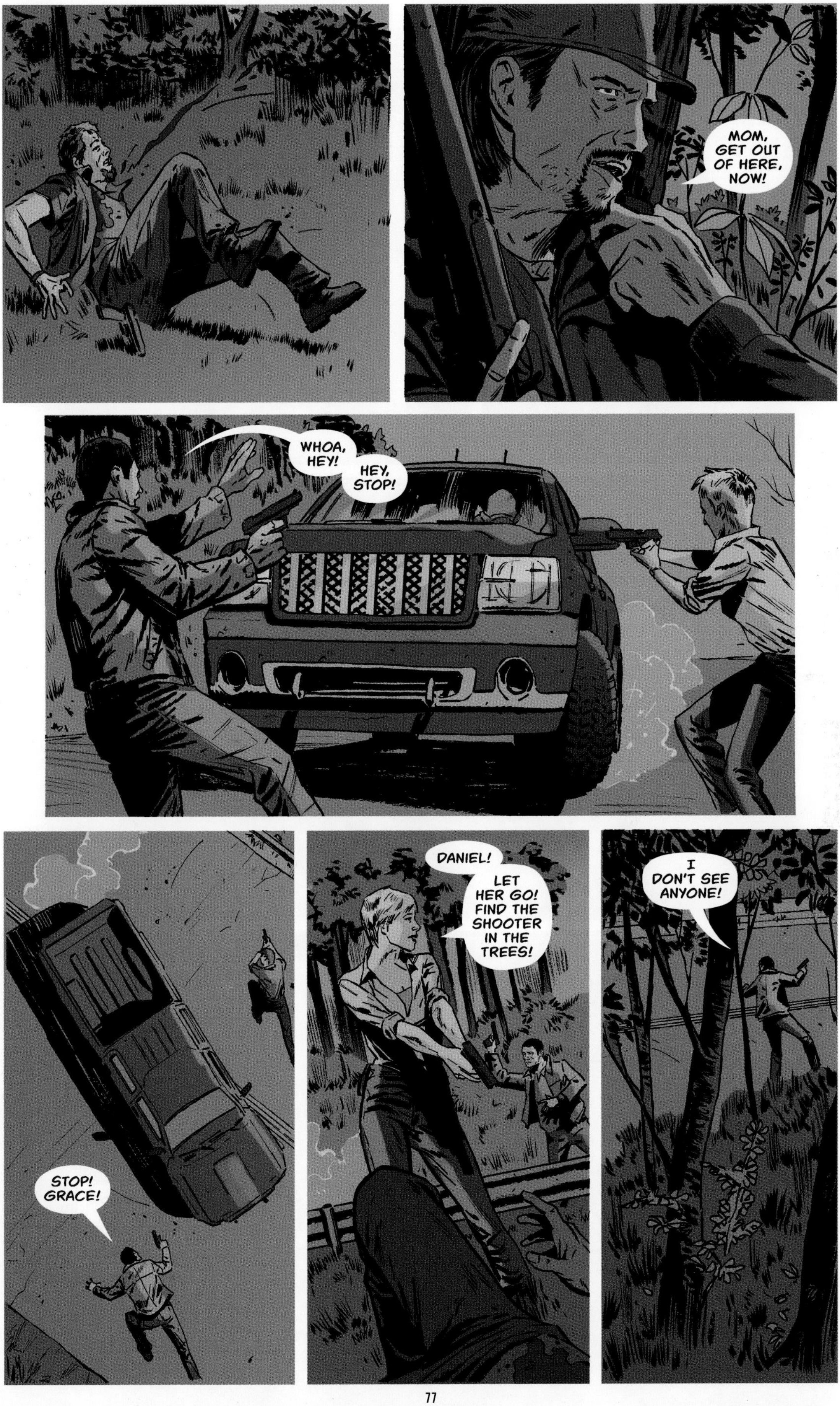

MOM, GET OUT OF HERE, NOW!
WHOA, HEY!
HEY, STOP!
STOP! GRACE!
DANIEL!
LET HER GO! FIND THE SHOOTER IN THE TREES!
I DON'T SEE ANYONE!

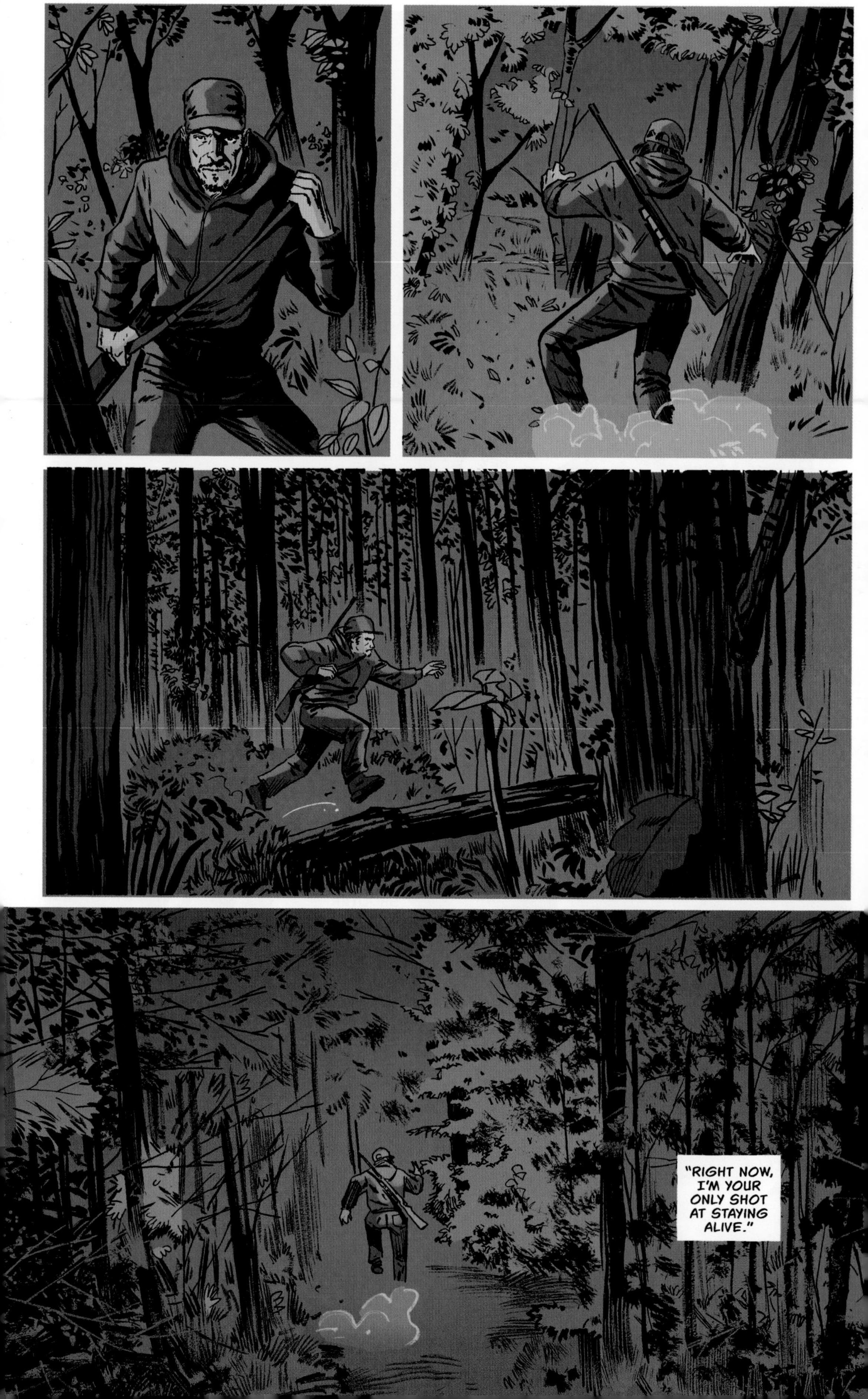
"RIGHT NOW, I'M YOUR ONLY SHOT AT STAYING ALIVE."

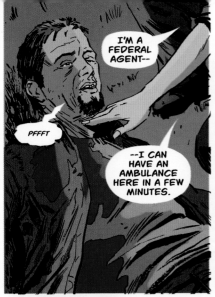

I'M A FEDERAL AGENT--

PFFFT

--I CAN HAVE AN AMBULANCE HERE IN A FEW MINUTES.

HE'S NOT GOING TO LAST THAT LONG.

HEY, BUDDY, LISTEN...

...JIM BRIGGS, YOU KNOW HIM? WHAT'S HE INTO? IS HE RUNNING THE FAMILY FROM PRISON?

DID YOU COME OUT HERE TO TAKE OUT GRACE? IS THE FAMILY AT WAR?

DO *YOU* HAVE A FAMILY? A WIFE? GIVE US SOMETHING. TALK TO US. WE CAN PROTECT HER.

HA...

...CAN'T DO SHIT...FUCKIN' FEDS...NOT YOUR FUCKIN' BUSINESS...

...JIM BRIGGS? WHAT A JOKE...

...FUCKIN' WIFE AT THE HELM, THE DUMB BITCH...WE'RE ALL DOOMED...

...⚡

THERE YOU GO. GRACE BRIGGS, HEAD OF THE FAMILY.

AND NOW SHE KNOWS YOUR FACE.

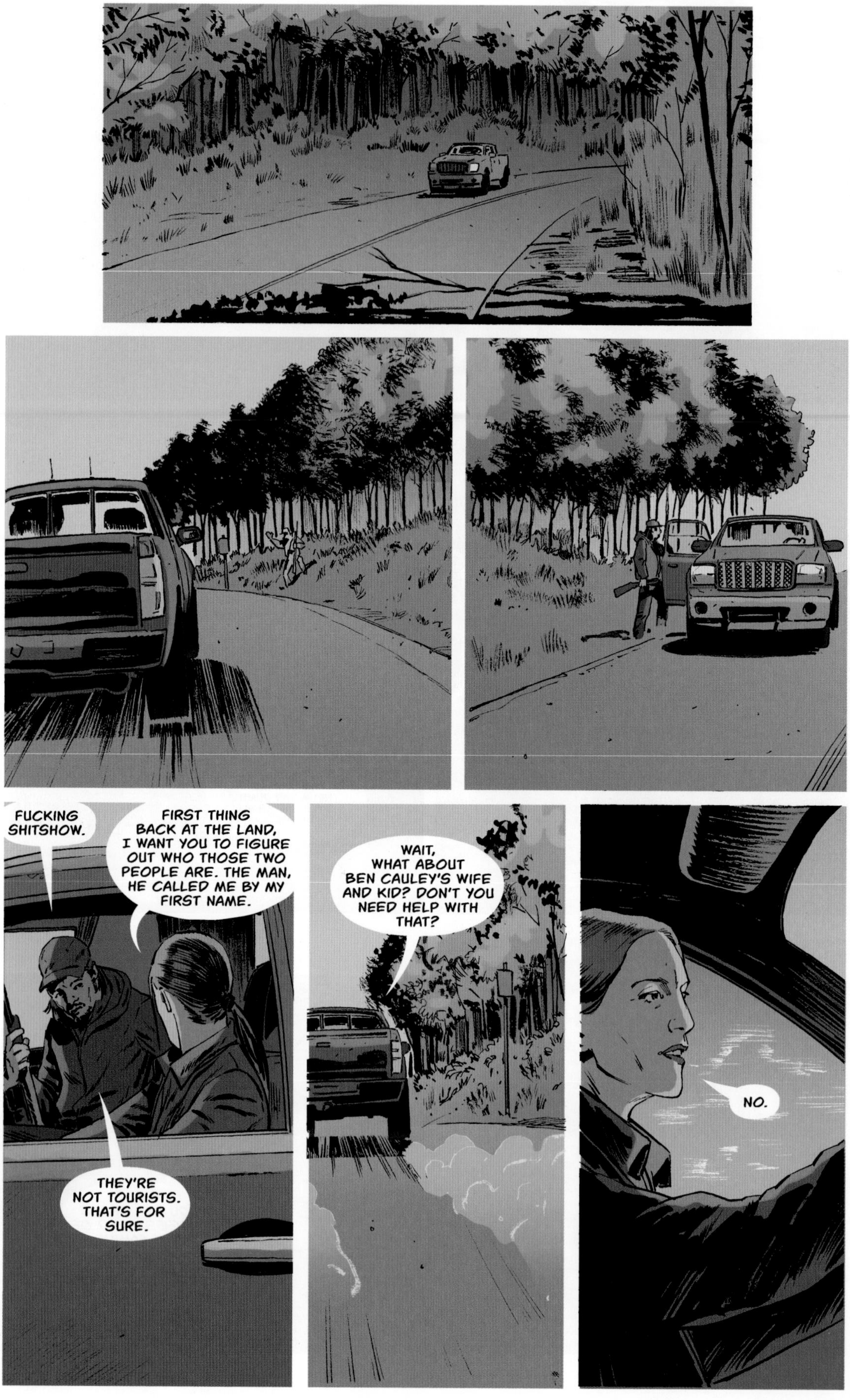
FUCKING SHITSHOW.
FIRST THING BACK AT THE LAND, I WANT YOU TO FIGURE OUT WHO THOSE TWO PEOPLE ARE. THE MAN, HE CALLED ME BY MY FIRST NAME.
THEY'RE NOT TOURISTS. THAT'S FOR SURE.
WAIT, WHAT ABOUT BEN CAULEY'S WIFE AND KID? DON'T YOU NEED HELP WITH THAT?
NO.

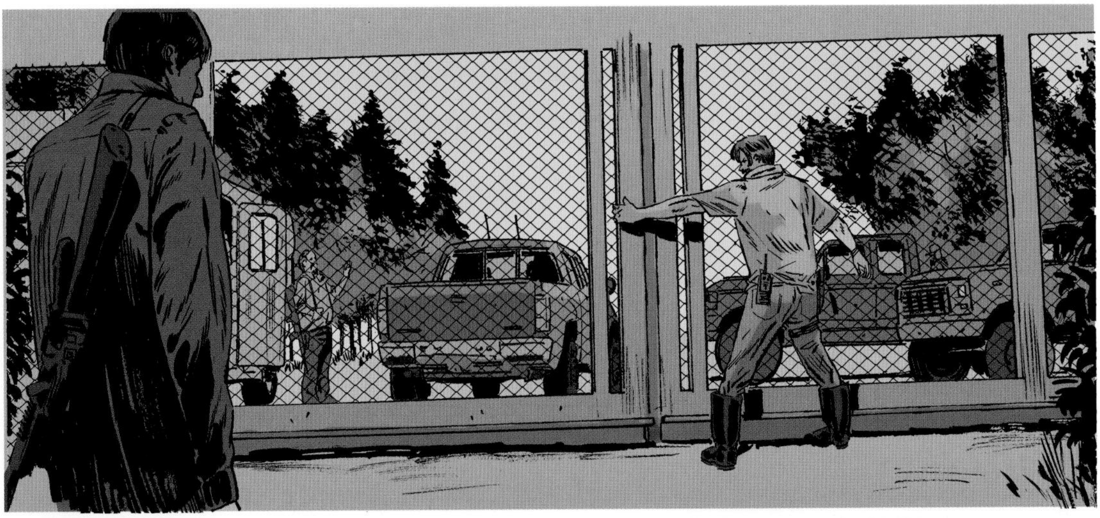

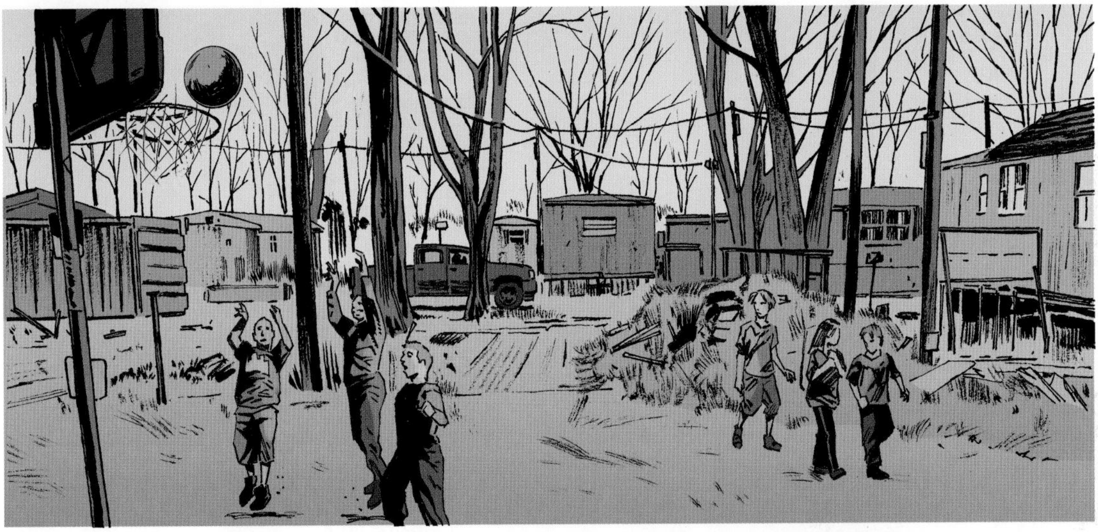

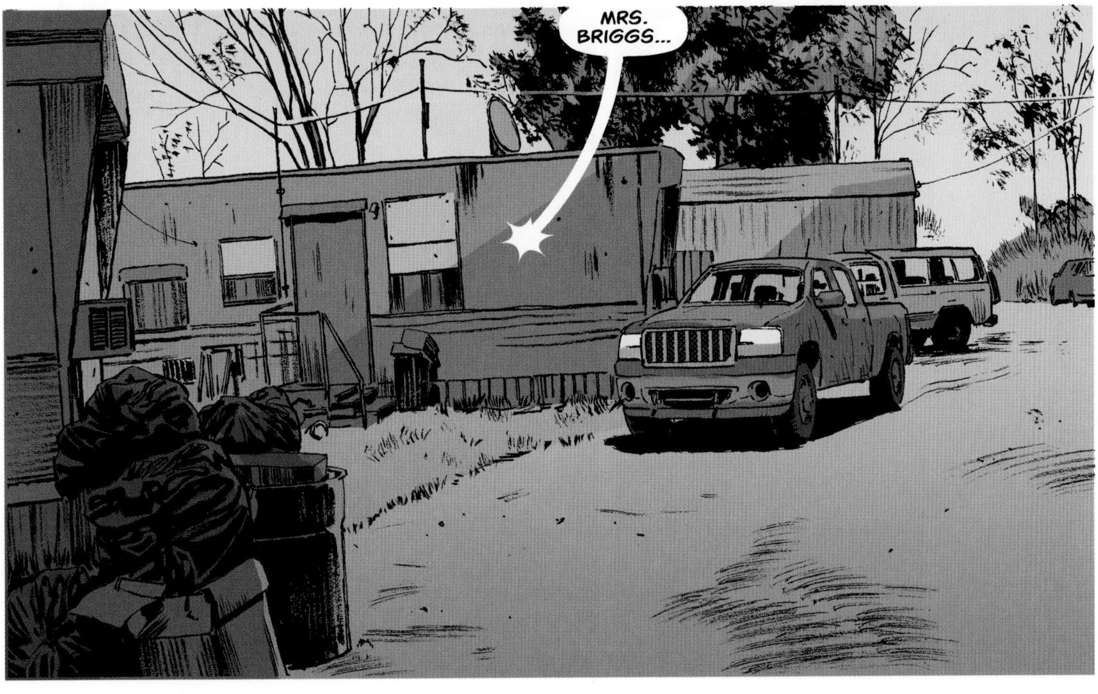
MRS. BRIGGS...

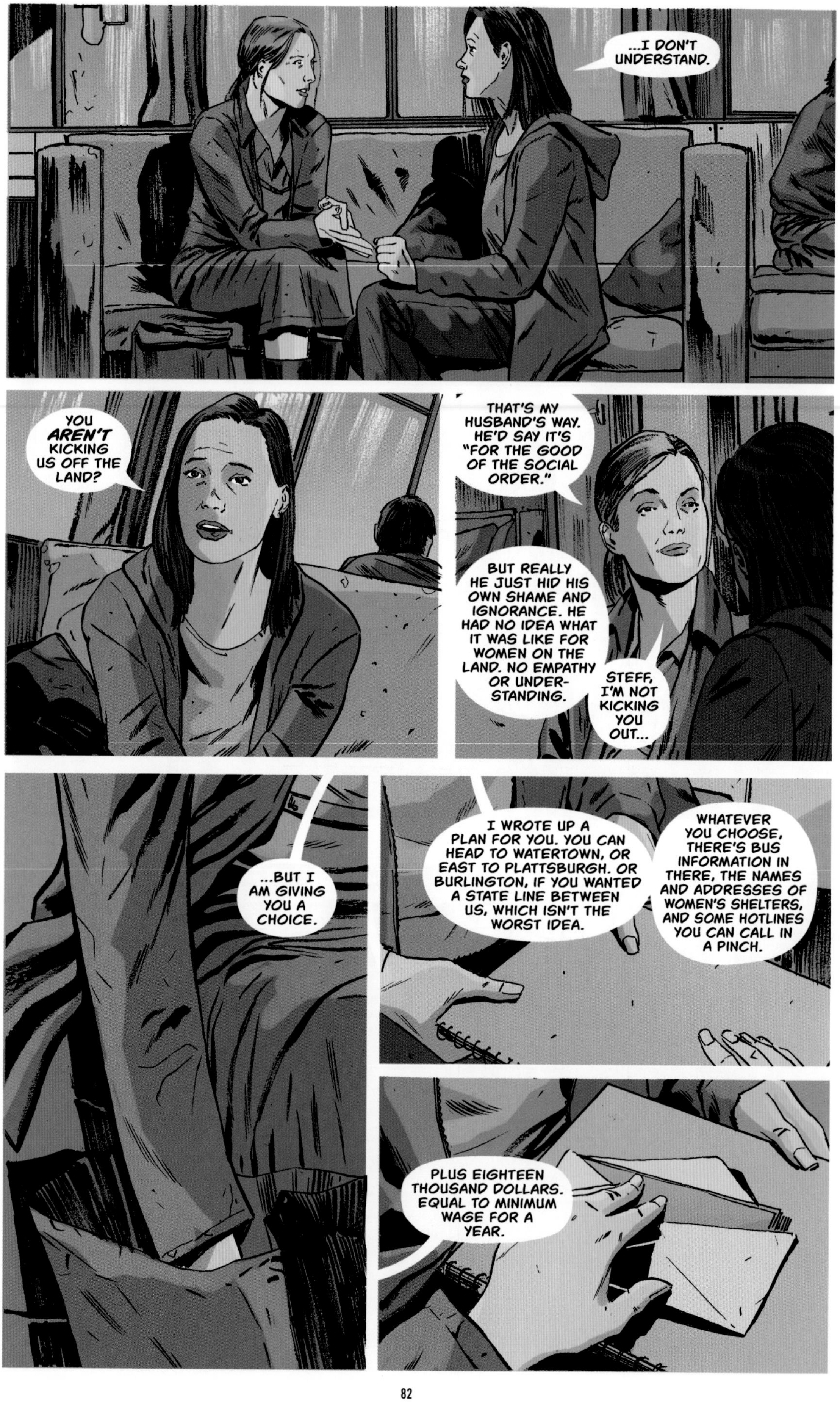

...I DON'T UNDERSTAND.
YOU *AREN'T* KICKING US OFF THE LAND?
THAT'S MY HUSBAND'S WAY. HE'D SAY IT'S "FOR THE GOOD OF THE SOCIAL ORDER."
BUT REALLY HE JUST HID HIS OWN SHAME AND IGNORANCE. HE HAD NO IDEA WHAT IT WAS LIKE FOR WOMEN ON THE LAND. NO EMPATHY OR UNDER-STANDING.
STEFF, I'M NOT KICKING YOU OUT...
...BUT I AM GIVING YOU A CHOICE.
I WROTE UP A PLAN FOR YOU. YOU CAN HEAD TO WATERTOWN, OR EAST TO PLATTSBURGH. OR BURLINGTON, IF YOU WANTED A STATE LINE BETWEEN US, WHICH ISN'T THE WORST IDEA.
WHATEVER YOU CHOOSE, THERE'S BUS INFORMATION IN THERE, THE NAMES AND ADDRESSES OF WOMEN'S SHELTERS, AND SOME HOTLINES YOU CAN CALL IN A PINCH.
PLUS EIGHTEEN THOUSAND DOLLARS. EQUAL TO MINIMUM WAGE FOR A YEAR.

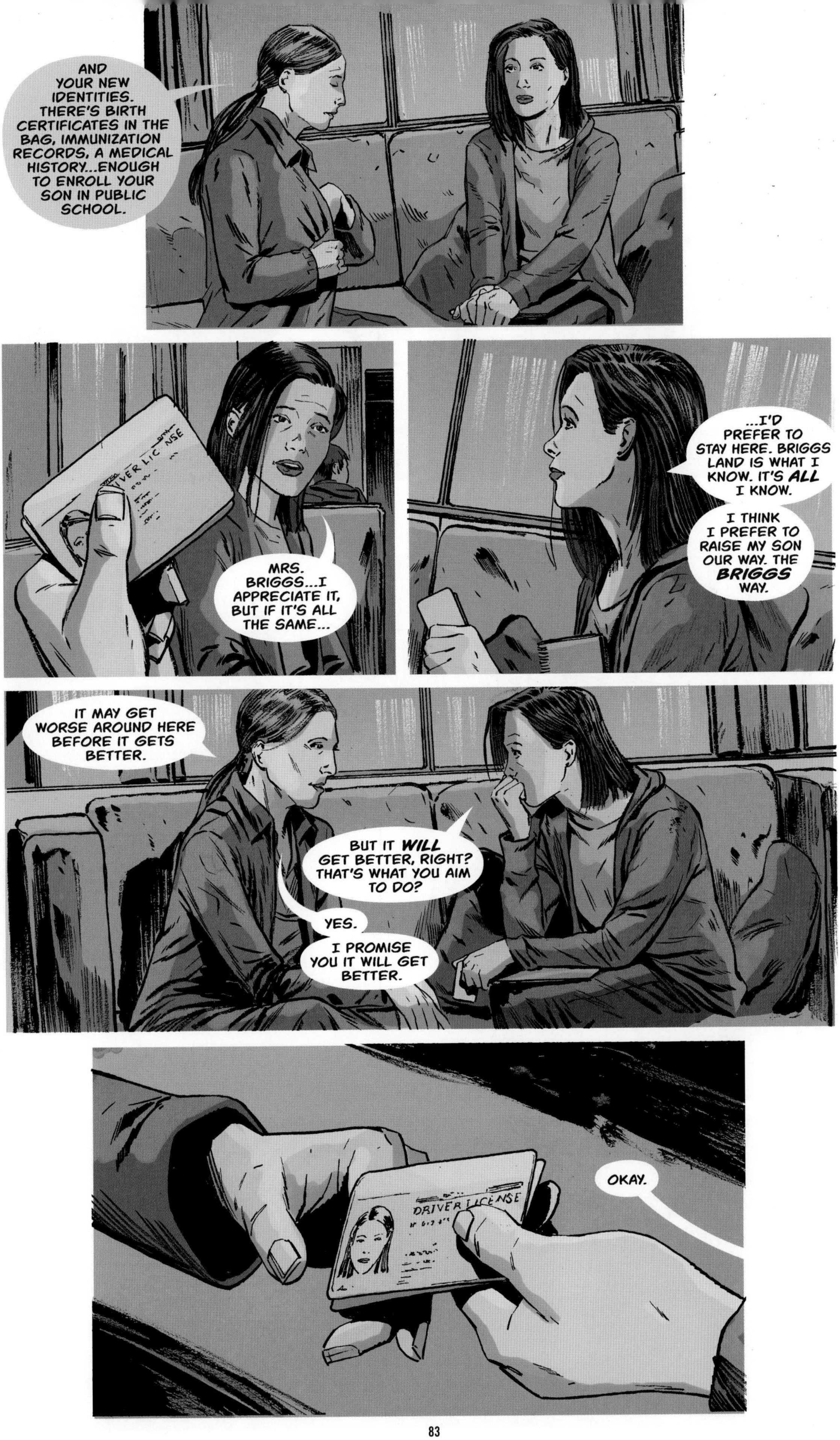
AND YOUR NEW IDENTITIES. THERE'S BIRTH CERTIFICATES IN THE BAG, IMMUNIZATION RECORDS, A MEDICAL HISTORY...ENOUGH TO ENROLL YOUR SON IN PUBLIC SCHOOL.
DRIVER LICENSE
MRS. BRIGGS...I APPRECIATE IT, BUT IF IT'S ALL THE SAME...
...I'D PREFER TO STAY HERE. BRIGGS LAND IS WHAT I KNOW. IT'S ALL I KNOW.
I THINK I PREFER TO RAISE MY SON OUR WAY. THE BRIGGS WAY.
IT MAY GET WORSE AROUND HERE BEFORE IT GETS BETTER.
BUT IT WILL GET BETTER, RIGHT? THAT'S WHAT YOU AIM TO DO?
YES.
I PROMISE YOU IT WILL GET BETTER.
DRIVER LICENSE
OKAY.

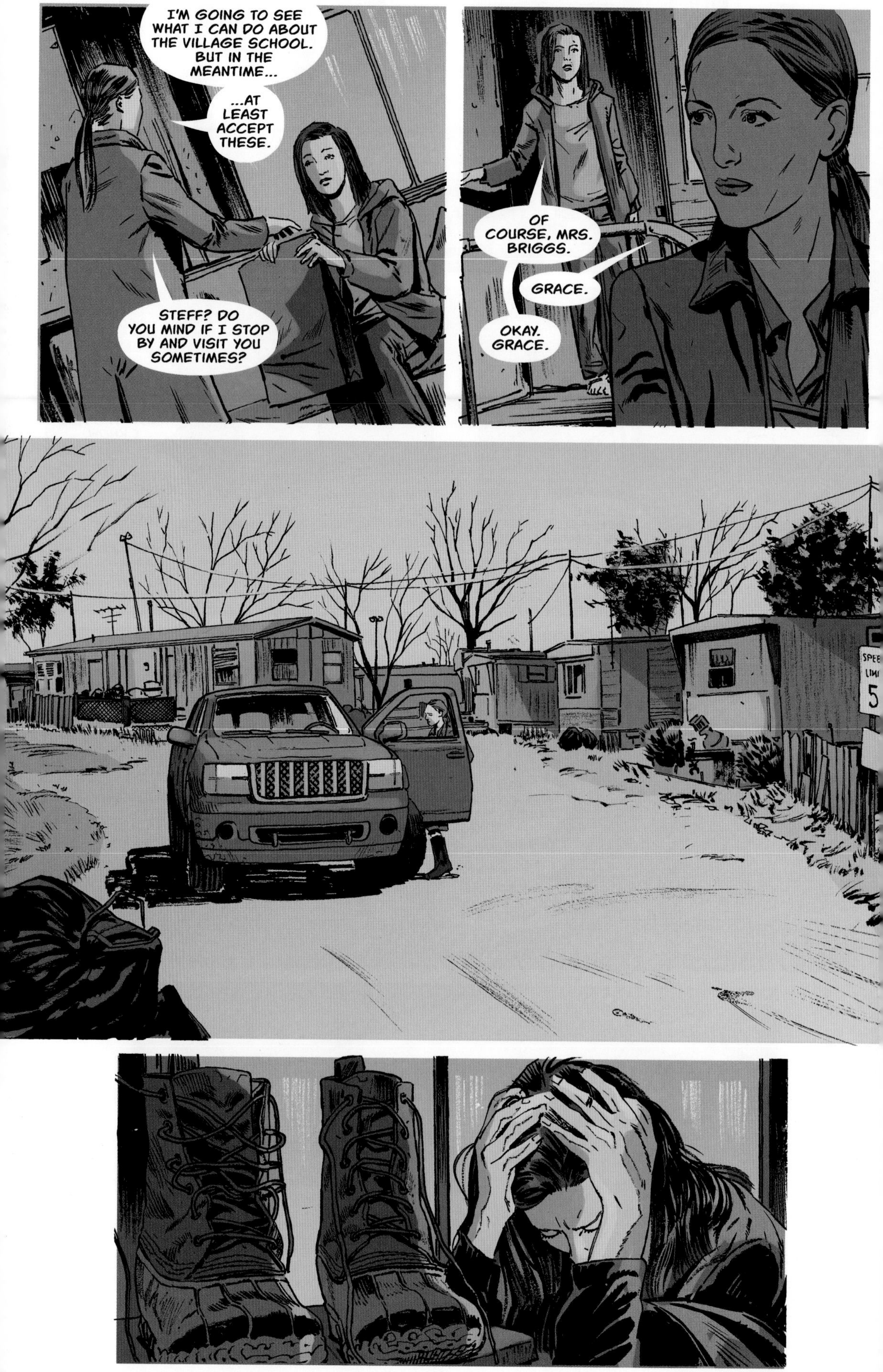
I'M GOING TO SEE WHAT I CAN DO ABOUT THE VILLAGE SCHOOL. BUT IN THE MEANTIME...
...AT LEAST ACCEPT THESE.
STEFF? DO YOU MIND IF I STOP BY AND VISIT YOU SOMETIMES?
OF COURSE, MRS. BRIGGS.
GRACE.
OKAY. GRACE.

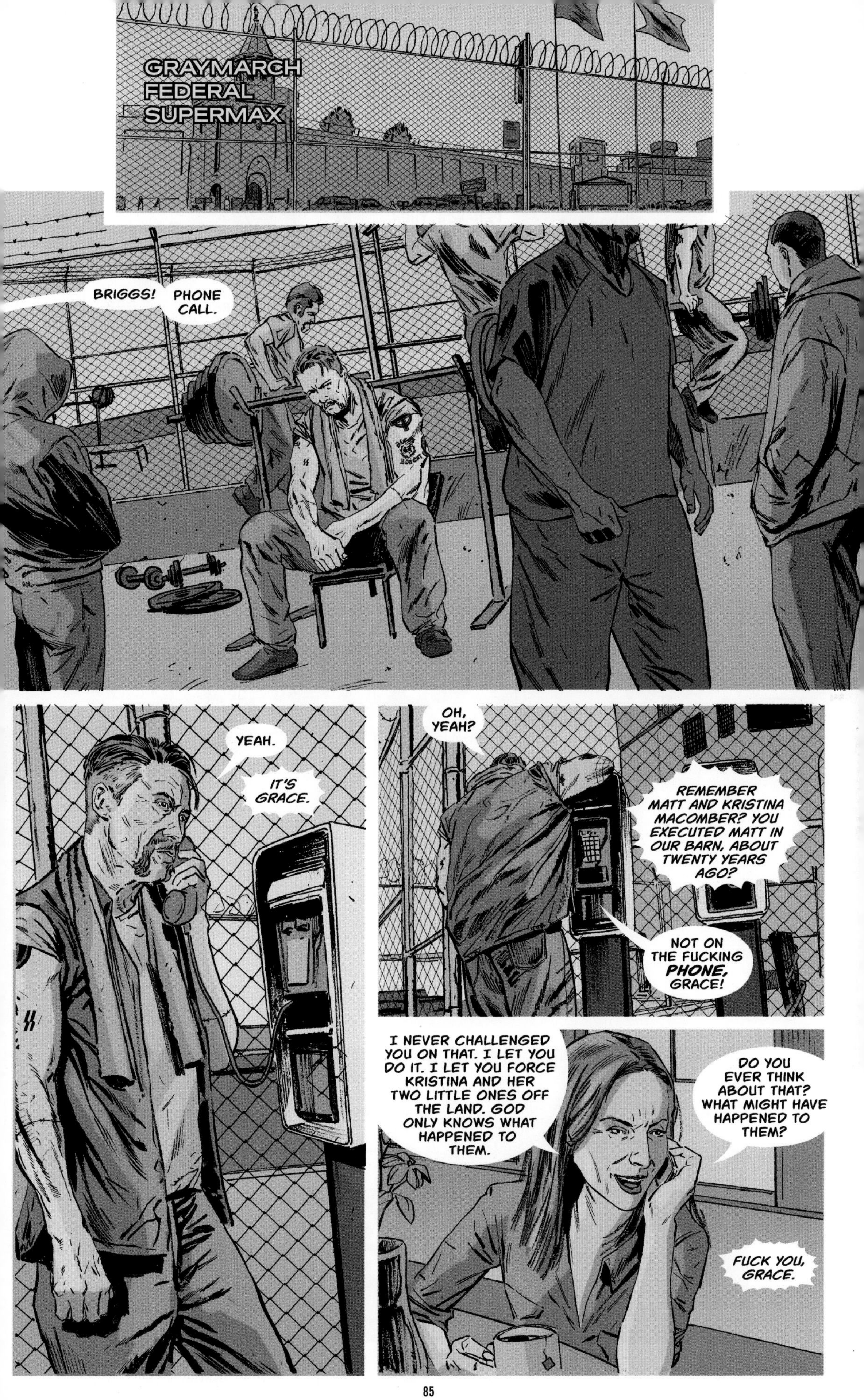
GRAYMARCH FEDERAL SUPERMAX
BRIGGS!
PHONE CALL.
YEAH.
IT'S GRACE.
OH, YEAH?
REMEMBER MATT AND KRISTINA MACOMBER? YOU EXECUTED MATT IN OUR BARN, ABOUT TWENTY YEARS AGO?
NOT ON THE FUCKING PHONE, GRACE!
I NEVER CHALLENGED YOU ON THAT. I LET YOU DO IT. I LET YOU FORCE KRISTINA AND HER TWO LITTLE ONES OFF THE LAND. GOD ONLY KNOWS WHAT HAPPENED TO THEM.
DO YOU EVER THINK ABOUT THAT? WHAT MIGHT HAVE HAPPENED TO THEM?
FUCK YOU, GRACE.

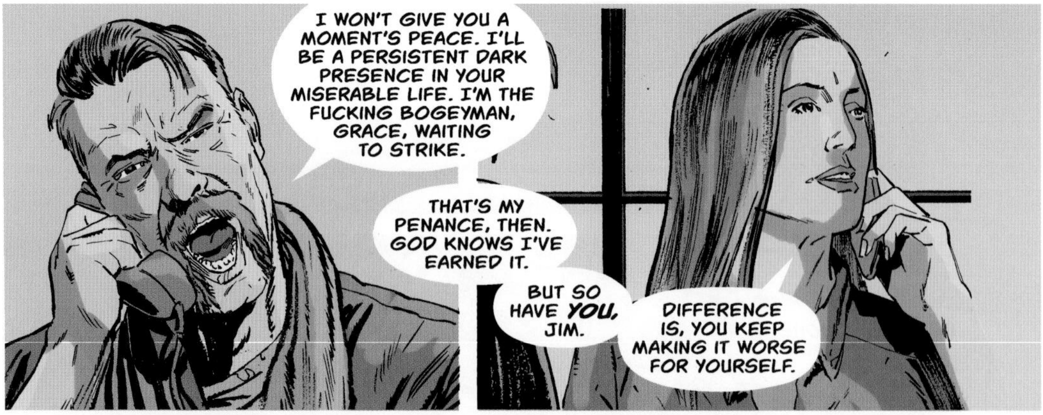
I WON'T GIVE YOU A MOMENT'S PEACE. I'LL BE A PERSISTENT DARK PRESENCE IN YOUR MISERABLE LIFE. I'M THE FUCKING BOGEYMAN, GRACE, WAITING TO STRIKE.
THAT'S MY PENANCE, THEN. GOD KNOWS I'VE EARNED IT.
BUT SO HAVE *YOU,* JIM.
DIFFERENCE IS, YOU KEEP MAKING IT WORSE FOR YOURSELF.

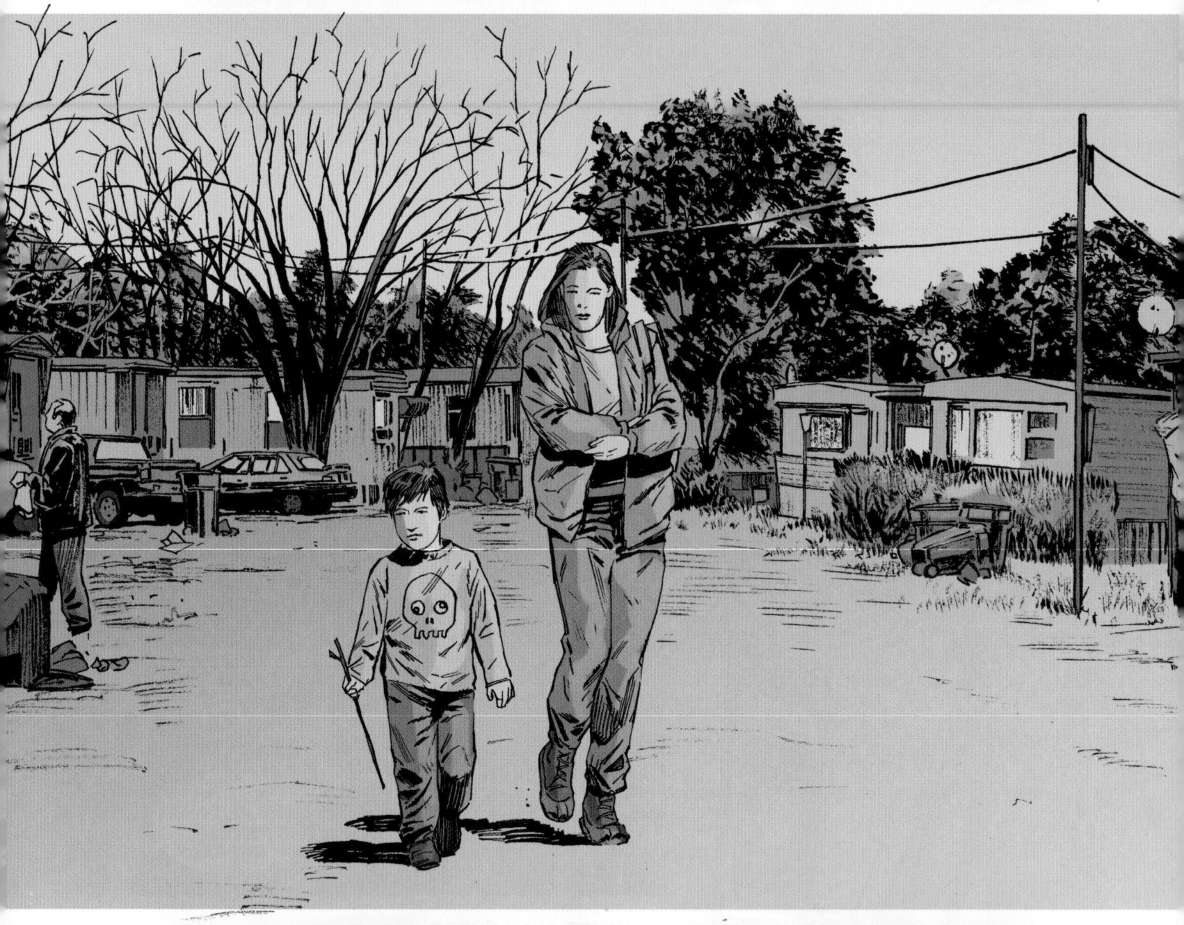

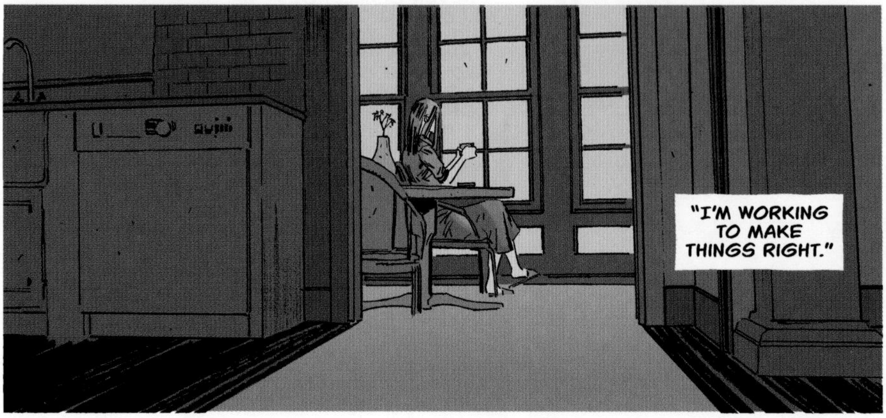
"I'M WORKING TO MAKE THINGS RIGHT."

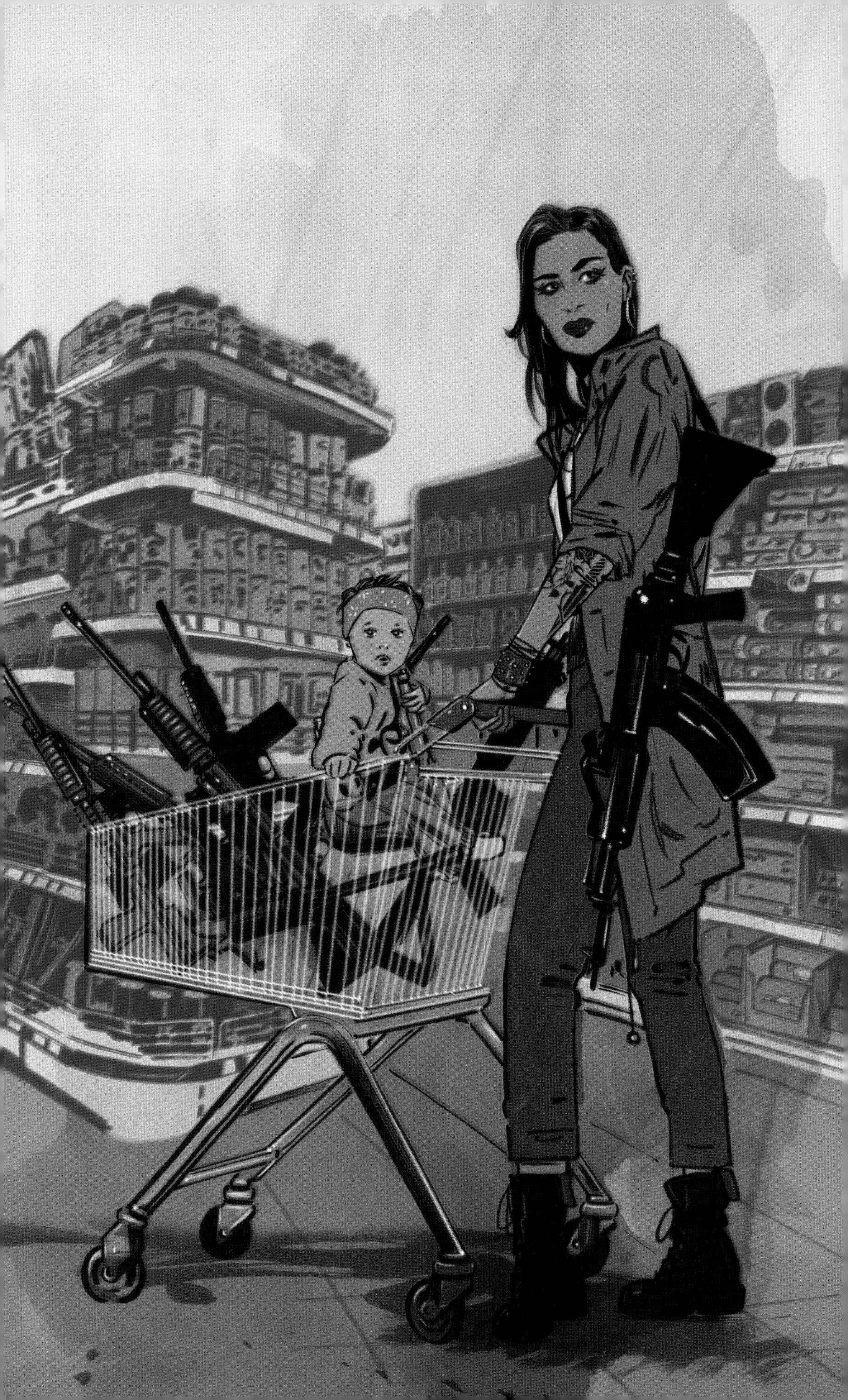

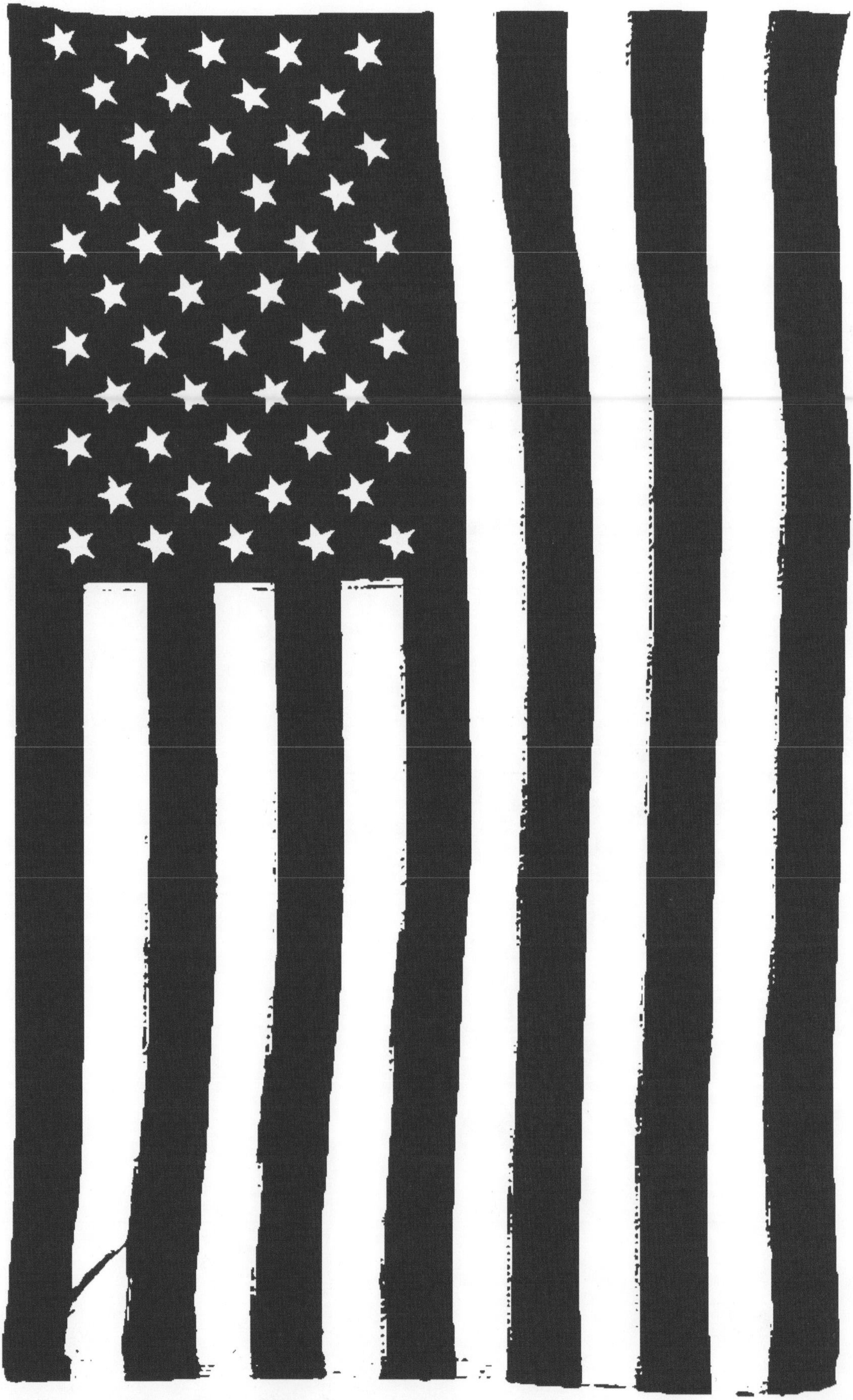

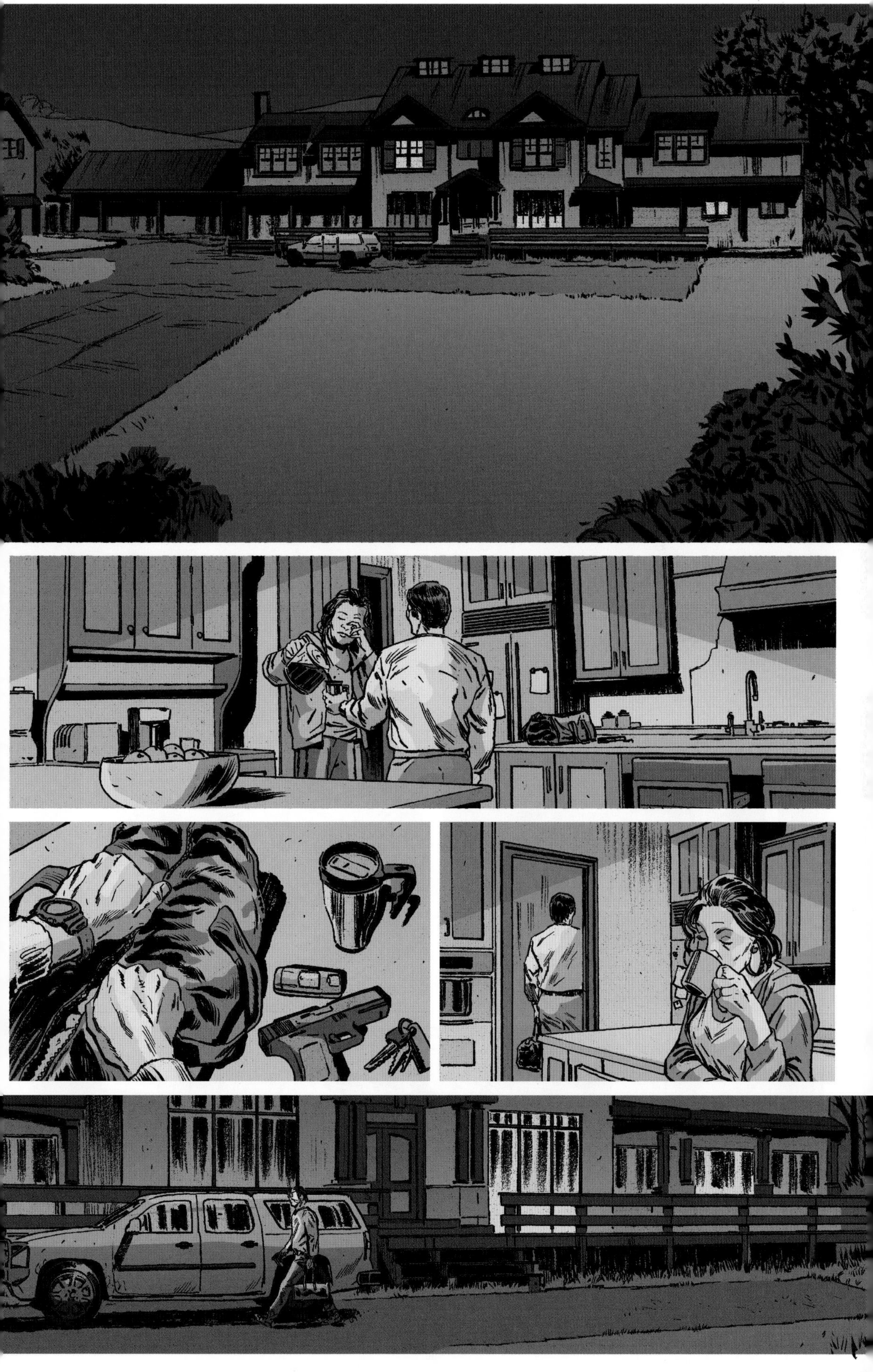

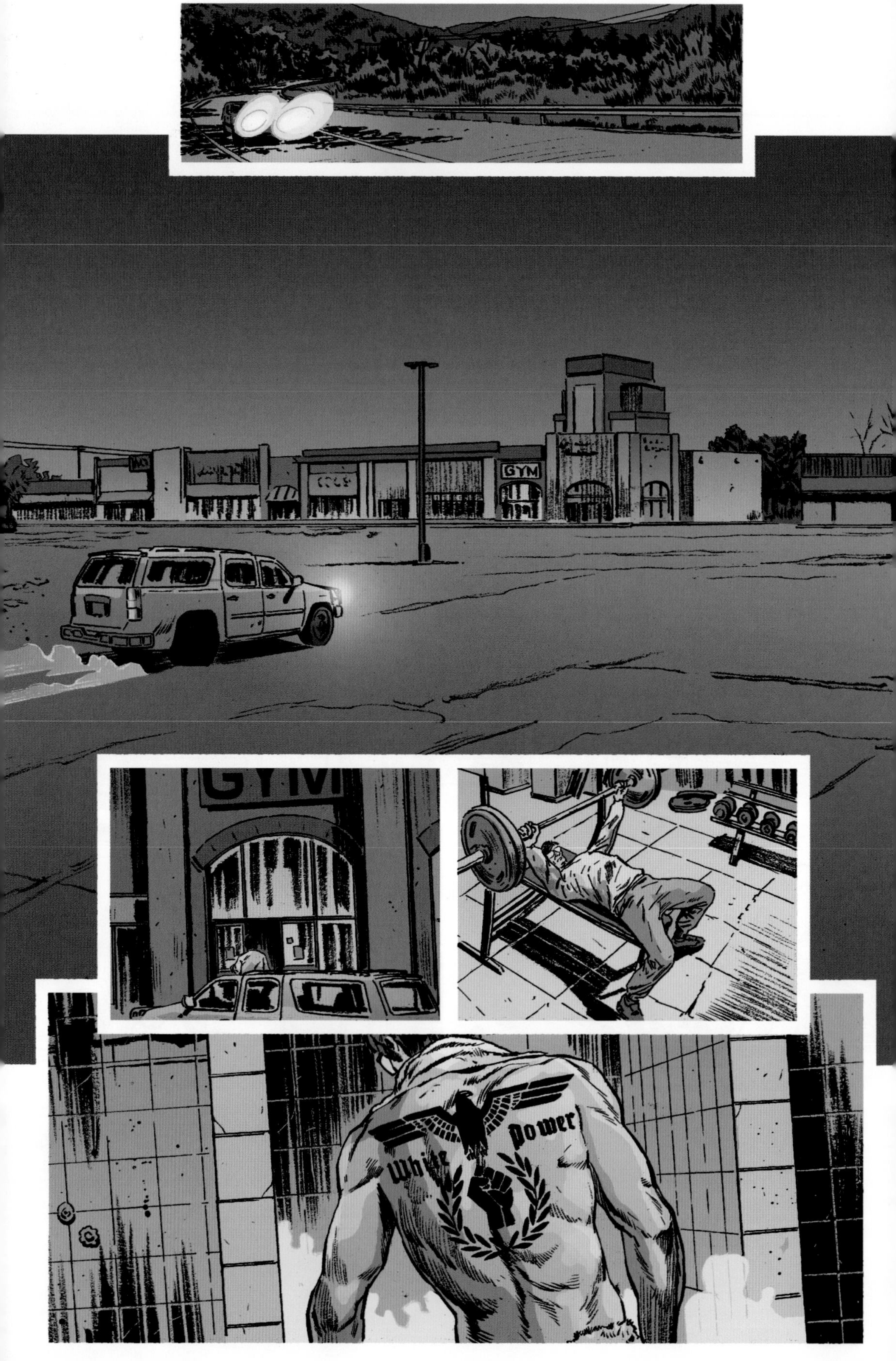
GYM
GYM
White Power

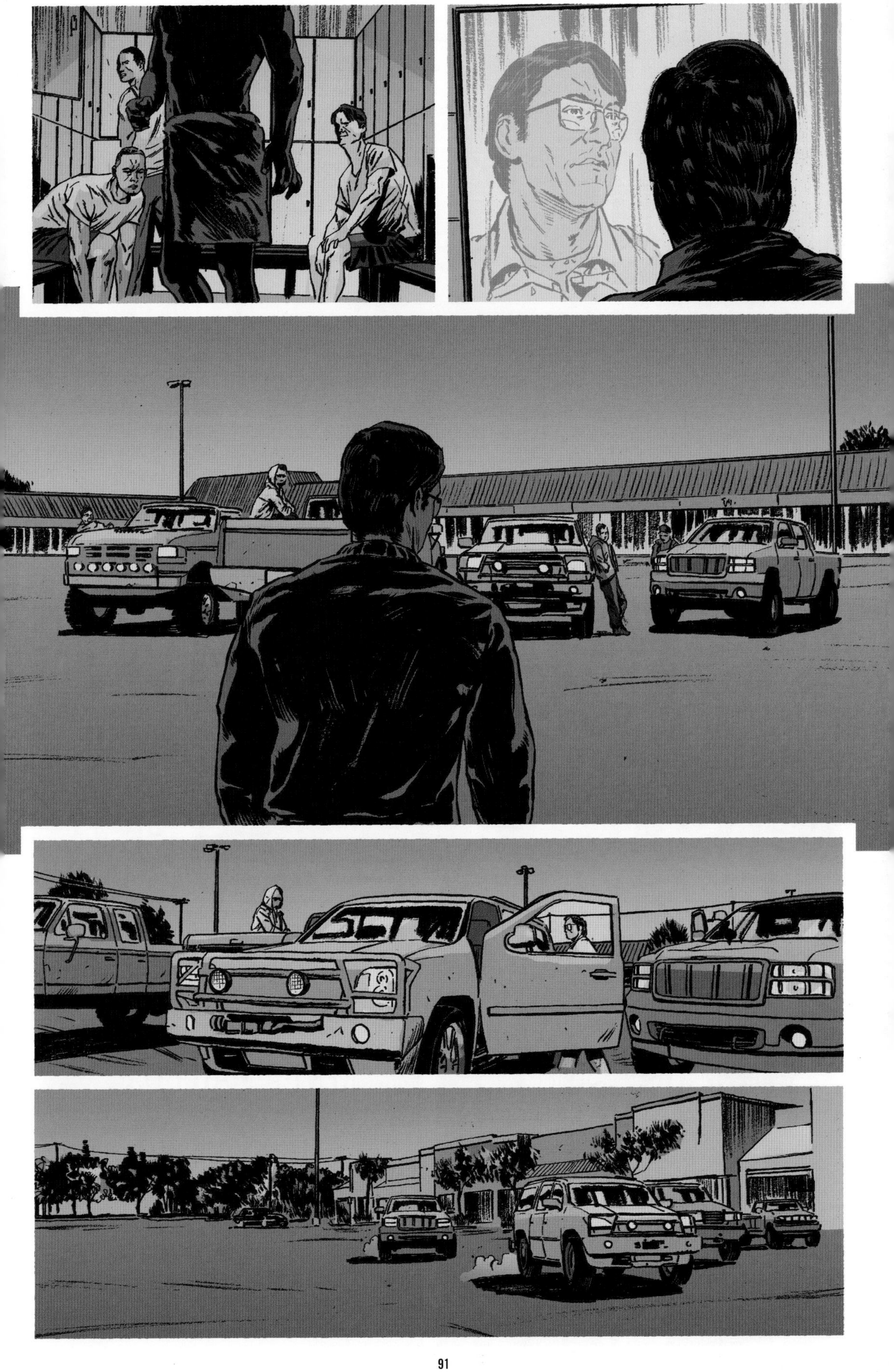

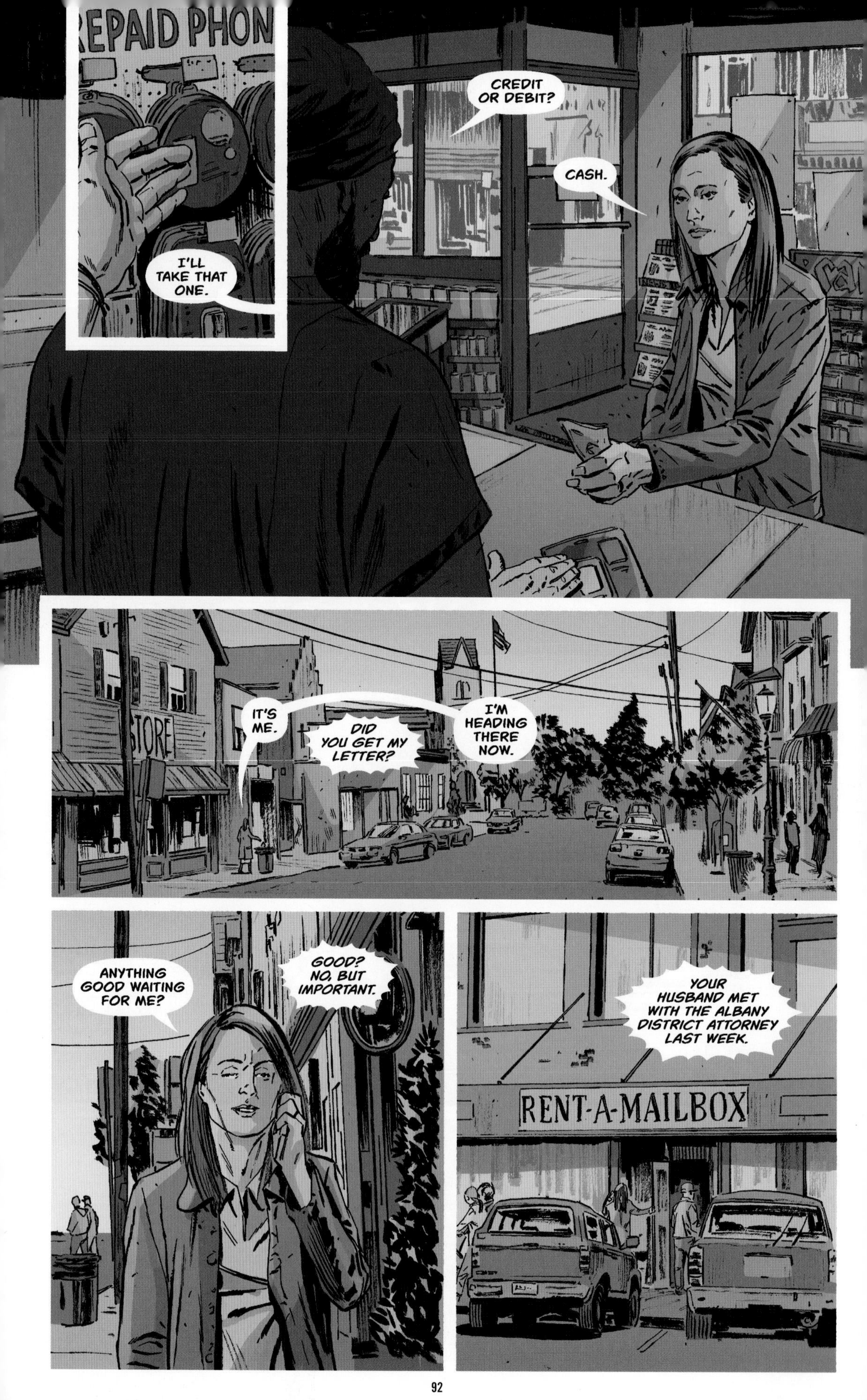

REPAID PHON
CREDIT OR DEBIT?
CASH.
I'LL TAKE THAT ONE.
STORE
IT'S ME.
DID YOU GET MY LETTER?
I'M HEADING THERE NOW.
ANYTHING GOOD WAITING FOR ME?
GOOD? NO, BUT IMPORTANT.
YOUR HUSBAND MET WITH THE ALBANY DISTRICT ATTORNEY LAST WEEK.
RENT-A-MAILBOX

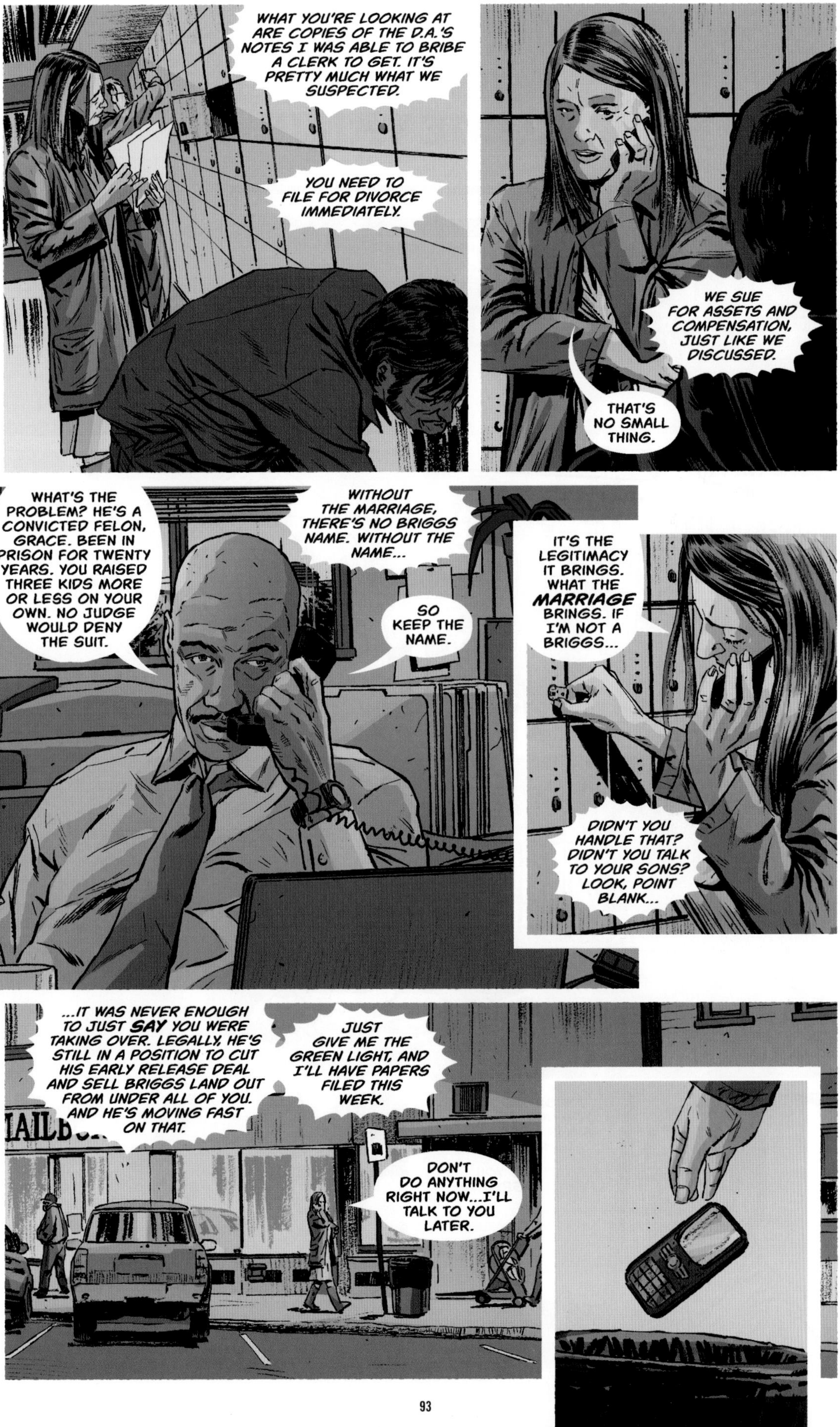
WHAT YOU'RE LOOKING AT ARE COPIES OF THE D.A.'S NOTES I WAS ABLE TO BRIBE A CLERK TO GET. IT'S PRETTY MUCH WHAT WE SUSPECTED.
YOU NEED TO FILE FOR DIVORCE IMMEDIATELY.
WE SUE FOR ASSETS AND COMPENSATION, JUST LIKE WE DISCUSSED.
THAT'S NO SMALL THING.
WHAT'S THE PROBLEM? HE'S A CONVICTED FELON, GRACE. BEEN IN PRISON FOR TWENTY YEARS. YOU RAISED THREE KIDS MORE OR LESS ON YOUR OWN. NO JUDGE WOULD DENY THE SUIT.
WITHOUT THE MARRIAGE, THERE'S NO BRIGGS NAME. WITHOUT THE NAME...
SO KEEP THE NAME.
IT'S THE LEGITIMACY IT BRINGS. WHAT THE MARRIAGE BRINGS. IF I'M NOT A BRIGGS...
DIDN'T YOU HANDLE THAT? DIDN'T YOU TALK TO YOUR SONS? LOOK, POINT BLANK...
...IT WAS NEVER ENOUGH TO JUST SAY YOU WERE TAKING OVER. LEGALLY, HE'S STILL IN A POSITION TO CUT HIS EARLY RELEASE DEAL AND SELL BRIGGS LAND OUT FROM UNDER ALL OF YOU. AND HE'S MOVING FAST ON THAT.
JUST GIVE ME THE GREEN LIGHT, AND I'LL HAVE PAPERS FILED THIS WEEK.
DON'T DO ANYTHING RIGHT NOW...I'LL TALK TO YOU LATER.

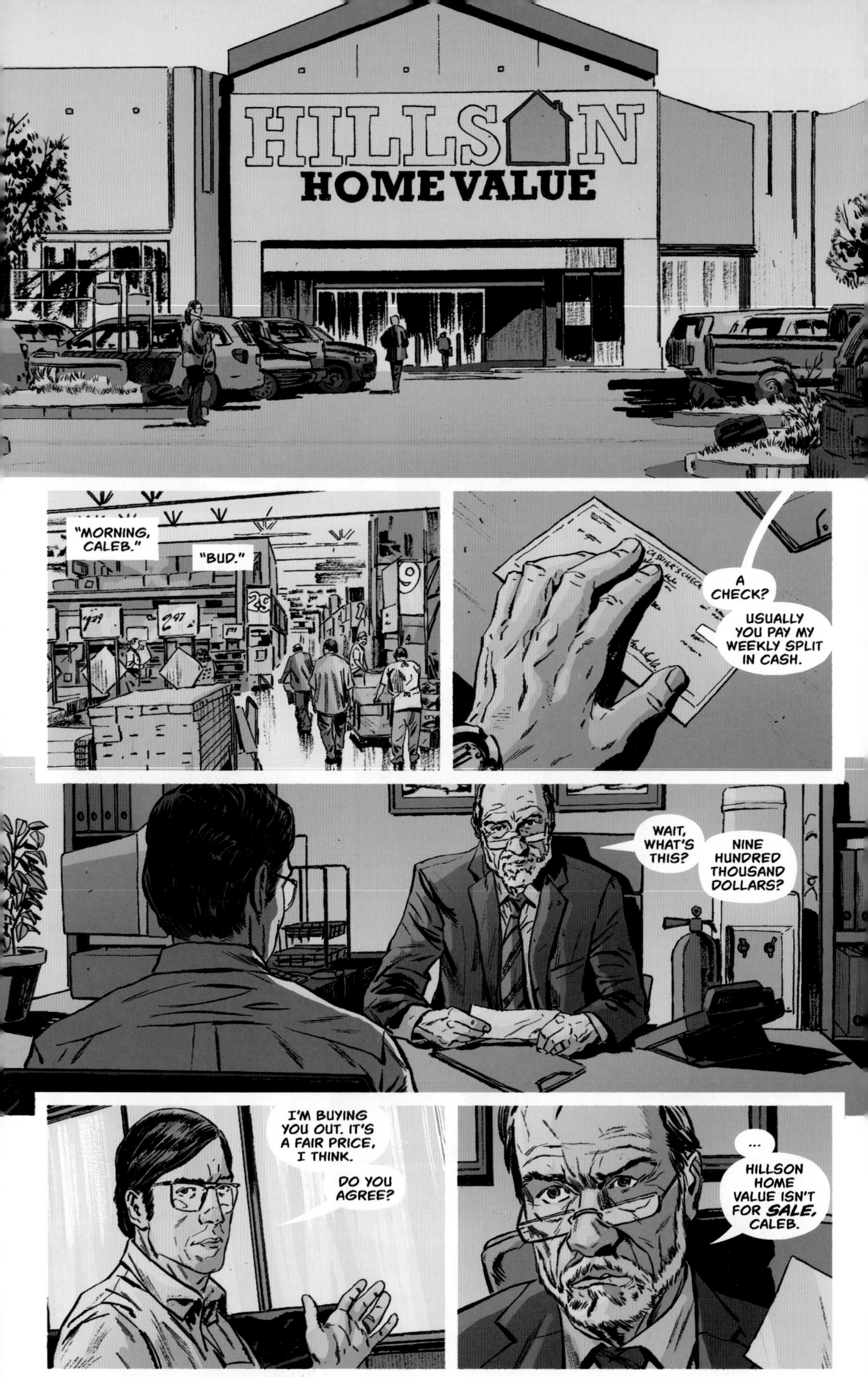
HILLSON
HOME VALUE
"MORNING, CALEB."
"BUD."
A CHECK?
USUALLY YOU PAY MY WEEKLY SPLIT IN CASH.
WAIT, WHAT'S THIS?
NINE HUNDRED THOUSAND DOLLARS?
I'M BUYING YOU OUT. IT'S A FAIR PRICE, I THINK.
DO YOU AGREE?
...
HILLSON HOME VALUE ISN'T FOR *SALE,* CALEB.

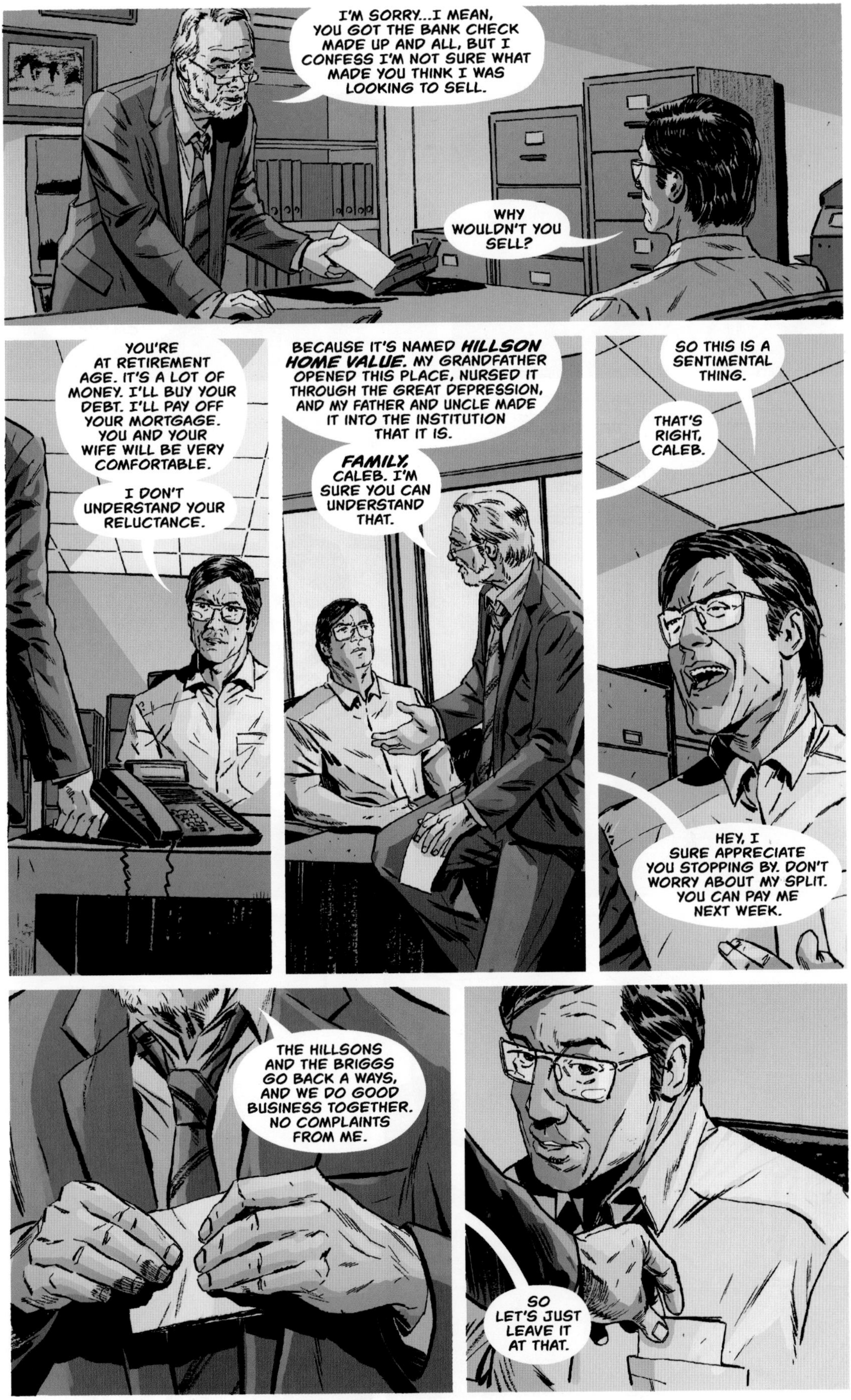
I'M SORRY...I MEAN, YOU GOT THE BANK CHECK MADE UP AND ALL, BUT I CONFESS I'M NOT SURE WHAT MADE YOU THINK I WAS LOOKING TO SELL.
WHY WOULDN'T YOU SELL?
YOU'RE AT RETIREMENT AGE. IT'S A LOT OF MONEY. I'LL BUY YOUR DEBT. I'LL PAY OFF YOUR MORTGAGE. YOU AND YOUR WIFE WILL BE VERY COMFORTABLE.
I DON'T UNDERSTAND YOUR RELUCTANCE.
BECAUSE IT'S NAMED ***HILLSON HOME VALUE.*** MY GRANDFATHER OPENED THIS PLACE, NURSED IT THROUGH THE GREAT DEPRESSION, AND MY FATHER AND UNCLE MADE IT INTO THE INSTITUTION THAT IT IS.
FAMILY, CALEB. I'M SURE YOU CAN UNDERSTAND THAT.
SO THIS IS A SENTIMENTAL THING.
THAT'S RIGHT, CALEB.
HEY, I SURE APPRECIATE YOU STOPPING BY. DON'T WORRY ABOUT MY SPLIT. YOU CAN PAY ME NEXT WEEK.
THE HILLSONS AND THE BRIGGS GO BACK A WAYS, AND WE DO GOOD BUSINESS TOGETHER. NO COMPLAINTS FROM ME.
SO LET'S JUST LEAVE IT AT THAT.

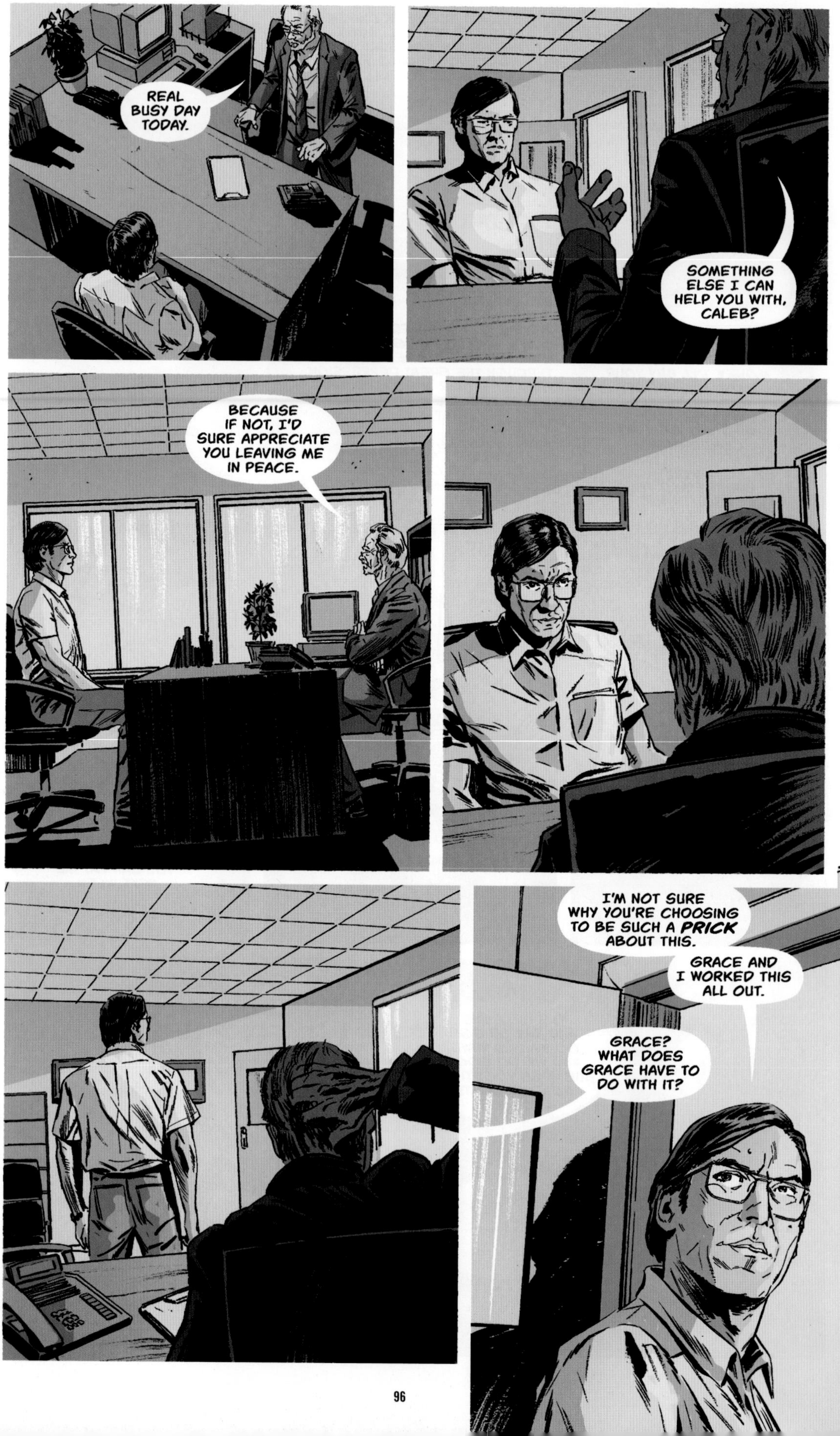
REAL BUSY DAY TODAY.
SOMETHING ELSE I CAN HELP YOU WITH, CALEB?
BECAUSE IF NOT, I'D SURE APPRECIATE YOU LEAVING ME IN PEACE.
I'M NOT SURE WHY YOU'RE CHOOSING TO BE SUCH A *PRICK* ABOUT THIS.
GRACE AND I WORKED THIS ALL OUT.
GRACE? WHAT DOES GRACE HAVE TO DO WITH IT?

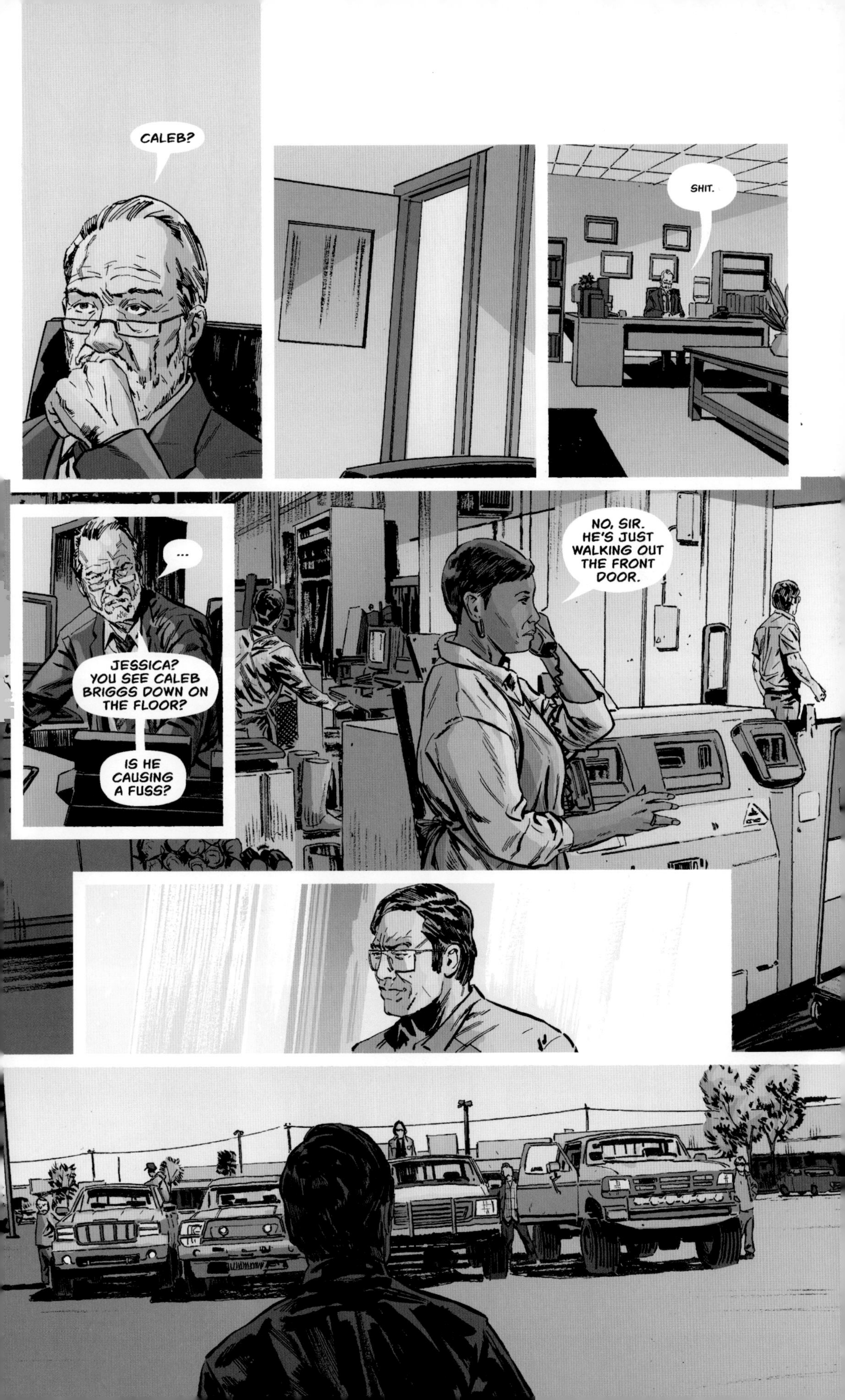
CALEB?
SHIT.
...
JESSICA? YOU SEE CALEB BRIGGS DOWN ON THE FLOOR?
IS HE CAUSING A FUSS?
NO, SIR. HE'S JUST WALKING OUT THE FRONT DOOR.

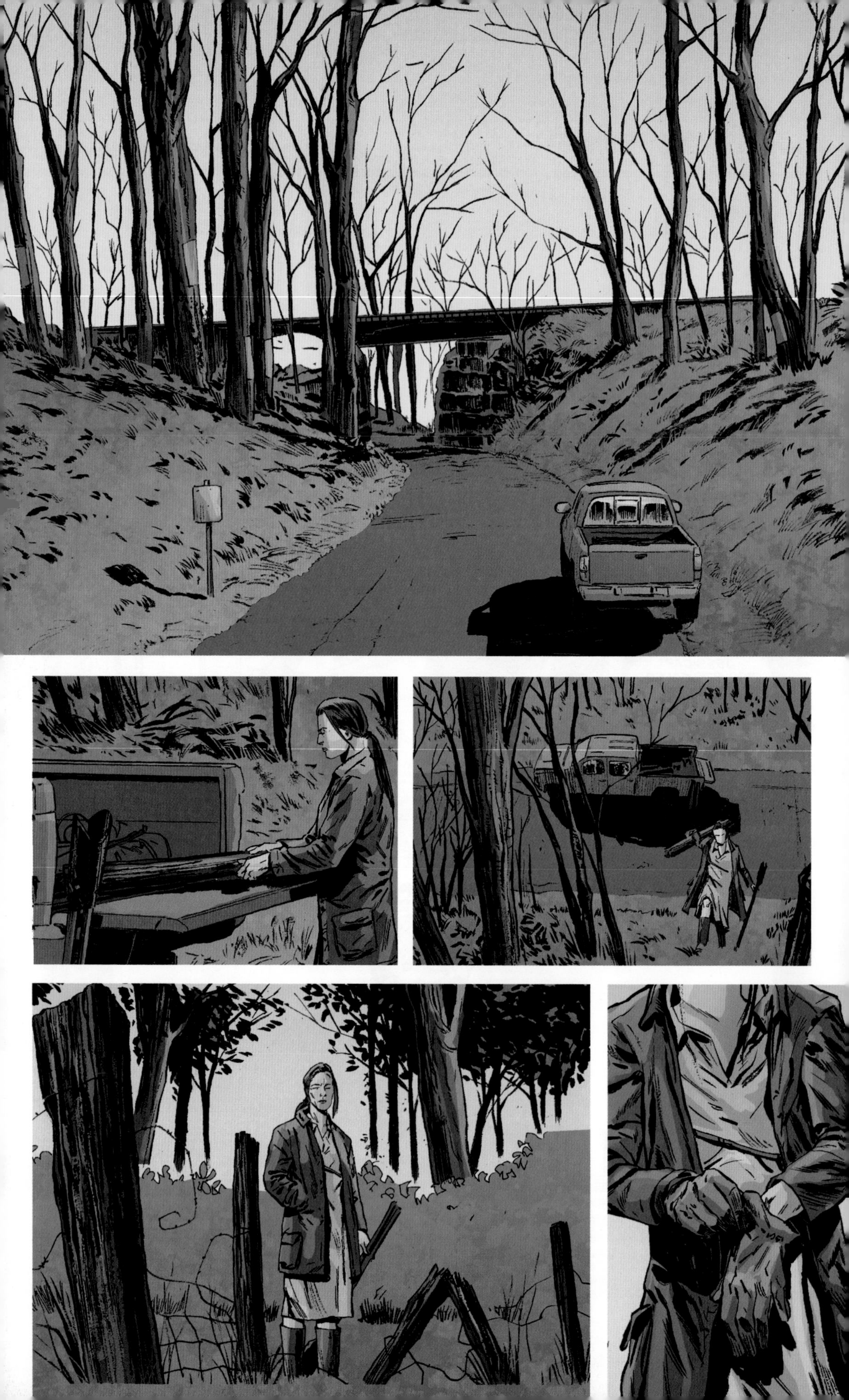

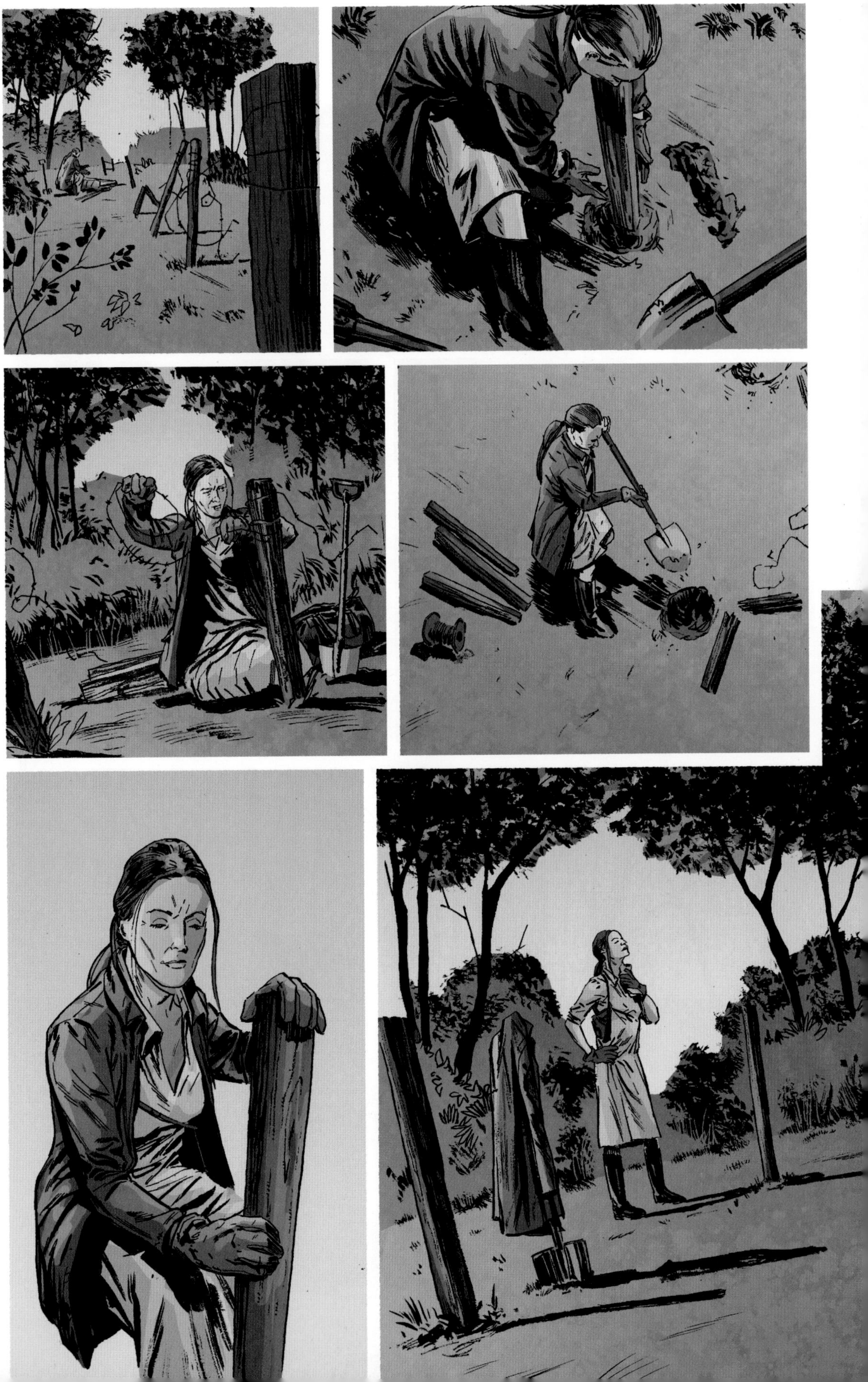

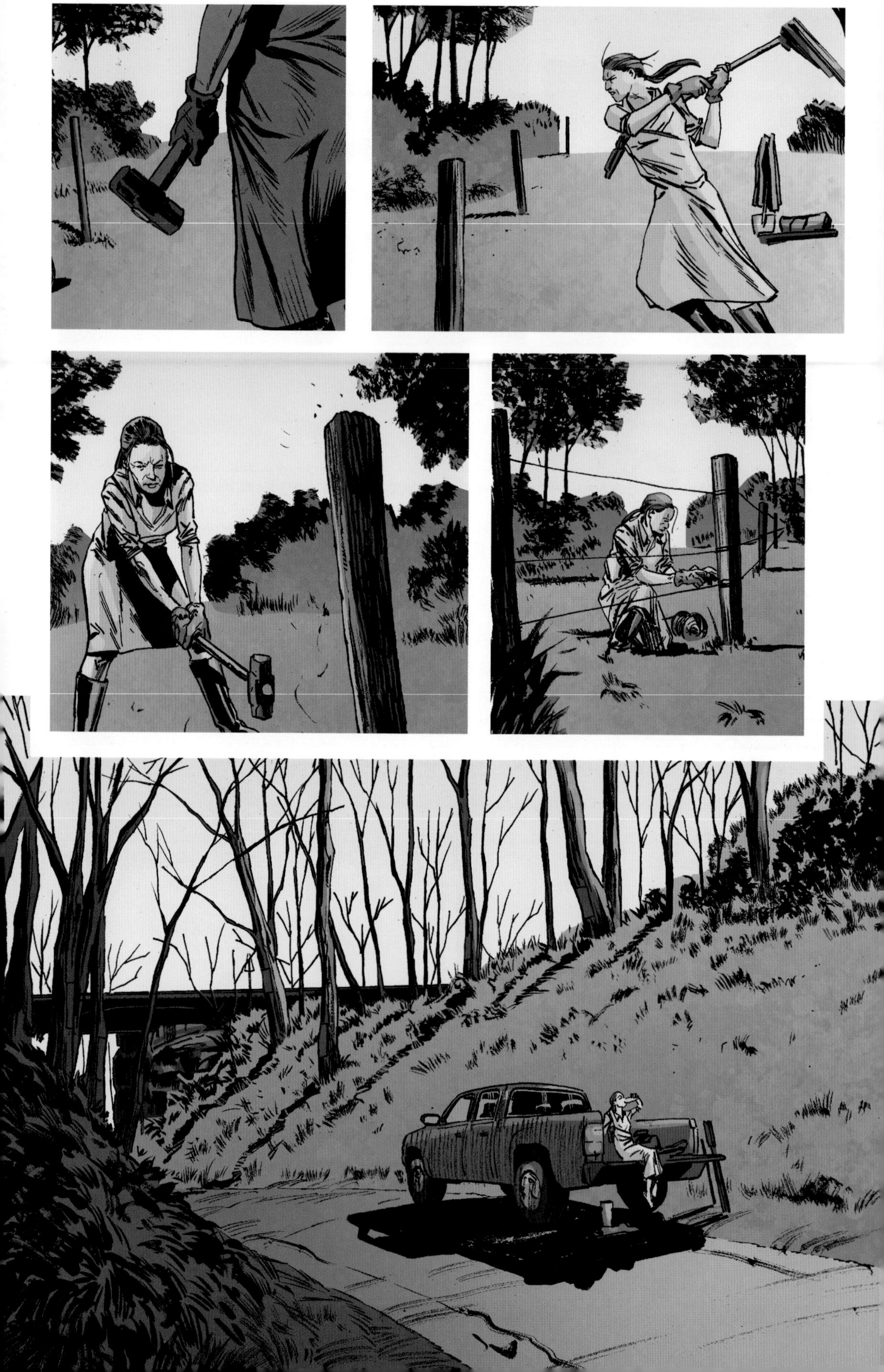

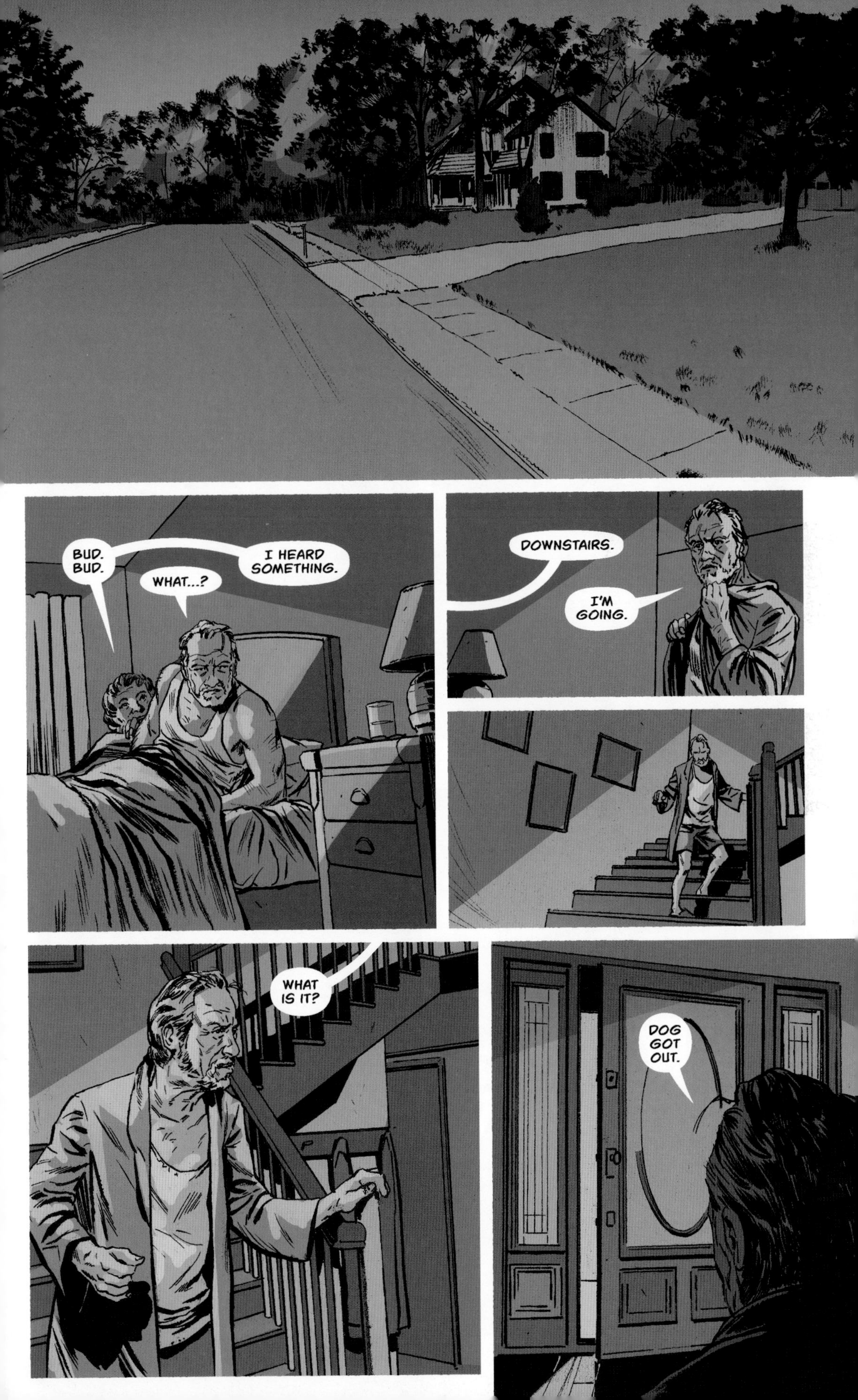
BUD. BUD.
I HEARD SOMETHING.
WHAT...?
DOWNSTAIRS.
I'M GOING.
WHAT IS IT?
DOG GOT OUT.

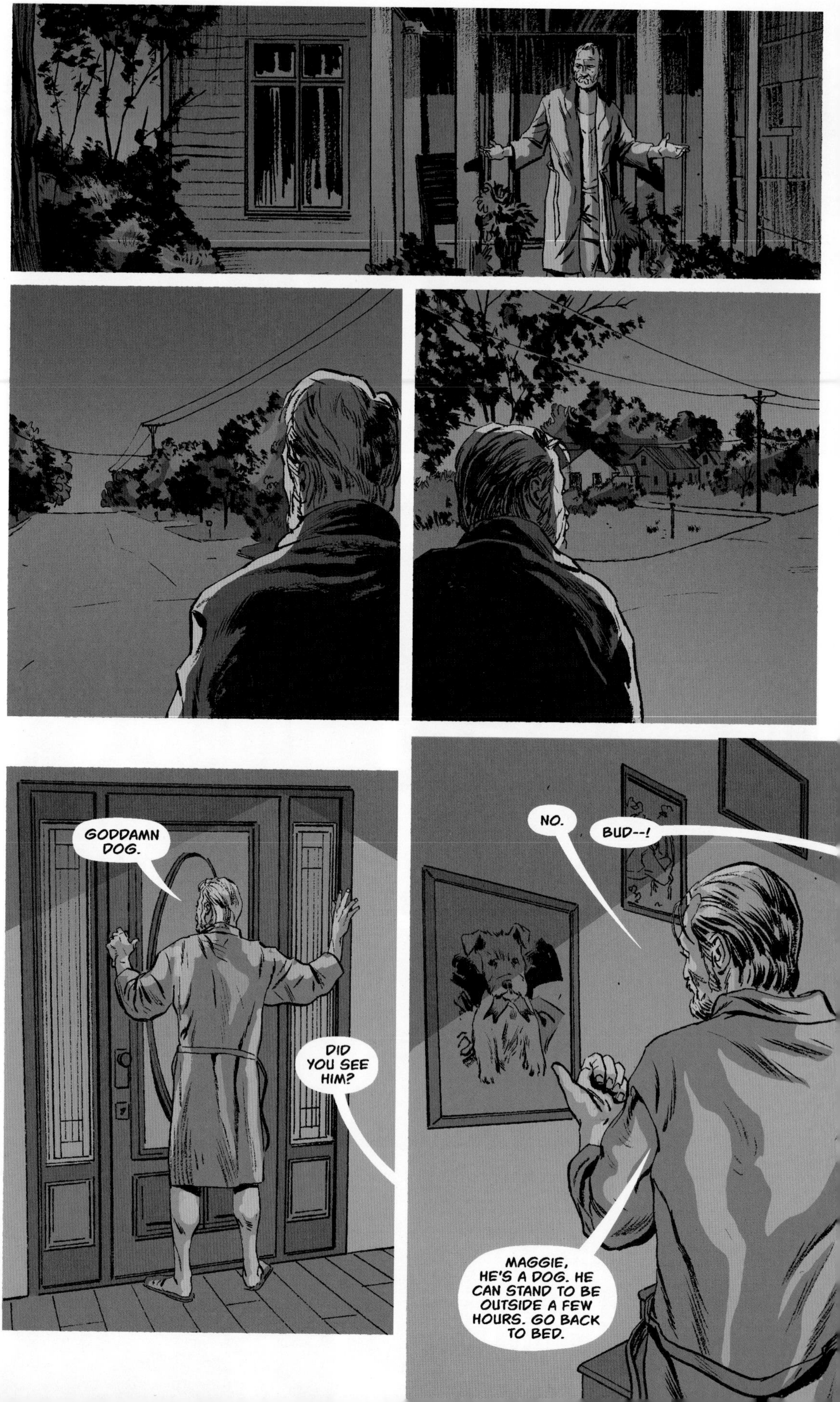
GODDAMN DOG.
DID YOU SEE HIM?
NO.
BUD--!
MAGGIE, HE'S A DOG. HE CAN STAND TO BE OUTSIDE A FEW HOURS. GO BACK TO BED.

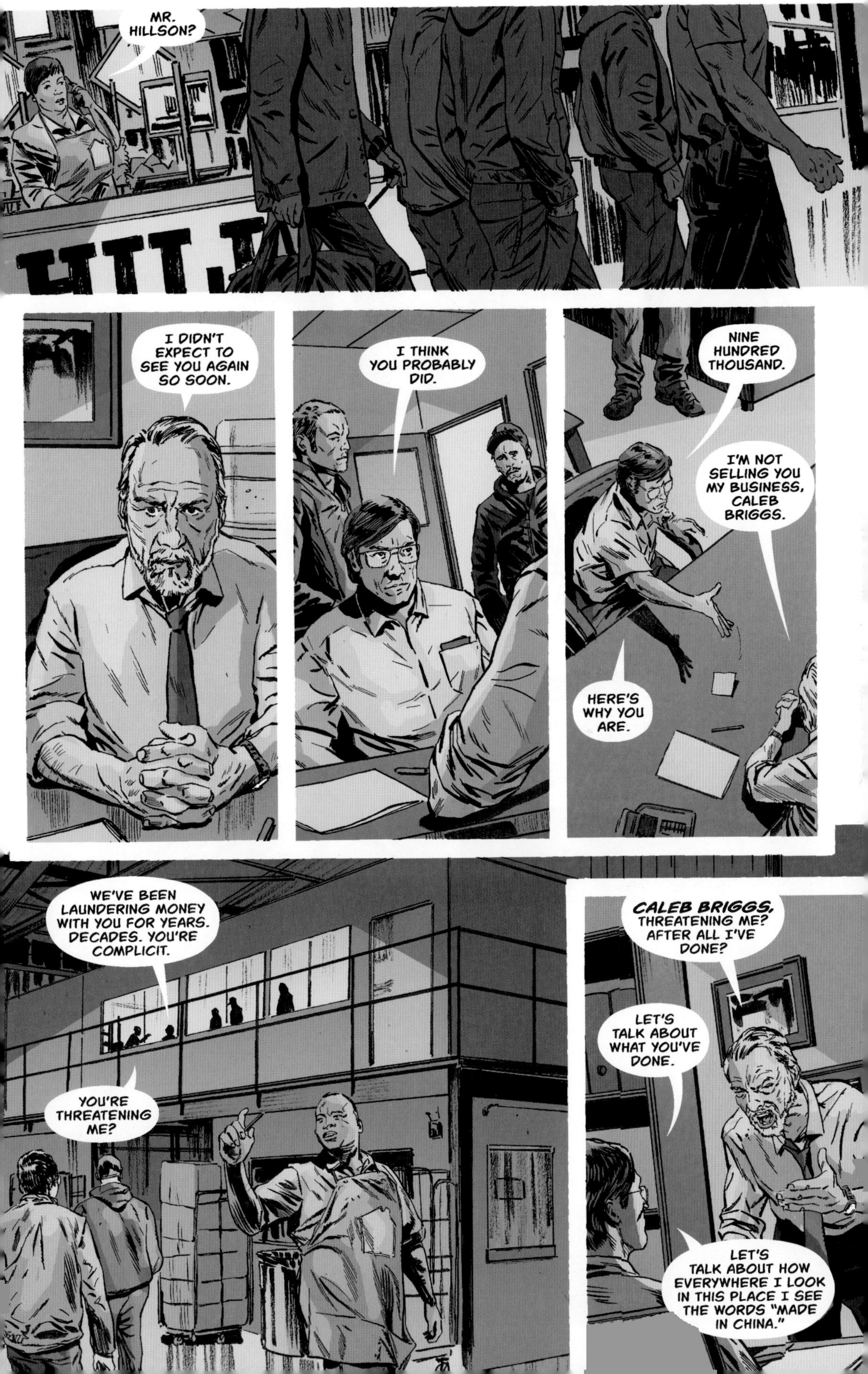
MR. HILLSON?
I DIDN'T EXPECT TO SEE YOU AGAIN SO SOON.
I THINK YOU PROBABLY DID.
NINE HUNDRED THOUSAND.
I'M NOT SELLING YOU MY BUSINESS, CALEB BRIGGS.
HERE'S WHY YOU ARE.
WE'VE BEEN LAUNDERING MONEY WITH YOU FOR YEARS. DECADES. YOU'RE COMPLICIT.
YOU'RE THREATENING ME?
CALEB BRIGGS, THREATENING ME? AFTER ALL I'VE DONE?
LET'S TALK ABOUT WHAT YOU'VE DONE.
LET'S TALK ABOUT HOW EVERYWHERE I LOOK IN THIS PLACE I SEE THE WORDS "MADE IN CHINA."

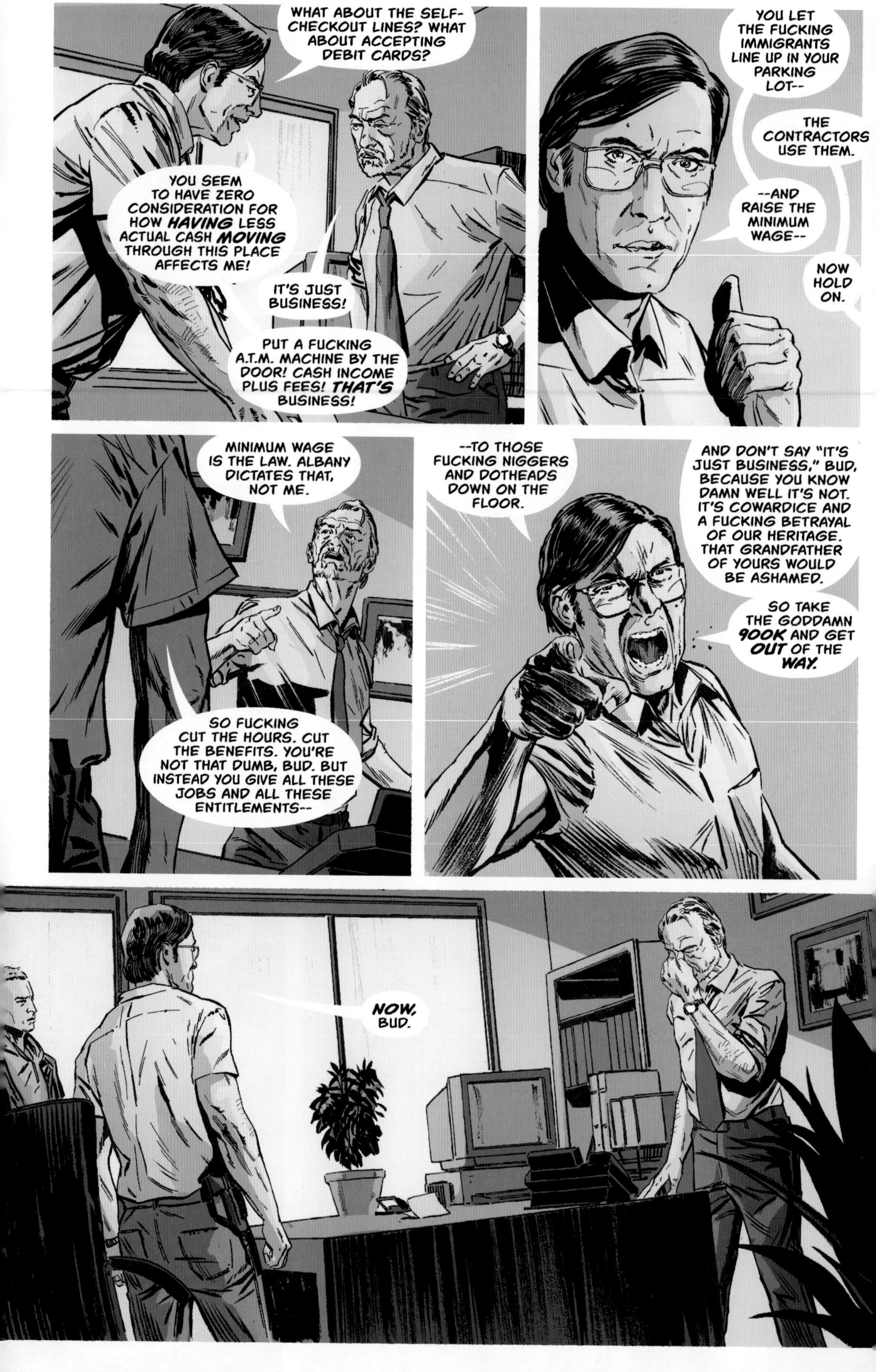

WHAT ABOUT THE SELF-CHECKOUT LINES? WHAT ABOUT ACCEPTING DEBIT CARDS?
YOU SEEM TO HAVE ZERO CONSIDERATION FOR HOW *HAVING* LESS ACTUAL CASH *MOVING* THROUGH THIS PLACE AFFECTS ME!
IT'S JUST BUSINESS!
PUT A FUCKING A.T.M. MACHINE BY THE DOOR! CASH INCOME PLUS FEES! *THAT'S* BUSINESS!
YOU LET THE FUCKING IMMIGRANTS LINE UP IN YOUR PARKING LOT--
THE CONTRACTORS USE THEM.
--AND RAISE THE MINIMUM WAGE--
NOW HOLD ON.
MINIMUM WAGE IS THE LAW. ALBANY DICTATES THAT, NOT ME.
SO FUCKING CUT THE HOURS. CUT THE BENEFITS. YOU'RE NOT THAT DUMB, BUD. BUT INSTEAD YOU GIVE ALL THESE JOBS AND ALL THESE ENTITLEMENTS--
--TO THOSE FUCKING NIGGERS AND DOTHEADS DOWN ON THE FLOOR.
AND DON'T SAY "IT'S JUST BUSINESS," BUD, BECAUSE YOU KNOW DAMN WELL IT'S NOT. IT'S COWARDICE AND A FUCKING BETRAYAL OF OUR HERITAGE. THAT GRANDFATHER OF YOURS WOULD BE ASHAMED.
SO TAKE THE GODDAMN *900K* AND GET *OUT* OF THE *WAY.*
NOW, BUD.

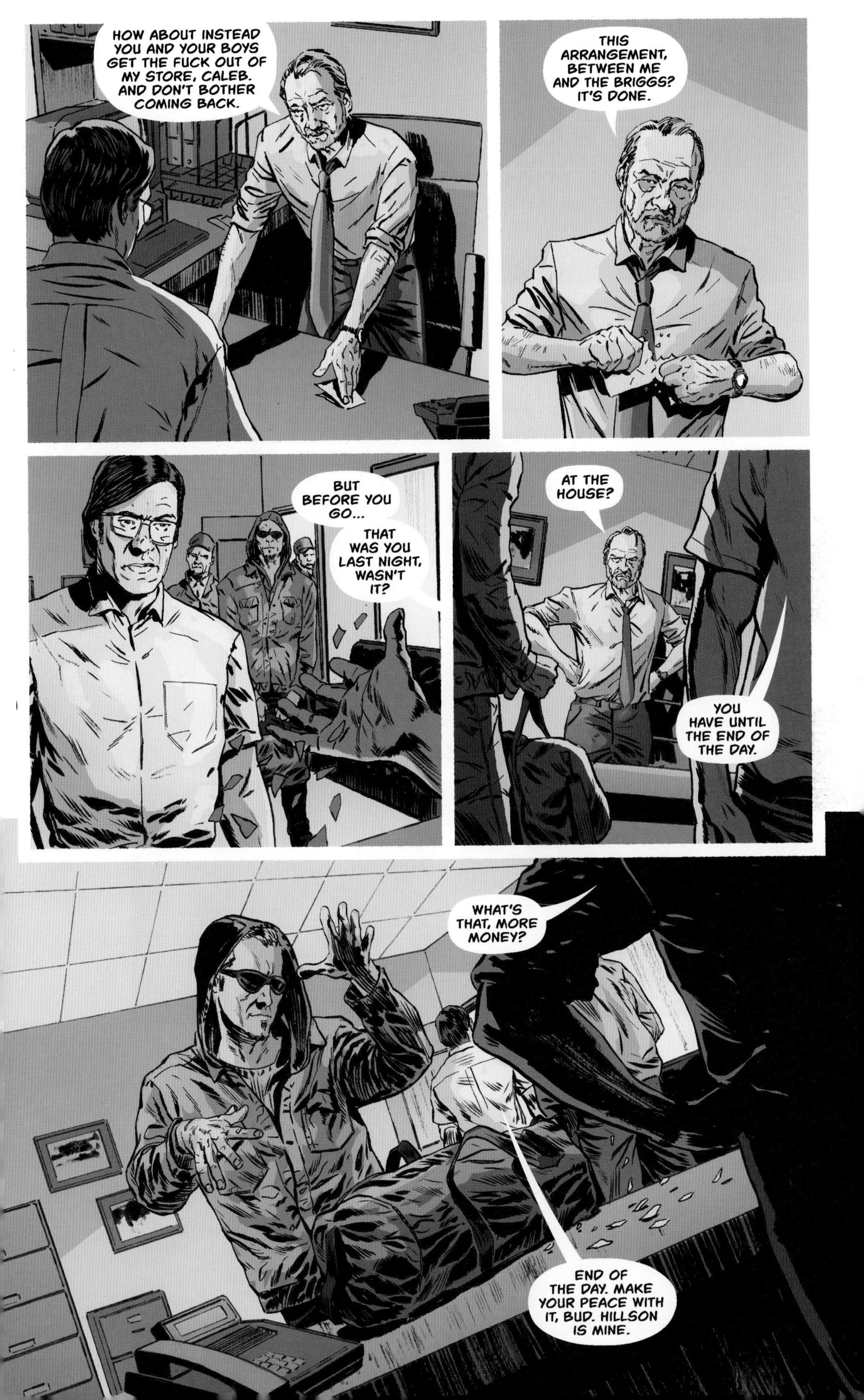
HOW ABOUT INSTEAD YOU AND YOUR BOYS GET THE FUCK OUT OF MY STORE, CALEB. AND DON'T BOTHER COMING BACK.
THIS ARRANGEMENT, BETWEEN ME AND THE BRIGGS? IT'S DONE.
BUT BEFORE YOU GO...
THAT WAS YOU LAST NIGHT, WASN'T IT?
AT THE HOUSE?
YOU HAVE UNTIL THE END OF THE DAY.
WHAT'S THAT, MORE MONEY?
END OF THE DAY. MAKE YOUR PEACE WITH IT, BUD. HILLSON IS MINE.

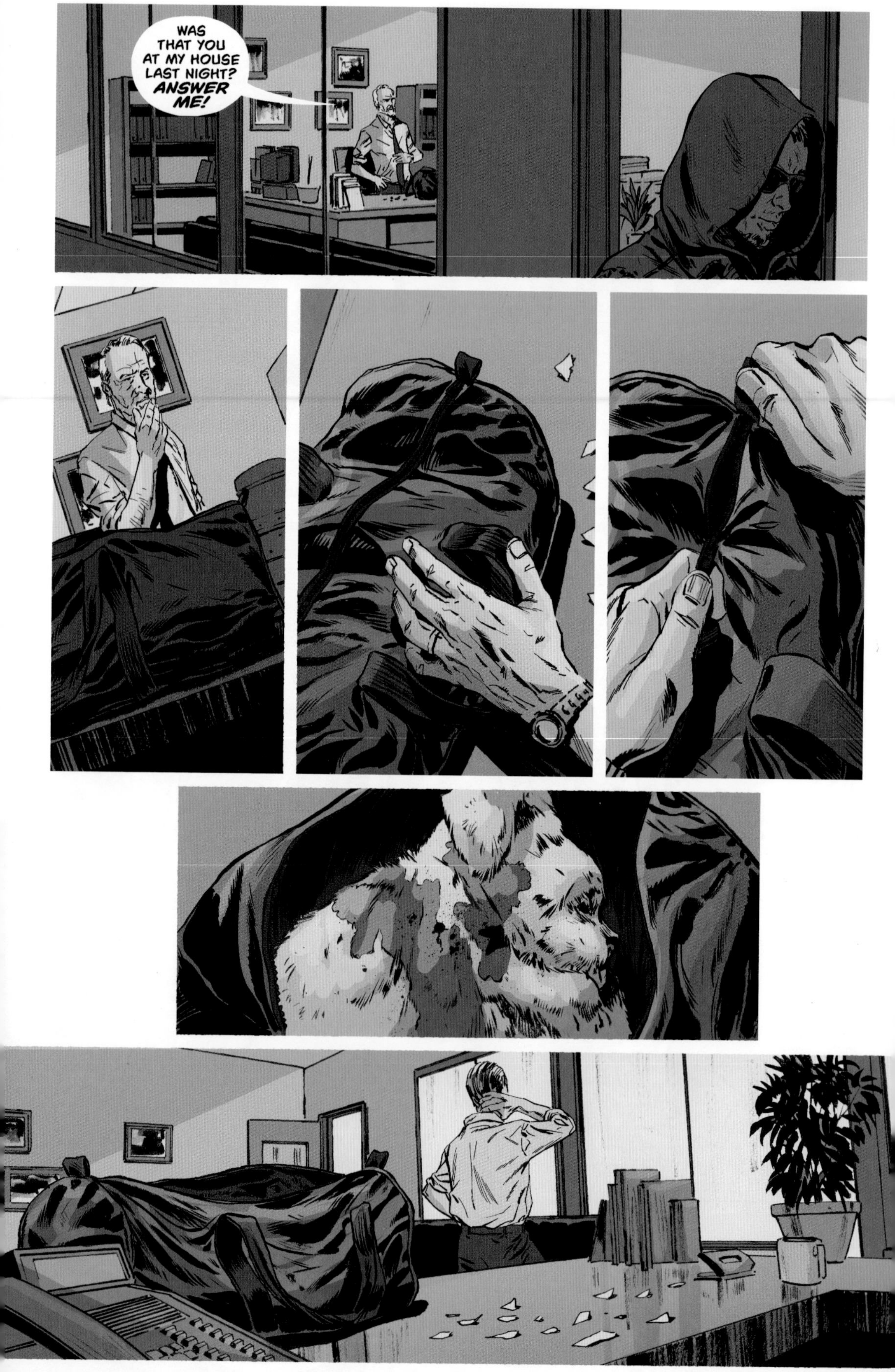
WAS THAT YOU AT MY HOUSE LAST NIGHT? ANSWER ME!

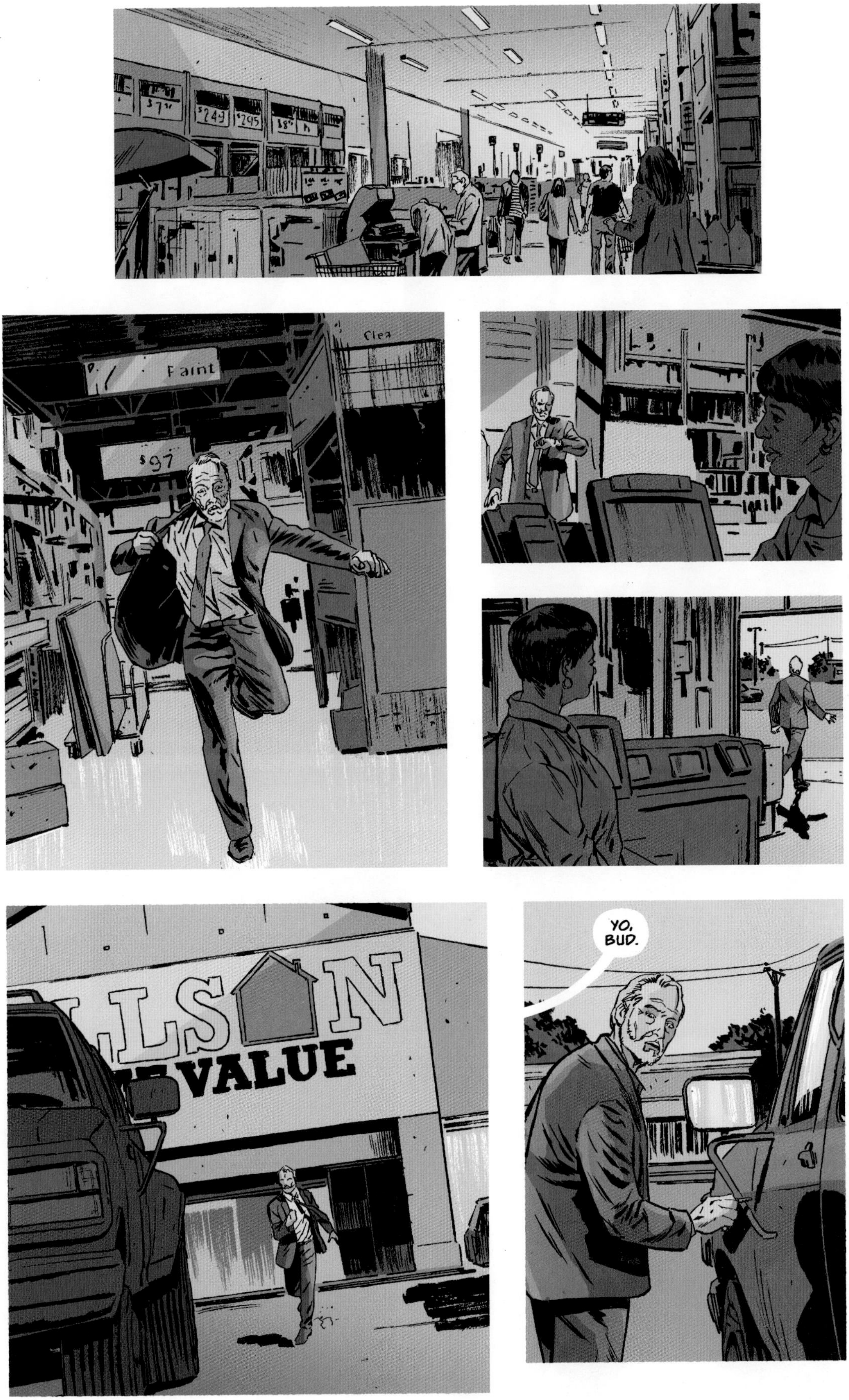
Paint
$97
VALUE
YO, BUD.

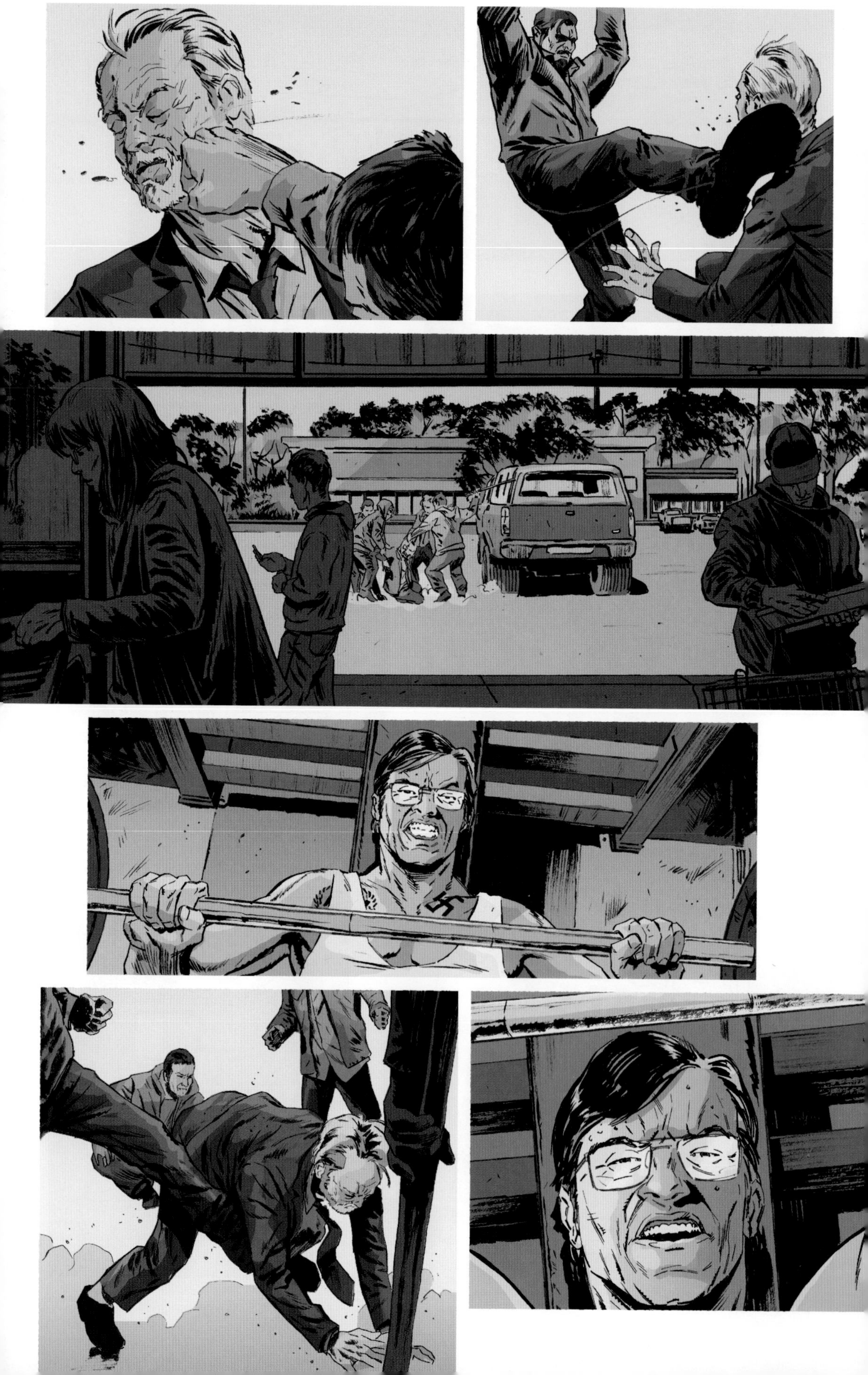

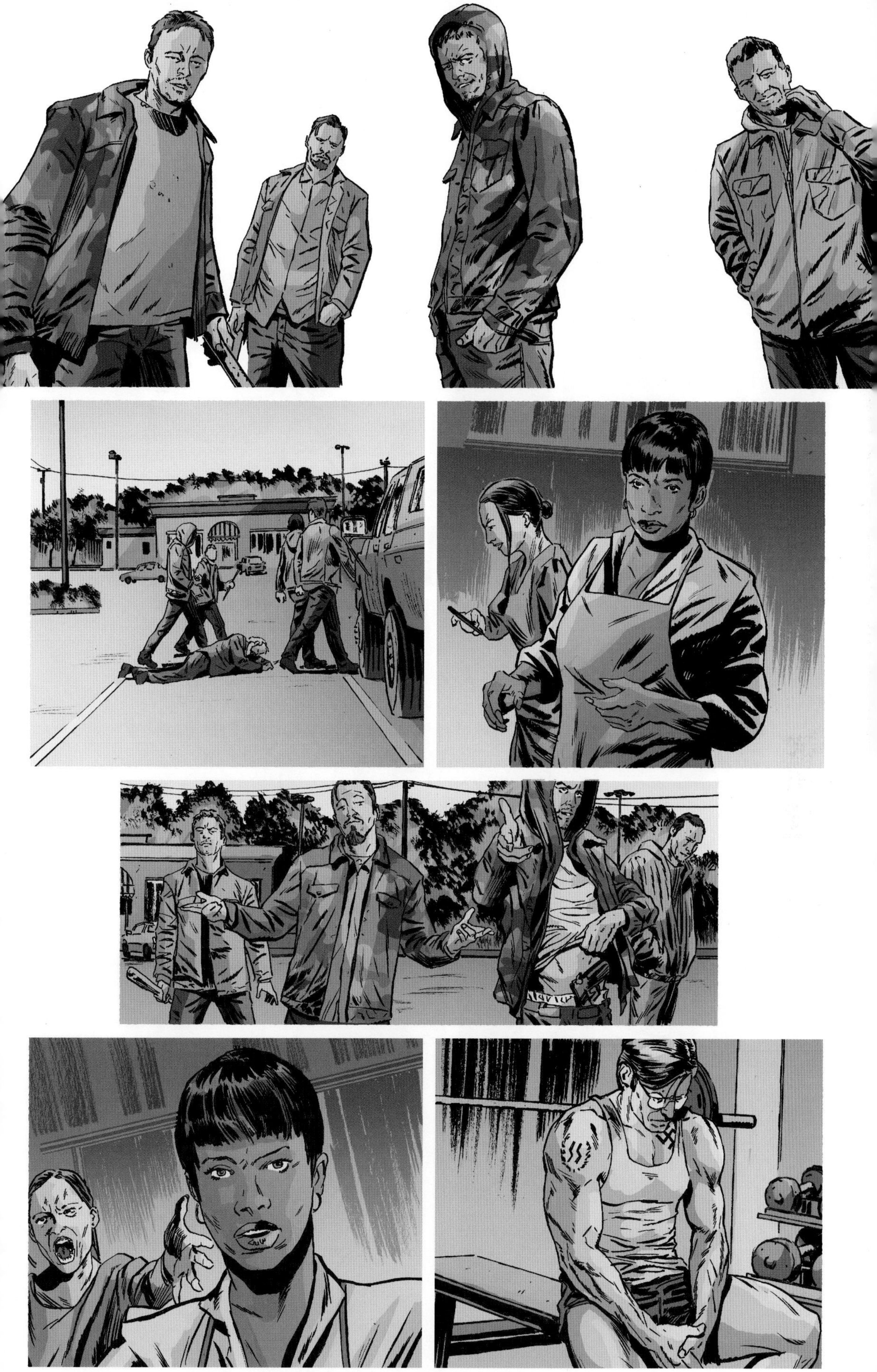

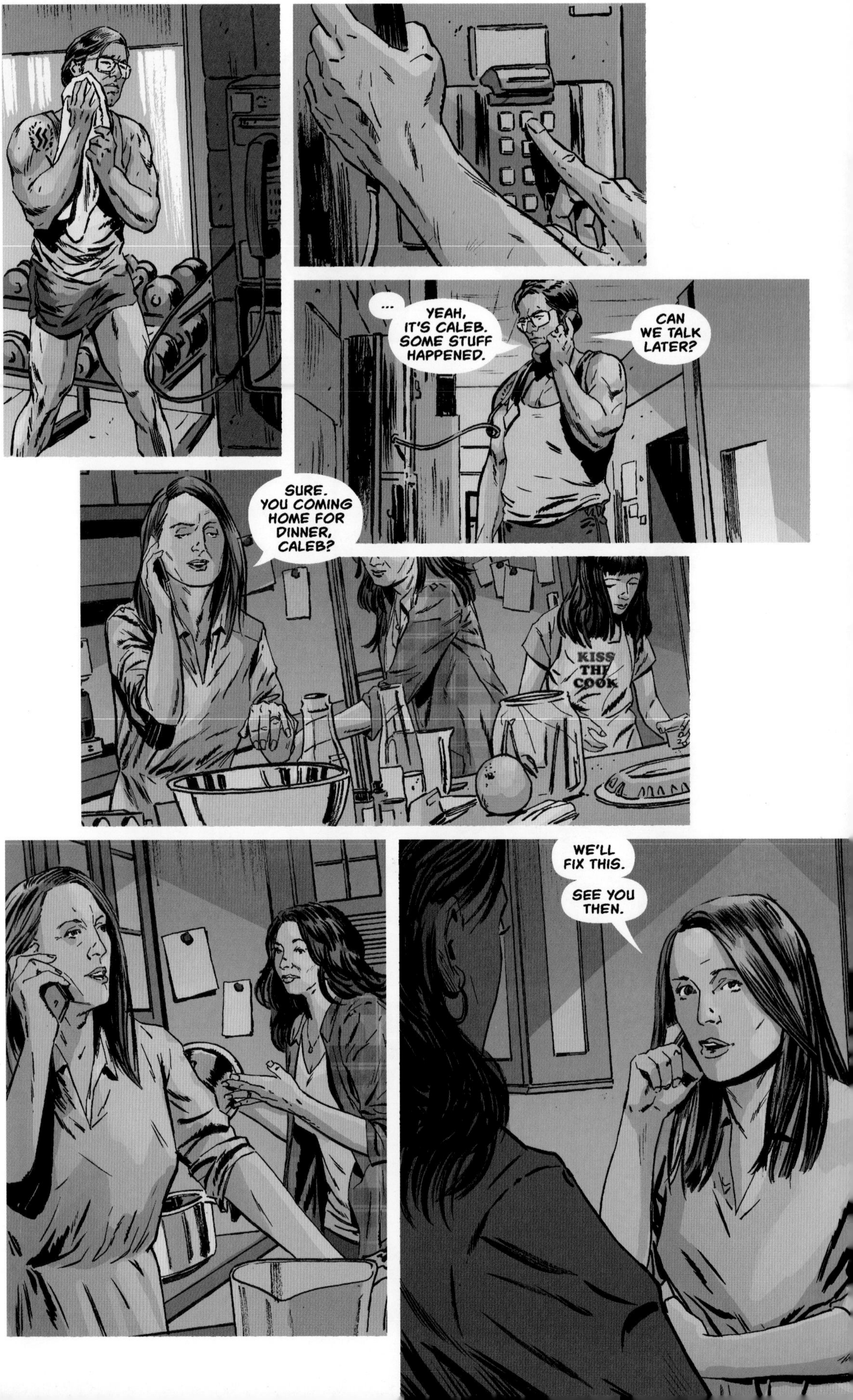
...
YEAH, IT'S CALEB. SOME STUFF HAPPENED.
CAN WE TALK LATER?
SURE. YOU COMING HOME FOR DINNER, CALEB?
KISS THE COOK
WE'LL FIX THIS.
SEE YOU THEN.

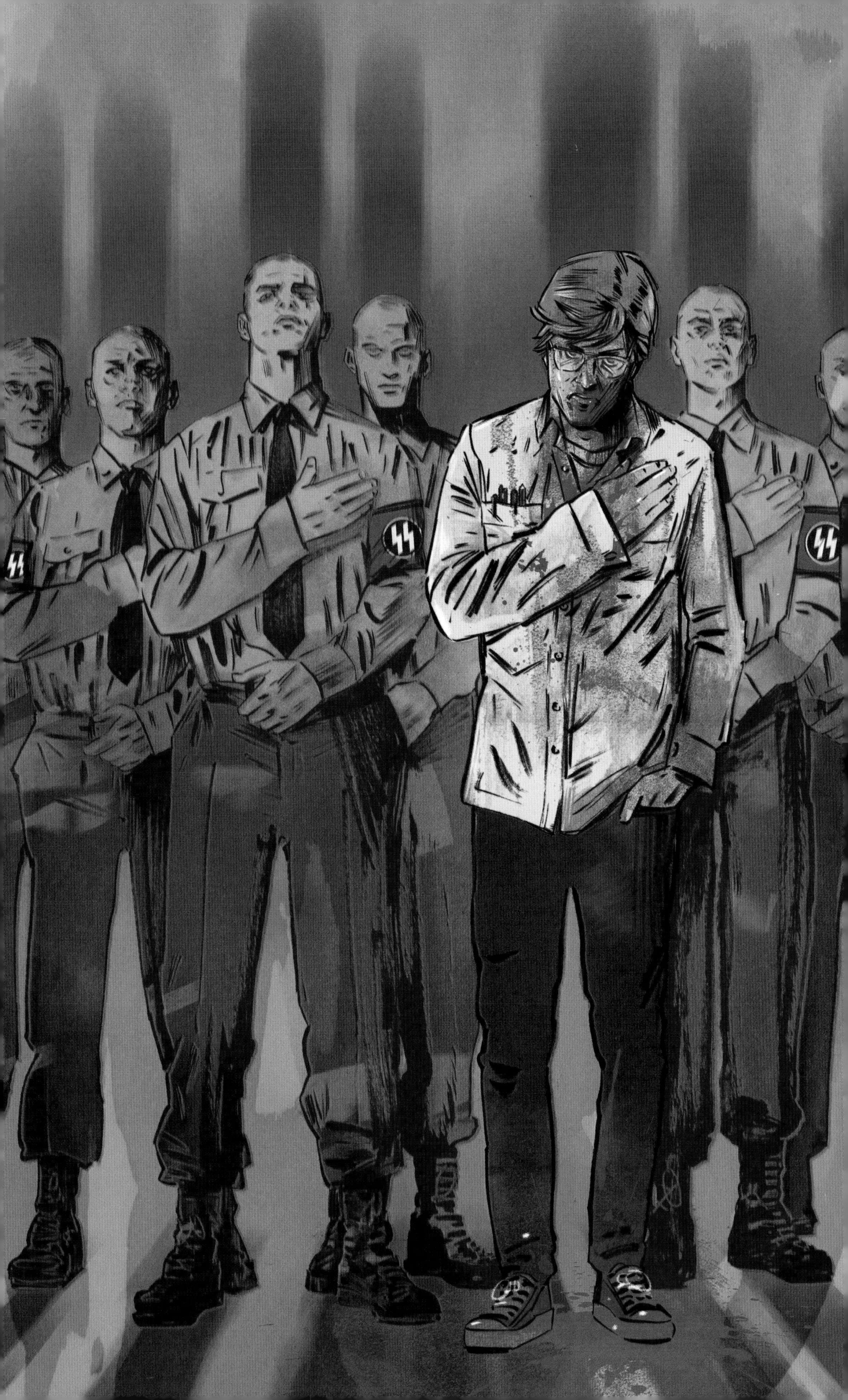

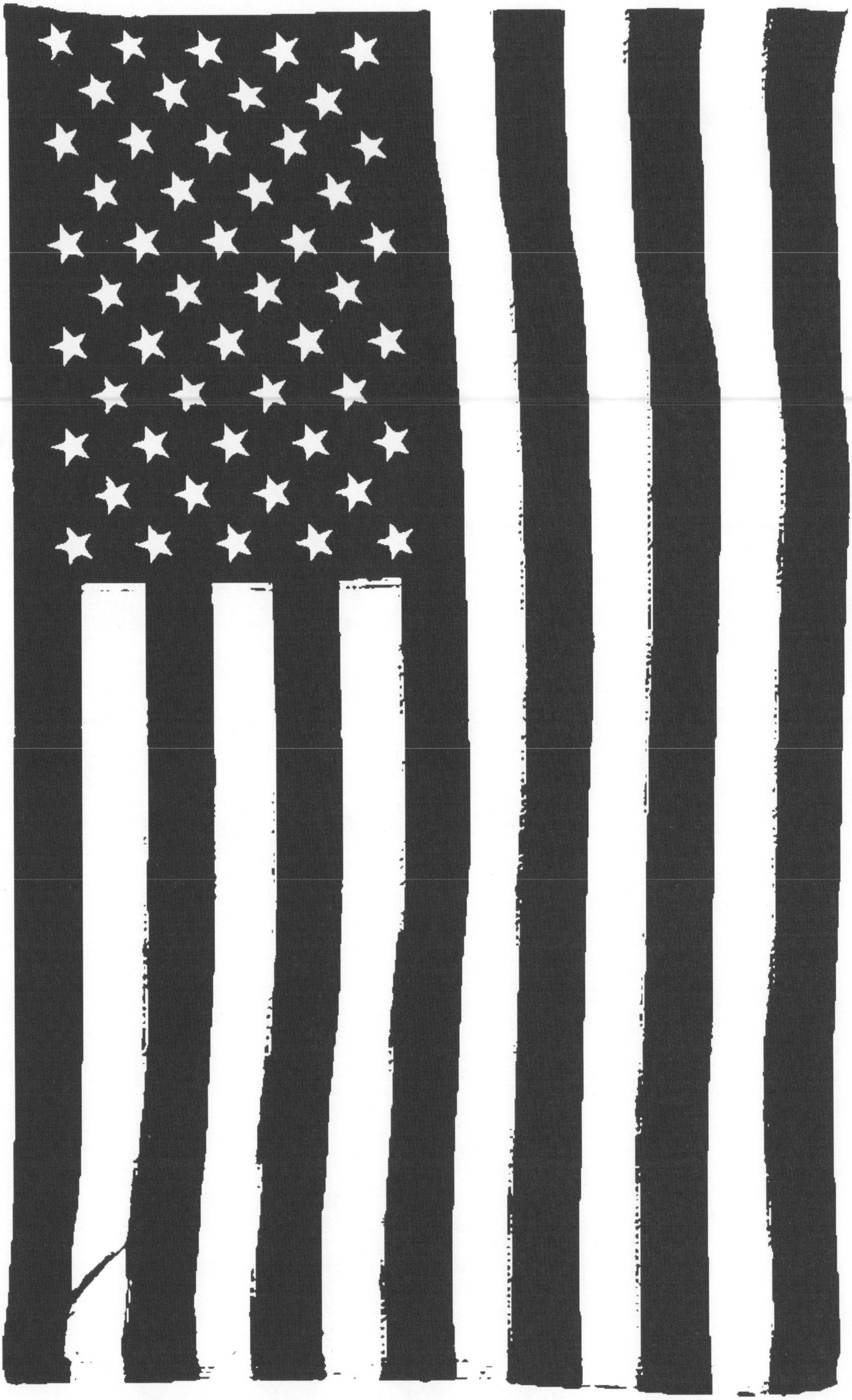

MAGGIE?
IT'S GRACE
BRIGGS.

HOW
IS HE?

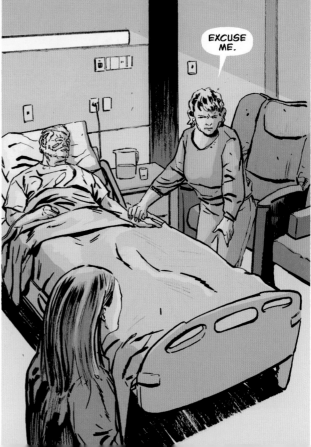

EXCUSE
ME.

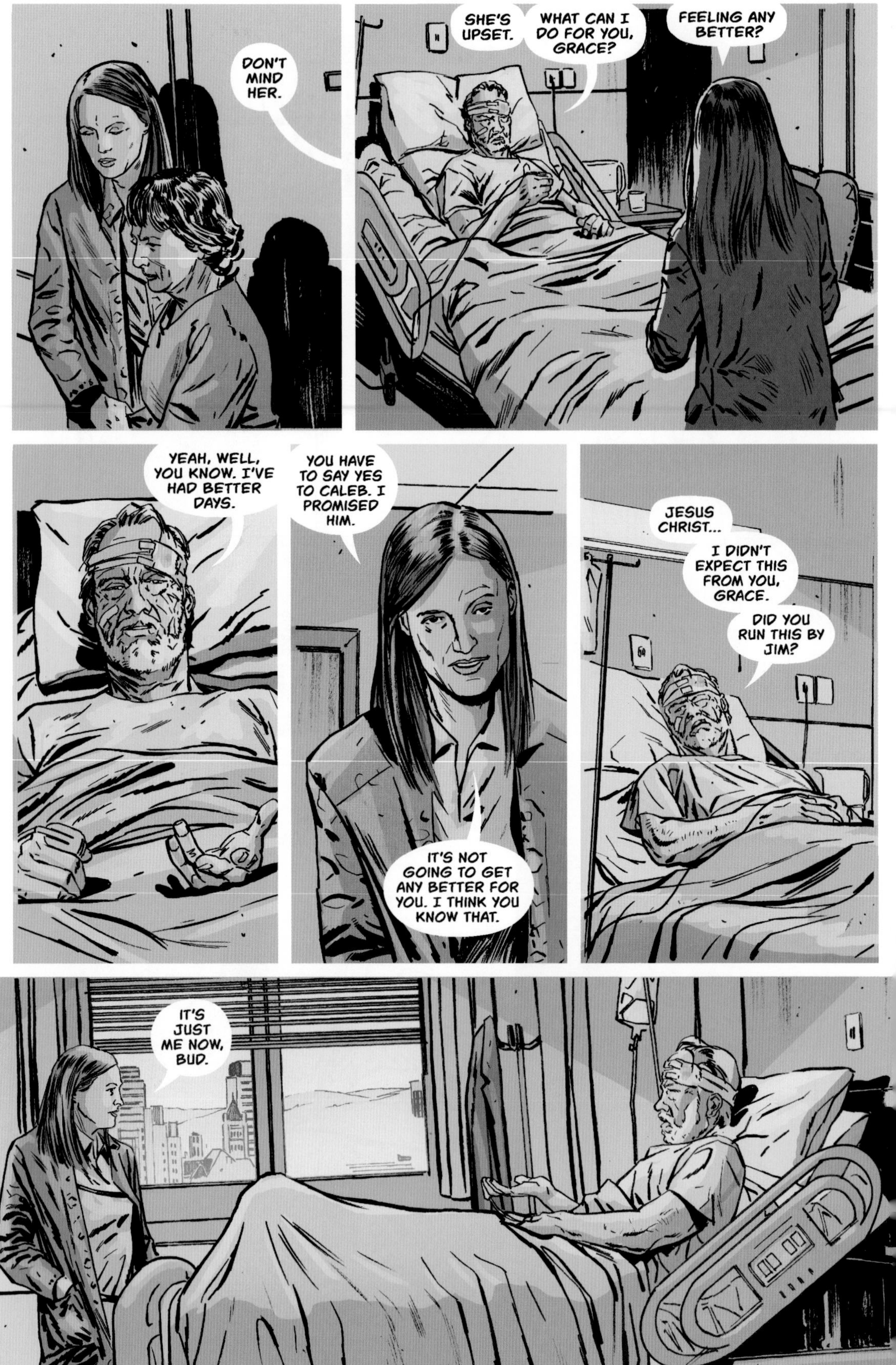
DON'T MIND HER.
SHE'S UPSET.
WHAT CAN I DO FOR YOU, GRACE?
FEELING ANY BETTER?
YEAH, WELL, YOU KNOW. I'VE HAD BETTER DAYS.
YOU HAVE TO SAY YES TO CALEB. I PROMISED HIM.
IT'S NOT GOING TO GET ANY BETTER FOR YOU. I THINK YOU KNOW THAT.
JESUS CHRIST...
I DIDN'T EXPECT THIS FROM YOU, GRACE.
DID YOU RUN THIS BY JIM?
IT'S JUST ME NOW, BUD.

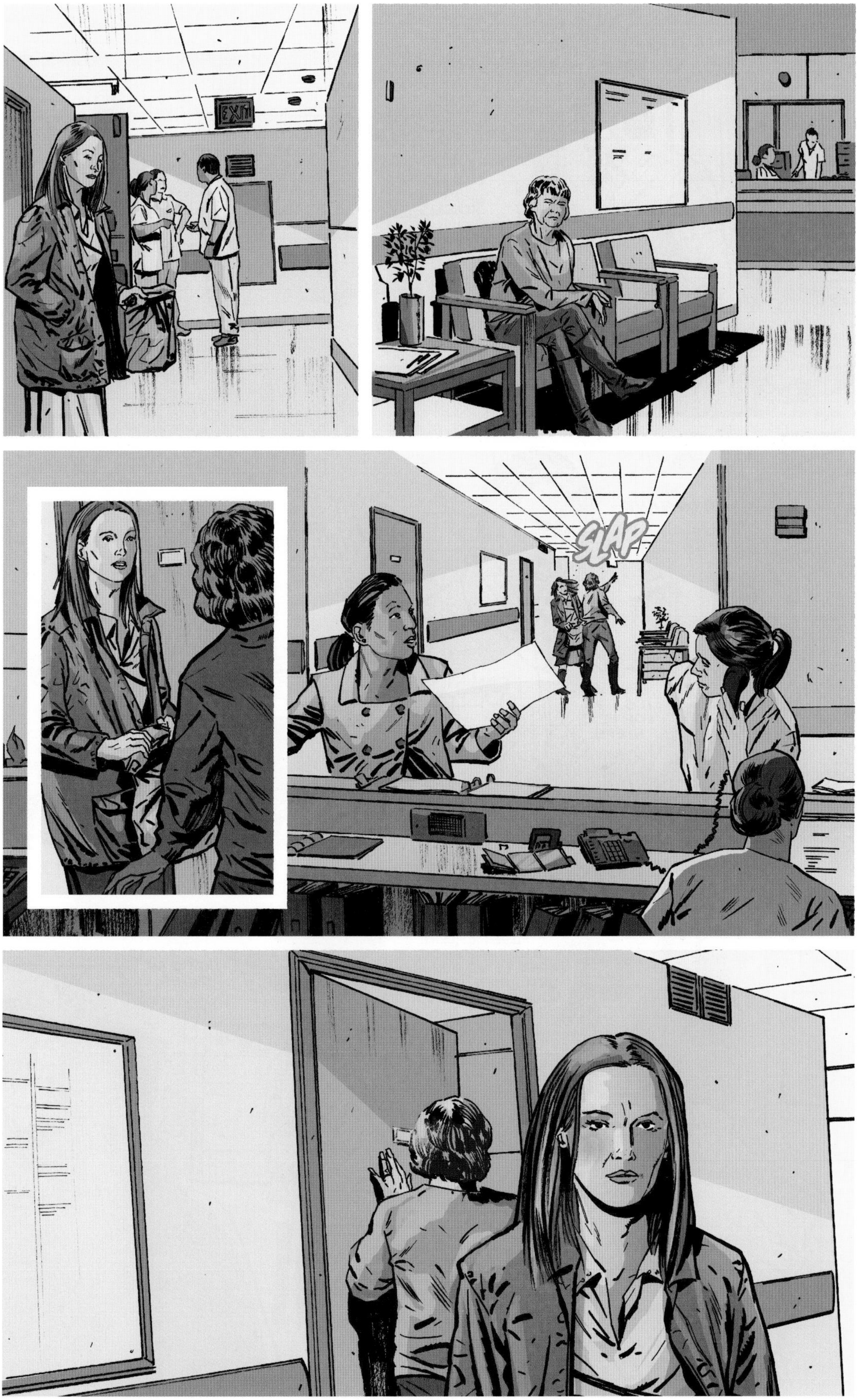
SLAP

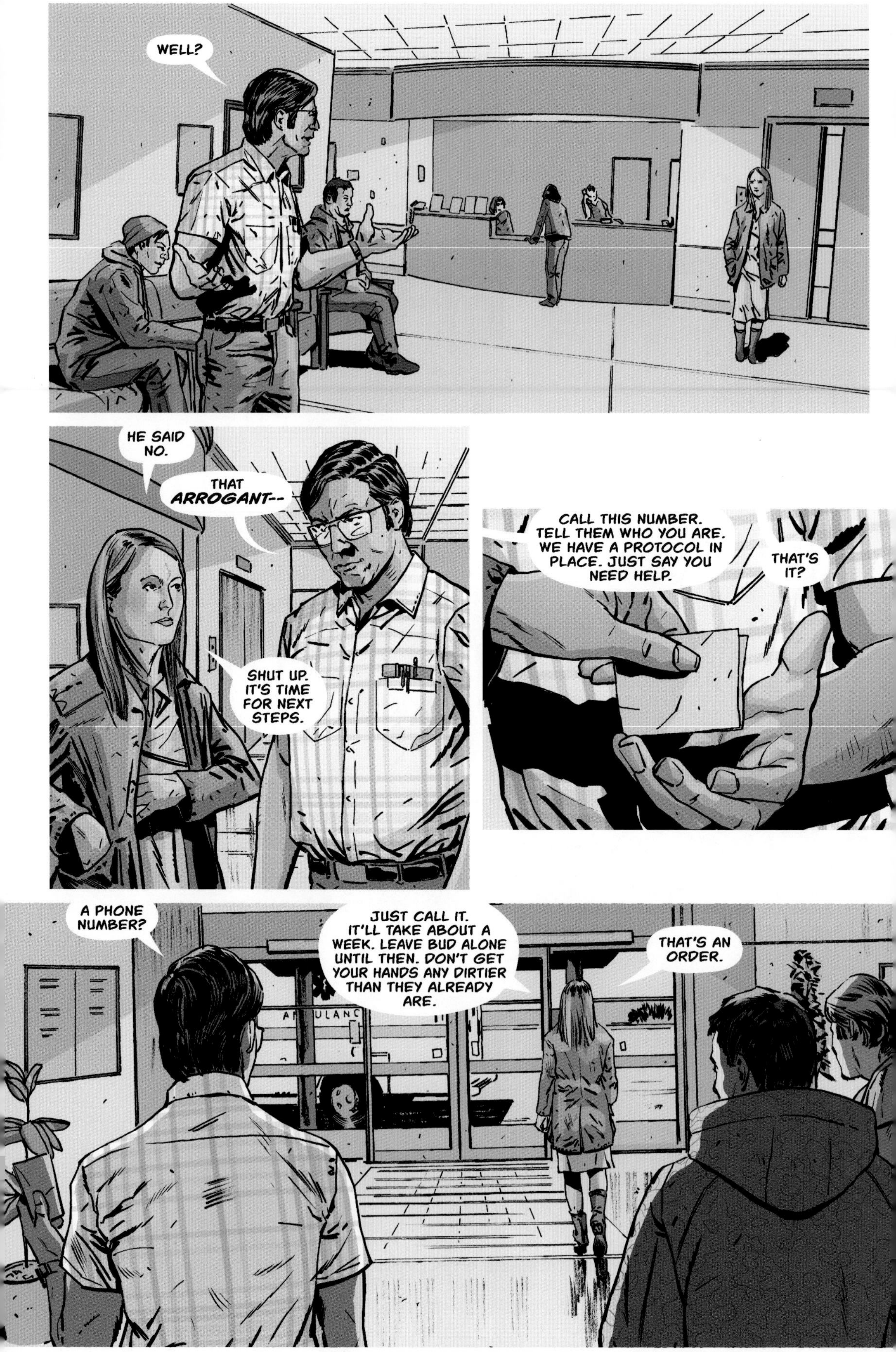
WELL?
HE SAID NO.
THAT ARROGANT--
SHUT UP. IT'S TIME FOR NEXT STEPS.
CALL THIS NUMBER. TELL THEM WHO YOU ARE. WE HAVE A PROTOCOL IN PLACE. JUST SAY YOU NEED HELP.
THAT'S IT?
A PHONE NUMBER?
JUST CALL IT. IT'LL TAKE ABOUT A WEEK. LEAVE BUD ALONE UNTIL THEN. DON'T GET YOUR HANDS ANY DIRTIER THAN THEY ALREADY ARE.
THAT'S AN ORDER.

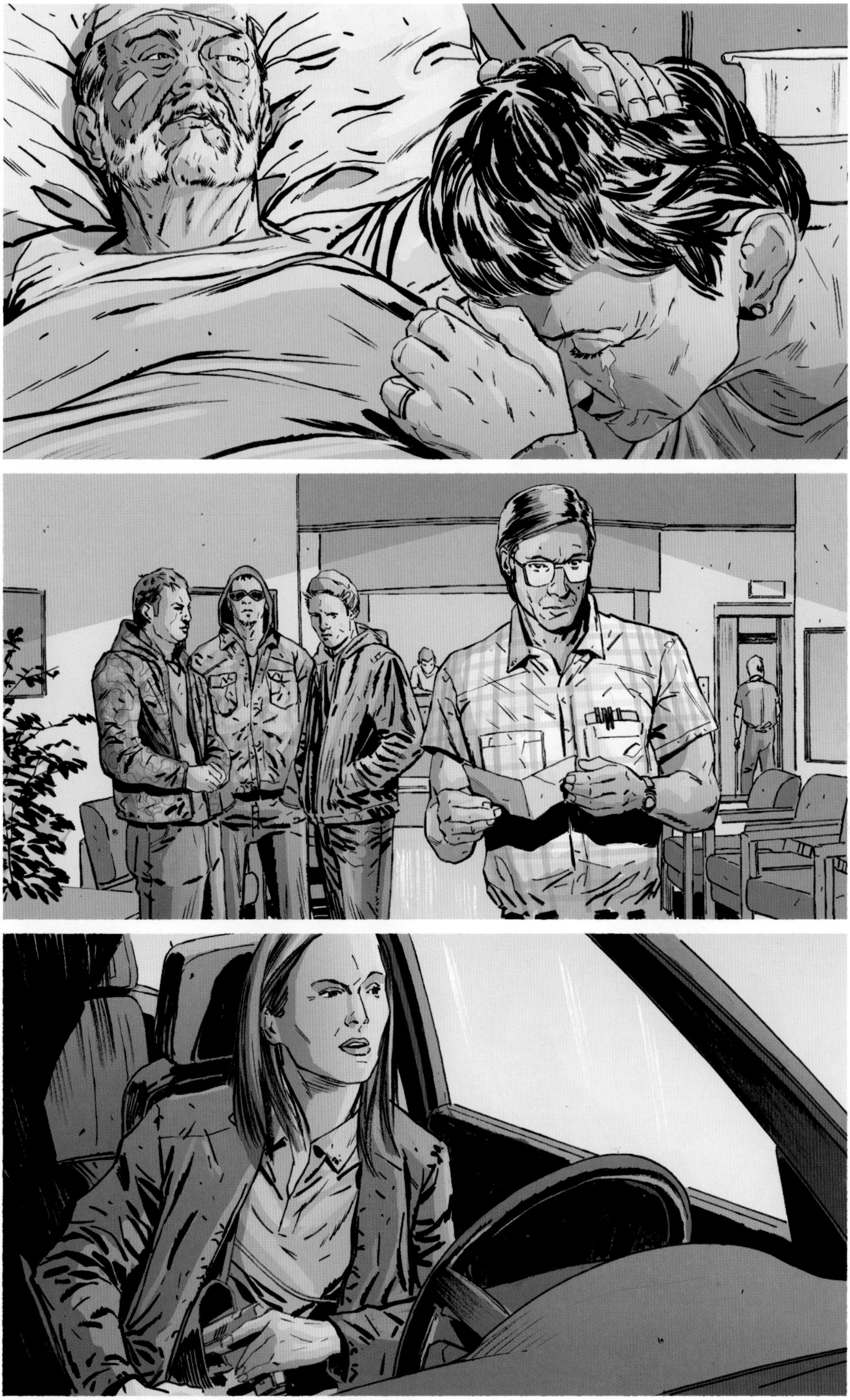

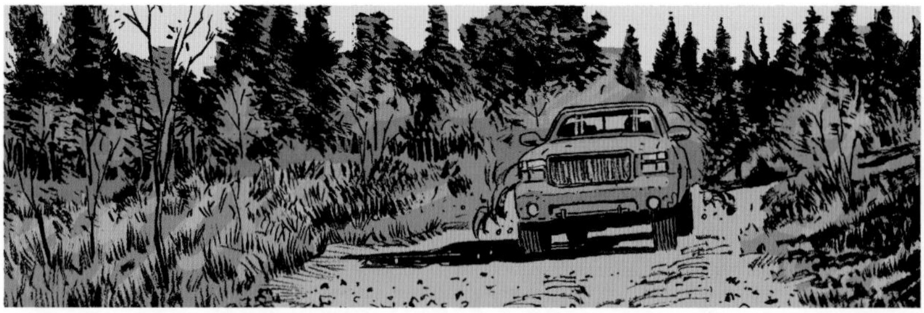

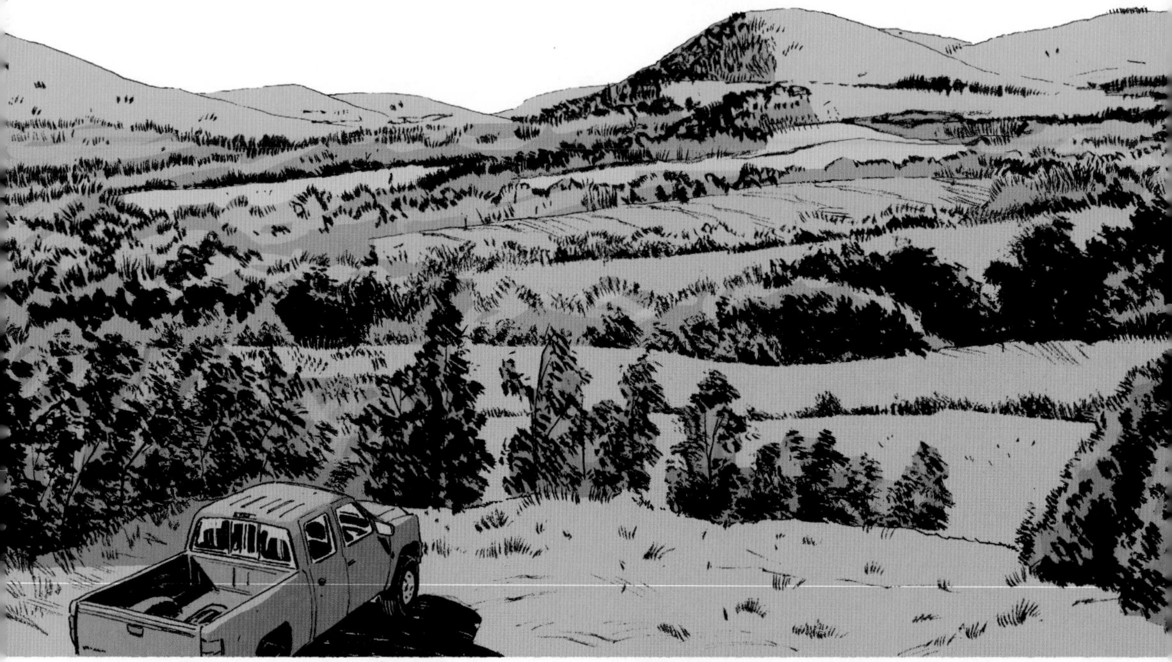

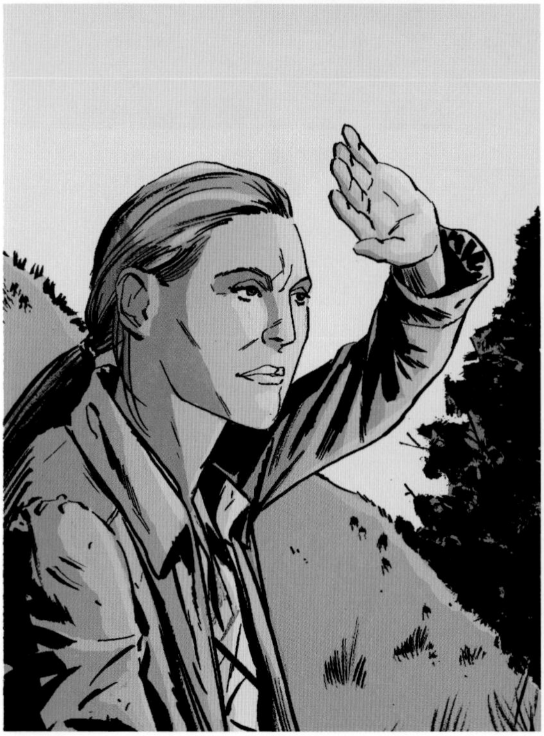

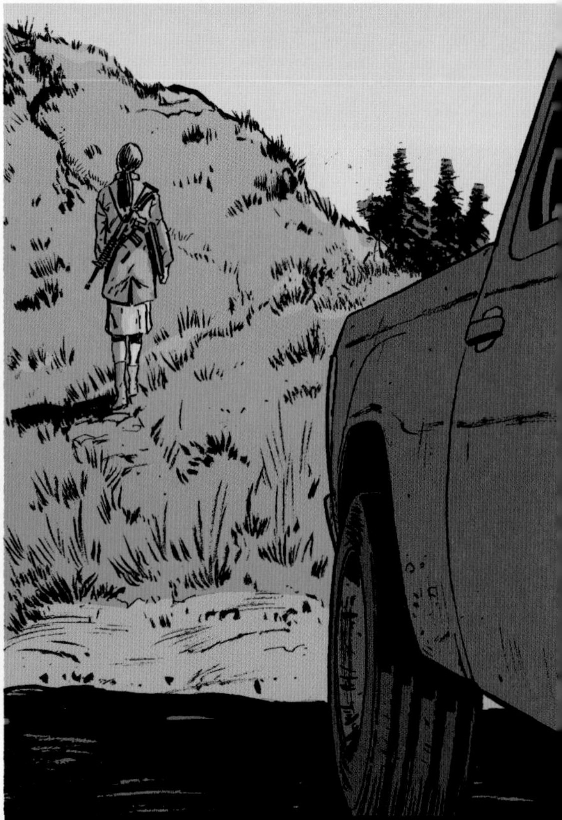

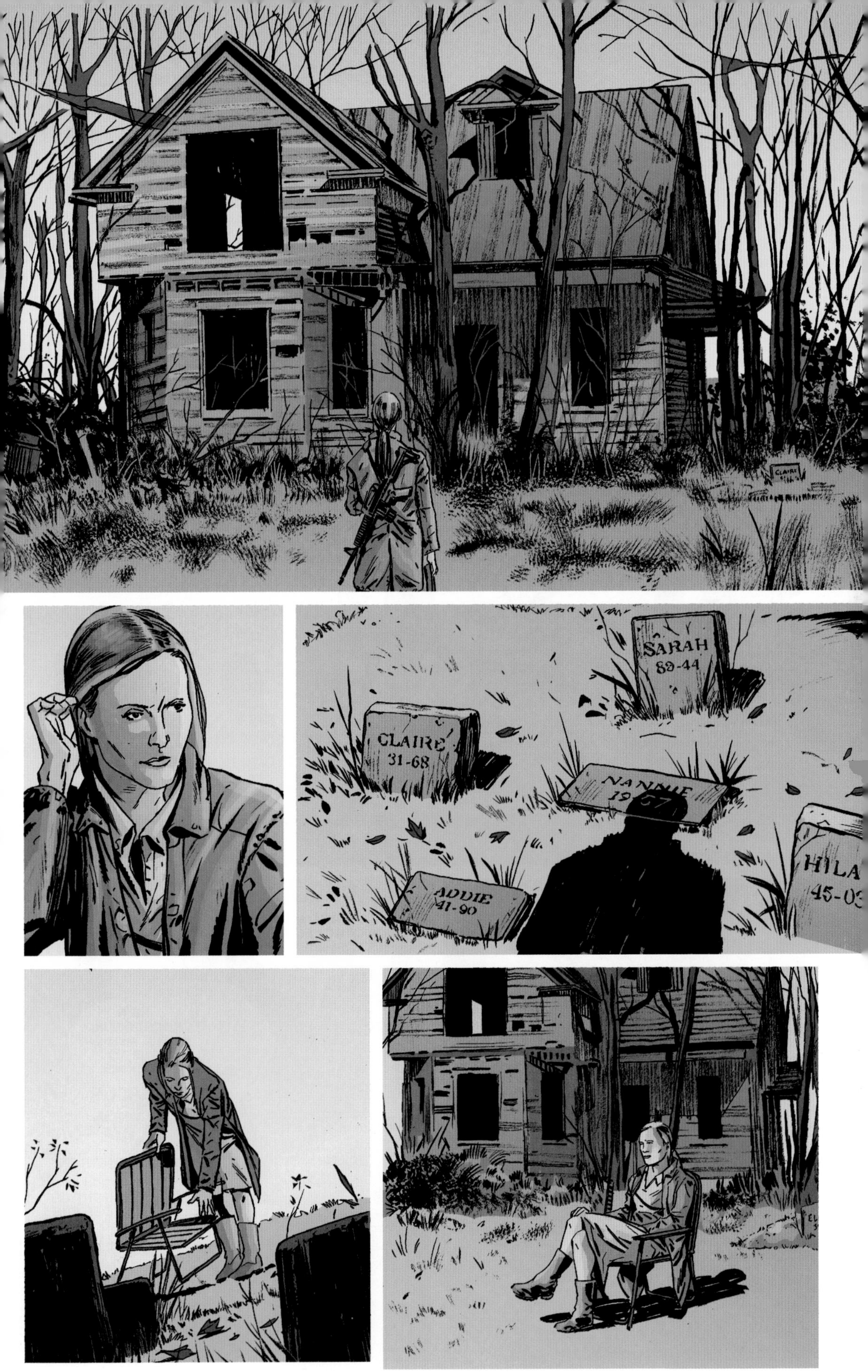
CLAIRE
SARAH
89-44
CLAIRE
31-68
NANNIE
ADDIE
41-90

YOU HAVE ONE TARGET INDIVIDUAL.

HE LIVES ALONE?

A MAN, NAME OF BUD HILLSON. HE LIVES OUTSIDE THE COMMUNITY, IN A RESIDENTIAL AREA ABOUT TWENTY MILES SOUTH OF HERE.

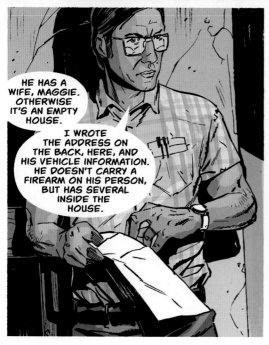

HE HAS A WIFE, MAGGIE. OTHERWISE IT'S AN EMPTY HOUSE.

I WROTE THE ADDRESS ON THE BACK, HERE, AND HIS VEHICLE INFORMATION. HE DOESN'T CARRY A FIREARM ON HIS PERSON, BUT HAS SEVERAL INSIDE THE HOUSE.

WHAT'S HIS DAILY SCHEDULE? HIS COMINGS AND GOINGS?

HE'S HOUSEBOUND AT THE MOMENT DUE TO INJURIES.

YOU BROUGHT US ACROSS THE COUNTRY TO DEAL WITH A LITTLE OLD MAN WHO CAN'T LEAVE THE HOUSE?

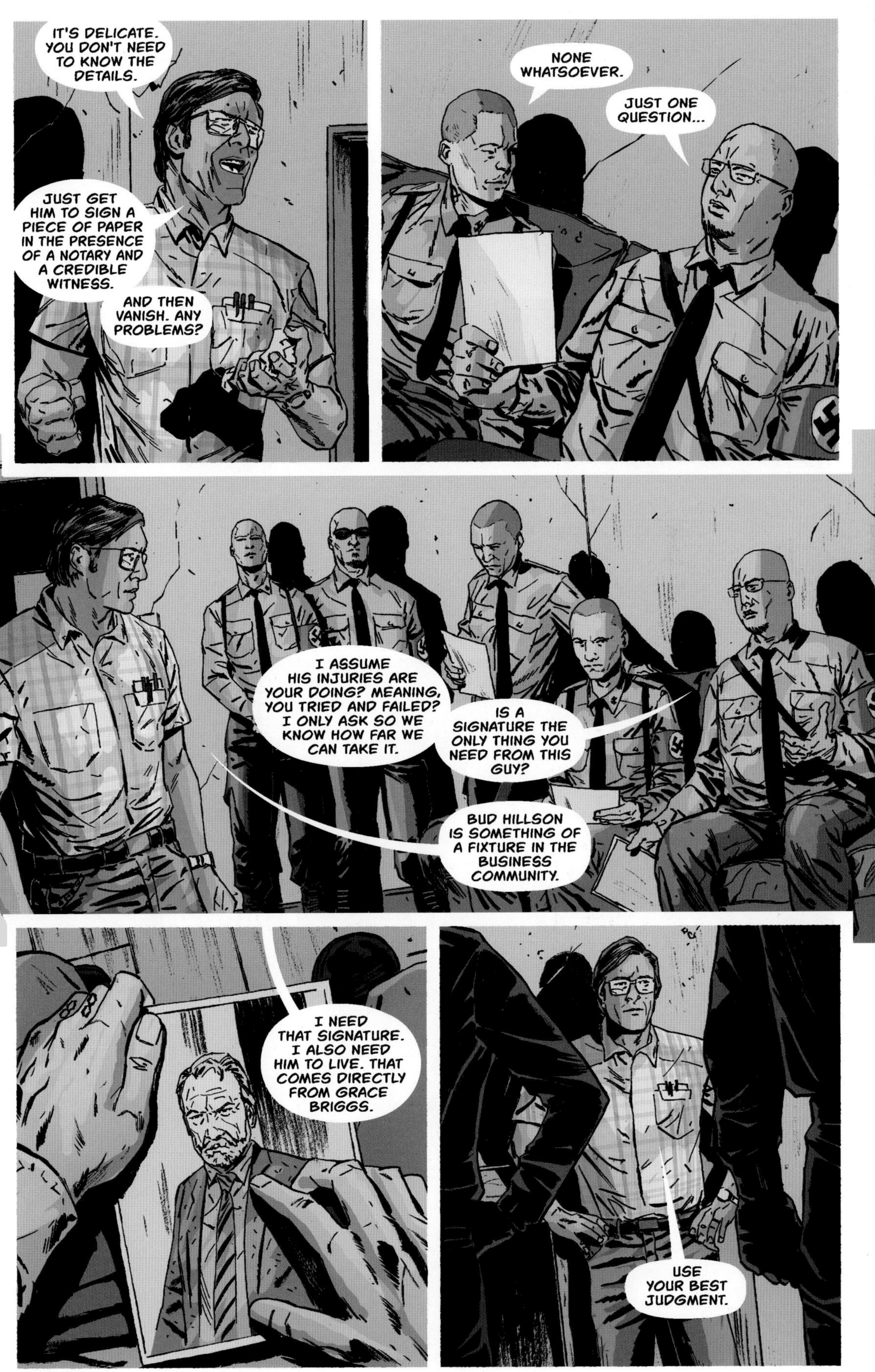
IT'S DELICATE. YOU DON'T NEED TO KNOW THE DETAILS.
JUST GET HIM TO SIGN A PIECE OF PAPER IN THE PRESENCE OF A NOTARY AND A CREDIBLE WITNESS.
AND THEN VANISH. ANY PROBLEMS?
NONE WHATSOEVER.
JUST ONE QUESTION...
IS A SIGNATURE THE ONLY THING YOU NEED FROM THIS GUY?
I ASSUME HIS INJURIES ARE YOUR DOING? MEANING, YOU TRIED AND FAILED? I ONLY ASK SO WE KNOW HOW FAR WE CAN TAKE IT.
BUD HILLSON IS SOMETHING OF A FIXTURE IN THE BUSINESS COMMUNITY.
I NEED THAT SIGNATURE. I ALSO NEED HIM TO LIVE. THAT COMES DIRECTLY FROM GRACE BRIGGS.
USE YOUR BEST JUDGMENT.

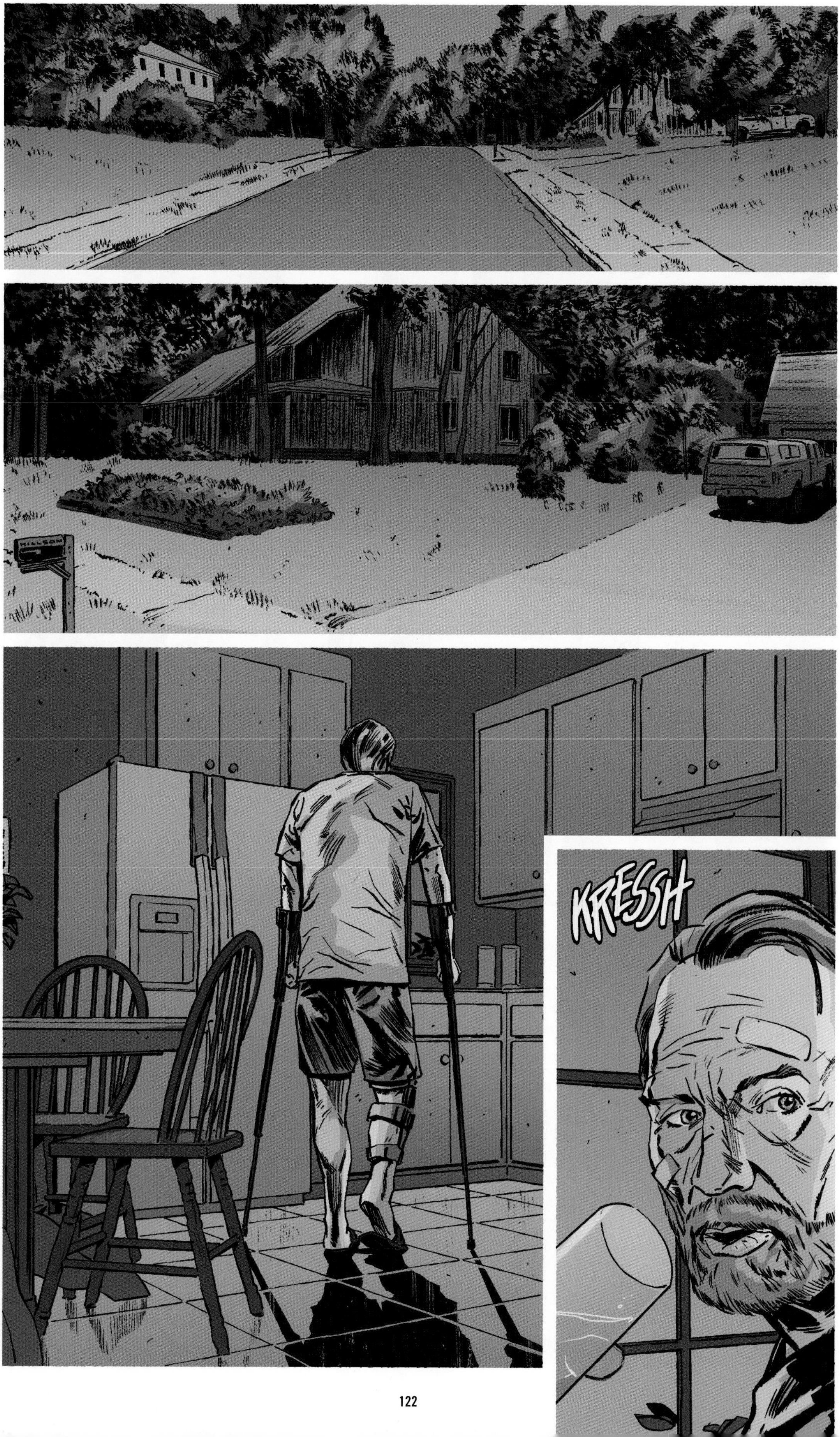
KRESSH

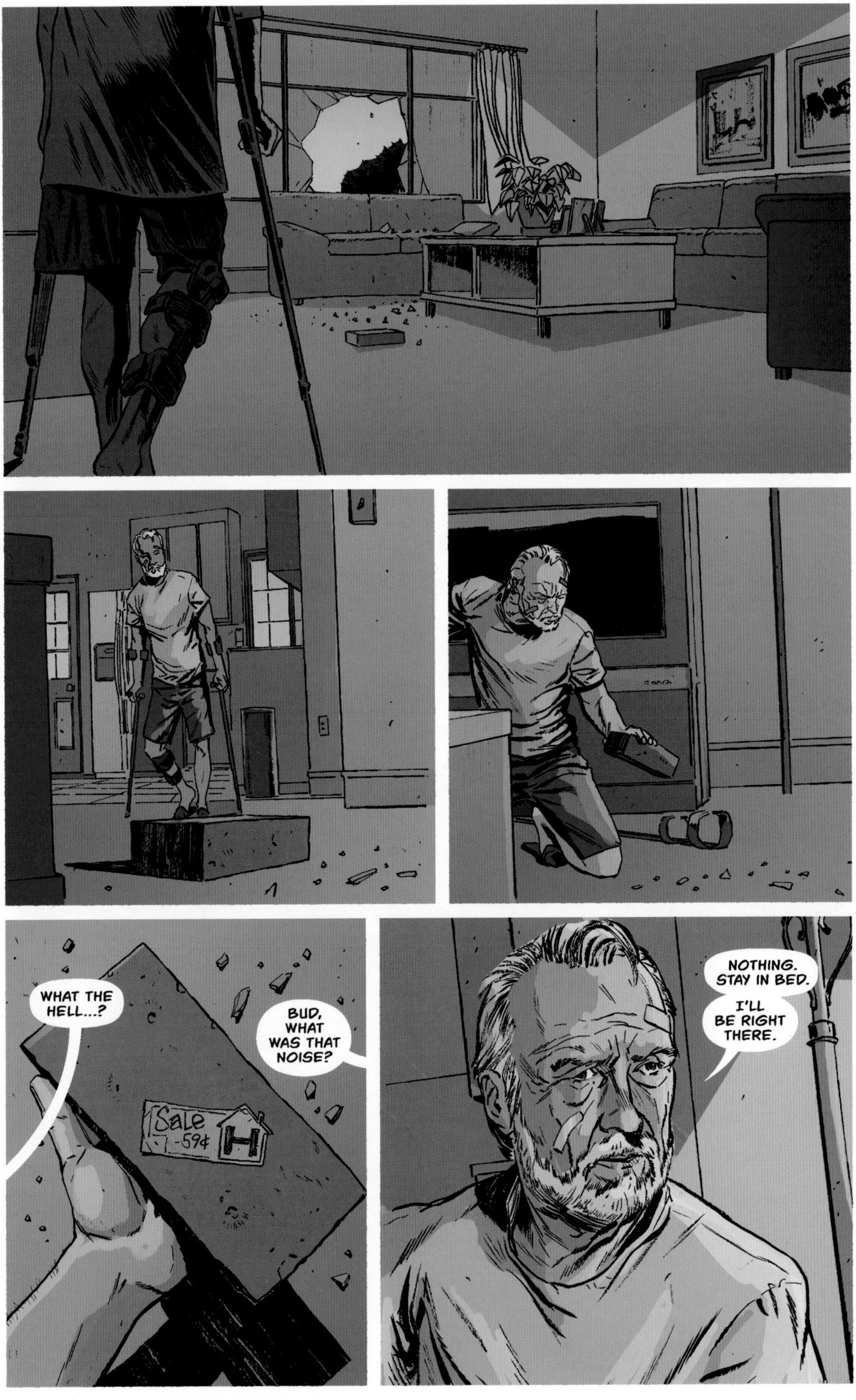
WHAT THE HELL...?
BUD, WHAT WAS THAT NOISE?
Sale -59¢
NOTHING. STAY IN BED.
I'LL BE RIGHT THERE.

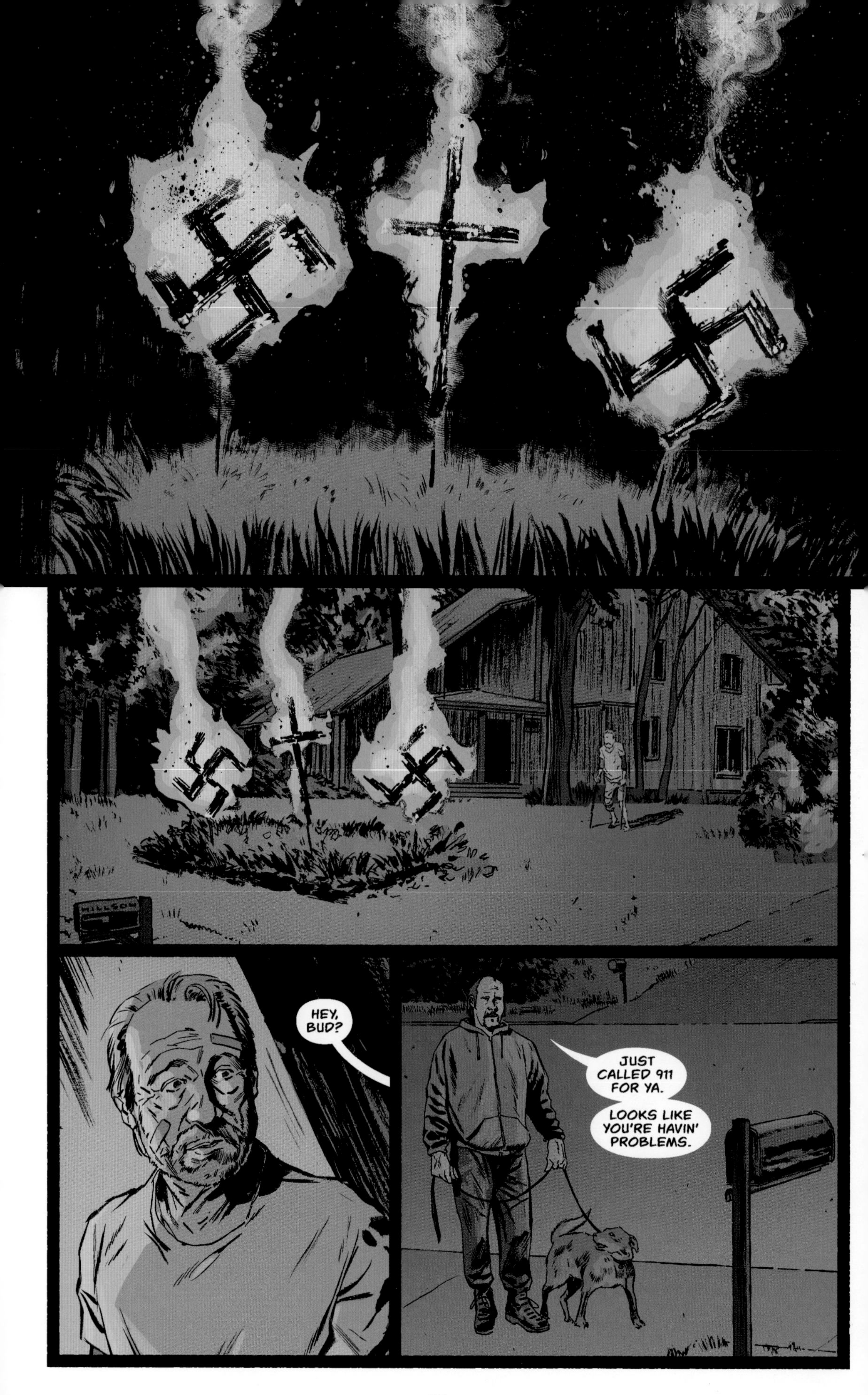
HEY, BUD?
JUST CALLED 911 FOR YA.
LOOKS LIKE YOU'RE HAVIN' PROBLEMS.

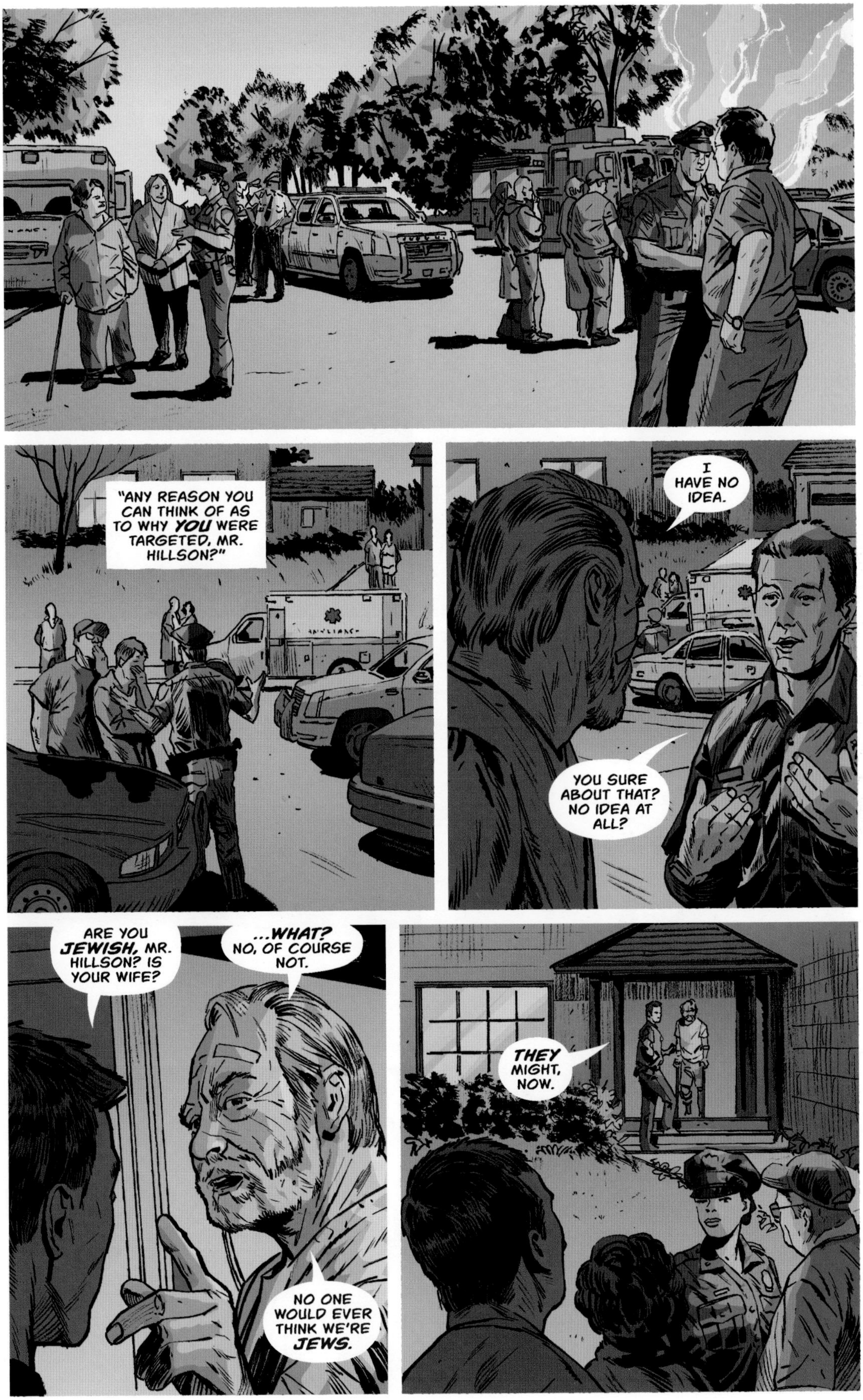
"ANY REASON YOU CAN THINK OF AS TO WHY *YOU* WERE TARGETED, MR. HILLSON?"
I HAVE NO IDEA.
YOU SURE ABOUT THAT? NO IDEA AT ALL?
ARE YOU *JEWISH*, MR. HILLSON? IS YOUR WIFE?
...WHAT? NO, OF COURSE NOT.
NO ONE WOULD EVER THINK WE'RE *JEWS.*
THEY MIGHT, NOW.

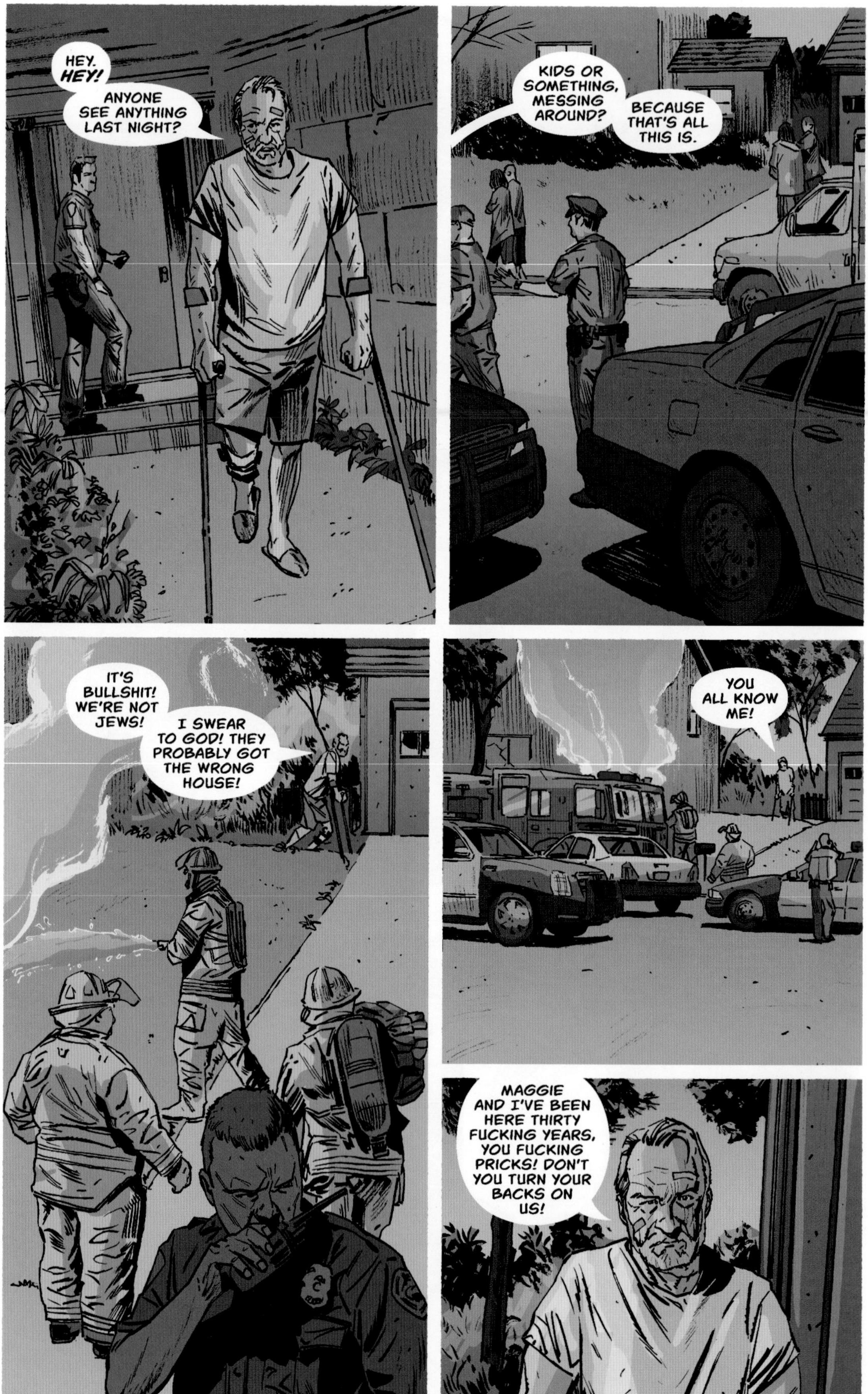
HEY. HEY!
ANYONE SEE ANYTHING LAST NIGHT?
KIDS OR SOMETHING, MESSING AROUND?
BECAUSE THAT'S ALL THIS IS.
IT'S BULLSHIT! WE'RE NOT JEWS!
I SWEAR TO GOD! THEY PROBABLY GOT THE WRONG HOUSE!
YOU ALL KNOW ME!
MAGGIE AND I'VE BEEN HERE THIRTY FUCKING YEARS, YOU FUCKING PRICKS! DON'T YOU TURN YOUR BACKS ON US!

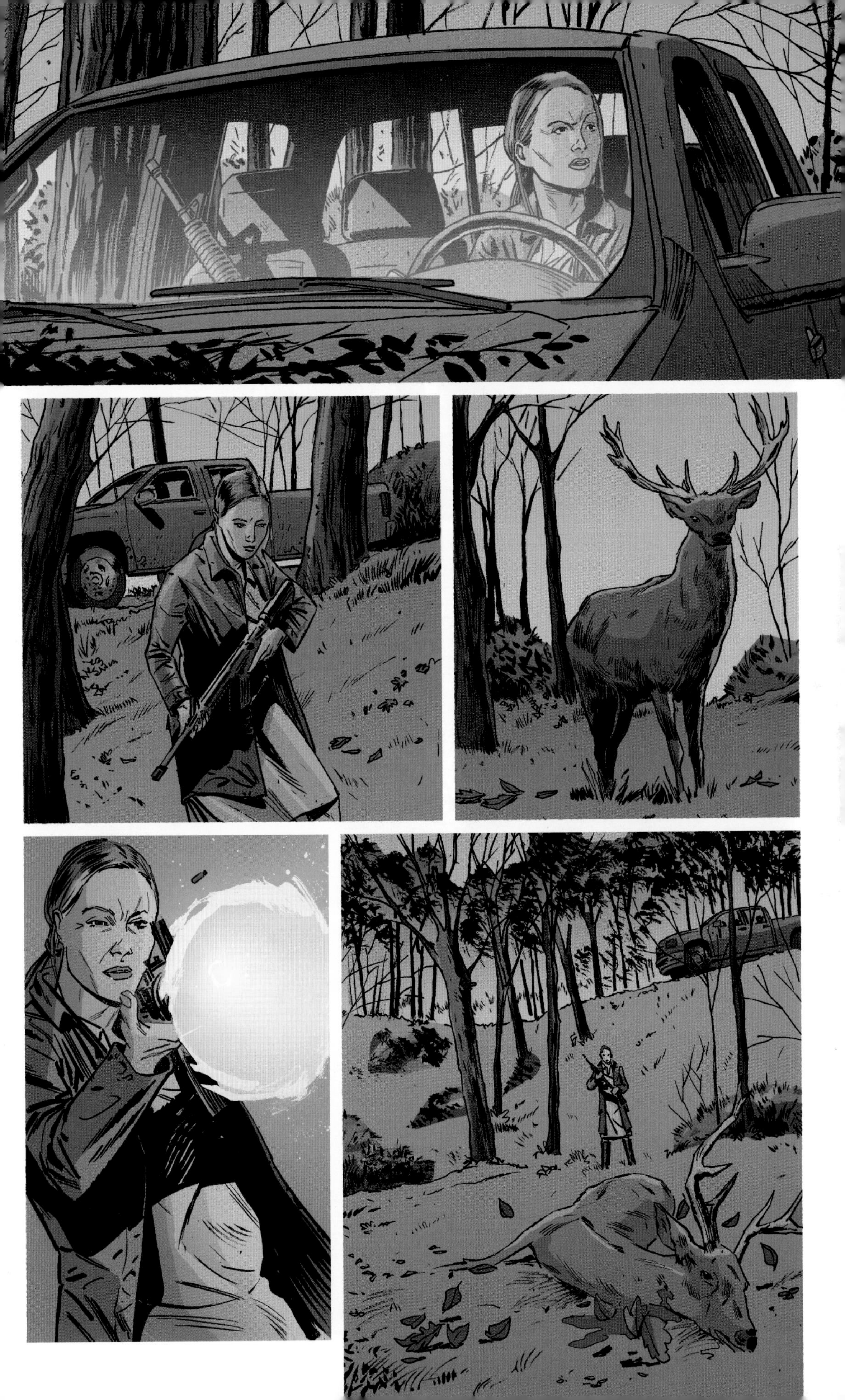

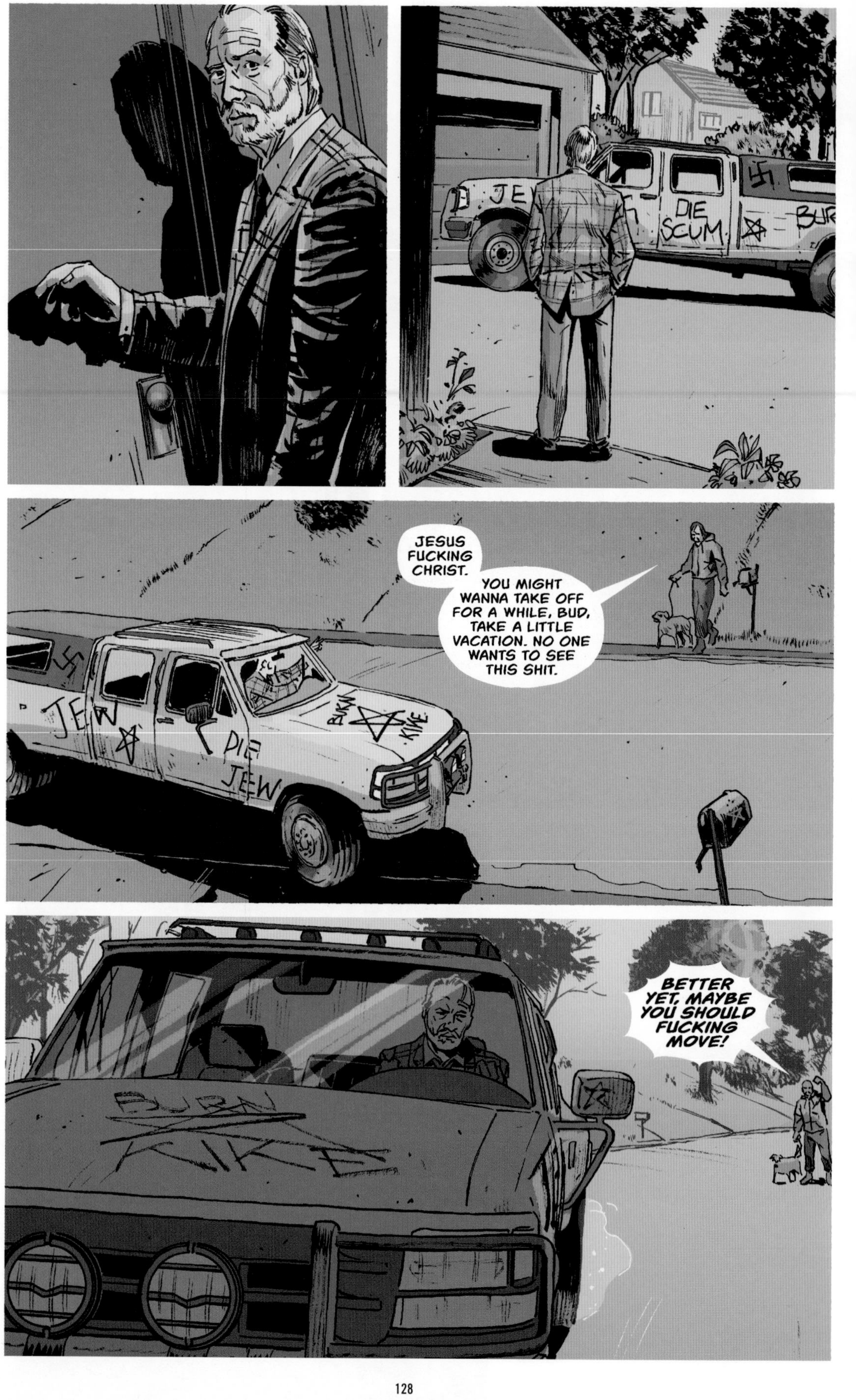
DIE SCUM
JEW
BURN KIKE
DIE JEW
JESUS FUCKING CHRIST.
YOU MIGHT WANNA TAKE OFF FOR A WHILE, BUD, TAKE A LITTLE VACATION. NO ONE WANTS TO SEE THIS SHIT.
BETTER YET, MAYBE YOU SHOULD FUCKING MOVE!

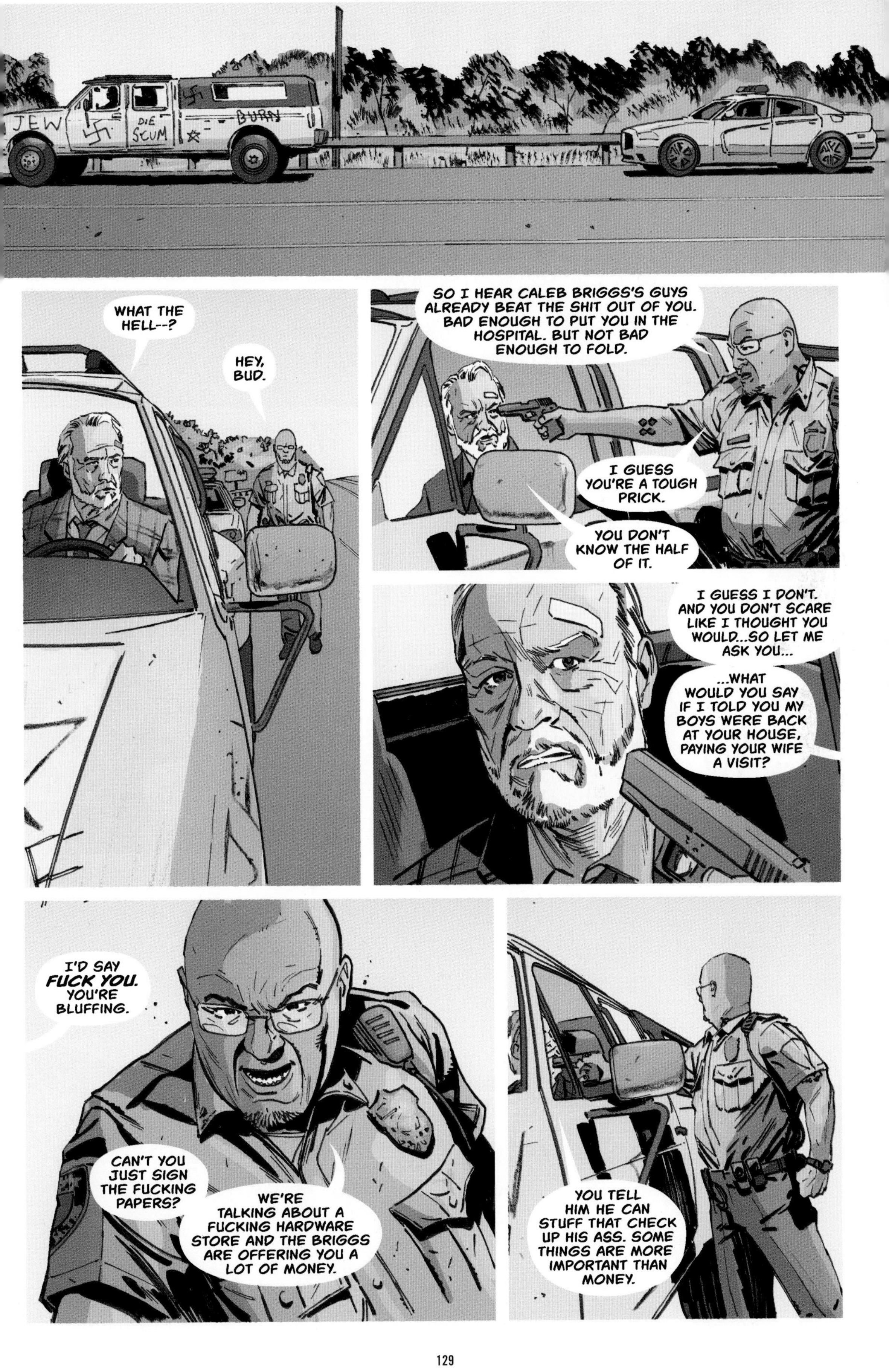
JEW
DIE SCUM
BURN
WHAT THE HELL--?
HEY, BUD.
SO I HEAR CALEB BRIGGS'S GUYS ALREADY BEAT THE SHIT OUT OF YOU. BAD ENOUGH TO PUT YOU IN THE HOSPITAL. BUT NOT BAD ENOUGH TO FOLD.
I GUESS YOU'RE A TOUGH PRICK.
YOU DON'T KNOW THE HALF OF IT.
I GUESS I DON'T. AND YOU DON'T SCARE LIKE I THOUGHT YOU WOULD...SO LET ME ASK YOU...
...WHAT WOULD YOU SAY IF I TOLD YOU MY BOYS WERE BACK AT YOUR HOUSE, PAYING YOUR WIFE A VISIT?
I'D SAY **FUCK YOU.** YOU'RE BLUFFING.
CAN'T YOU JUST SIGN THE FUCKING PAPERS?
WE'RE TALKING ABOUT A FUCKING HARDWARE STORE AND THE BRIGGS ARE OFFERING YOU A LOT OF MONEY.
YOU TELL HIM HE CAN STUFF THAT CHECK UP HIS ASS. SOME THINGS ARE MORE IMPORTANT THAN MONEY.

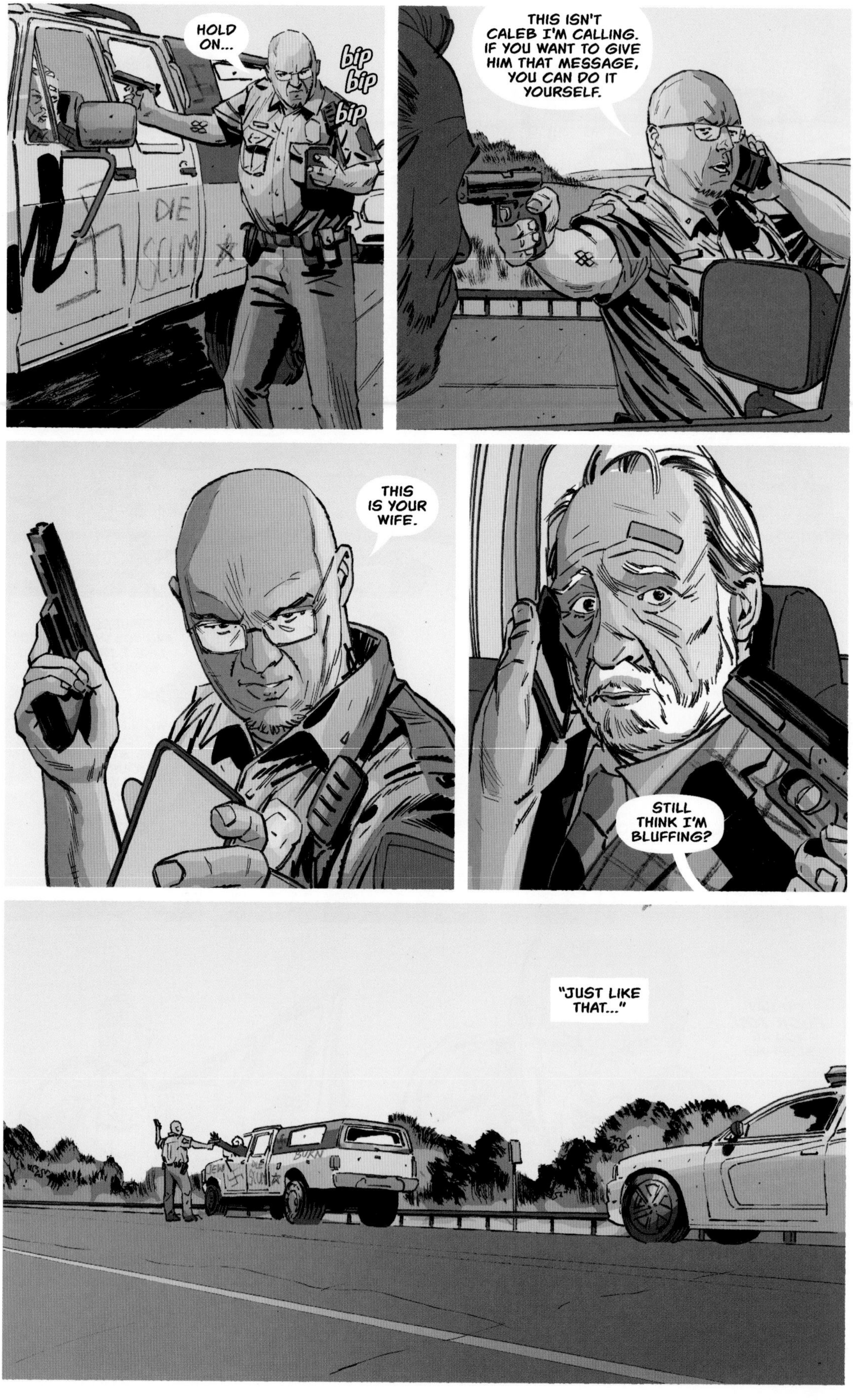
HOLD ON...
bip
bip
bip
DIE SCUM
THIS ISN'T CALEB I'M CALLING. IF YOU WANT TO GIVE HIM THAT MESSAGE, YOU CAN DO IT YOURSELF.
THIS IS YOUR WIFE.
STILL THINK I'M BLUFFING?
"JUST LIKE THAT..."

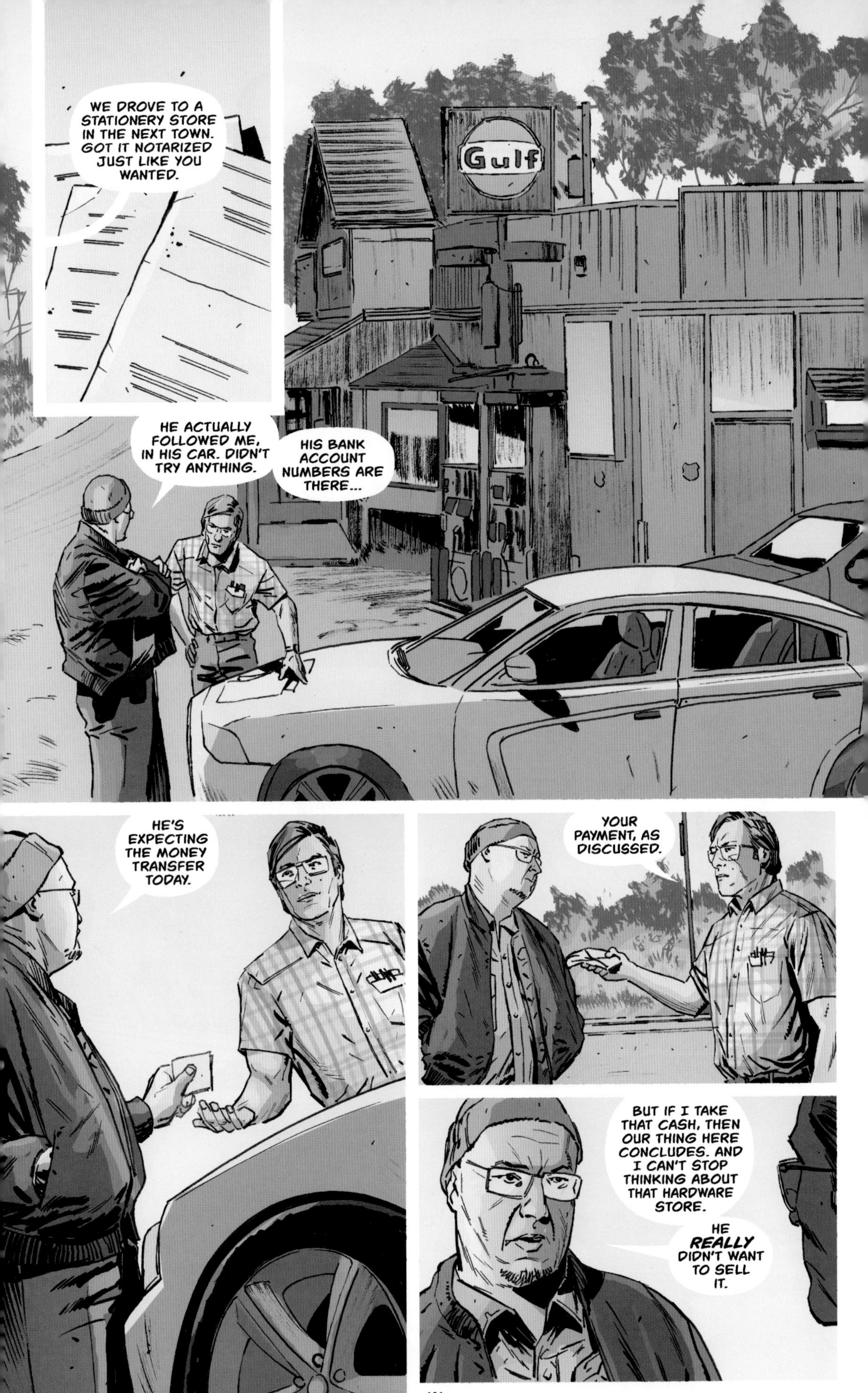
WE DROVE TO A STATIONERY STORE IN THE NEXT TOWN. GOT IT NOTARIZED JUST LIKE YOU WANTED.
Gulf
HE ACTUALLY FOLLOWED ME, IN HIS CAR. DIDN'T TRY ANYTHING.
HIS BANK ACCOUNT NUMBERS ARE THERE...
HE'S EXPECTING THE MONEY TRANSFER TODAY.
YOUR PAYMENT, AS DISCUSSED.
BUT IF I TAKE THAT CASH, THEN OUR THING HERE CONCLUDES. AND I CAN'T STOP THINKING ABOUT THAT HARDWARE STORE.
HE *REALLY* DIDN'T WANT TO SELL IT.

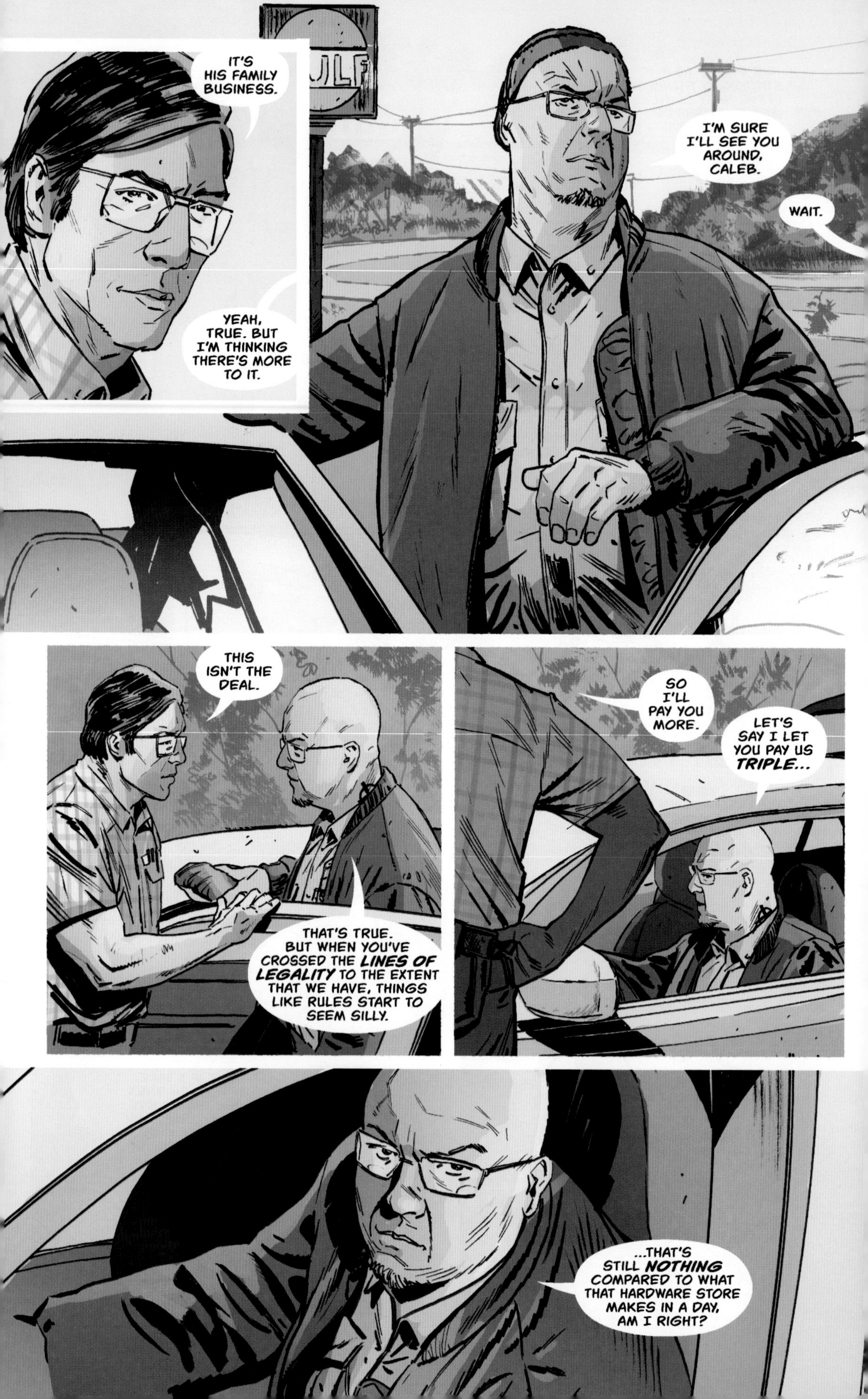
IT'S HIS FAMILY BUSINESS.
YEAH, TRUE. BUT I'M THINKING THERE'S MORE TO IT.
I'M SURE I'LL SEE YOU AROUND, CALEB.
WAIT.
THIS ISN'T THE DEAL.
THAT'S TRUE. BUT WHEN YOU'VE CROSSED THE LINES OF LEGALITY TO THE EXTENT THAT WE HAVE, THINGS LIKE RULES START TO SEEM SILLY.
SO I'LL PAY YOU MORE.
LET'S SAY I LET YOU PAY US TRIPLE...
...THAT'S STILL NOTHING COMPARED TO WHAT THAT HARDWARE STORE MAKES IN A DAY, AM I RIGHT?

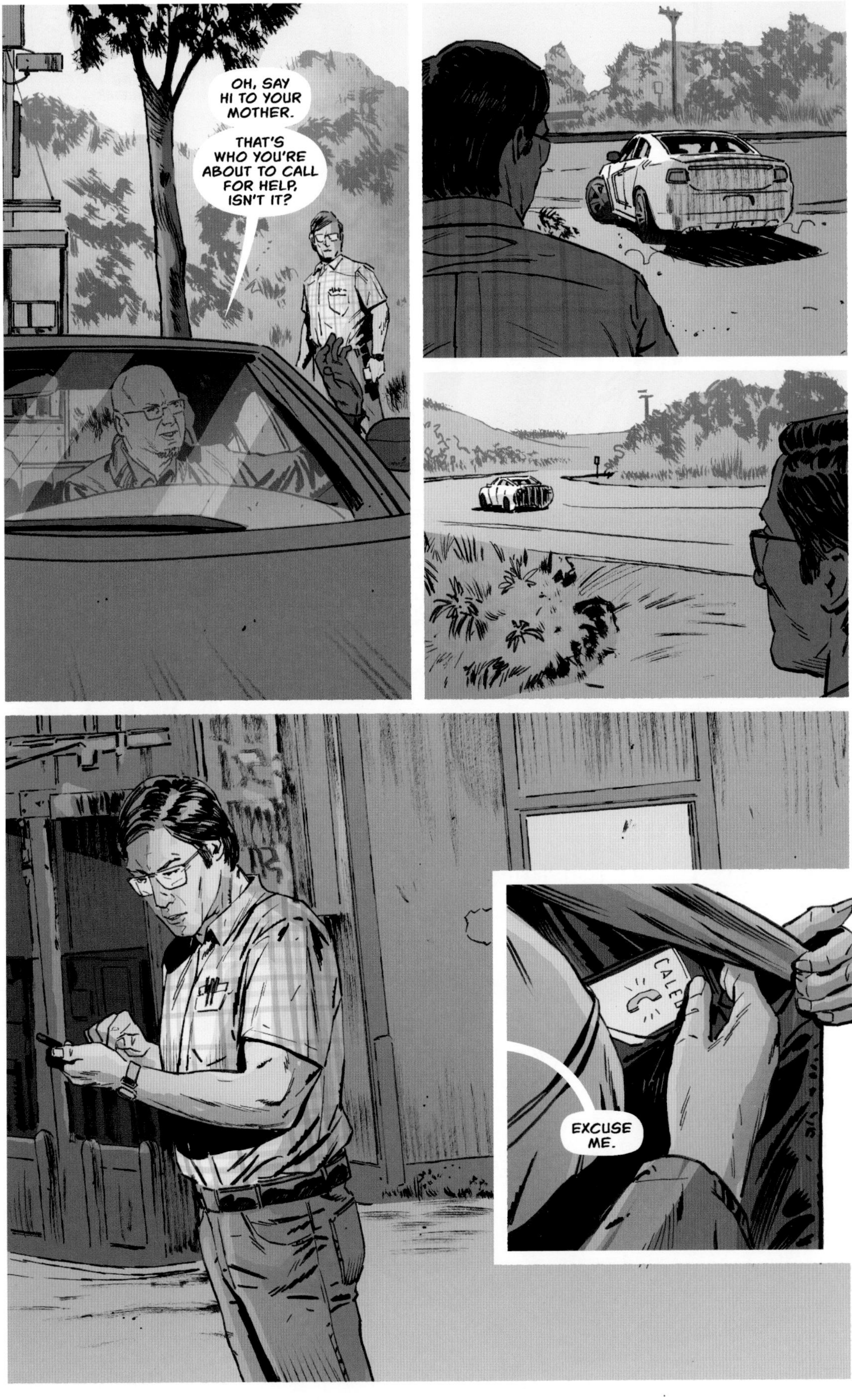
OH, SAY HI TO YOUR MOTHER.
THAT'S WHO YOU'RE ABOUT TO CALL FOR HELP, ISN'T IT?
EXCUSE ME.

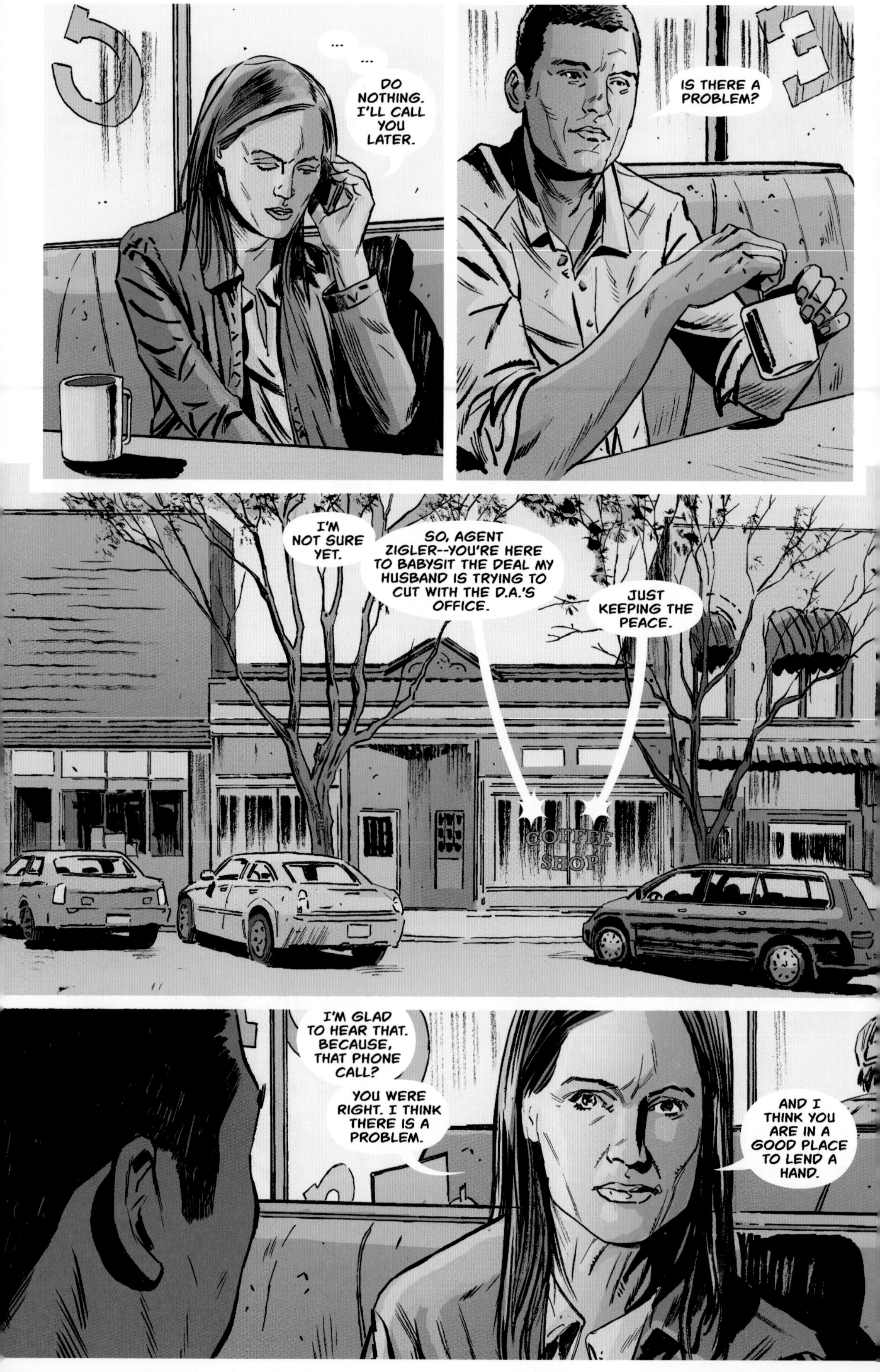
...
...
DO NOTHING. I'LL CALL YOU LATER.
IS THERE A PROBLEM?
I'M NOT SURE YET.
SO, AGENT ZIGLER--YOU'RE HERE TO BABYSIT THE DEAL MY HUSBAND IS TRYING TO CUT WITH THE D.A.'S OFFICE.
JUST KEEPING THE PEACE.
COFFEE SHOP
I'M GLAD TO HEAR THAT. BECAUSE, THAT PHONE CALL?
YOU WERE RIGHT. I THINK THERE IS A PROBLEM.
AND I THINK YOU ARE IN A GOOD PLACE TO LEND A HAND.

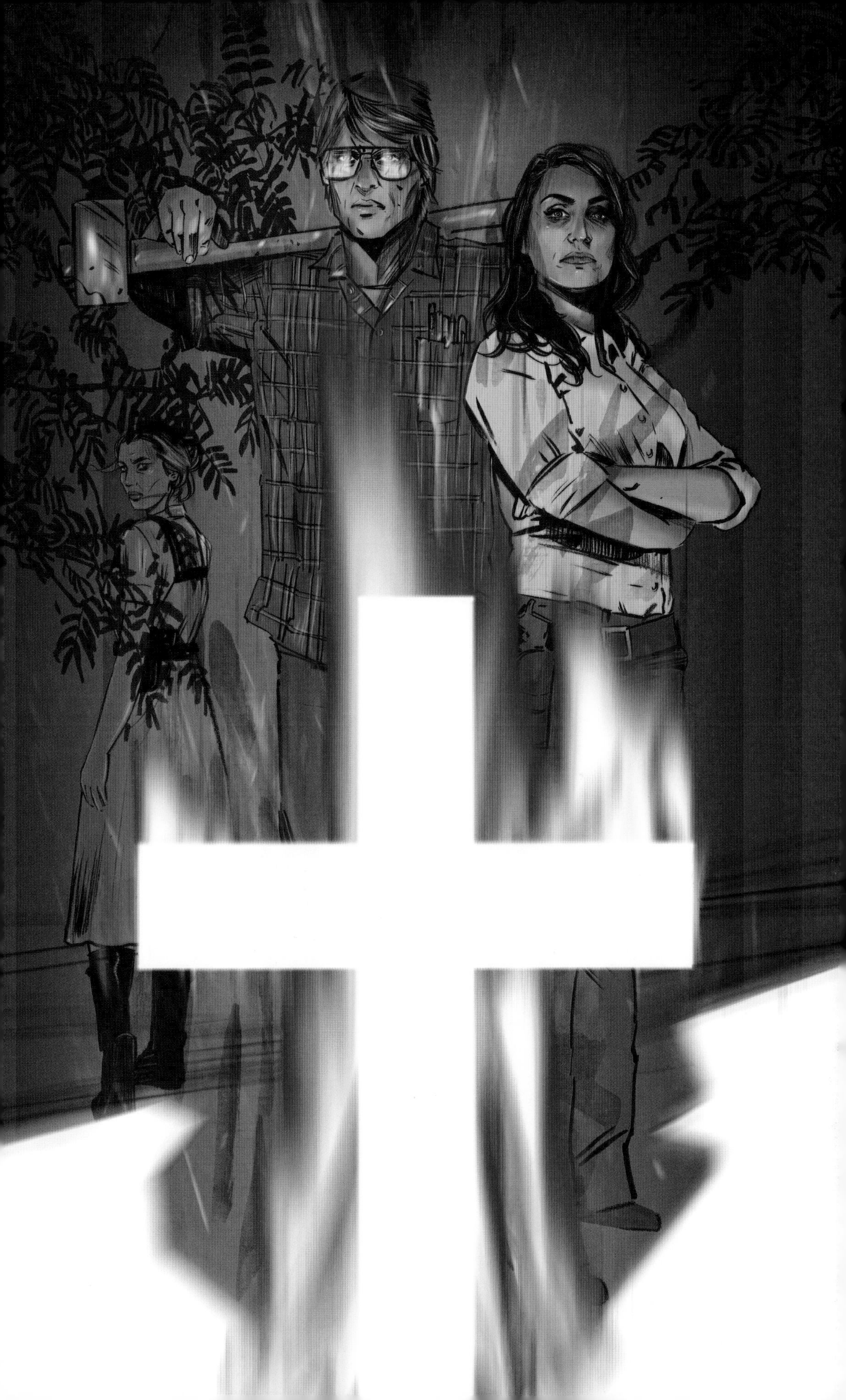

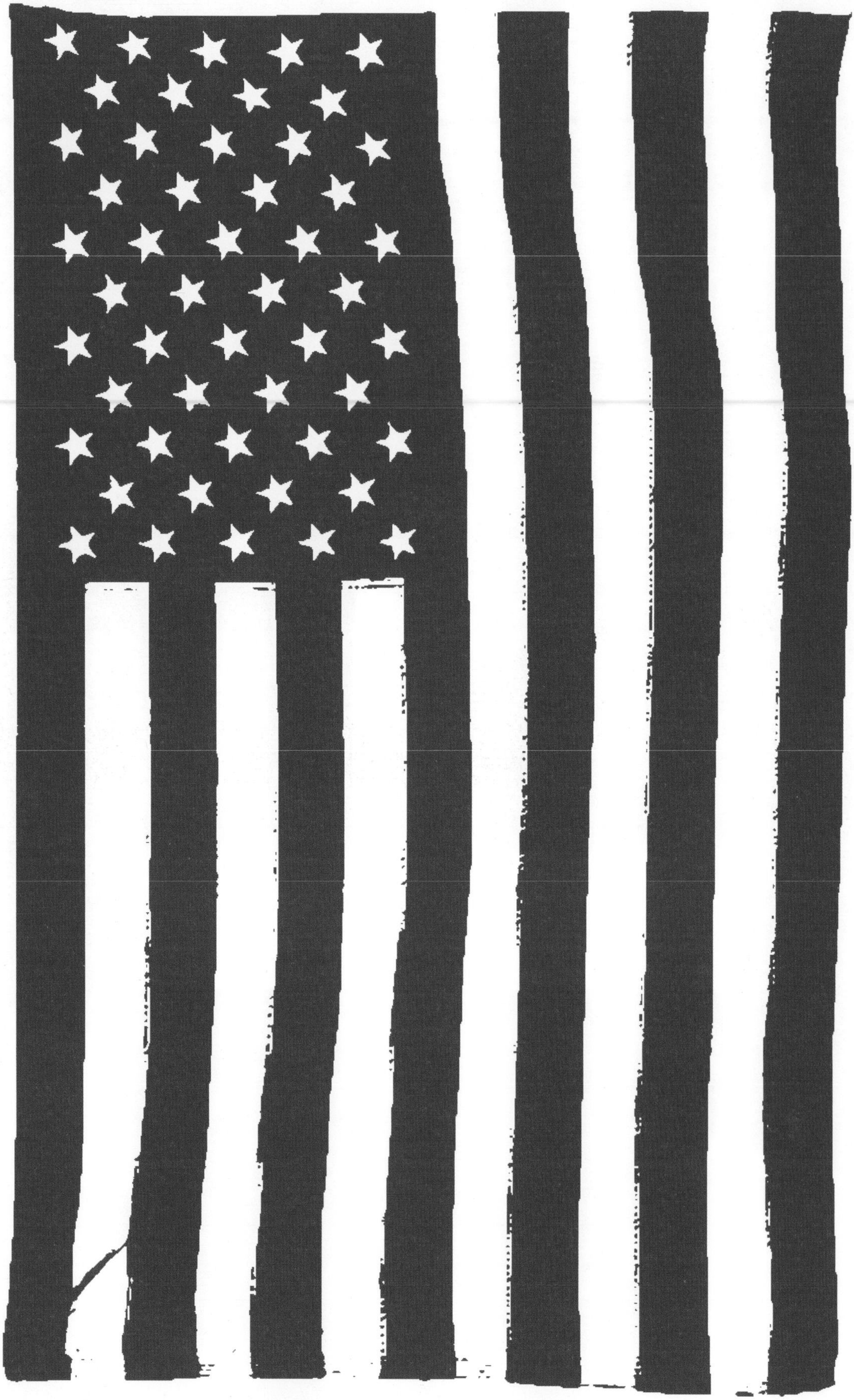

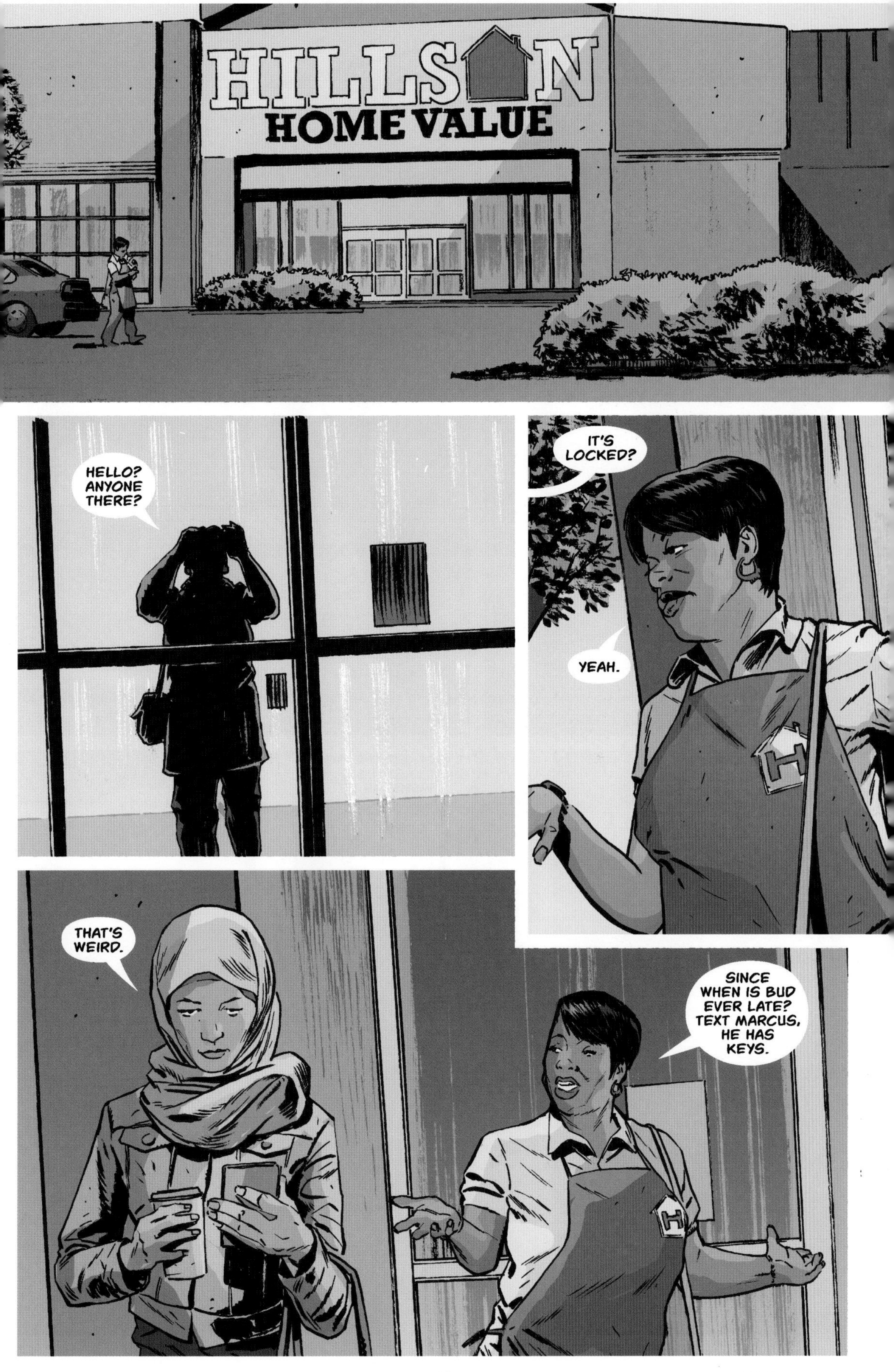
HILLSON
HOME VALUE
HELLO? ANYONE THERE?
IT'S LOCKED?
YEAH.
THAT'S WEIRD.
SINCE WHEN IS BUD EVER LATE? TEXT MARCUS, HE HAS KEYS.

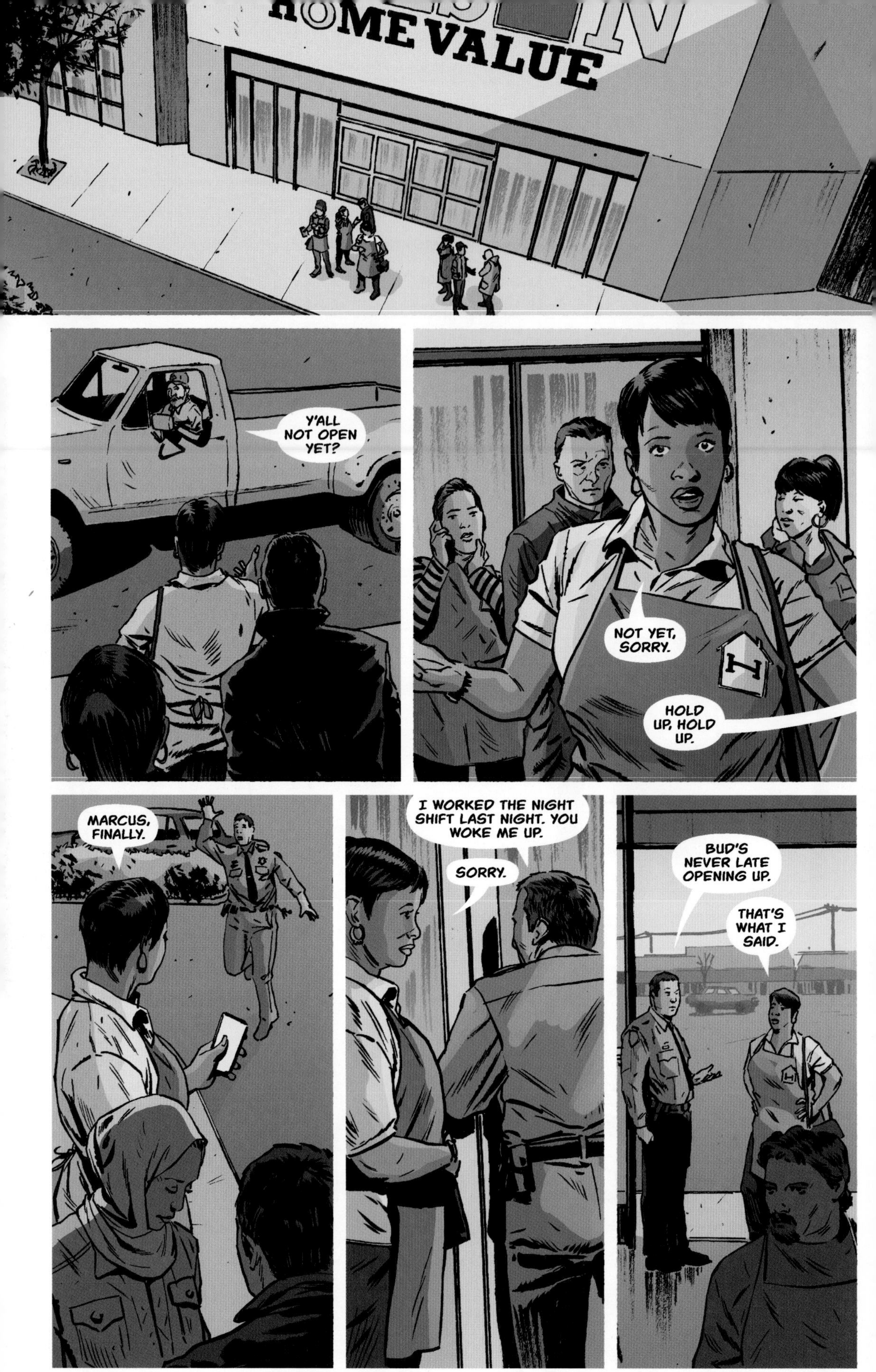
ʜOME VALUE
Y'ALL NOT OPEN YET?
NOT YET, SORRY.
HOLD UP, HOLD UP.
MARCUS, FINALLY.
I WORKED THE NIGHT SHIFT LAST NIGHT. YOU WOKE ME UP.
SORRY.
BUD'S NEVER LATE OPENING UP.
THAT'S WHAT I SAID.

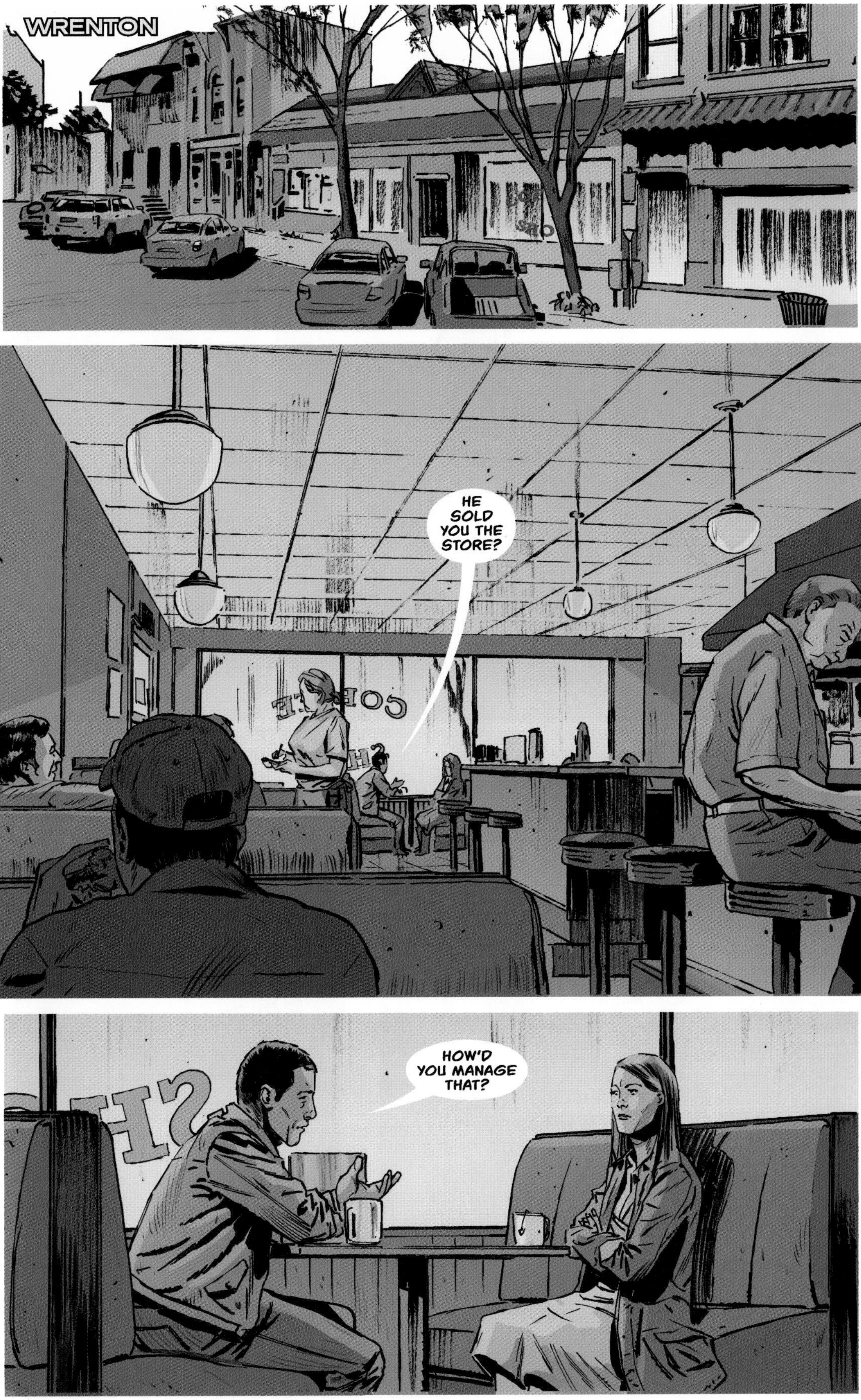
WRENTON
HE SOLD YOU THE STORE?
HOW'D YOU MANAGE THAT?

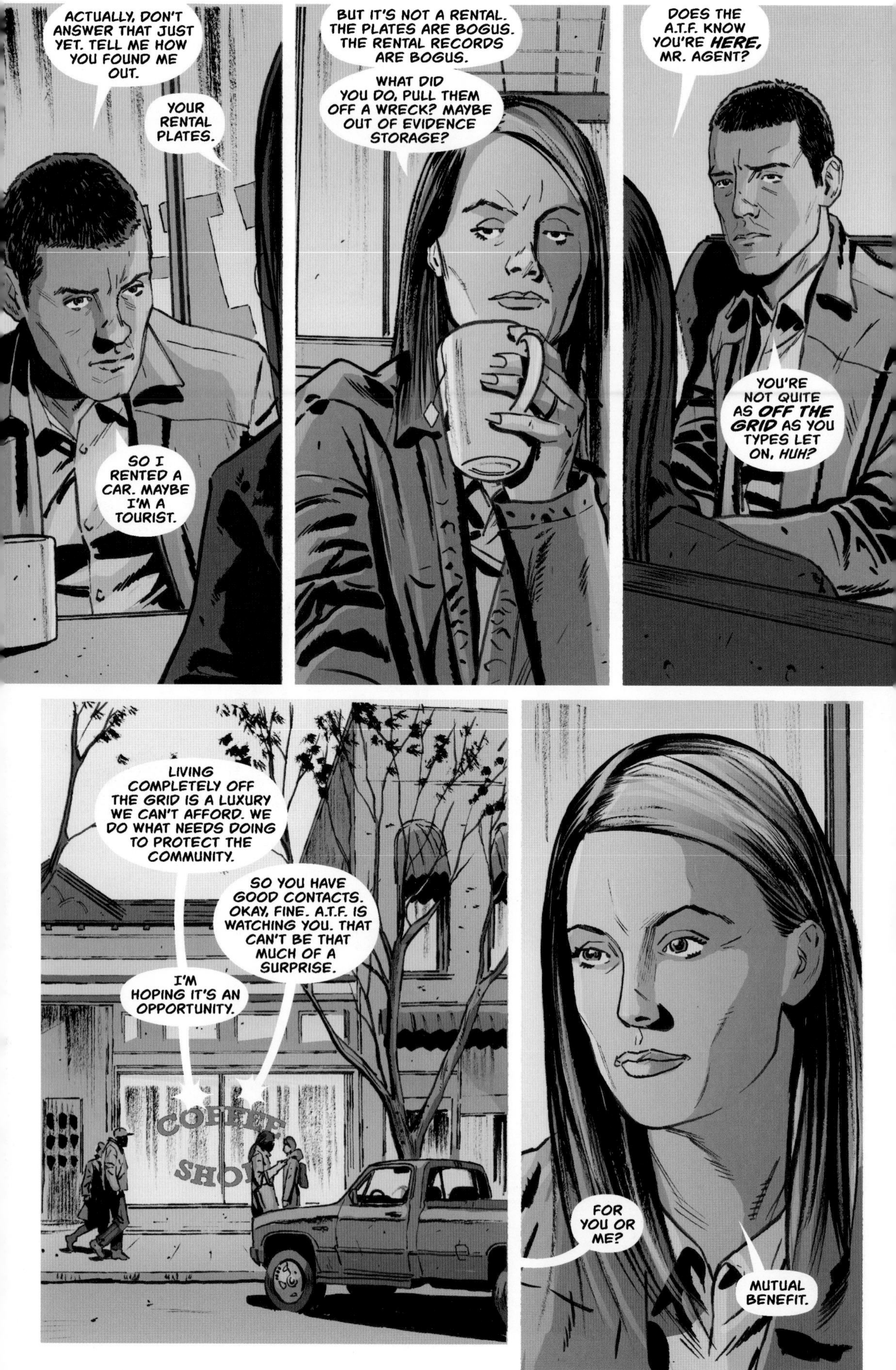
ACTUALLY, DON'T ANSWER THAT JUST YET. TELL ME HOW YOU FOUND ME OUT.
YOUR RENTAL PLATES.
SO I RENTED A CAR. MAYBE I'M A TOURIST.
BUT IT'S NOT A RENTAL. THE PLATES ARE BOGUS. THE RENTAL RECORDS ARE BOGUS.
WHAT DID YOU DO, PULL THEM OFF A WRECK? MAYBE OUT OF EVIDENCE STORAGE?
DOES THE A.T.F. KNOW YOU'RE HERE, MR. AGENT?
YOU'RE NOT QUITE AS OFF THE GRID AS YOU TYPES LET ON, HUH?
LIVING COMPLETELY OFF THE GRID IS A LUXURY WE CAN'T AFFORD. WE DO WHAT NEEDS DOING TO PROTECT THE COMMUNITY.
SO YOU HAVE GOOD CONTACTS. OKAY, FINE. A.T.F. IS WATCHING YOU. THAT CAN'T BE THAT MUCH OF A SURPRISE.
I'M HOPING IT'S AN OPPORTUNITY.
FOR YOU OR ME?
MUTUAL BENEFIT.

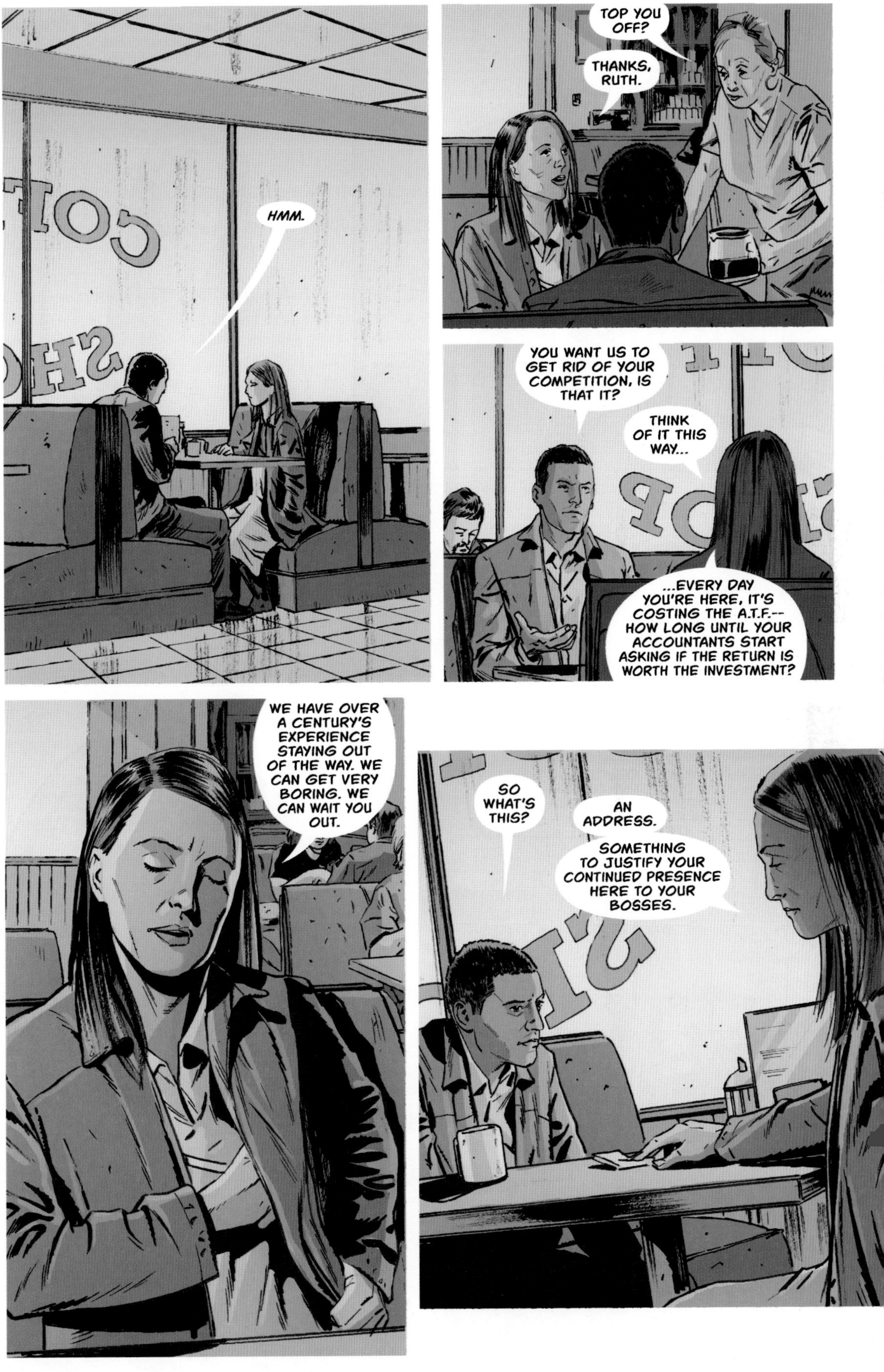
HMM.
TOP YOU OFF?
THANKS, RUTH.
YOU WANT US TO GET RID OF YOUR COMPETITION, IS THAT IT?
THINK OF IT THIS WAY...
...EVERY DAY YOU'RE HERE, IT'S COSTING THE A.T.F.-- HOW LONG UNTIL YOUR ACCOUNTANTS START ASKING IF THE RETURN IS WORTH THE INVESTMENT?
WE HAVE OVER A CENTURY'S EXPERIENCE STAYING OUT OF THE WAY. WE CAN GET VERY BORING. WE CAN WAIT YOU OUT.
SO WHAT'S THIS?
AN ADDRESS.
SOMETHING TO JUSTIFY YOUR CONTINUED PRESENCE HERE TO YOUR BOSSES.

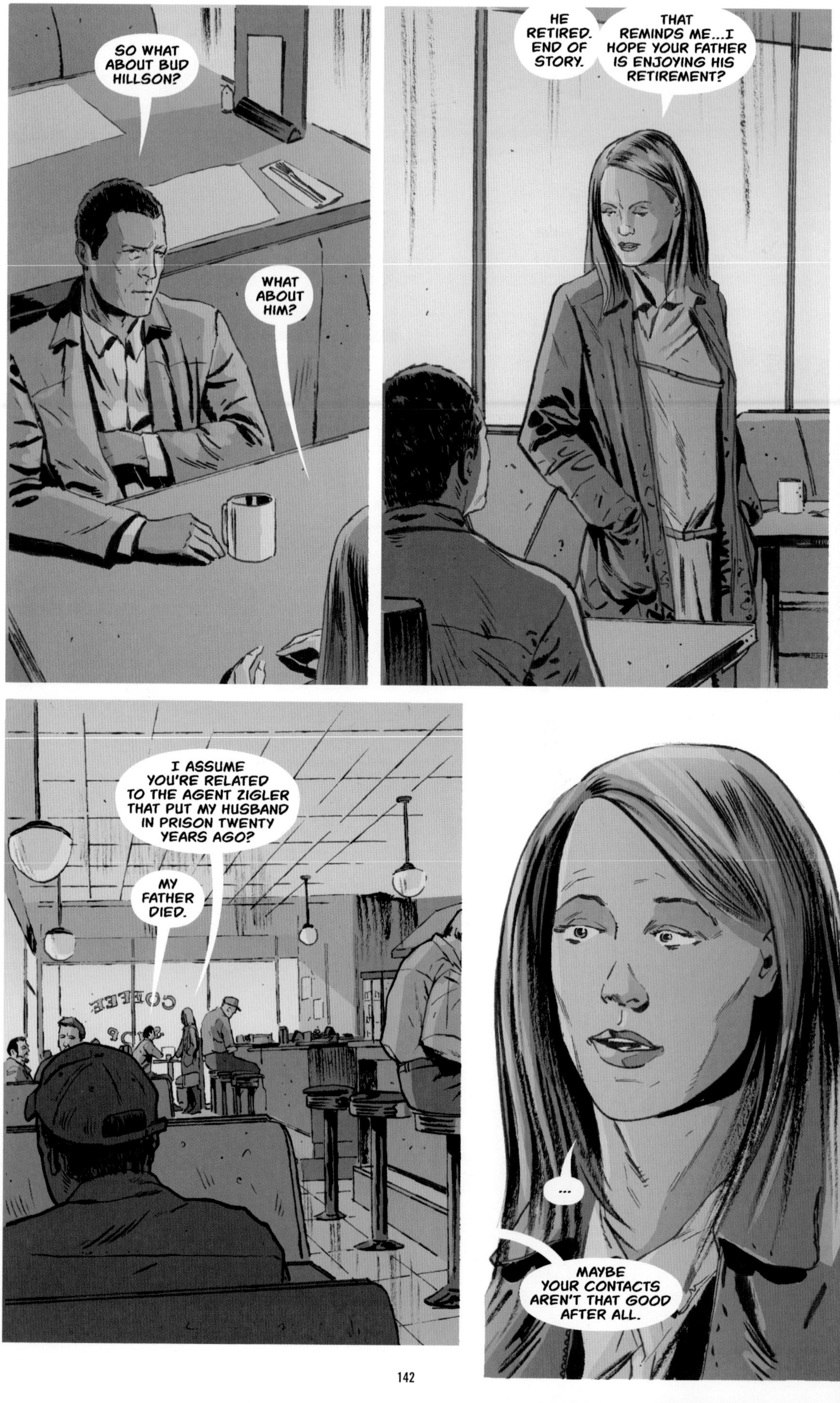
SO WHAT ABOUT BUD HILLSON?
WHAT ABOUT HIM?
HE RETIRED. END OF STORY.
THAT REMINDS ME...I HOPE YOUR FATHER IS ENJOYING HIS RETIREMENT?
I ASSUME YOU'RE RELATED TO THE AGENT ZIGLER THAT PUT MY HUSBAND IN PRISON TWENTY YEARS AGO?
MY FATHER DIED.
COFFEE SHOP
...
MAYBE YOUR CONTACTS AREN'T THAT GOOD AFTER ALL.

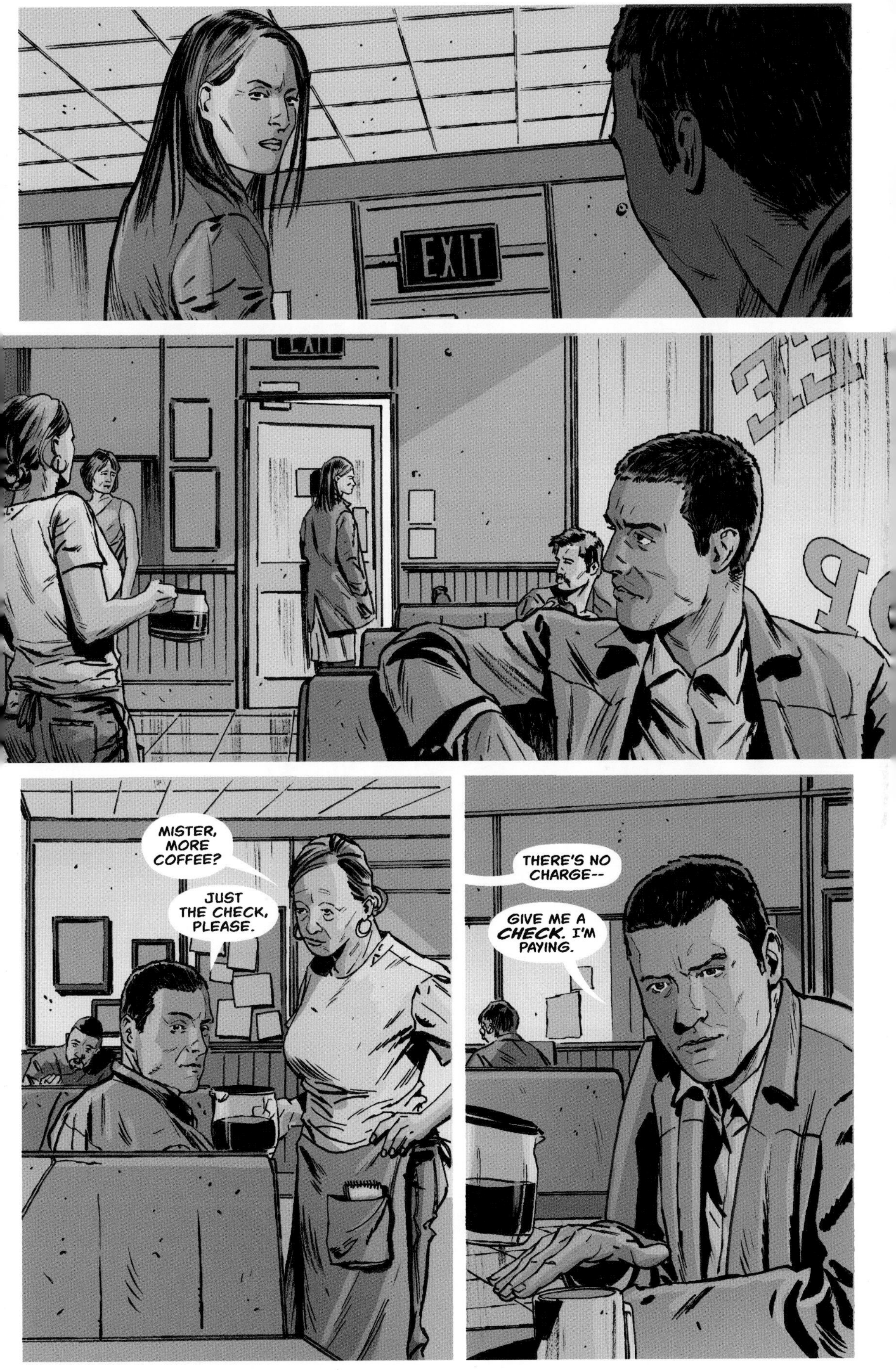
EXIT
MISTER, MORE COFFEE?
JUST THE CHECK, PLEASE.
THERE'S NO CHARGE--
GIVE ME A **CHECK**. I'M PAYING.

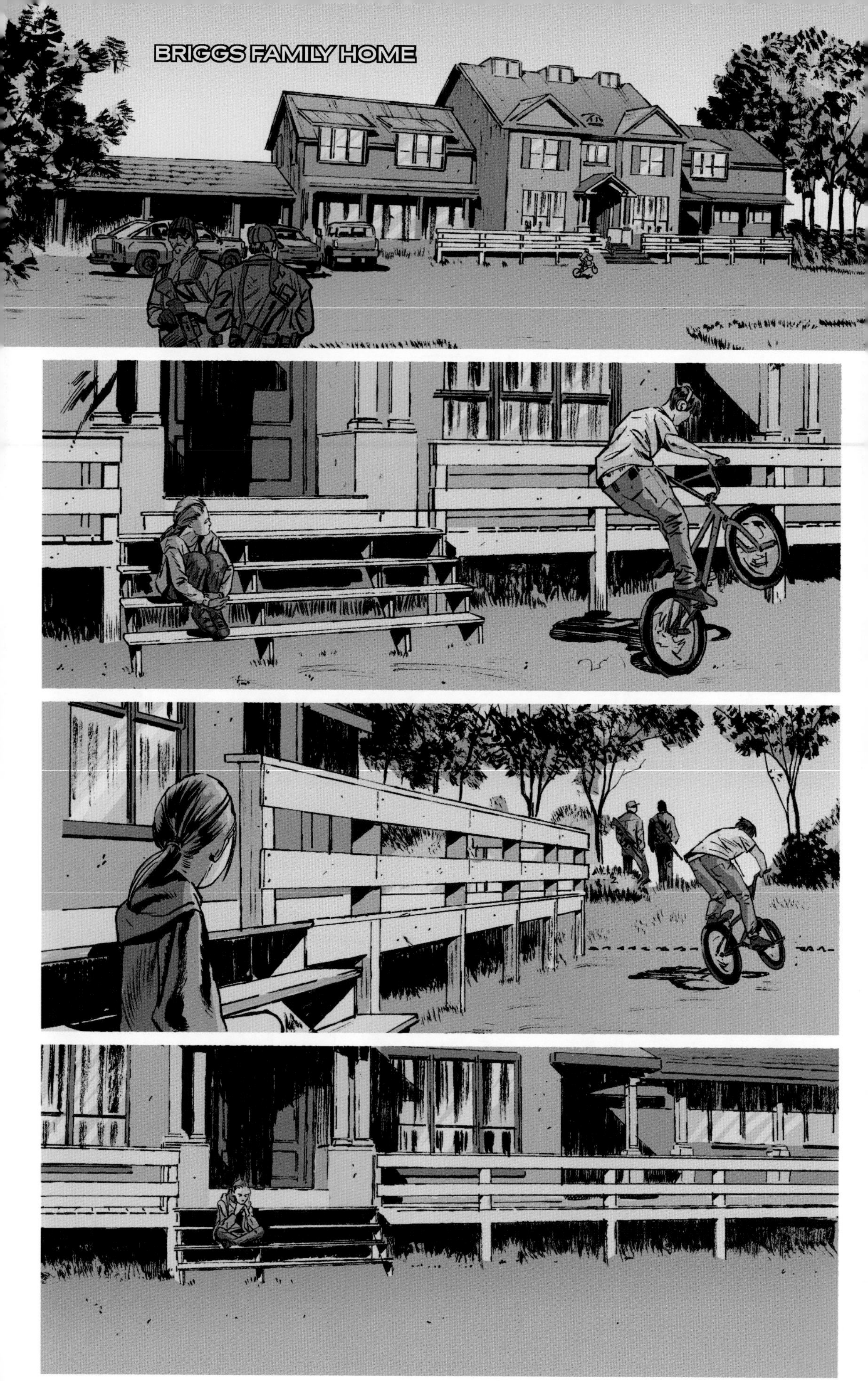
BRIGGS FAMILY HOME

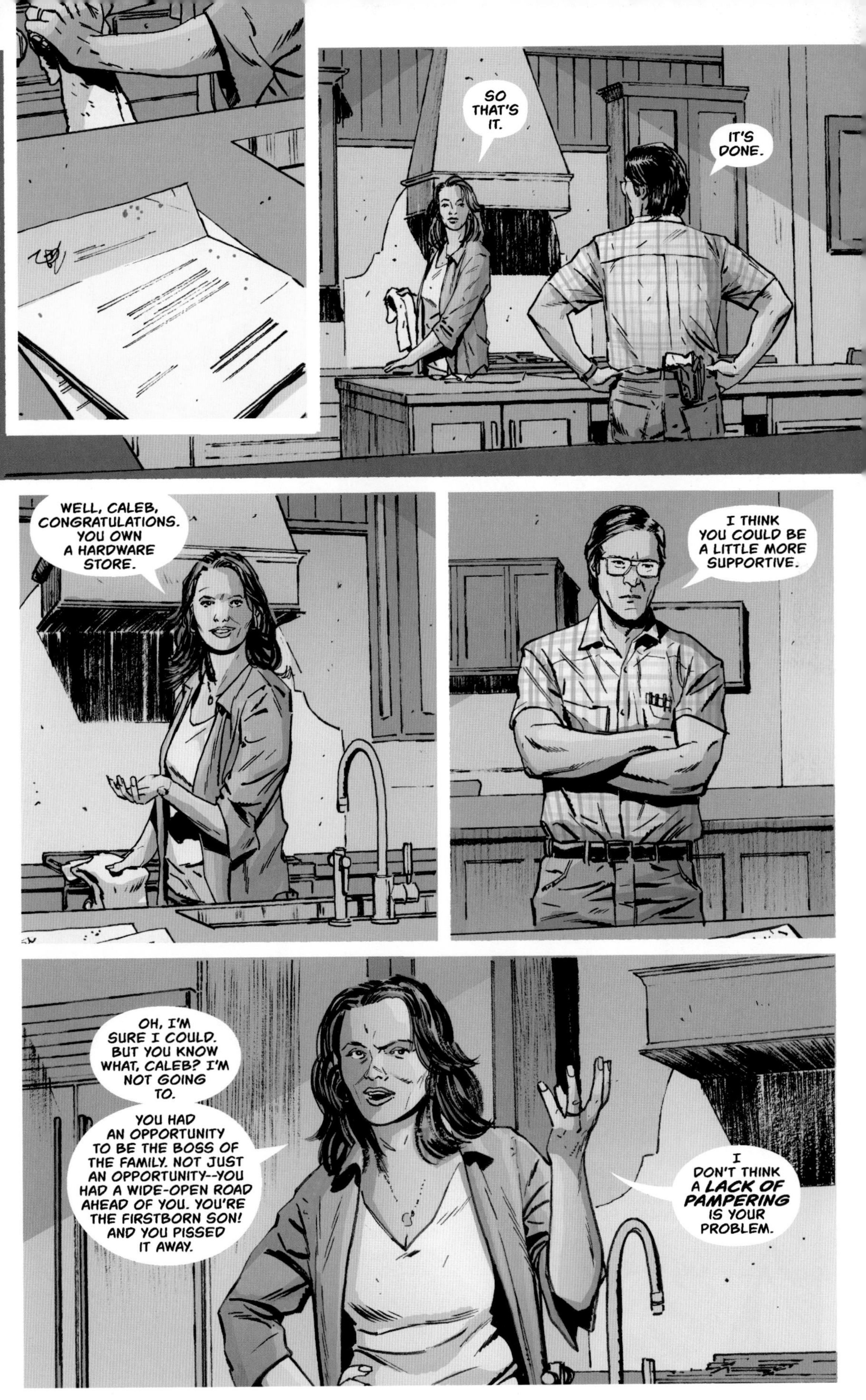

SO THAT'S IT.
IT'S DONE.
WELL, CALEB, CONGRATULATIONS. YOU OWN A HARDWARE STORE.
I THINK YOU COULD BE A LITTLE MORE SUPPORTIVE.
OH, I'M SURE I COULD. BUT YOU KNOW WHAT, CALEB? I'M NOT GOING TO.
YOU HAD AN OPPORTUNITY TO BE THE BOSS OF THE FAMILY. NOT JUST AN OPPORTUNITY--YOU HAD A WIDE-OPEN ROAD AHEAD OF YOU. YOU'RE THE FIRSTBORN SON! AND YOU PISSED IT AWAY.
I DON'T THINK A *LACK OF PAMPERING* IS YOUR PROBLEM.

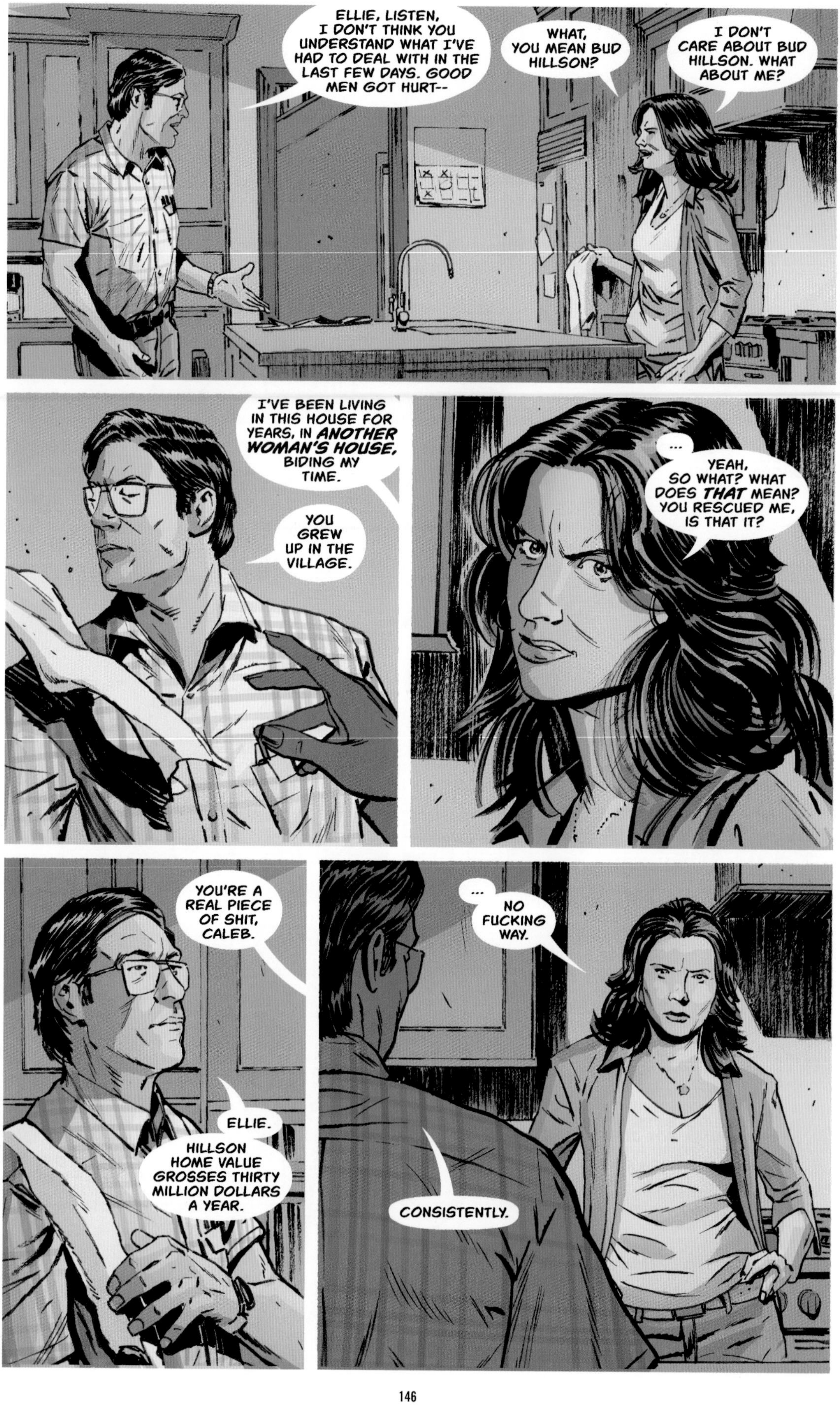
ELLIE, LISTEN, I DON'T THINK YOU UNDERSTAND WHAT I'VE HAD TO DEAL WITH IN THE LAST FEW DAYS. GOOD MEN GOT HURT--
WHAT, YOU MEAN BUD HILLSON?
I DON'T CARE ABOUT BUD HILLSON. WHAT ABOUT ME?
I'VE BEEN LIVING IN THIS HOUSE FOR YEARS, IN ANOTHER WOMAN'S HOUSE, BIDING MY TIME.
YOU GREW UP IN THE VILLAGE.
...
YEAH, SO WHAT? WHAT DOES THAT MEAN? YOU RESCUED ME, IS THAT IT?
YOU'RE A REAL PIECE OF SHIT, CALEB.
ELLIE.
HILLSON HOME VALUE GROSSES THIRTY MILLION DOLLARS A YEAR.
CONSISTENTLY.
...
NO FUCKING WAY.

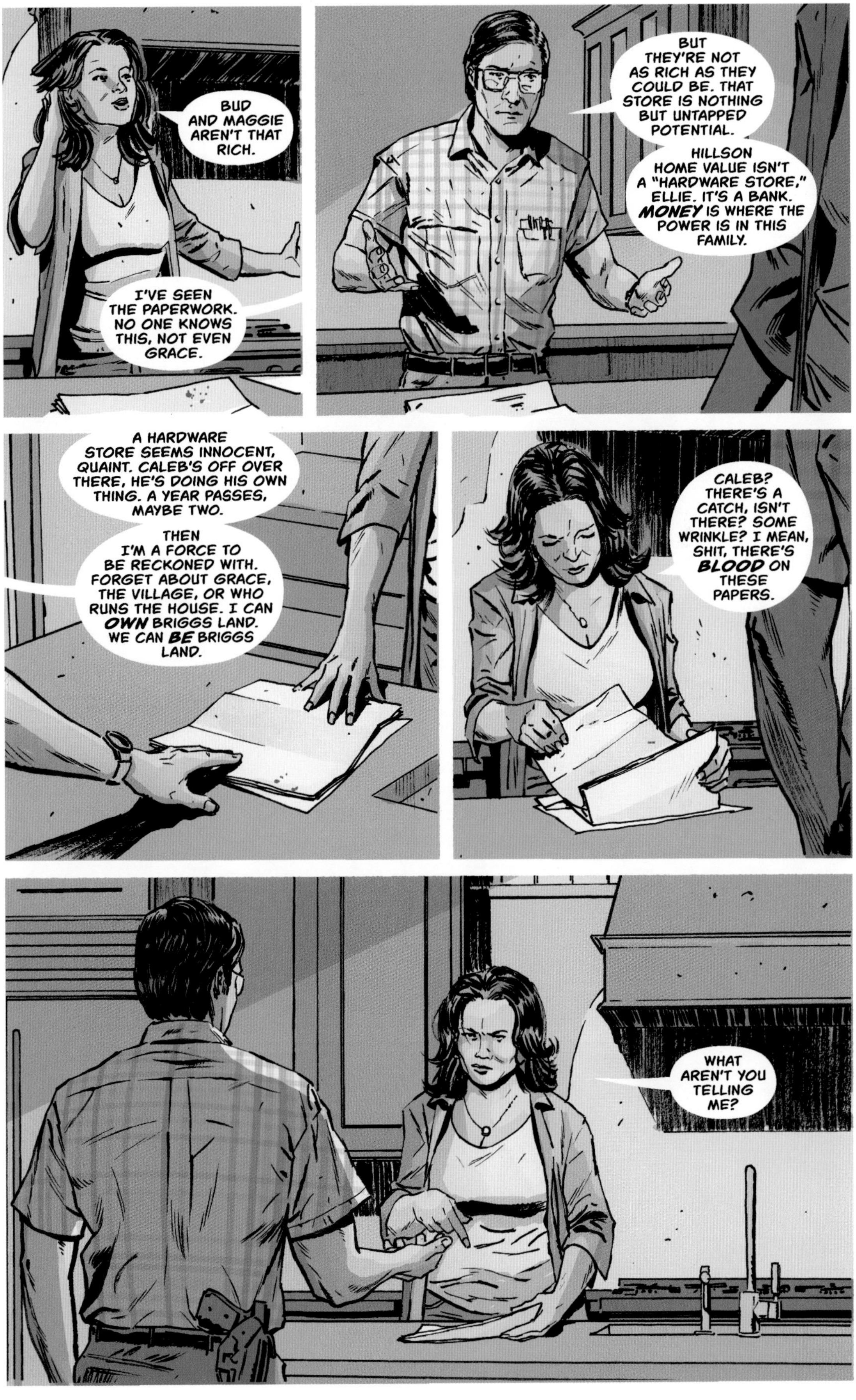
BUD AND MAGGIE AREN'T THAT RICH.
I'VE SEEN THE PAPERWORK. NO ONE KNOWS THIS, NOT EVEN GRACE.
BUT THEY'RE NOT AS RICH AS THEY COULD BE. THAT STORE IS NOTHING BUT UNTAPPED POTENTIAL.
HILLSON HOME VALUE ISN'T A "HARDWARE STORE," ELLIE. IT'S A BANK. MONEY IS WHERE THE POWER IS IN THIS FAMILY.
A HARDWARE STORE SEEMS INNOCENT, QUAINT. CALEB'S OFF OVER THERE, HE'S DOING HIS OWN THING. A YEAR PASSES, MAYBE TWO.
THEN I'M A FORCE TO BE RECKONED WITH. FORGET ABOUT GRACE, THE VILLAGE, OR WHO RUNS THE HOUSE. I CAN OWN BRIGGS LAND. WE CAN BE BRIGGS LAND.
CALEB? THERE'S A CATCH, ISN'T THERE? SOME WRINKLE? I MEAN, SHIT, THERE'S BLOOD ON THESE PAPERS.
WHAT AREN'T YOU TELLING ME?

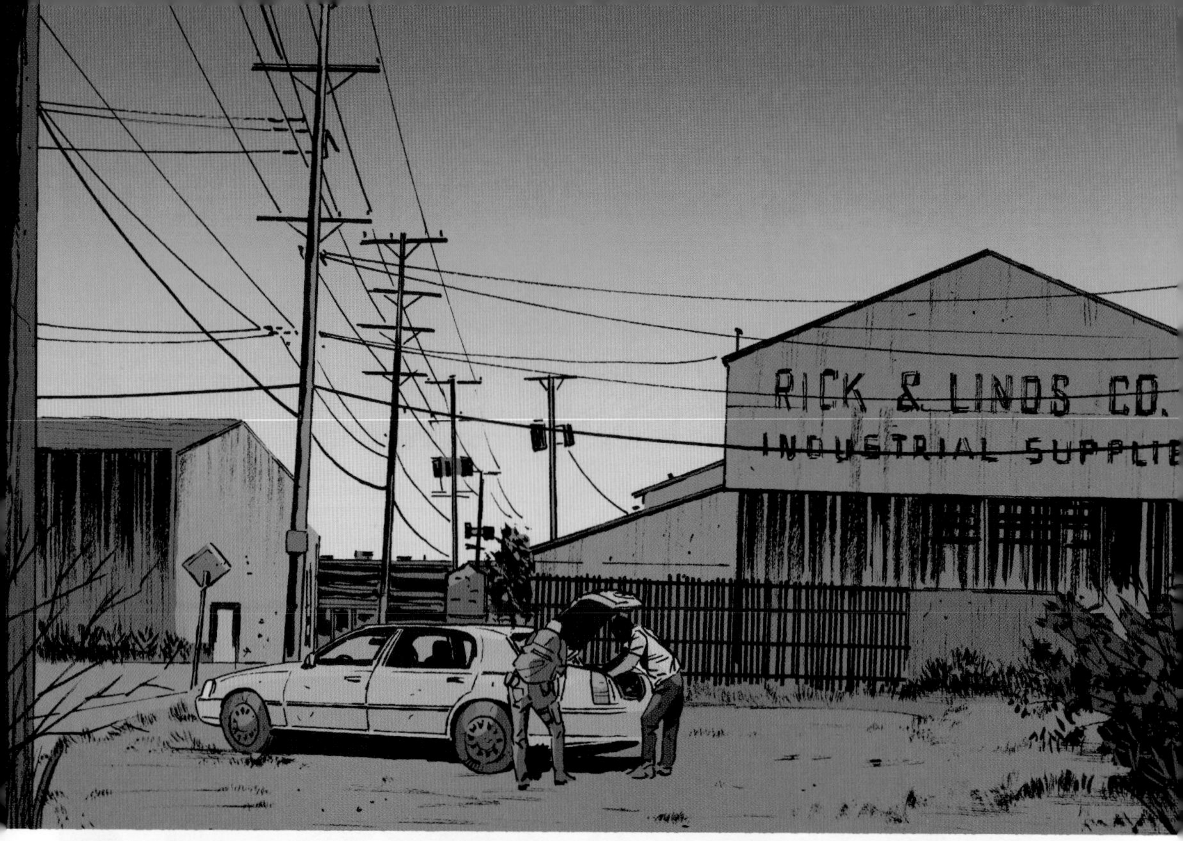
RICK & LINDS CO.
INDUSTRIAL SUPPLIE
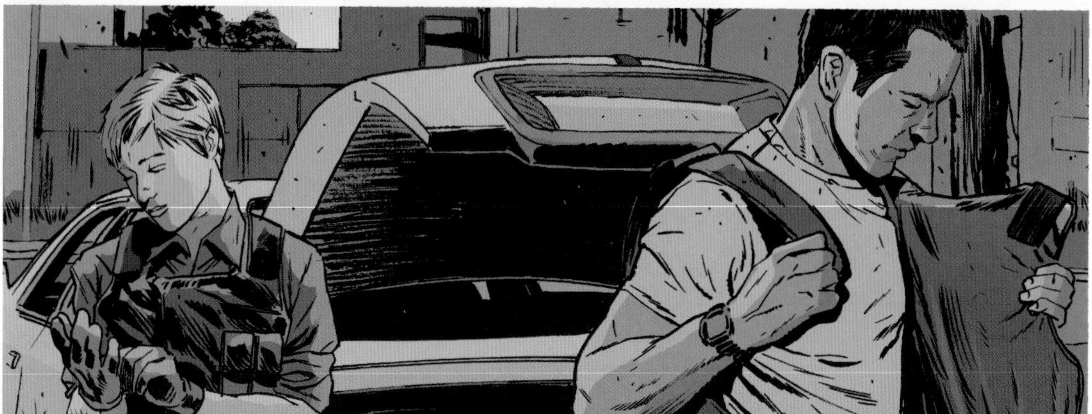
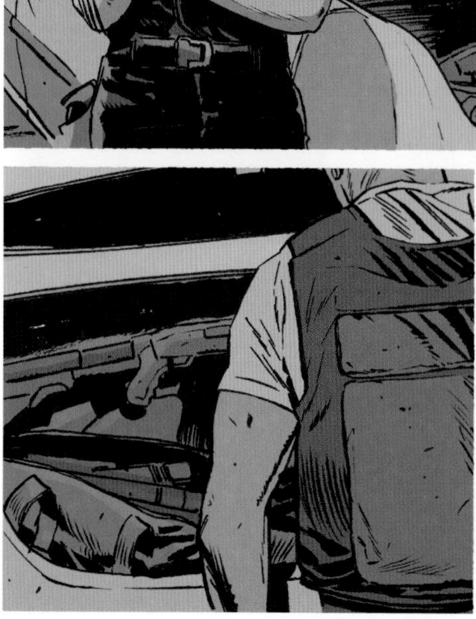
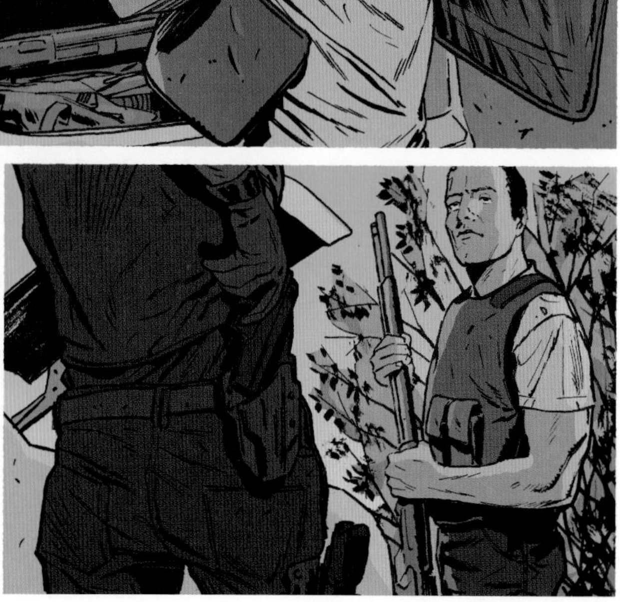

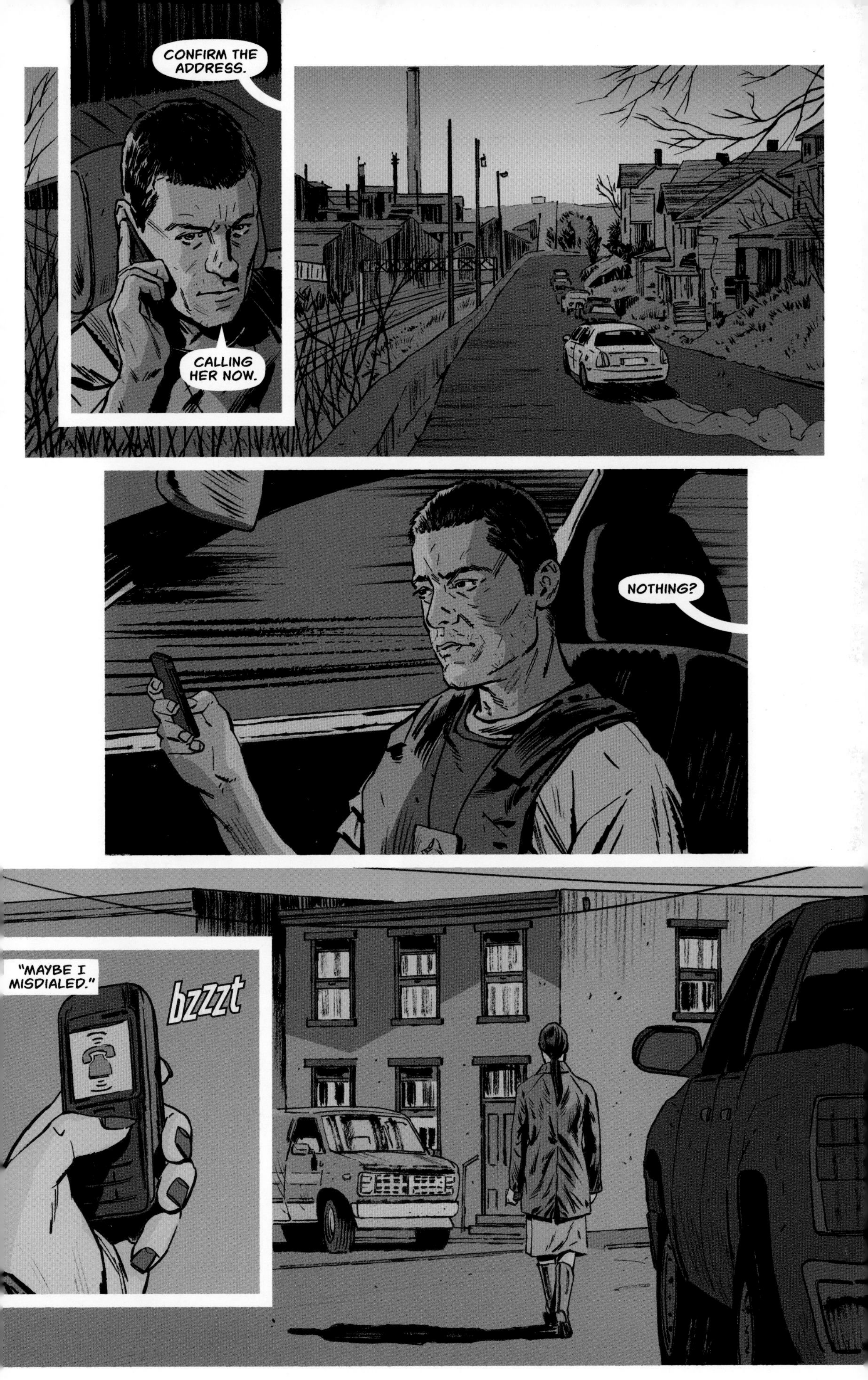
CONFIRM THE ADDRESS.
CALLING HER NOW.
NOTHING?
"MAYBE I MISDIALED."
bzzzt

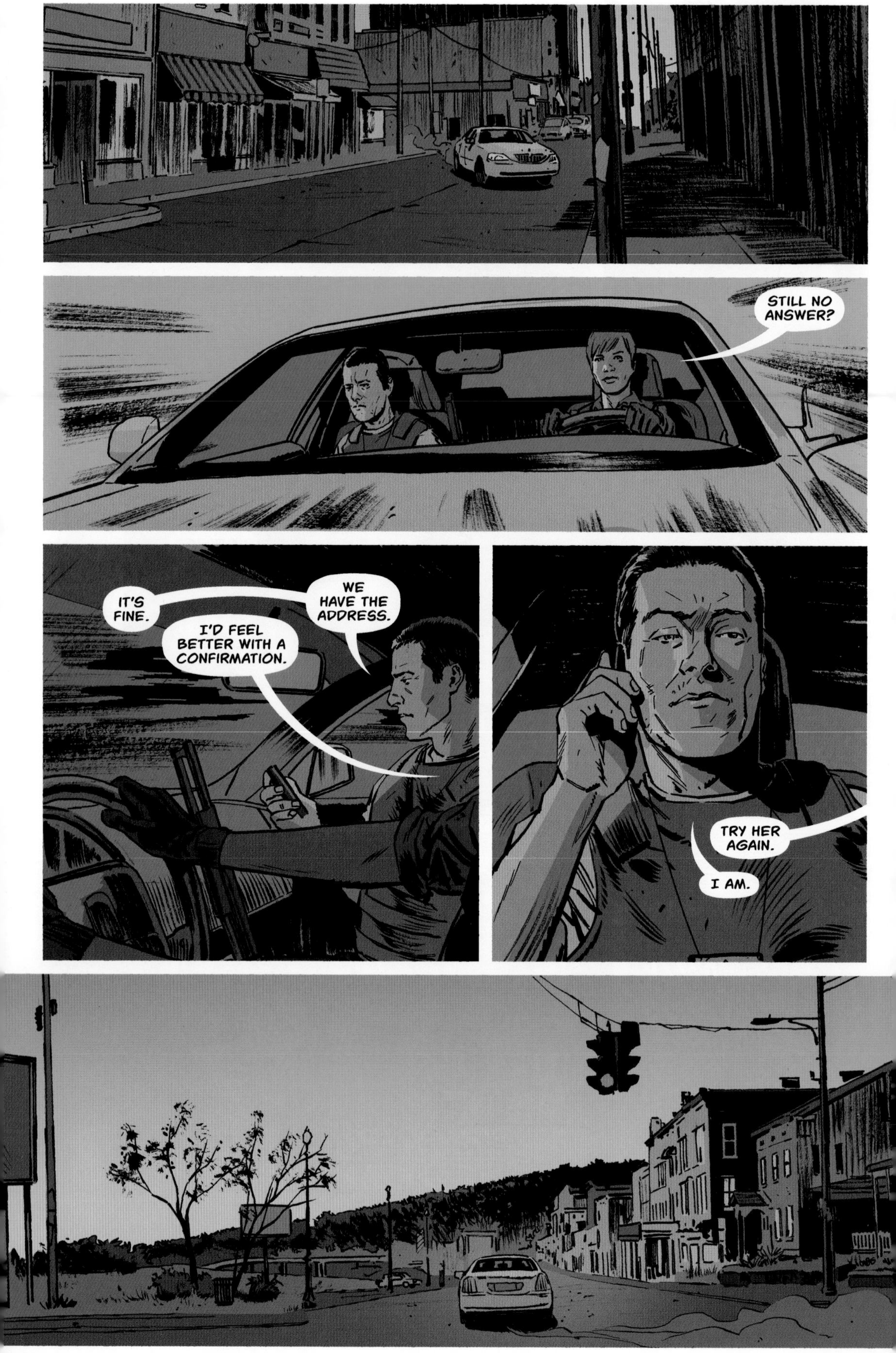
STILL NO ANSWER?
IT'S FINE.
WE HAVE THE ADDRESS.
I'D FEEL BETTER WITH A CONFIRMATION.
TRY HER AGAIN.
I AM.

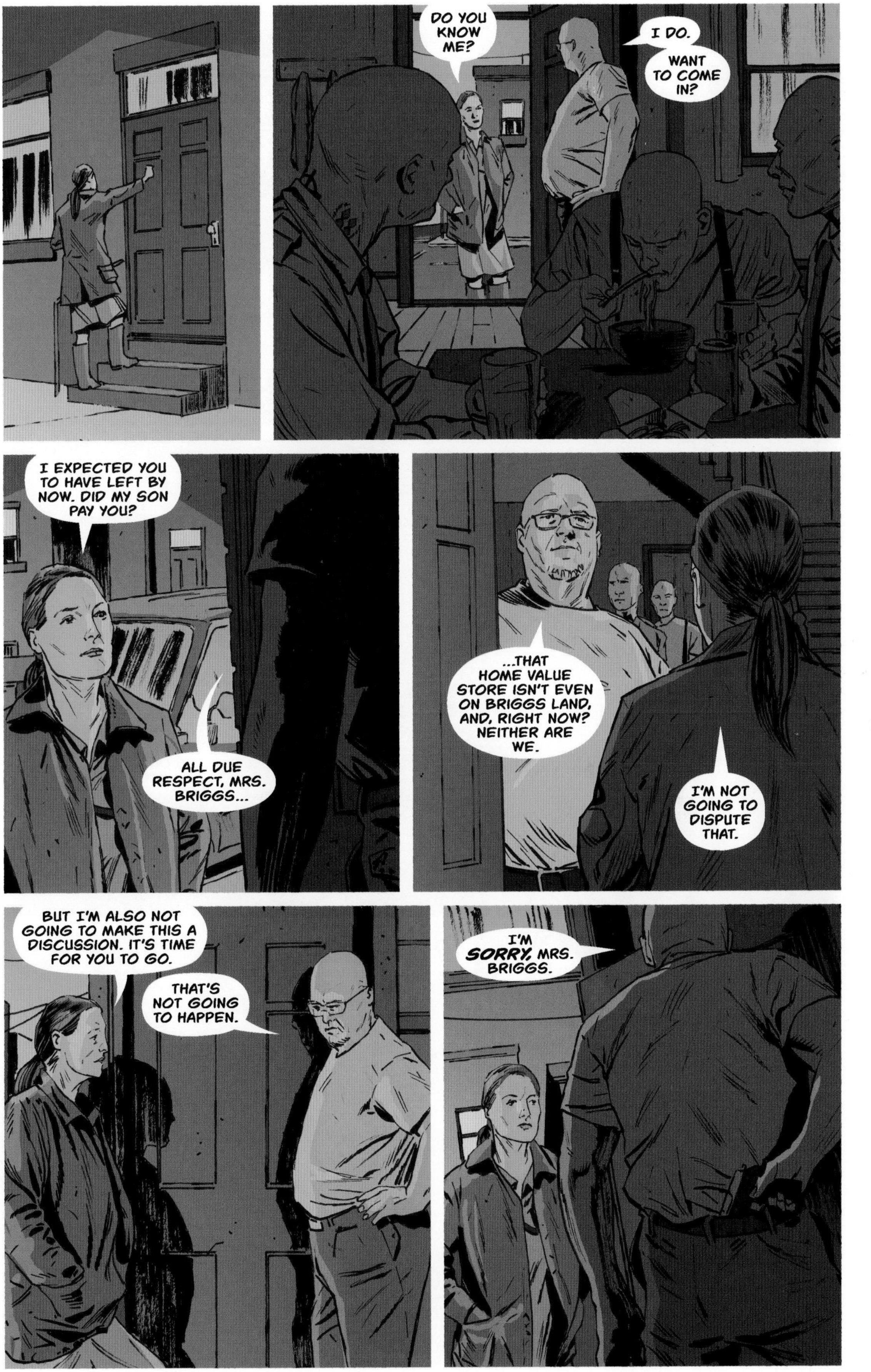
DO YOU KNOW ME?
I DO.
WANT TO COME IN?
I EXPECTED YOU TO HAVE LEFT BY NOW. DID MY SON PAY YOU?
ALL DUE RESPECT, MRS. BRIGGS...
...THAT HOME VALUE STORE ISN'T EVEN ON BRIGGS LAND, AND, RIGHT NOW? NEITHER ARE WE.
I'M NOT GOING TO DISPUTE THAT.
BUT I'M ALSO NOT GOING TO MAKE THIS A DISCUSSION. IT'S TIME FOR YOU TO GO.
THAT'S NOT GOING TO HAPPEN.
I'M SORRY, MRS. BRIGGS.

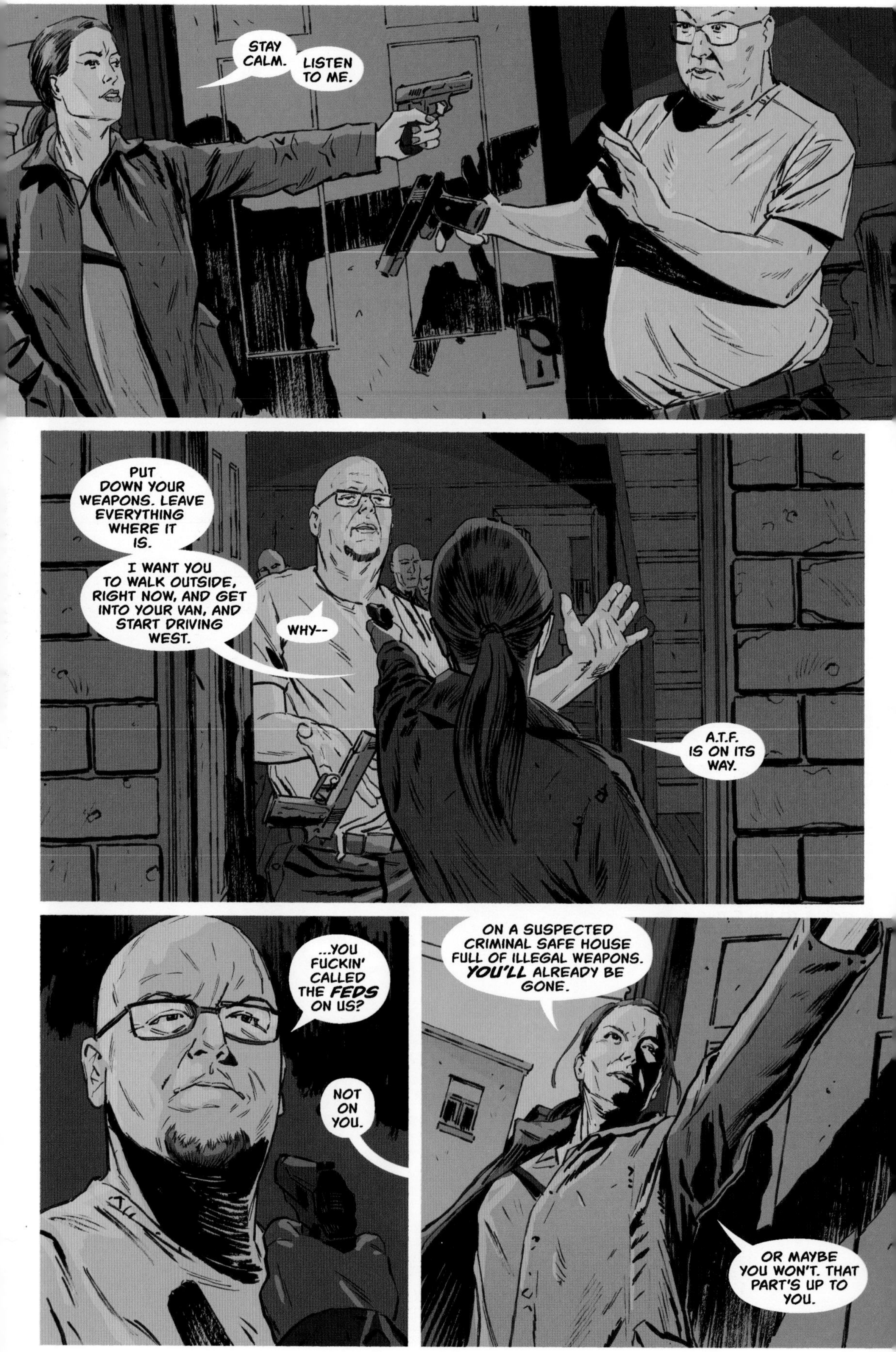
STAY CALM.
LISTEN TO ME.
PUT DOWN YOUR WEAPONS. LEAVE EVERYTHING WHERE IT IS.
I WANT YOU TO WALK OUTSIDE, RIGHT NOW, AND GET INTO YOUR VAN, AND START DRIVING WEST.
WHY--
A.T.F. IS ON ITS WAY.
...YOU FUCKIN' CALLED THE *FEDS* ON US?
NOT ON YOU.
ON A SUSPECTED CRIMINAL SAFE HOUSE FULL OF ILLEGAL WEAPONS. *YOU'LL* ALREADY BE GONE.
OR MAYBE YOU WON'T. THAT PART'S UP TO YOU.

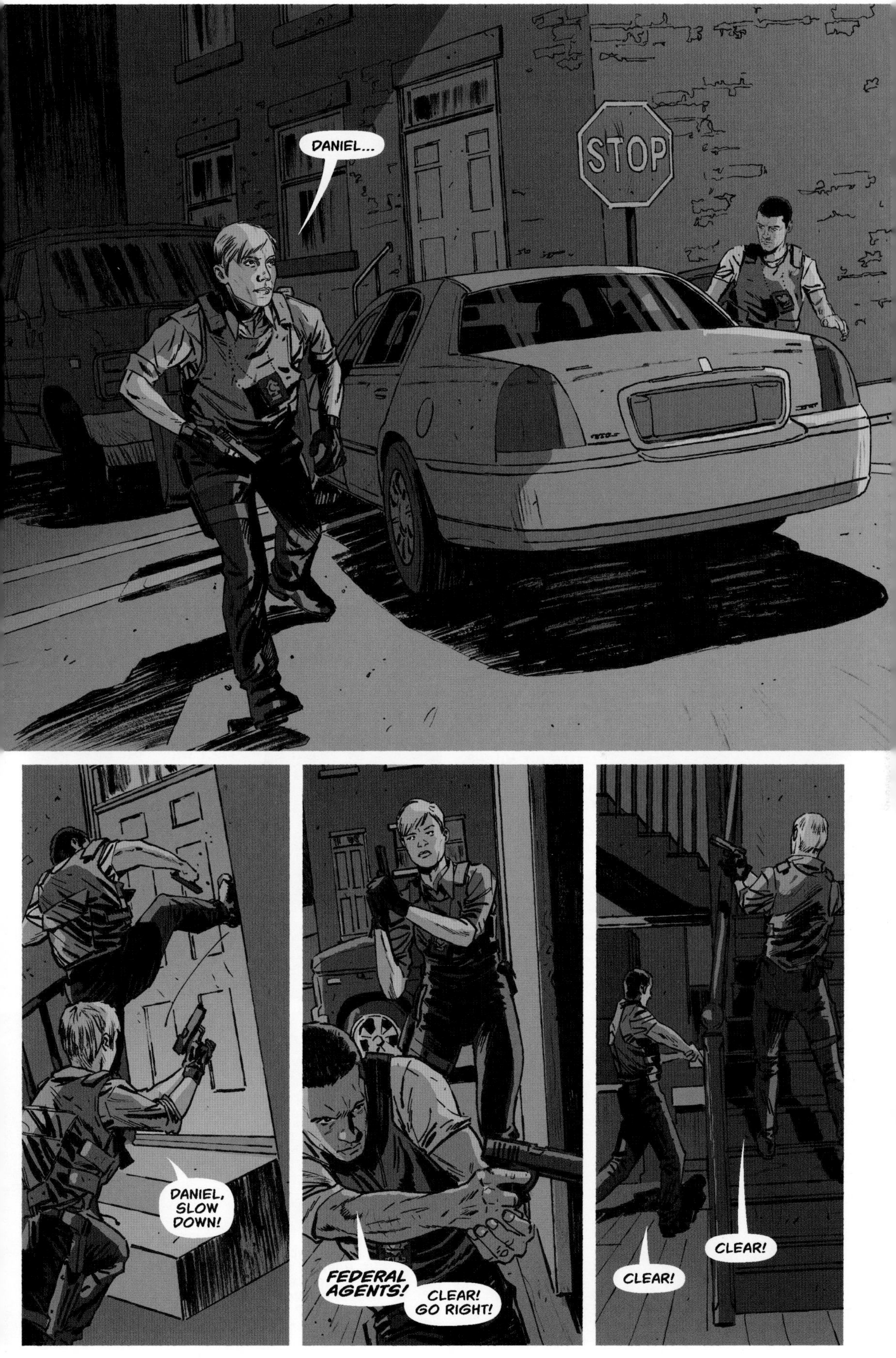
DANIEL...
DANIEL, SLOW DOWN!
FEDERAL AGENTS!
CLEAR! GO RIGHT!
CLEAR!
CLEAR!

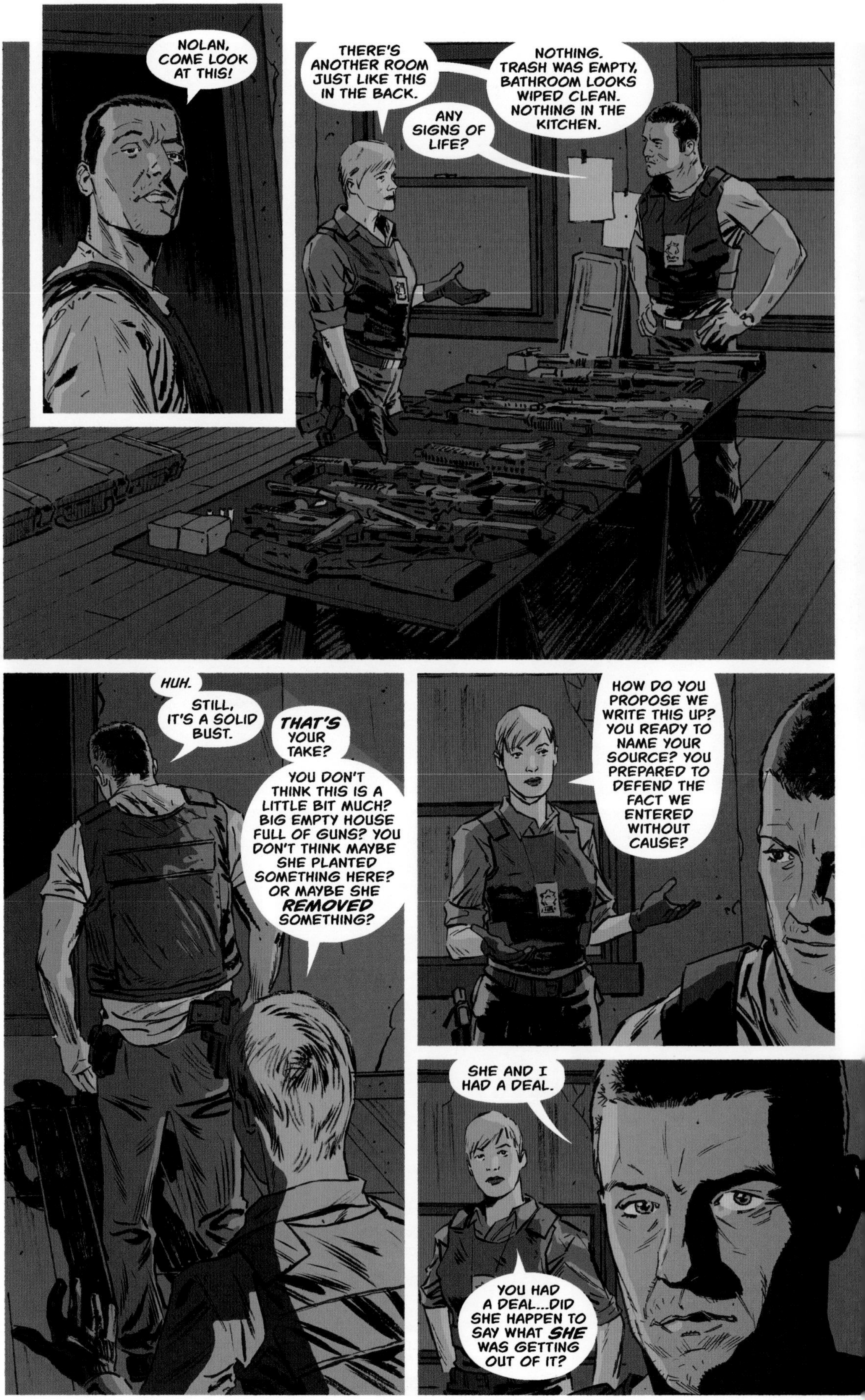
NOLAN, COME LOOK AT THIS!
THERE'S ANOTHER ROOM JUST LIKE THIS IN THE BACK.
NOTHING. TRASH WAS EMPTY, BATHROOM LOOKS WIPED CLEAN. NOTHING IN THE KITCHEN.
ANY SIGNS OF LIFE?
HUH.
STILL, IT'S A SOLID BUST.
THAT'S YOUR TAKE?
YOU DON'T THINK THIS IS A LITTLE BIT MUCH? BIG EMPTY HOUSE FULL OF GUNS? YOU DON'T THINK MAYBE SHE PLANTED SOMETHING HERE? OR MAYBE SHE REMOVED SOMETHING?
HOW DO YOU PROPOSE WE WRITE THIS UP? YOU READY TO NAME YOUR SOURCE? YOU PREPARED TO DEFEND THE FACT WE ENTERED WITHOUT CAUSE?
SHE AND I HAD A DEAL.
YOU HAD A DEAL...DID SHE HAPPEN TO SAY WHAT SHE WAS GETTING OUT OF IT?

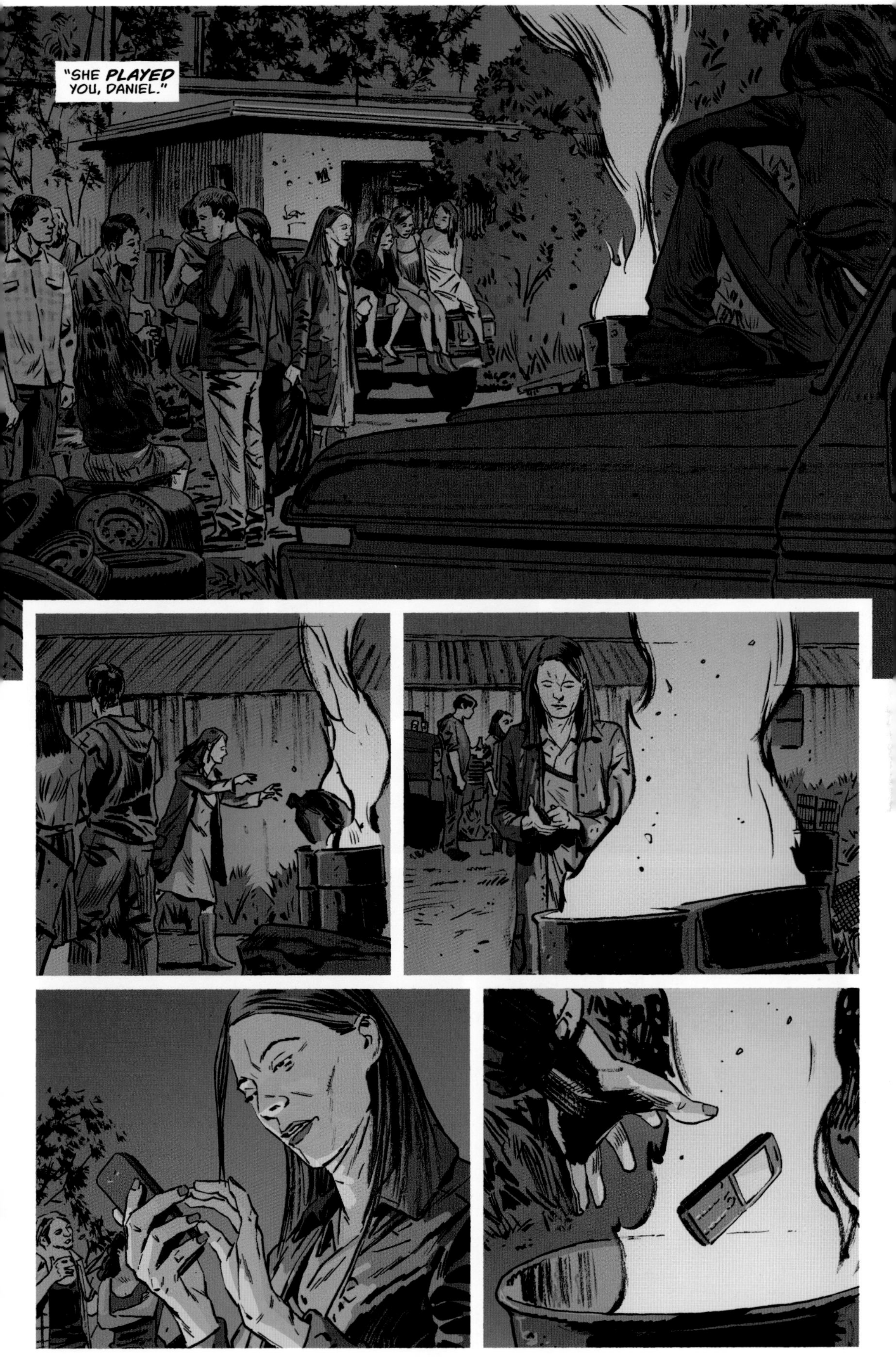
"SHE PLAYED YOU, DANIEL."

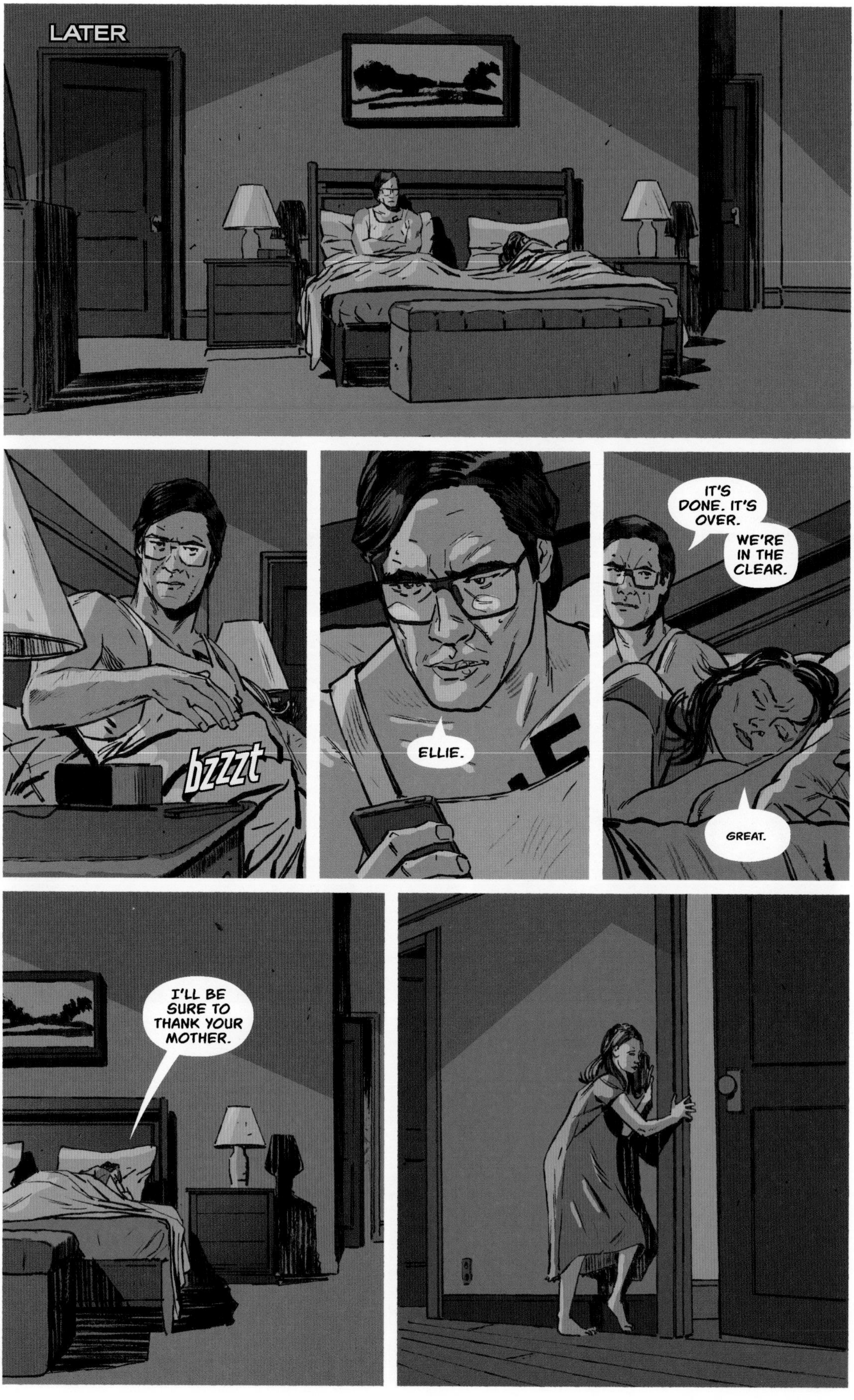
LATER
bzzzt
ELLIE.
IT'S DONE. IT'S OVER.
WE'RE IN THE CLEAR.
GREAT.
I'LL BE SURE TO THANK YOUR MOTHER.

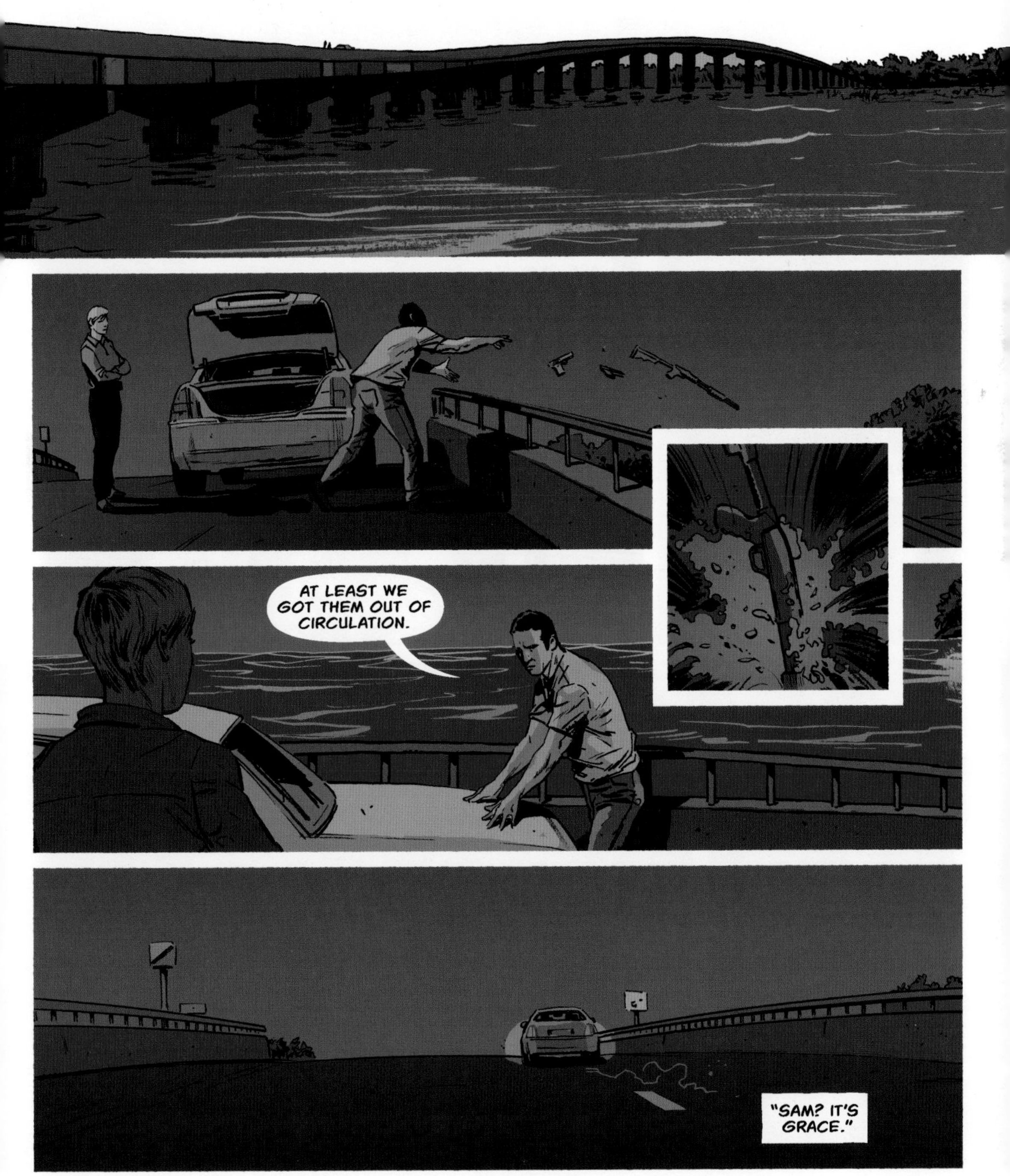
AT LEAST WE GOT THEM OUT OF CIRCULATION.
"SAM? IT'S GRACE."

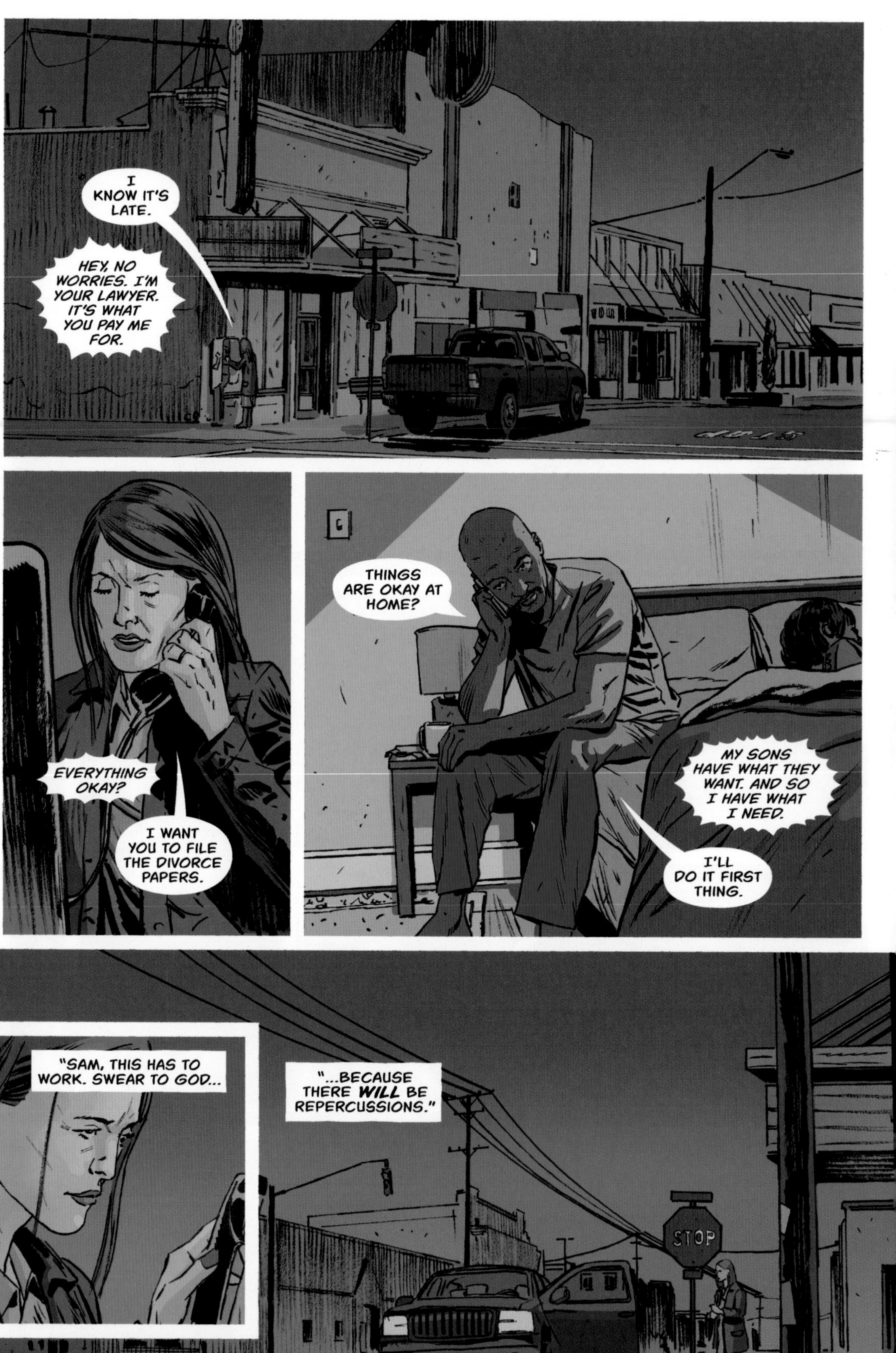
I KNOW IT'S LATE.
HEY, NO WORRIES. I'M YOUR LAWYER. IT'S WHAT YOU PAY ME FOR.
THINGS ARE OKAY AT HOME?
EVERYTHING OKAY?
I WANT YOU TO FILE THE DIVORCE PAPERS.
MY SONS HAVE WHAT THEY WANT. AND SO I HAVE WHAT I NEED.
I'LL DO IT FIRST THING.
"SAM, THIS HAS TO WORK. SWEAR TO GOD...
"...BECAUSE THERE ***WILL*** BE REPERCUSSIONS."
STOP

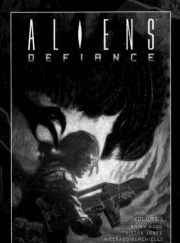
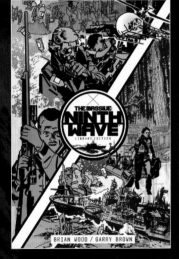

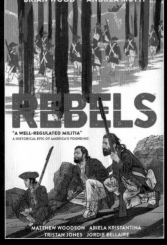

More great

NOIR AND ESPIONAGE

from Dark Horse Books

BLACKSAD
DÍAZ CANALES GUARNIDO

BLACKSAD

JUAN DÍAZ CANALES AND JUANJO GUARNIDO

The *Blacksad* books first took Europe by storm in 2000 and sold over 200,000 copies in France alone. Now Dark Horse presents the beautifully painted stories of private investigator John Blacksad, up to his feline ears in mystery, digging into the backstories behind murders, child abductions, and nuclear secrets.

ISBN 978-1-59582-393-9
$29.99

MIND MGMT
matt kindt
VOLUME ONE: THE MANAGER
FOREWORD BY DAMON LINDELOF

MIND MGMT VOLUME 1

MATT KINDT

A young journalist stumbles onto a big story — the top-secret Mind Management program. Her ensuing journey involves weaponized psychics, hypnotic advertising, talking dolphins, and seemingly immortal pursuers. But in a world where people can rewrite reality itself, can she trust anything she sees?

ISBN 978-1-59582-797-5
$19.99

THE BLACK BEETLE
IN
"NO WAY OUT"
A Mystery Tale by FRANCESCO FRANCAVILLA

THE BLACK BEETLE VOLUME 1: NO WAY OUT

FRANCESCO FRANCAVILLA

Follow Francesco Francavilla's critically acclaimed pulp hero the Black Beetle — Colt City's sleuthing sentinel — as he searches island prisons, dank sewers, and swanky nightclubs for the mysterious man known as Labyrinto.

ISBN 978-1-61655-202-2
$19.99

GREEN RIVER KILLER
A TRUE DETECTIVE STORY
JEFF JENSEN | JONATHAN CASE

GREEN RIVER KILLER: A TRUE DETECTIVE STORY

JEFF JENSEN AND JONATHAN CASE

The story of one of America's most notorious killers is revealed in this true-crime comic unlike any other! Written by case detective Tom Jensen's own son, acclaimed entertainment writer Jeff Jensen, this is the ultimate insider's account of America's most prolific serial killer.

ISBN 978-1-59582-560-5
$24.99

DARK HORSE BOOKS
DarkHorse.com

AVAILABLE AT YOUR LOCAL COMICS SHOP OR BOOKSTORE • TO FIND A COMICS SHOP IN YOUR AREA, CALL 1-888-266-4226
For more information or to order direct: • On the web: DarkHorse.com • E-mail: mailorder@darkhorse.com • Phone: 1-800-862-0052 Mon.–Fri. 9 AM to 5 PM Pacific Time.

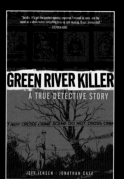